THE BOOK OF TRESPASS

Crossing the lines that divide us

Nick Hayes

BLOOMSBURY PUBLISHING

LONDON · OXFORD · NEW YORK · NEW DELHI · SYDNEY

BLOOMSBURY PUBLISHING
Bloomsbury Publishing Plc
50 Bedford Square, London, WC1B 3DP, UK
29 Earlsfort Terrace, Dublin 2, Ireland

BLOOMSBURY, BLOOMSBURY PUBLISHING, and the Diana logo are trademarks
of Bloomsbury Publishing Plc

First published in Great Britain 2020
This edition published 2021

A catalogue record for this book is available from the British Library

ISBN: HB: 978-1-5266-0469-9; EBOOK: 978-1-5266-0471-2; PB: 978-1-5266-0472-9

2 4 6 8 10 9 7 5 3 1

Typeset by Newgen KnowledgeWorks Pvt. Ltd., Chennai, India
Printed and bound in Great Britain by CPI Group (UK) Ltd, Croydon CR0 4YY

To find out more about our authors and books visit www.bloomsbury.com
and sign up for our newsletters

for my two mothers,
Cornelia and Cristine,
without whom there would have been
neither nurture nor nature
— with love
xx

'There have existed men who had the power to hold or to give exclusive possession of portions of the earth's surface, but when and where did there exist the human being who had the right?'
                                        — Henry George, *Progress and Poverty*

CONTENTS

LIST OF ILLUSTRATIONS

BADGER

Fires, tracks, lines and legislation

'Any friend of mine walks where he likes in this country,
or I'll want to know the reason why'
— Mr Badger, *The Wind in the Willows*

On the morning of St George's Day 1932, a teenager called George Beattie Elliot took the train from his home in Preston. With his climbing ropes and enough supplies for a couple of days' camping and roaming, he travelled the sixty miles to the brim of the Peak District and set off on foot.

He was not alone. Every weekend, thousands of men and women would stream from the blackened, industrialised cities of Sheffield, Manchester, Bolton and Preston to catch a breath of fresh air and clean the chimneys of their lungs. Freed from the beat of the working week, they sought scenery and self-determination. They walked twenty miles up and down dale, and then back to the pub on a Sunday night for huzzahs, huzzoohs and a socialist singsong. Rambling, cycling and climbing clubs had spawned across the area, train companies were offering group discounts, and, with the new Youth Hostel Association offering cheap accommodation for the overnighters, the thirty-seven square miles of Bleaklow were a honey pot for the worker bees of the north.

George cut off the busy main paths and, trespassing now, he sneaked across the open moorland. He was heading to the Laddow Rocks, where he would spend the night in a cave halfway down a steep scree slope, a small pocket of secret space, silent and snug beneath the heavens. He slept, and must have woken early, because by mid-afternoon the next day he had already covered thirteen miles, passed Bleaklow, gone through Snake Pass and was ascending the north face of Kinder Scout, the highest point of the Peak District. The cities of Manchester and Bolton rolled beneath him and if the day had been crystal clear he would have been able to see, over a hundred miles away, the white peaks of Snowdonia. The rocks at the summit, silhouetted by the bright sky, ran like the turrets of a ransacked stone fort, and, as he approached them, he heard a commotion from the other side of the peak.

He climbed further and as the hill flattened out he saw a crowd of a few hundred, mostly around his age, singing and shouting, advancing towards a line of a dozen gamekeepers. As soon as the crowd saw George, their shouts inexplicably turned to cheers, they waved their caps at him and urged him on like a sporting hero. The keepers turned and, as several rushed towards him, George saw the broad sticks they were holding. George's confusion intensified as the keepers circled him, even more so as they began to punch him to the ground. The crowd arrived, the keepers were hauled off him and George was pulled to his feet, slapped on the back and praised for his heroic work for the good old cause. The scene ended as quickly as it had sprung upon him, the crowd moved on and poor George was left, as before, to the silence of the Peaks. Bruised, utterly bemused, stars spiralling around his head, George continued his walk as planned, descending into the Goyt Valley and out of history.

It was only at work on Monday that he would have uncovered the meaning of this bizarre and briefly violent encounter. It was all over the papers. Four hundred ramblers had met at Hayfield, a few miles west of Kinder, and, amid a large police presence, had walked up the William Clough pass to protest for a greater right of access to the moors. Because it was well publicised in advance, the Duke of Devonshire's men were ready with their sticks and hired men, and at the precise time George had crested the peak the crowd were beginning to break bounds, spill off the Right of Way and pile up the hill. Only a small proportion of the crowd made it onto the forbidden land, and only by about four hundred metres, before the violence George experienced spread into a tussle with the keepers. Some trespassers had hoiked away the keepers' sticks and exchanged a few blows, causing one keeper to fall and break his ankle. The crowd had its climax and merrily they rolled along, singing 'The Red Flag' and 'The Internationale' back to Hayfield. The constabulary emerged from their hiding place in the local picture house, and the plain-clothed bobbies who had accompanied the trespassers pointed out the ringleaders, six of whom were arrested and taken for trial at the Derby assizes. Entirely unwittingly, George had fallen upon one of the most notorious land protests in English history, the Kinder Trespass.

We reach the dell and lay our fire. Scuffing away the black leaves with the toe of my boot, I scrunch a manger of newspaper on the wet earth and balance brittle twigs on top. My friend is off in the distance, crashing around in the bracken, gathering fallen wood. I touch a flame to an edge of the newspaper and a line of blue wriggles along its edge, blackening it, gaining ground like a tiny rising tide. I light the other available corners and begin to pile thicker twigs into a wigwam around the flame, black-tipped ash and brittle pencil twigs from a long-fallen elder.

An owl hoots, cool and spooky, and it suddenly seems much colder. I drop to my knees, hands on the wet earth, and I lay my head alongside the fire and I blow long gentle streams of air into its centre. The twigs glow red like the filament of a bulb, and, as my breath runs out, the flames reappear, stronger than before. I breathe in and blow, breathe and blow, and there is a warm crackling noise as the fire takes. I blow harder and the fire roars, comes alive, and is soon ready to fend for itself. My friend piles on shin-length logs that he has cracked underfoot from the fallen limbs of ash, oak and cherry. We both blow, then step back to watch the flames rise up the wooden scaffold, searing at the rough bark, unlocking decades of stored sunlight into our damp, gloomy dell.

The air is smoky, charcoal-blue, smudging the outline of the trees. The winter sky is dark and bright, a blank cinema screen projected into an empty theatre. A stillness has descended. Three miles beyond the wood, in the pit of the glacial valley, by the River Thames, the boundary between West Berkshire and Oxford, the geese start their honking.

The fire orchestrates the space. The thrumming light gives a rhythm to the static features of the dell, as if seen through water, causing the shadows cast from the exposed roots around us to seethe like snakes; its orange glow simmers up and down the steep slopes of the pit, and lights the underside of the yew tree bright white. The fire has the motion of a busy engine, a generator of light and heat, whirring and flaring. Thin gusts of air sweep through a heavy white mist in its glowing rib cage. Shafts of gas burst and squeal from the old wood, the spiky yew sticks hiss and spit, drooping into the growling hearth beneath them. The rough packing of the cherry and birch trees cracks and splits and flakes of its skin rise with ghostlike motion into the air, like flaring Amaretti wrappers, disappearing into the black above.

When the wind comes we hear it from miles away: a low timpani roll, sweeping up the steep valley slopes through the empty wood, pouring into our dell and rushing the fire into clouds of sparks, drawing deep on its furnace. Noise returns to the blackness around us. The owls are hunting, screeching, the undergrowth skitters and rustles and every so often there is a chilling cry, hoarse and insistent, that echoes through the woods. We roll a joint, pop the caps of bottled beer and follow rambling lines of conversation. We are comfortable, easy with each other and with our surroundings, and it is only when we go to piss, stepping outside the orange glow, that we remember the coldness and inhospitality of the night.

In time, the fire is sleepy. Fiery furnace fades to starry constellation and its orange bulb extends only as far as its ash perimeter. Snug in my sleeping bag I can hear a steady breathing and can't see if my friend is sleeping or entranced. My eyes close.

I discovered our dell a decade ago. I had returned from London to the village I grew up in. I had a notion for a book, a graphic novel, and needed a couple of months to draw up the idea and tout it around publishers. It was a leap in the dark: I wasn't at that stage an illustrator, hadn't studied it, hadn't practised it, and to try and get a book on the shelves seemed a lot like hubris. I didn't want to tempt fate or trumpet something that didn't yet exist, so had told few people of my plans. Leaving the city at night, with my books stored in a friend's loft and everything I needed on my back, I felt like I was sneaking away, eloping, just me and my idea.

I was sleeping once again in my old single bed. A miniature desk, a beanbag and a wall papered with the flyers of nineties indie gigs. Every day I drew, legs squeezed under the desk by the window, and at the weekends I went for long walks linking the various haunts and dens of myself and my childhood friends. Back then, we weren't particularly interested in the great outdoors. We didn't skip through the long grass with butterfly nets, we never went fishing or bird-spotting, we barely climbed a tree. The countryside around our homes was important chiefly because it offered us a space outside of adult rule. The steep basins in the woods that we dared each other to bike down, and where later we set small fires for aerosol cans that would explode and come singing through the air like ragged ninja stars. The benches on the Recreation ground, by the woods that sloped down to the river, where we listened to trance tracks on mini-disc speakers and rolled our first joints. But on my return these friends were now living ten miles away in Reading, and these spaces, though resonant, were empty. So I walked on.

I went further into the country around our village than we had ever thought to go as kids. Several weeks in, just before Christmas, I was walking across the Rec to the valley woods. Snow had fallen, just a couple of inches, but it was a weekday and no one was around, so the playing field was a blank canvas. I cut across it to the woods and took the Right of Way, winding steeply down the hillside to the road at the trough of the valley. I could see right through the woods to the farm on the opposite side: lorries, barns, white fields and grey sheep. The woods felt like an empty marquee, hushed, the party long gone.

At the valley bottom another path emerged, a thin ridge of earth marked by an indent in the snow, a line veering off the

Right of Way. A badger track. Because I was alone and had the day to myself, and because it led me into the woods, not out of them, I followed it. It took me to a wide gap cut through the trees for the pylons, blocked by a wire fence. The path ploughed straight through the dead bracken under the fence and stumbled and swerved across the field, barging again beneath the fence beyond. I climbed the fence, crossed the field, in full view of the farmhouse on the facing slope, climbed a broken metal gate and, under cover of trees again, continued along this ghost of a path.

I passed the badger sett and continued along a ledge tyre-marked by the farmer's 4x4. Through the trees I could see a large white slope, like the roof of a gingerbread cottage frosted with sugar. My heart gripped: this might be someone's home. I stopped. There was a tree growing right out of its apex and still I couldn't work out what I was seeing. I turned from the track and moved slowly towards it. The roof was in fact a steep hill, an island of earth that ran from its peak at ground level some forty feet down into a disused clay pit cut from the valley slope. Its rim was lined with the roots of thin, reedy ash trees that led up to an aperture of grey sky. Secreted away from the roads and paths, there was a calmness here. It felt like a place I would return to.

When, finally, I had sent off my proposal for the graphic novel and, mercifully, it had been accepted, I asked my parents if I could stay for the year. I had a book to draw but, better, I suddenly had a licence, a temporary artist's permit, which gave me the right to sit and read and draw outside of the shadow of idleness. As the year progressed, I followed the badger tracks that crossed the woods, cutting through the clouds of bluebells, the forests of ferns and nettles, the clumps of bramble, on tracks that barrelled through the bracken, bust under fences and burrowed through hedges. Every now and then the paths would lead me to their homes, large mounds of greenish chalk, clannish compounds, like Iron Age forts, some of which were inhabited, some of which were empty. Just so long as I kept up with the book, I felt free to wander at will, and sit until my legs went numb, drawing whatever I saw before me.

I returned in particular, again and again, alone and with friends, by day and by night, to the dell I had discovered. There was a new bond growing between myself and this place, one which came from simply being there, through looking, listening and sketching. In mind and body, drawing stills you. Sitting at ground level, hidden by nettle and fern, making studies of the trees and topography, it was as if the animal world would drop its state of high alert and come out of hiding. Small packs of deer would rest in the shade, birds would scuff around in the leaf litter, yards from my feet. Rooted to the spot, silent and motionless, I saw more of this countryside than ever before. And as the sketches I made began to cover my bedroom walls, I began to internalise the world outside of me. A relationship was forming: I was drawing closer to the land.

I pulled books from the shelf that hadn't been opened since they were given as birthday presents decades before: *Wild Birds of Britain*, the Usborne *Guide to English Wildflowers*, *The Observer's Book of Trees*. When I finally cracked their spines, and started to recognise the pictures on the paper as details I had drawn on my walks, my perspective changed: I began to see the trees from the wood. Oak, ash and hazel became distinct from each other, elder, hawthorn, birch and cherry stepped forward from the fray, with temperaments and idiosyncrasies, like characters from a play.

There were other books on the shelf. One, by a local amateur historian, details a history of the village so comprehensive that it begins: 'In Africa some 4.5 million years ago, a species of primate started walking upright ...' Reading that book was like

watching a light sinking down a mineshaft into the earth, illu-
minating Mesolithic communities, sacred groves of Neolithic
pagan worship, Celtic tribes, Roman forts and pitched battles
between Saxons and Viking invaders, all buried beneath the neat
gardens and greens of the village. King Sweyn and the Viking
army had sailed up the Thames and pillaged everything from
Reading to Wallingford. Sixty years later, Duke William had
just won the Battle of Hastings and, aiming to ford the Thames,
was drawn by Wallingford and was the next to raze my village
to the ground. It was non-stop ransack.

Now my eyes had focused, I kept finding books in the local
Oxfam, or pamphlets for a quid in the library, all written by
the unacknowledged heroes of England – the local amateur
historians. I read now about the legends specific to our village.
The giant stone, riddled with holes, twenty miles from my
parents' home, onto which King Alfred pursed his lips and blew
a horn that gathered the militia from miles around to face the
Vikings. Old Farmer Nobes, whose tomb was now a pile of
ancient mossy stones by the gates of the shooting school, whose
spectre rode a white horse around the woods. The witch, Nan
Carey, whose name was recorded on the tithe maps, who had
owned what was now the deserted chalk pit by the B-road; steep,
crumbling ivy-clad cliffs hidden in a copse, an inconspicuous
non-place that was now charmed by folklore. There was no path
to this learning, no structure and no signposts; this was wayward
wandering and wondering. Like the badger tracks in the wood,
I cut lines through tracts of land and text, entirely oblivious to
partitions between history, myth and ecology.

There was another layer to this land: the literature. Just
across the river, the countryside of Oxfordshire had been the
inspiration for J. R. R. Tolkien's *The Lord of the Rings*. The
land held the spirit of Frodo and Aragorn and that modern
Merlin: Gandalf. But closer to home, my mother had grown up

outside Newbury, in a Nissen hut for prisoners of war, on the verge of Watership Down, thirty years before Richard Adams immortalised the place with his book of the same name. It was the first book I'd ever read all by myself. Returning to it now, the legends of Hazel and Fiver, the dark spirits of El-ahrairah and the Black Rabbit poured out of the book like Jumanji, enchanting the woods around me.

Another book was even closer to home. Kenneth Grahame wrote *The Wind in the Willows* just twenty miles upriver, in Cookham Dean, but came to the next village on from mine to retire. In 1931, following the book's success, the publishers commissioned Ernest Shepard to illustrate the new edition of the book and the artist, already famous for his depiction of Winnie-the-Pooh, came to Pangbourne to sketch the countryside.

This was all it took for Pangbourne to claim the book, slap its title on the village sign and brand its café after a song from Chapter Two. In the book, the Wild Wood above Ratty's river lodge was full of 'copses, dells, quarries and all hidden places, which had been mysterious mines for exploration'. The woods above the River Thames in Pangbourne were my woods and exactly the same. *The Wind in the Willows* bridged the gulf between reality and fiction and now the luscious description of Mr Badger's warm-hearted home, hanging hams and brick floors, shabby, dishevelled, gruff and welcoming was an apt description of our dell: 'it seemed a place where heroes could fitly feast after victory, where weary harvesters could line up in scores along the table and keep their Harvest Home with mirth and song, or where two or three friends of simple tastes could sit about as they pleased and eat and smoke and talk in comfort and contentment.'

Then, one day, the real world caught up with me. I was walking with my mother after lunch at the local pub; we were crossing the perimeter of the pig farm, where the River Pang cuts a straight line between fields on its way to meet the Thames. There's a lightning-cracked willow with a wild beehive, a deserted house almost entirely sunk in clematis and honeysuckle, and among the surge of spring flowers the scene is chocolate-box pretty, John Constable on sherbet. At the time it was the only place I'd ever seen a kingfisher.

But we never got there. A quad bike came chugging across the paddock and parked itself, just a little too close, in our way. More often than not, the opening line is the facetious: *are you lost?* But this guy came right out with it: 'You've no right to be here. You're trespassing.'

Without a moment's thought, we apologised and left the land. I walked with my mother back to the car, promised to show her the kingfisher lair on some other occasion, and opted to walk the five miles home. I crossed the grass fields and made my way home, marvelling at the power of the words he had spoken. In two sentences he had managed to reverse the direction of two free-willed adults, imposing his will over ours: he got his way and we redirected ours. It was as if his words had cast a spell that had tied our feet and dragged us away.

In Harry Potter there is a rarely used spell called *mobilicorpus*: 'The person who casts the spell can control the recipient almost like a puppet; it is as though invisible strings are supporting them.' The professors of Hogwarts are comfortable calling this a spell, but in the real world, professors of linguistics prefer the euphemism 'speech-act', which refers to any utterance that causes manifest changes in the world. Linguistics divides the speech-act into three sections: first, *locution*, the actual words uttered: *you're trespassing*. There were many ways to cut the cake on what my mum and I were doing. To a literalist, we were walking, putting one foot in front of another; to a romantic, we were bonding, sharing the world as we met it; to a nutritionist we were digesting our meal in the recommended method of a stroll, and to a more metaphysical bent of mind we were offering ourselves to the magic of the world, to the possible glimpse of a kingfisher. But this man had managed to reframe all these subjective assessments into one objective assertion: we were trespassing. None of these other perspectives counted quite so much as his.

The second part of a speech-act is the *illocution*, or the intention behind the words, very clearly: *get off this land, now*. And the third part is the *perlocution*, the influence of the words on the listener. We felt a flush of guilt, a moral sense of being in the wrong, but there was also a sense of being wronged: the abruptness of the intrusion, the absolutism of his approach. Finally, of course, his words caused the reversal of our direction. I wondered what these puppet strings were that yanked us away from the field, how they worked and where their power came from.

When I got home I typed 'trespass' into the search engine. The definition of trespass from the House of Commons library is: 'any unjustifiable intrusion by a person upon the land in possession of another'. And that's the last clear statement you'll get. From here onwards, you have a muddy trek through thick legalise, a language obfuscated by its very precision. You might like to purchase one of the 800-page law textbooks that deals with trespass, the most popular being *Winfield and Jolowicz on Tort* (although other breezeblocks are available) or call up your local law firm, and have them look into it for you, for 200 quid an hour.

I'll save you the bother. The first thing you should know is that the famous sign 'Trespassers Will Be Prosecuted' is an out-and-out lie. Jolowicz calls such signs 'wooden falsehoods', a neat phrase he borrowed from the arch-trespasser of the 1920s, G. H. B. Ward. Since 1694, the misdemeanour of trespass has resided in the province of civil, not criminal, law, and can only be brought to court if damages have been incurred. However, if you resist the landowner's command to leave, if you are impolite, the police can be called and if you resist them, you can be done for a breach of the peace, or for obstructing a police officer.

A landowner is allowed to use reasonable force to encourage you to leave the land, though no one can agree what that means. They are not allowed to detain you, nor are you compelled to give out your name and address. When they do ask you to leave, you don't necessarily have to retrace your steps; it is your right to leave at the closest available exit. If you return to the property, the landowner is allowed to apply for an injunction, which they have to send to you by post, which will be impossible, because they don't have your address. If they do manage to serve you with an injunction and you are caught back on the land, you will now be in contempt of court, which most likely means paying a fine but, in theory at least, can mean prison.

However, owing to two relatively recent pieces of legislation, trespassing can be scaled up into the criminal sphere. In 2005 the Serious Organised Crime and Police Act (SOCPA) extended the arrest powers for the police and allowed them to keep DNA evidence of suspects, even after they had been cleared. Perhaps most controversially of all, it criminalised unauthorised demonstrations in Parliament Square, finally clearing the ten-year anti-war demonstration of activist Brian Haw, emptying the square and silencing his protest. Following the advice of the Armstrong report of July 2003, an extra section was sneaked into the Act, which as a statutory instrument required no new debate from Parliament. Its purpose was to 'create a deterrent to intrusions at high-profile secure sites and to provide police officers with a specific power of arrest of a trespasser at such sites where no other apparent existing offence had been committed'. On these sixteen sites alone, walking is a criminal act.

Armstrong's report came off the back of a publicity stunt by a comedian called Aaron Barschak who had climbed into Windsor Castle during Prince William's twenty-first birthday party. Dressed as Osama Bin Laden, he had mounted the stage, stolen the mic and lifted up the hem of the pink skirt he was wearing to reveal a dark wig of pubic hair, shouting 'Here's the heir apparent'. Even those that didn't find this remotely funny could not have denied the satire when, two years later, it would be classified as serious and organised; clearly, it was neither. But from 2005, Buckingham Palace and fifteen other properties were charmed with a twelve-month jail sentence. The list includes various high-security GCHQ sites, Westminster, Parliament Square, sites of national security interests, but also large areas of land owned privately by the queen and her offspring, with nothing to do with the state.

But the real hocus pocus had come a decade before. The Criminal Justice and Public Order Act 1994 introduced criteria to arrest people for the newly invented crime of 'aggravated trespass'. In 1992, 20,000 ravers and travellers met on common ground for an impromptu May Day rave in the Malvern Hills. It lasted a week and prompted police from the surrounding districts to descend on the land, searching diligently, desperately, for something to arrest them for. In the absence of any actual crime, this proved both difficult and embarrassing. So the bobbies lobbied hard, and two years later, *alakazam!* – trespass stepped up a gear.

The lawyers define 'aggravated' in their own breezy way as 'any circumstance attending the commission of a crime or tort which increases its guilt or enormity or adds to its injurious consequences'. A hidden knife would be aggravated assault; and from 1994, a hidden intention had the same effect. Section 61 of the Act legislated that a police officer could remove two or more people from any private land, if they have met for

a common purpose. That's for the ramblers. Section 63 crim-
inalises any gathering of twenty people or more who meet to
dance to amplified music. That's for the ravers. Section 68 crim-
inalises the intimidation, deterrence, obstruction and disruption
of lawful activities on land, which turns all protest on land not
owned by the protesters into an illegal activity. At the time, this
was primarily to restrict the hunt saboteurs, but is used in the
vast majority of protests of all flavours, from fracking, to animal
rights, to war. Your right to protest is secured by Articles 10 and
11 of the European Convention on Human Rights, but for the
last twenty years, if you do it anywhere but your back garden or
a highway, you can be arrested and sent to jail. On top of this,
since 2014, a common ruling has inserted the phrase 'additional
conduct'. If you are trespassing on land and engaging in any
additional conduct, literally anything, it can now be classed as
intimidation. In the words of the Crown Prosecution website:

> There is no requirement that the additional conduct should
> itself be a crime, so activities such as playing a musical
> instrument or taking a photograph could fall within any-
> thing. What limits the scope of anything is the intention
> that must accompany it: the intention to obstruct, disrupt
> or deter by intimidating.

In short, if you are doing something that is not illegal (photography, dancing, playing the flute), while doing something that
is not criminal (trespassing) you can be automatically arrested,
and liable to six months in prison and a level-four fine. In this
equation, two rights combine and somehow make a wrong.

But there is another dimension to trespass that runs deep
beneath the scaffold of the law. 'Trespass' is one of the most
charged words in the English language. For such a small legal
infraction, the notion of crossing a fence line, wall or invisible

boundary is wrapped in a moral stigma that runs to the heart of English political and civil life. Many of our liberties and the restrictions on them are expressed in terms of land, parameters and property, so much so that it is hard to tell which is a metaphor for the other.

If someone has *crossed the line*, they have strayed over the limits of acceptable action and their words or deeds are deemed to be *beyond the pale* (the old Saxon word for fence). We talk of *access* equally in terms of the physical, with disability rights and the right to roam, and in the abstract realm, in terms of education, health and opportunity. Segregation, which directs the mindset of race and gender, is a word whose Latin root means to be cast out of the flock, and which reinforces the prejudice that racial groups that can be distinguished by a line alone. The legal texts are full of variants of an old word *seisin*, whose origin lies in the French word *saisir*, to seize. This word was the French version of the Latin *rapio*, which leads us to the word rape, where our understanding of sexual politics is structured through metaphors of *personal space* and *acceptable boundaries*.

To *wander* and to *roam* are implicitly connected with moral failings and the word 'vagrancy' has as much sense in morality as it does in legal cases concerning homeless people. A *deviant* is someone who has turned off the right way. To *stray from the path* suggests a clearly marked line of righteousness, signposted by societal or religious doctrines. And the most fundamental link between the physical world of trespassing and its moral parallel, is the origin of the word itself. *Trespasser* is the French verb meaning to cross over, which came from the Latin word *transgredior*, from whose past participle we get the English word: *transgression*. Transgression, which carries with it that pungent whiff of candle smoke and incense, that sense of religious damnation, is the reason Christians pray for the Lord to *Forgive us our trespasses*.

There are boundaries in nature. There are rivers, forests, escarpments, ravines and mountain ranges; there are cellulose walls. But these boundaries are in fact areas of transaction, semi-permeable membranes. The notion that a perimeter should be impenetrable is a human contrivance alone.

When the concept of trespass first entered the law records in the thirteenth century it was meant to establish some reparation for damage – damage to person or land. Over the years, the requirement for damage has disappeared, and a landowner can be compensated, hypothetically, for the breach of his property alone. In a court ruling in 1874, a horse had leaned over a fence in Glamorgan and bitten the plaintiff's mare. There was a debate as to whether the horse had trespassed, so leaving its owner liable for damages. The judge, Lord Coleridge CJ, made what came to be a defining statement: 'If the defendant place a part of his foot on the plaintiff's land unlawfully, it is in law as much a trespass as if he had walked half a mile on it.'

With this ruling, the absolute inviolability of property, a notion that had been hardening for 500 years, was finally consolidated into law. A property, whether your back garden, or 20,000 acres of grouse moor in the Peak District, had become a hypothetical space, a legal force field, a man-made spell. Whether marked by a wall, fence, sign or just an imaginary line, crossing over it turns the inclination of the law against you. The concept of property really is a bubble, a hallucination conjured by a history of privatisation, whose hard, impenetrable border is in fact a flimsy meniscus – one foot over the line, you pierce its logic and the bubble bursts.

Perhaps this goes some way to explaining the response of both the keepers and the crowd to George Beattie Elliot as he blithely walked over Kinder Scout all those decades ago. To cheer a man for walking through heather and likewise to beat him up for it are both absurdly disproportionate to the act itself. But inside the logic of the bubble, such an act is tantamount to anarchy, because it threatens the spell. When the Kinder Trespass was reported in the press, the bare facts of the case were sunk beneath a seething froth of outrage. The *Manchester Evening Chronicle* led with the headline 'MOB LAW ON THE MOORS', stating that 'the danger of mob law usurping the constitutional methods in the ventilation of grievances, real or imagined, is viewed with apprehension not only by landowners, but by thousands of ramblers'.

In their sputtering indignation at the trespass, both sides of the land access debate had finally, with delicious irony, found common ground. To the rambling associations, these kids were naïve upstarts, too brassy to negotiate the slippery political terrain, and had set the campaign for open access back several decades. To the landowning establishment, both the national water boards and the aristocracy, these kids were out of line, bold, impudent commie hooligans threatening to take down the entire state. They must be taught a lesson, slapped with the patrician's rod.

The six young men arrested on the day were taken to the Derby assizes, sixty miles from their families in Manchester, and held there for several months until the trial. Five of them were sentenced to a total of seventeen months behind bars. Because it was not then a crime, none of the men was charged with trespass, but instead with the ancillary charges of the breach of the peace and assault, for which the keepers, who brought the batons and who some might say had started the fight, were not even accused.

This spell was only recently cast upon the moors. The uncultivated land of the Peaks had for centuries been classed as King's Land, free to roam. When it was enclosed in 1836 and parcelled off to the surrounding landowners, the Eyres, Norfolks, Shrewsburys and the Duke of Devonshire were suddenly able to exercise their right to exclude. Only twelve tracks of more than two miles were left open to the ramblers of the surrounding cities, and a private security force uniformed in tweed jackets was brought in, acolytes to light the lines of this enchanted, indicted land.

In 1953, the battle to free Kinder Scout was finally won. The 5,624 acres of land belonging to the Duke of Devonshire were signed over to the Peak District National Park, which had been set up two years earlier. Keepers were now replaced by professional rangers and volunteer wardens whose job was to protect not the ownership of the land, but the land itself. With a wave of a wand, or a judge's hammer, the spell was lifted.

To those in the rambling community who consider themselves in the know, the Kinder Trespass has never been anything but a footnote to this victory. They point instead to the actions of a Liberal MP named James Bryce, who in 1884 brought the first open access act to Parliament. They point to G. H. B. Ward, who set up the first rambling clubs in the north and scoured the old tithe maps of the Peaks for forgotten Rights of Way, or Octavia Hill, who set up the National Trust, or any number of politically minded activists across the country, who worked tirelessly to keep up the pressure on the government, lobbying, pamphleteering, repeatedly pushing bastardised versions of Bryce's bill into Parliament, only to have them rejected by the members. Because it was only with the constitutional success of the 1949 National Parks and Access to the Countryside Act that a structure was secured for the land to be returned to the people. Yet to dismiss the power of legend is to miss the need we have for stories, however fanciful. The Kinder Trespass challenged the power of ownership right at its narrative source. In the myth of property, for all to see, the land had been unspelled.

I went to see the farmer, the one whose house was nestled into the facing flank of the valley of my firepit. Those woods of mine were his, not mine. And his right to eject me from Mr Badger's Wild Wood had become strikingly apparent. He could meet me one day on his land and, on a whim, ask me to leave. If I refused, the police could be called. If I was drawing, mad as it might seem, they could charge me on aggravated trespass. If I came back within three months and was caught again, I would be liable for a fine of £2,500. It wouldn't take many more meetings like that for me to blow the advance on the book I was working on. Yet just as he had the right to deny me, I had the right to ask for 'permissive access', so I knocked on his door.

We spent fifteen slightly awkward minutes in his front garden, rocking on our heels, looking out across the valley. There was a heritage to his presence on this side of the valley that carried an authority I couldn't deny. He had been born in the front room behind us and had taken over the farm from his father. He had known that land for seven decades longer than me. We discussed the various parts of the wood we both knew and he told me that our firepit had in fact been a clay mine for bricks in the 1800s, and maybe even 2,000 years before, since the Romans were also fond of a good brick. Beside us, in the yard, covered in creepers, was a large boulder, a Sarsen stone, which, more than 10,000 years ago, had been carried from Liverpool by a glacier. It was a historical pin in the landscape and the succession of houses and barns of the property had been built around it. He was happy to let me make fires in the dell, and didn't mind me drawing on his land.

Standing by his side, I looked over the valley in front of me and saw for the first time my woods from his side of the road. They seemed smaller, neater, enclosed on all sides by fence and field. Behind the woods are private houses and their gardens, marked by wooden fences. To the north, over the hill, there is the shooting school, and north-east, hidden in the woods behind ten-foot-high electric fences, the deer enclosure. Follow the path east through the woods and you come to Basildon Park, an estate now held by the National Trust. Its 400 acres of parkland were enclosed by Francis Sykes, the former MP for Wallingford and Governor of Cossimbazar, whose fortune was amassed through his work for the British East India Company. Ten miles south of us run the razor-wire fences of Burghfield and Aldermaston's nuclear weapons facilities. The interests of agriculture, hunting, aristocracy, colonialism and war were laid out before me in the undulating valley, like a series of open books.

E. P. Thompson, the historian of the working class, said of the eighteenth century that 'land remained the index of influence, the plinth on which power was erected'. Turn the past tense to present, and his words still apply. I had no interest in the gardens of strangers, but in the rest of the wide, open landscape, I couldn't see a single place I was allowed to be.

'You have no right to be here' moves easily, with the slip of a comma, to 'you have no right to be, here, there, or anywhere'. If those that own the land can dictate what happens on the land, then this private elite can conduct those in society who have nowhere else to be but the land. Race, class, gender, health, income are all divisions imposed upon society by the power that operates on it; if this power is sourced in property, then the fences that divide England are not just symbols of the partition of people, but the very cause of it.

In the gaps between our conversation you could just make out the hum of the pylons that cut through the wood, crossed the road and ran over our heads to the horizon behind us. Buzzing with 400,000 volts of electricity, they distribute power across England. But the fence lines below were charged with a different kind of power, a national and international grid of control whose effect was to divide the people of its land from its worth – its minerals, its game, its goods, its kingfishers – and from each other. You can follow these fence lines and walls all across the country on your Rights of Way, you can keep to your codes of conduct and never question this status quo. Or you can cross these lines, look inside this system and find out who put them there, and how. Because someone cast the net; something cast the spell.

The day is mine: I am free. So I thank the farmer for his time and tea, and follow the drive down to the bottom of the valley, out onto the road, up the tunnel of trees and left along the ghost-path. I climb the fence, cross under the pylons in full view of the farmer's house, climb the broken gate and make my way along the tyre tracks. I pass our dell and continue up through the empty woods to meet the Right of Way. I join the main road for a corner and immediately come to the closed gates of Basildon Park. I put my hands on the flint wall and climb over.

FOX

Possession, property, power and dominion

'There is nothing which so generally strikes the imagination,
and engages the affections of mankind, as the right of property;
or that sole and despotic dominion which one man claims
and exercises over the external things of the world, in total
exclusion of the right of any other individual in the universe.
And yet there are very few, that will give themselves the
trouble to consider the origin and foundation of this right'
— William Blackstone, *Commentaries on the
Laws of England* (1765–9)

It's December 1802. We're in America, in Southampton, just
south of Long Island, on a 'wild and uninhabited, unpos-
sessed and waste land, called the beach' and we're watching a
young man by the name of Lodowick Post gallop through the

scrub with his pals. They're chasing a fox. The fox in question was later to be described by a judge from the Supreme Court of America as both a 'saucy intruder' and, slightly more hysterically, '*hostem humani generis*', the enemy of all mankind. So, alongside their manly pleasure, galloping through the unseasonably warm winter air, these men are also performing something of a public service. The fox cuts across the beach and goes to ground by a disused well in a squelch of watery land known as Peter's Pond. A shot rings out. Lodowick and his chums stop up short, surprised – it was none of them. They watch as a young man called Jesse Pierson steps out of the reeds, picks up the limp corpse and carries it home to flay its pelt.

Now, who owns the fox? The guy who was chasing it or the one who shot it? The fox is in Jesse's hands but Lodowick is a sporting chap with a sporting mindset and thinks that the chase alone declared his ownership of it, if not actual possession. The men have an altercation. Both have guns, although one is on horseback and surrounded by his mates, but neither is backing down. Instead of violence, they choose the right and proper action: they go home and tell their dads.

Jesse goes home to Captain Pierson, a farmer from a line of educated gentlemen landowners, long established in the area, leaders of the town. Lodowick goes home to Captain Post, a veteran of the Revolutionary War, who had gone on to make a fortune in the Dutch West Indies and was a rising star of the nouveau riche (which in America was very nouveau indeed). Like son like father: neither of the daddies was prepared to give ground.

Being true Americans, they went to court. The Posts brought an action of 'trespass on the case' against the Piersons, claiming the fox was rightfully theirs before Jesse had even seen it. By killing the fox, Jesse was trespassing Lodowick's property. The court found in their favour, ruling that the value of the fox, 75 cents, should be paid to Lodowick, plus $5 costs. But the Piersons weren't giving up. They appealed to the Supreme Court of New York, questioning how the act of pursuit alone could have legitimised Lodowick's right of ownership to the fox. Could a child chasing pigeons be said to own them? Besides, when did Lodowick's chase start – the moment he saw the fox, the moment he got on his horse that morning, or the weeks and months and years before that it took to train the dogs? And so began a case that today is taught in almost all Anglo-American property law courses, a case that tested one of the most fundamental questions of civil society: what makes this mine, and not yours; or, in other words, what is property?

Of ownership, the legal dictionary says: 'it is either so simple as to need no explanation or so elusive as to defy definition'. Which doesn't really help. It continues: 'At its most extreme and absolute, it means the power to enjoy and dispose of things absolutely.' Yet for ownership to exist, possession must first be claimed, and of possession, the US Supreme Court has stated: 'there is no word more ambiguous in its meaning than possession'.

For three years, three judges trawled through European case law, chasing a paper trail all the way back to the Norman conquest of England, searching for legal precedents concerning how something free can become something owned. The costs of the case escalated from $5 to $1,000 for each side, but the damages remained the same – 75 cents for a carcass. The fox itself is lost in history, rotting on melting ice, because it had become symbolic of a much wider concern: land.

I arrive at the King's Arms too late for a hot meal, so when I've dumped my bags I swallow a pint, stuff packets of peanuts into my pockets and head out into the cold night. It's a twenty-minute walk to Worcester Lodge, where tomorrow hundreds of people will gather to celebrate the annual meet of the most prestigious fox chase in England, the Duke of Beaufort's Hunt.

In deep darkness I creep along the A-road. With the village behind me I walk along the Beaufort estate perimeter, past woods and fields, until the land on my left opens up. There is a large semi-circle of grass, the road at its diameter and, in the centre of its circumference, Worcester Lodge, a four-storey stone archway. There is a balcony above the arch, where tomorrow people will sup their sherries, and on either side there are rooms that are curtained and dark. Quietly, not quite sure where my trespass begins, I turn off the road and crunch up the gravel path until the iron gate of the archway blocks my way.

The story of land ownership, or, rather, the fable that land can be owned exclusively, goes all the way back to the moment that humans turned from nomadism to a settled, agricultural existence. Important resources such as natural springs, fishing lakes and fertile pastureland became properties of a sort, something to be defended and contested. Aristotle thought that property served to make men more virtuous, giving them a responsibility to the earth that made them serious citizens. Plato, that proto-communist, thought that property corrupted men, and in *The Republic* sketched a vision where nothing was owned, and each man received a daily salary for his work. Two hundred years later, Virgil wrote of a halcyon age where:

No fences parted fields, nor marks nor bounds
Distinguished acres of litigious grounds
But all was common.

He must have been suffering from a severe bout of nostalgia, because the very foundation myth of Rome was built upon the defence of a boundary. In what is probably the first reported incident of the disproportionate treatment of trespassers, the historian Livy reports that 'Remus contemptuously jumped over the newly raised walls and was forthwith killed by the enraged Romulus, who exclaimed, "So shall it be henceforth with every one who leaps over my walls."'

When the Romans invaded Britain they brought with them the Emperor Justinian's categories of land ownership which described four different resources that should not, could not, be privatised. The *res communes* – the air and the sea – were the natural property of all humanity; the *res publicae* – the rivers, parks and public roads – belonged to all citizens. The *res universitas* were the public baths or theatres, essentially council amenities, and the *res nullius* referred to wasteland, cattle pasture, woodland and wild animals, including, 2,000 years later, our famous fox.

When the Roman occupation finally collapsed, like a soggy cardboard box left out in the English rain, the land reverted to clan rule. Kings, thanes and ceorls ruled their demesnes, offering protection and order to the peasants who were tied to the land in complex webs of exchange of military service and offerings of produce. By the eighth century, peasants were practising collective farming, an open-field system where plots of land were allocated on rotation, sowing and harvesting was a communal endeavour and the resources of the land were shared by those that lived on it.

The laws of King Ine, who ruled Wessex from AD 688 to 726, have survived to this day. The legislation reads like basic modern tort law, standardising redress and compensation for various acts of harm and damage inflicted by one on another. They contain rules over fighting in church, blood feuds, regulating the actions of traders, forfeiture of land due to lack of military service. Fences and hedges existed, but for the purpose of containing livestock, not for the restriction of free movement. Nowhere is trespass mentioned.

I have in my hands the cold iron bars of the arch gate, my face pressed through the gaps like a cartoon prisoner in a cowboy jail. In front of me is a wash of darkness, with a tiny speck of light dead centre: a brazier perhaps, or a bonfire. Though I can't see a thing, I know from the satellite map that what lies before me is a two-mile-long drive that cuts through woodland all the way to Badminton House. Inside live the Beauforts, a family who can trace their bloodline back through the years to the one man who imported the notion of private property as we know it now: William the Conqueror. When William first set foot on English sand, he proclaimed to his men: 'I have seized England with both my hands.' From that moment on, a new logic bound England, the logic that saw the vast majority of its inhabitants barred from its lands, the logic that fenced fields, walled parkland and led right up to the locked iron gate in my hands. But tomorrow, this gate will be open.

The next morning, I'm sitting in a corner of the semi-circle, watching the cars fill up the space around me. I'm drawing in my sketchbook, a useful technique that somehow legitimises public loitering. The heavy silence of last night has disappeared and there is a jolliness embellished with the pride of pageantry. People step out of their cars, stretch their legs and walk blithely through the gate.

The fashion is royal dress-down – the queen posing for photographs at Balmoral – silk headscarves and blue gilets, Le Chameau wellies and stout tweed jackets. The balcony is lined with people chit-chatting and, below, car boots double as buffet tables for wicker baskets full of picnic pieces. Though the faces are cheerful and warm, I feel self-conscious, conspicuously out of place, for here is something tribal and I don't belong.

The debate surrounding fox hunting has long been the line drawn between warring factions of England. It posits animal

welfare groups against traditionalists and the idealism of inter-
fering City types against a romanticised countryside realpolitik,
nature red in fang and paw. Most dramatically of all, it is the
fulcrum of a bitter class war in England: the toffs parade on
horseback while the plebs run around in the mud. But today, in
the crowds, not everyone talks like Bertie Wooster. Among the
caviar-and-smoked-salmon accents, there is a thick Gloucester
burr, the oral expression of a cheddar and chutney pub lunch.
Here on the ground, away from the spin of politics and media,
there is something that is less binary, or at least more nuanced,
than the classic cartoon of Class.

I walk through the gate to join the throng. A field of lush
green grass is speckled with groups of people. Plush dogs and
pedigree children run around, and some men and women are
already perched on glossy horses. The avenue runs through the
trees, undulating over the valleys, and, right at the very end,
miles away, gleaming whenever the clouds part: Badminton
House. In the far distance, a troop of horses is cantering towards
us, with a pack of dogs at their hooves, an impressive, magnificent and anachronistic sight. When the phalanx arrives,
the hundreds of people in the field crowd around a temporary
fenced enclosure where inside, the dogs now gambol and leap
over each other. The Duke of Beaufort is there, nursing an inch
of sherry in a plastic pint glass, and three horsemen stand as still
as their horses permit, two young and dashing, the third a port-
stained Humpty-Dumpty.

The dogs, or *hounds* as the tribe calls them, are beautiful
creatures, with snowy markings on their cream backs like fallow
deer and a clownish and captivating energy. They have a world-
famous (and highly profitable) bloodline that runs back almost
400 years, when they were used to hunt down deer, boar and
hare, and the occasional fox. In 1762 the 5th Duke of Beaufort
returned home empty-handed from a stag hunt, in an area now

part of the Westonbirt Arboretum, and the pack took up the scent of a fox. The team had such a fine run of it that the duke focused on foxes from then on. Today the hunt covers an area of 2,000 square kilometres, and has become renowned across the globe. In spite of the Labour government's ban in 2004 of hunting wild game with dogs, or perhaps because of it, fox hunting is thriving: today there are over 180 different hunt packs in Britain and subscriptions are up nationwide, most noticeably with younger riders.

The dogs are bored. Two of them have inexplicably dug deep holes in the grass, and now most are sitting as one, impatiently facing the horses. They're ready. There is a brief flurry of activity, the gates to the enclosure are opened, children are lifted onto dads' shoulders, the horns blow, there are cheers, and the pack thunder off to the woods at the bottom of the field. Since the ban, these hunts have officially given up on live quarry, and instead they chase a trail of fox urine or chemical compounds laid by a hunt member twenty minutes before the chase. I watch them disappear into the woods, pursuing, like Proust's madeleines, the essence of the past, or more literally, a pungent bag of piss.

Like a shoplifter I loiter around the gate to the main estate, unsure of what happens next. People begin folding up their hampers, closing the boot doors and saying their goodbyes. Some wander past me for a quick stroll in the grounds – they keep mainly to the first slope of the valley, still two miles away from the house. And this seems to be my chance. I slip through the gate into a murky grey ground of trespass law: the duke has given his permission for the grounds to be open today, but to a limit, and now the line is not one of property, but propriety. I start walking.

Once William the Conqueror had defeated Harold on Senlac Hill in Hastings, he advanced on London. He crushed Edgar

Atheling in as little as two weeks and balanced the crown upon his head on Christmas Day, 1066. The coronation was the first of his spells to be cast upon the land, a PR stunt – he wasn't conquering England, but asserting his rightful claim to the throne. Over the next few years, he distributed the land to his French barons, about 180 of them, who went on to build castles in strategic locations to monitor the Anglo-Saxons and suppress their uprisings. The land, however, was only owned by the consent of the king. It could be taken back at any time. England had a new centralised source of power, bound by the notion of sole dominion, underpinned by the threat of eviction.

William kept about a fifth of England for himself. And this long avenue of open grassland that leads to Badminton House, the width of a football pitch and the length of forty, is a record of what he did with his lands. It is a *chase*, a long section of land cut through the woods to facilitate horseback hunting. As a Norman noble, hunting was what you did with your day: not only was it practice for armed combat, it was also a highly effective source of revenue. In a land without a standardised coin, venison was a valuable trading commodity; as his dogs sniffed out another hind, William was chasing petty cash through the woodlands. But under Anglo-Saxon rule, these tracts of land were recognised as the vital source of subsistence for all peasants of the area and governed by strict localised customs. Commoners, the people who used these commons, had long-established rights not just to graze their cattle and pigs, but to take wood (estovers), dig peat and gravel (turbary) and fish the ponds (piscary). The problem for William was that deer are easily spooked and require large tracts of land to live comfortably – and so to protect them, and for the first time in English history, the commoners and their cattle were barred from the land they used. These areas became known as forests, from the Latin *foris*, meaning 'outside of', because they were areas that operated *outside of* common law.

Within these forests, another set of laws applied, ones that were intended not to promote equality and justice, but simply to fatten the deer for the king.

And so began the cult of exclusion. William's love of hunting (and of petty cash) was shared by his barons, and a hundred years after the Battle of Hastings a quarter of England was forested, including most of Essex, Sussex, Surrey and Hampshire. Villages were burned, roads re-routed and farmed fields left to grow wild. By the 1200s, there were almost 2,000 deer parks across England, breeding grounds for these flighty cash-sacks, protected and guarded areas outside the common laws of the land. It is here that we start to come across references to trespass in its most primitive form: *quare intrusit*.

The assizes of *novel disseisin* were the local courts devoted to cases regarding new dispossession, or unlawful seisin. Seisin was what Jesse Pierson did to the fox and what William the Conqueror did to England (with both his hands). Literally translated as rape, it is the definitive term for the moment of possession. It was William's grandson, Henry II, who established the first court of novel disseisin, which became hugely popular due to its speed and expediency – rather than dealing with the messy business of proving who actually owned the land, it sought simply to give redress to those whose property had recently been seized by other parties. Cases included anything from burglary to cattle rustling or violent assault. Decisions were made, damages paid, the property was recovered, the King's Peace restored. But over time the notion of the violation of property expanded, so that simply to cross the boundary was deemed damage enough. Through the increment of various cases, the cult of exclusion hardened into common law: it had precedence.

I am now approaching the end of the ride. Two miles of grass cut through working woodland, the spine of the 52,000-acre estate, has led to its heart, the parkland and the manorial seat,

Badminton House. Twenty-five windows wide, the two turrets and grand Vitruvian façade curtain a large multi-faceted estate office, with gardens of symmetrical hedges, roses and tulips, the world-famous dog kennels and its own private church.

All the other celebrants of the hunt have disappeared behind me, the house is silent and I am alone before a long netted wire fence, and a wooden slatted gate, six foot high with a latch at the top, for riders on horseback to open. The gate is locked, and I don't fancy scaling it directly in front of the house, so I follow the fence round to the east, where a road sweeps up to the front porch. The land before me was seized just as the notion of tres-pass was emerging in the late thirteenth century; but it took another hundred years or so, and a new dynasty on the throne, to legitimise fully the fence around it.

The Tudor era was the goldrush for private property. Common land was being privatised not only by barons of Norman heri-tage, but by any number of squires and gentry who saw the vast profits to be made in turning the land over to sheep. The watch-word of Tudor enclosure was 'improvement', a euphemism for privatisation that councils and building contractors use to this day. It contains the idea that unowned space was a waste of potential profit, and that society at large could be bettered by the private regulation of land.

This new philosophy was ratified by the emergence of a new tradesman, the surveyor, who was able to make use of new technologies to map out the exactitudes of what was owned. A multitude of books, pamphlets and lectures drew out the new terms of land ownership. The concept of property was soon divorced from localised tradition and instead standardised into textbook definitions that applied across the land. The purity of mathematics was used to sanctify the purity of property, as John Dee describes in the preface to his work *Elements of Geometry*, published in 1570: 'the perfect Science of Lines, Plaines, and Solides which like a divine Justicier, gave unto every man, his owne'. In the Reformation, maths was God, and those who held the numbers held the land. Land ownership itself became a profession, and supported a raft of other jobs – lawyers, surveyors, estate agents – each generating reams of paperwork to prove their own viability. When Hamlet is skulking around the graveyard in Act V of Shakespeare's play, he picks up a skull, stares into its hollow sockets and ponders that 'this fellow might be in's time a great buyer of land, with his statutes, his recognisances, his fines, his double vouchers, his recoveries. Is this the fine of his fines, and the recovery of his recoveries, to have his fine pate full of fine dirt?'

Aside from Hamlet's teenage nihilism, Shakespeare, himself a modest landowner, gives us some insight into the mechanics of this new perception of property. The fence lines that were rolled out across England were the manifestation of lines of legal prose, and each justified the other. As these fences went up around England, what lay inside them was partitioned from the web of social ties and responsibilities to the communities that surrounded them and became abstracted into commodity alone – something to be bought and sold on the market.

There was push-back, both in government and Church. In 1601, Edward Glascock rebuked Robert Johnson, MP for Monmouth and a professional surveyor, saying, 'I think the gentleman that last spake hath better Skill in Measuring of Land, than Men's Consciences.' The necessary displacement of people from within the fences, and their subsequent estrangement from the wealth of the land, was decried as an immoral act, kicking away the crutches that the peasants leaned on for their subsistence. One Puritan preacher and polemicist, Robert Crowley, levelled this accusation against the gentry in 1548: 'God hath not sette you to surveye hys lands, but to playe the stuardes in his householde of this world, and to se that your pore below tenants lacke not theye necessaries.'

There is a cattle grid where the fence parts for the driveway. And a sign that says DEER IN RUT. It is late autumn, mating season, and this sign points to the very prominent danger of being skewered by a horny stag, amorously or otherwise. I can't see the herd, so I chance it, and cross the fence line into the duke's private park. Among the various follies of the estate is an ancient hermitage made from the roots of trees. Built during a brief fad for root houses, the landscape designer and astronomer Thomas Wright designed it to accommodate a part-time fancy-dress hermit. On the back end of the hut is a bench under an alcove of a forked bough, with an inscription that reads: 'Here loungers loiter – here the weary rest', and a few nights before, circling it on the map, this had seemed as good a place as any to sit and draw.

With the house to my right, I cut a diagonal across the parkland, a landscaped, picture-book Arcadia of undulating lawns and statuesque oaks. A dried-up, grassed-up dyke runs to my left, and I cross it on a small stone bridge, my gaze sweeping the land for the root house. It emerges through the trunks of the trees, a thatched roof squat beneath a circle of grand oaks. From a distance, it has the look of a gingerbread fairy-tale cottage, home to a craggedy old witch. It is, in fact, dedicated to the deity of Badminton House, a little-known sorceress by the name of Urganda, who was a Portuguese version of Circe, the witch that Odysseus encountered halfway through his journey home from Troy. I circle the hut, and find an inscription above its front door, which has been graffitied by generations of dukelets: 'Here Urganda, in woods dark and perplexed, inchantments mutters with her magic voice.' The place *is* enchanting, a make-believe theatre prop that has weathered into something real, and I want to draw it, while sitting under one of its oaks.

I circle it again, to find the best angle, and not 200 yards away I notice the herd of deer which have been watching me all along. Each and every one of them is paused, poised, posed, one foot in the air, a troupe of dancers waiting for the music to begin. They are a knee jerk away from bolting, streaming across the parkland, sending a visual alarm to anyone in the great house that an intruder is at large. But I sense the greater danger when I see three stags at the head of the herd. Two are already on their feet, but the third, still sitting on his haunches, is the Marlon Brando of the bunch, heavy and hulking, sexy in the calm assurance of his own dominance. It is instantly apparent that in this rutting season, as with many before, he's been getting most of the action.

In the year he died, English philosopher Thomas Hobbes wrote: 'my mother gave birth to twins: myself and fear'. The moment she heard that the Spanish were on their way, coming over to colonise England, her waters broke and out came Thomas. He went on to write *Leviathan*, a treatise on how best to structure a society and nation state, which was published the year that the English civil war ended. He later claimed that this war had been brought about by 'the new belief in unconditional property right' and much of *Leviathan* is a study of his concept of property, and where it gained its legitimacy.

For Hobbes, property was a man-made construct, designed to lift us out of our 'state of nature', which was one of conflict and precarity. This is the foundational text of what is now called libertarianism, and 300 years later was neatly summarised by Robert Frost in his sardonic poem 'Mending Wall': 'Good fences make good neighbors.' For Hobbes, property and its strict delineation was the basis of all civil society, a social contract that ensured human interaction be peaceful and civil, superior to that of the wild animals; without it our lives would be 'solitary, poor, nasty, brutish, and short'. And out here, caught in the beam of Marlon's steady gaze, these words seem more than theoretical: I decide to channel Hobbes, and leave this state of nature for the protection of the fence. I don't look back until I'm almost there, and while the two young stags have disappeared, Marlon is on his feet, adding a final exclamation mark to his silent threat. *Turn, piddly human, and do not make me gore you against an eighteenth-century Grade II listed building.*

I pass through a ten-foot gate into another sweeping valley dotted with isolated oaks. I walk along a path lined with trees that form another one of the chases emanating from Badminton House like rays of the sun. I'm calm again, safe behind the fence, and I stop to draw an enormous tree stump that looks like an inverted moon crater. Inside it is an oasis of wet rot and green life, ferns and flowers, and as it appears on the page of my sketchbook it turns into a table-topped dormant volcano, a private Eden walled from the field by its bulky outer layer of crumbling cambium and hard bark.

From the Middle Ages onwards, theorists of property worked from the premise of the Garden of Eden, the original walled park of western philosophy. In Genesis 1.28, God instructs Adam and Eve to 'Be fruitful, and multiply, and replenish the earth, and subdue it: and have dominion over the fish of the sea, and over the fowl of the air, and over every living thing that moveth upon the earth.'

The anthropocentric authors of the Bible state that everything on earth was created by God for the sole use of Adam; in other words, for all of humanity. In Tudor England, this was the unquestioned consensus, a given. However, the problem that followed was how any one member of this group could justify enclosing a common wealth for their own private gain. This was a problem taken up by a range of Tudor philosophers, jurists and

theologians and continues to the modern day, in a snowstorm of thuslys, moreovers, therefores and furthermores, otherwise known as logic. Carol M. Rose, Professor Emeritus of Law at Yale University, has encapsulated these arguments in a neat phrase she calls 'ownership anxiety', the compulsion to validate the central crux of the argument, the origin myth at the base of every area of private land on earth: the moment of 'first possession'.

Hugo Grotius was a Dutch statesman and jurist writing in the early seventeenth century. He worked from the principle of Eden – that all land was given to all people. But he gave himself the authority to extend God's claim that those who were able to 'replenish the earth and subdue it' had earned their right to exclude others from it. He saw private property as an institution invented by man but which, once created, had become a law of nature, that is, an issue of inherent morality: 'property (dominium) ... was introduced by Man's Will, and being once admitted, this law of Nature informs us, that it is a wicked Thing to take away from any Man, against his Will, what is properly his own.'

Samuel von Pufendorf elaborated on this theory in 1673, explaining how the first person to occupy an area of land had a moral right to it simply because they did not have to displace anyone else to claim it as their own. In modern terms: if you arrive at a waiting room at a railway station and take an empty seat, it is fair for you to defend that seat if someone tries to throw you off. You have occupied that space peacefully and the law should defend your right to maintain occupancy. In other words: *finders, keepers*.

For John Locke, writing in 1689, 'finders, keepers' did not justify the right to exclusive possession. But you could earn it by working. For Locke, private property in land was an extension of the fundamental ownership of one's body, and the labour it exerted. Once you have combined the earth's natural resources with your own sweat and skill, ploughed the fields, sowed the seeds, then the land and its wealth should be yours and no one else's:

> Though the earth and all inferior creatures be common to all men, yet every man has a property in his own person; this no body has any right to but himself. The labour of his body and the work of his hands, we may say, are properly his. Whatsoever then he removes out of the state that nature hath provided and left it in, he hath mixed his labour with, and joined to it something that is his own, and thereby makes it his property.

For Locke, the notion of property was a natural law, one that applied to men and beasts alike; it is a natural inclination to guard the resources that make life possible. Locke disagreed with the Hobbesian idea that the state of nature was a brutish dog-eat-dog existence, preferring instead the idea of an inherent morality that obliges one not 'to harm another in his life, health, liberty or possessions'. However, he conceded that this moral or natural law was fragile, and so required a consensus agreement to safeguard it, an artificial creation called the rule of law. The role of law, therefore, was to protect a citizen's right to protect their own life, and thusly, moreover, therefore and furthermore, the role of law was to protect private property: 'The great and chief end, therefore, of men's uniting into commonwealths and putting themselves under government is the preservation of their property.'

This was a key moment in property philosophy, not unlike the creation of the forests: one small step of logic for man, one giant leap for mankind. Suddenly, the law of the land lurched from protecting the rights of all citizens to protecting the rights of those with property – logic had led Locke from the natural law of self-preservation to the artificial law of property protection, and by extension, 400 years later, he had reframed this walk of mine on a field in Gloucestershire, into a direct assault on the Duke of Beaufort.

I have walked up the slope of the parkland, through a beguiling sculpture park of fallen oaks – great canopies that have, over the years, come crashing down, had their leaves and brush cleared and been left to create striking silhouettes against the sky. I come to the end of the field to find myself enclosed by another fence. A tall slatted gate is chained at the bottom, and to leave this parkland I must climb ten feet into the air. I'm taking the bag off my shoulders when I hear a voice, the classic opener: 'Are you lost?'

I look up, and on the other side of the fence are six horses with their riders. They are on their way back from the hunt but they are dressed in blue coats, not green, a sign that they are subscribers to the hunt and have no property here. They neither represent the duke nor have anything more than his permission to be on the land. But their authority comes from their horses. An infamous YouTube video flashes through my mind, filmed in 2017 during the Middleton Hunt. Members of the West York Sabs are being confronted by George Winn-Darley, owner of Staunton Moor and Representative of the Moorland Association, on a track through a dour piece of land in North Yorkshire. Winn-Darley is mounted on a beautiful, incredibly well-behaved horse, and is driving it repeatedly into the gaggle of anoraked hunt saboteurs, kicking one in the chest with his black leather boot. When the Sabs accuse him of assault, he responds that he is using 'reasonable force', availing himself of a semantic grey ground of property law that favours those with pockets deep enough to argue their case in court. In just over a minute of footage, he manages to shout 'Go back to the highway' thirty-two times, all the while emphasising his words with little jerks of the foot, still attached to the stirrups. His performance is a masterclass of surrealist repetition and a reminder of how, throughout history, horses have been used to assert authority.

Ironically, the fence protects me: trespassing the duke's land, with his representatives on the other side of the fence, I'm safe from the heft of their horses. I take the option they offer me, because it's easier for everyone, and say, 'Yes, could you help?' They spend a while redirecting me, and I watch them gallop off, punching deep crescent dents into the mud as they go. I climb the gate and drop down to the other side.

Directly beneath where the speaker's horse was standing is something I have never seen before. Among the brown oak leaves, almost camouflaged against the grass, is the head of a deer — black muzzle, grey fur, eyes shut. Its jawbones are visible beneath the torn fur and a knotted rope of vertebrae runs from the base of the skull, bright pink like cherry yoghurt, turns a right angle at the ribs and extends the full length of its spine to its hip bone and two thigh bones. It is a ravaged carcass, almost no meat left on the bone, and other than the pack of dogs currently ranging the Beaufort hunt I can't think what could have done it. *Jus abutendi*, I think. 'The right to destroy is an inherent component of the right to property. It has traditionally been called the *jus abutendi*: the right to consume, transform, and abuse ... An owner is entitled to consume or transform the thing that is the object of property rights, and the same theme is evident in international law.'

And this vision somehow clarifies the mysterious rite of fox hunting. The red fox is a red herring that leads you on a chase away from the real meaning of the hunt. Instead, it is the liveries the hunters wear that speak more directly to the source of this ritual: the green jackets and leather boots are relics from the uniforms worn by the duke's yeomen, the private army that each lord kept to underscore his rule of the land. Yeomen were used to mete out justice, the arm of the rule of law that in feudal times was the whim of the landowner. Just as the Catholic Church used to consecrate the boundaries of land, in a village ritual where youngsters would walk the edges of fields, blessing what lay within with fertility for next year's crop, so fox hunting is a ritual, an elaborate display of total dominion within the land. The hunt is a reassertion of the right to go anywhere the fox takes them, over hedges, fences, farmed fields and public highways. The power of the horses' hooves, that deranged baying of the hounds, the bloodlust that has survived through the ban, is a fet-ishisation of that moment of possession, the moment that dogs encircle the fox, the moment the land is seized.

Grotius, Pufendorf, Locke and their like were unable, or unwilling, to confront the true mechanism of land seizure, that the notion of peaceful first occupancy is a lie, that the land was already held by the people that used it, relied on it and lived upon it. But when the cult of exclusion met the philosophy of the commons, exclusion won because it rode a horse.

England was not seized when Harold fell from his horse. Nor was it seized when the crown was placed on William's head. The following year, William embarked on a military campaign called the Harrying of the North, an assault on the commoners just shy of genocide. It was a sustained campaign that began in the north of England and set a precedent that was to be followed right up to the nineteenth century. It was a campaign that relied on brute force, the power of the sword and the horse cutting the ties between the people and the land. In the words of the Conqueror himself:

In mad fury I descended on the English of the north like a raging lion, and ordered that their homes and crops with all their equipment and furnishings should be burnt at once and their great flocks and herds of sheep and cattle slaughtered everywhere. So I chastised a great multitude of men and women with the lash of starvation and, alas! was the cruel murderer of many thousands, both young and old, of this fair people.

I'm sitting in Room 35 of the National Gallery. It's a weekday, but it's still busy with tourists, using the room as a corridor to the selfie-scrum, two rooms on, before a still life of some sunflowers. In front of me there is a painting by Thomas Gainsborough, small and chocolate-box twee, which is largely ignored.

A man stands before a tree, leaning on a bench, a shotgun tucked under his right arm, a hunting dog at his heel. He wears a tricorn hat and a silver dress coat, and his eyes link with the viewer. A woman sits on the bench, her eyes caught by something behind us. She wears a shimmery sky-blue dress, her feet poking out from the golden hem of her petticoat. To the right, the landscape rolls out behind the couple, a full two-thirds of the picture, telling us everything they want us to know about them. They're doing well for themselves: the land they own has just been harvested, they've sheep in the fields (money in the bank) and they're in the flush of young adulthood. They are Mr and Mrs Andrews, newlyweds.

The art critic John Berger had a pop at this painting in his television series *Ways of Seeing*. Through Berger's prism we see a pair of haughty privileged kids, flaunting their wealth, challenging us to the one aspect of the land behind them that made it completely theirs: the right to exclude us.

They have become not a couple in nature, as Rousseau imagined nature, theirs is private land ... If a man stole a potato at that time, he risked a public whipping. The sentence for poaching was deportation. Without a doubt, among the principal pleasures this painting gave to Mr and Mrs Andrews was the pleasure of seeing themselves as owners of their own land.

As Berger delivers his monologue, the camera pans out to a new version of the portrait, vandalised by Berger, or one of his art department. The tree trunk that roots the composition has a sign painted on it, above Mrs Andrews' head, which reads: TRESPASSERS KEEP OUT.

The painting is itself a form of private property, Gainsborough's labour and skill hardened into a desirable object, a commodity that can be bought or sold and held behind locked doors. It would have hung above the marital bed of the Andrews, for their eyes only, a poetic version of the surveyors' maps in a Tudor landlord's office, a mirror of their magnificence. The public were granted access to the painting in the 1960s, when it was sold to the National Gallery, but the land it depicts remains out of bounds. However, while the two-dimensional realm of the painting is literally impenetrable, the land it depicts is not.

So, in the hot hum of high summer, me and a friend drive out to Sudbury, on the border between Essex and Suffolk. I have read online that the current owner of the estate receives so many pilgrims that he let one spend an entire day painting the wrong tree. My friend sympathises, as she lives on the farm once owned by the nature writer Roger Deakin, and has had her fair share of pilgrims; depending on her mood, she will either receive them courteously or hide in a hedge.

We walk up the gravel drive and ring the bell of the large house. The owner tells us where to find the tree, we thank him and drive round to the back fields. As we approach a tree, a hare turns out of the long grass and simultaneously a barn owl drops, wide-winged from the leaves, and soars low across the field. A good start.

From the size of the trunk in the painting, the tree was already a couple of hundred years old when Gainsborough turned up with his brushes. That makes the tree before us now almost 500 years old, and it looks its age. Its crown is thinning and several boughs have fallen, leaving great gaps in its canopy and old worn holes in the trunk, perfect homes for barn owls. There is a large crack down the trunk, and the wood inside has turned to red dust. My friend and I stretch out on the dry grass at its base, like cats on an Aga. I pull out my sketchbook and draw the tree as flies thud onto the cartridge paper. Time passes and eventually my friend has to leave, so we hug and, as her car pulls out of the drive, she takes our permission to be there with her. For John Berger, in memoriam, I'm staying; I want to cross the forbidden line of the painting and enter its real space.

You can tell Gainsborough had a sense of humour because he called his dog 'Fox'. And when you know a little more about his private life, that his wife was the bastard child of Henry Somerset, the 3rd Duke of Beaufort, this twinkle-eyed pun garners an altogether more subversive tone – you can guess which side of the fence he was on.

When Justice Livingstone referred to the fox in the Pierson and Post case as 'the enemy of all mankind', we can presume he was referring to foxes in general. The fox has always been the archetypal trespasser, the wanton destroyer of fowl, the white-gloved invader of the hen house. By the eighteenth century, Bold Reynard, the character of the fox sourced from twelfth-century French and Germanic folklore, was a firmly established peasant-hero character, either gypsy or vagabond, outwitting the lords and gentry with his wily ways. Perhaps this adds an extra hue to the tradition of fox hunting, giving it a symbolic meaning on top of the ritualistic display of land ownership – by flushing the fox from the forest, these huntsmen are re-enacting the cult of exclusion.

I am sitting by the lake, drawing the scene. The sun is hammering hard on the earth, filtering colours with its glare: all greens are yellows, all shadows are pitch black and the sky is so blue it throbs like a bruise. There is an occasional plip from the lake, from the lips of big fish that rise like brown mud from the shallows. Dragonflies are knitting soft nets of noise above my head and the wood pigeons repeat their earnest cry: *my toes hurt Betty, my TOES hurt Betty*. For forty minutes or so I sit in a perfect reverie, a kind of loose concentration that turns streams of distinct thoughts into pools of passive rumination. Breath deepens, slows, holds and lengthens, the body calms into that moment just before sleep. Drawing is meditating with your eyes open – it turns the self into something permeable: no longer are you the end point of sight, but, with the paper as the final destination, you become simply a catalyst, your mind only a midpoint in a transformation.

The Heythrop Hunt is an offshoot of the Beaufort and uses the same pack of dogs. In 2011, it was the first hunt to fall foul of the new fox-hunting legislation brought in by the Labour government, when its members pleaded guilty to four counts of 'unlawfully hunting a wild fox with dogs'. The case gained considerable publicity, though largely in criticism of the RSPCA, who brought the case and had spent £327,000 on the proceedings. Again, class warfare clouded the debate – David Cameron, posh boy of posh boys, used to ride with the Heythrop, and the hunt faction declared the case a war on tradition, an act of inverted snobbery. Even District Judge Tim Pattinson criticised the RSPCA, saying, 'Members of the public may feel that RSPCA funds can be more usefully employed', adding (somewhat fatuously): 'It is not for me to express an opinion.'

The Heythrop Hunt was fined £4,000 with £15,000 costs, and two of their members had to pay £1,800 and £1,000 respectively. The footage that convicted these men was filmed by the Cotswolds' animal rights group Protect Our Wild Animals, who operate in a similar manner to the Sabs that Winn-Darley was filmed kicking, following the hunt and monitoring it for illegal activity. Outside the court one of the convicted huntsmen said that he had only pleaded guilty to avoid the escalating costs of the RSPCA's case. His following comment was aimed at the Sabs who had filmed his crime, but is a useful text in the psychology of property: 'These people are vigilantes following me around and filming me ... I'm not allowed to follow them around Tesco and see if they steal a tin of beans.'

No, but Tesco do employ security guards for precisely that purpose. What stands out in this quote is that for the huntsman and his sporting chums the body of a fox, alive or dead, is analogous to a tin of beans. It is an object excised from its context, a thing, reified by the principle of property.

By the time Gainsborough had painted his portrait of Mr and Mrs Andrews, land had followed the same logic that the huntsman projected onto his fox. It had become fully commodified, pulled from the roots of human relations, bagged and tagged like a tree in a garden centre. The fence, which had for so long existed to keep things in, had by now had its dynamic reversed, and was the primary technology of keeping things out. If the Andrews were anything like their landowning counterparts, the hedges and greenery of Gainsborough's portrait would have concealed an artillery of anti-trespass technology: man-traps in the hedges, spring-loaded iron-toothed thigh-crunchers that snared playing children and creeping poachers alike. There were tripwires that set off shotguns hidden in the brush, spraying the area with lead shot. And, long before any official police force had been established, teams of private security guards, gamekeepers, prowled the land, armed with shotguns and flails, or swinges, long oak staffs with heavy cudgels hinged by leather straps, weapons designed primarily for the defence of property rights. And the law was fully onside. E. P. Thompson explained that 'Since property was a thing, it became possible to define offences as crimes against things, rather than as injuries to men. This enabled the law to assume with its robes, the postures of impartiality: it was neutral as between every degree of man, and defended only the inviolability of the ownership of things.'

Words had also changed their meaning. The original meaning of the word 'acre' was 'open country, untenanted land', but by Gainsborough's time it had come to refer to an exact measurement of land, standardised across the country to facilitate valuations and sales. The most significant change was in the definition of the word property itself. In feudal times, property meant rights *in* a piece of land, referring to the customs of permissible actions and their reciprocal duties. Medieval lawyers never spoke of owning land, but, rather, of holding the land – an aspect echoed in the terms still used today of 'freehold' and 'leasehold'. The land was yours to use, according to local custom and to the ecology of what each particular site had to offer – you held it, but you didn't have it. When the commons were *particularised* (to use a popular euphemism of the time), that is, divided up and sold, these rights were part of the deal and became the sole right of the owner of the land – rights *in* land became rights *to* land. Property had come to be understood less as a network of relations between community and land, and now referred simply to the land itself. The space without the community. This is the origin of the phrase real property, having nothing to do with the nature of truth, but instead deriving from *res/realis*, the Latin word for *thing*.

But what about the wild animals? These wild-eyed ramblers have no regard for the lines of land ownership. Smoots, meuses and smeuses are ancient terms for the same phenomenon seen today across England – those little pathways that run through hedges and under fences made by foxes, badgers and hares. These lawless critters move between estates as if trespass laws don't exist, and in the eighteenth century this raised concerns about who held the rights to hunt them. Was hunting a lease granted by the sovereign, or was it a right that came with land ownership? As communities excluded from privatised land sought to re-establish their rights to hunt the wild animals that fed them, poaching became the crime that defined the eighteenth century, and caused another bout of Ownership Anxiety.

This time, the defence fell to William Blackstone, jurist, judge and Tory politician, whose quote opens this chapter. Like Hobbes, he argued that the rights of property came from the sovereign, and that, in the case of wild animals, a person's right to hunt them came from a grant, issued by Parliament or local government. His magnum opus, *Commentaries on the Laws of England*, was divided into four sections and the second, 'The Rights of Things', dealt almost exclusively with real estate.

> The only question remaining is, how this property became actually invested: or what it is that gave a man an exclusive right to retain in a permanent manner that specific land, which before belonged generally to everybody, but particularly to nobody. And, as we before observed that occupancy gave the right to the temporary use of the soil, so it is agreed upon all hands, that occupancy gave also the original right to the permanent property in the substance of the earth itself; which excludes every one else but the owner from the use of it.

Once again, like Pufendorf and Locke before him, Blackstone cannot find a moral argument for the moment of first possession – like his forebears he invents the notion of a community consensus: *so it is agreed upon all hands*. Like his forebears, he also assumes that the land which was first occupied was not already taken: it 'belonged generally to everybody, but particularly to nobody'. History tells us otherwise.

'All the world was America,' wrote John Locke in his *Two Treatises of Government*. He meant that every area on earth was, at some point, unowned and therefore, in Locke's perspective, ownership could be justified by that land having been improved to turn a profit. But, of course, the land of America *was* owned: by hundreds of Native American tribes. They had rights *in* the land, and had fought each other viciously to maintain them. Similarly, the wasteland of Jesse Pierson's fox was not, as Locke would have it, unoccupied property. It was originally occupied by the Shinnecock Indian Nation who paid protection tributes to the most powerful tribe of the area, the Pequot. When the Pequot were slaughtered and enslaved by British colonialists in the war of 1637, their vested interests were washed away in blood. The land became hotly contested by the Dutch government and the English Crown and by the time Lodowick Post had climbed on his horse it was not a wasteland but common land, with a multitude of property claims. These days, this wasteland around Peter's Pond has been almost exclusively parcelled up and sold, common rights entirely subsumed by private rights, and the prices of property on the Southampton Bay now average at around $1.3 million.

From Locke to Blackstone, these tracts of logic are not as objective as their authors made out. Grotius was writing his defence of property in direct support of the Dutch claim to fish in British sea territory. Hobbes was writing under the patronage of the Duke of Devonshire, who later came to own the land targeted by the Kinder Trespass. Pufendorf, the guiding light to Locke and Blackstone, dedicated his first book to Charles Louis, the nephew of Charles I of England and palatine of much of modern-day Germany. Locke was under the patronage of the Earl of Shaftesbury, and writing essentially in defence of colonialism. And Blackstone himself was writing under the financial patronage of George III and was a Member of Parliament for a rotten borough, which put him in Parliament by virtue of his landholdings alone. It's pretty clear what side of the fence he was on. Logic, in its pure definition, means the use of reason, validated by empirical data. However, modern-day computer technicians define it slightly differently, and more appropriately to these dusty polemics: a system, or set of principles, aligned in such a way that they can perform *a specific task*. What these highly influential texts sought to do was reimagine the world according to their own interests.

Which brings us back to Gainsborough, and his portrait of Mr and Mrs Andrews. You have to go to the land itself to see the artifice of the image. Standing by the tree, taking in the view with my friend, nothing in front of us correlated with the version Gainsborough had painted. This isn't just the effect of time, or that great catch-all excuse of 'artistic licence'. The topography has changed. Villages have moved. The church that Gainsborough painted through the trees is All Souls Church, which is actually at a right angle from the painter's view. In real life, the land falls sharply away and rises to the crest of another hill, which blocks out anything but a few distant trees. In the painting you can see at least four fields, plus the distant blues of hills in the background. It is as if Gainsborough has tilted the land, like a waiter would present a cheeseboard, for your inspection. And this is precisely the aim of the painting. For all its realism of rendition, this painting of the newlyweds is in fact a symbolic representation of a contract of land ownership, marriage as business merger.

The land once belonged to a convent, where local commoners would have had rights in the wood and grazing. When Henry VIII sacked the convent and sold the land on to its highest bidder, he particularised the common into private property and divested the commoners of their livelihood. The land was eventually sold to two men, Mr Andrews and Mr Carter, the fathers of the couple in the painting. When Mr Andrews died in 1735, his share of the land was left to his wife to 'hold' until their ten-year-old son came of age. She had the use but not the ownership of the property, on the strict proviso of her dead husband that she would lose everything if she remarried. When the young couple were married in 1748, the two halves of the land were joined in one dynasty, but it was a year later, when Robert's mother died, that he gained full title of the land. The picture was not in fact commissioned to commemorate the marriage, but the succession of ownership rights.

With this in mind, the rest of the picture falls into place. The gun and the dog, like the sheep and wheat, are symbols of the rights conferred by land ownership, hunting and farming. These were the same rights that were removed from the community when the land was enclosed (the community who are themselves absent from the picture) and given to the only two people who remain: its owners. This is a painting not of people and their property, but a portrait of property itself, as it was now conceived, an icon of the cult of exclusion.

My sketch is done. I have been snoozing in the shade of the oak, moving only to flick off the flies as they tickle my skin. The day feels as endless as the sky, as if time has loosened its grip; it feels like the school holidays. I gather my crayons, brushes and ink, fold the sketchbook and leave the lake through a cool green copse. I head for Sudbury, where the Andrews were married, where Gainsborough grew up and where I will eventually take the train home.

I walk out into a machine-sculpted landscape, a gravel track running along its side into arable fields beyond. Not a fence in sight. Several hundred yards in front of me is a man-made lake glistening like a golden ticket. I am walking around its perimeter, past banks messy with goose shit and large grey feathers, eyes tranced by the dance of the sun on the water. It's very tempting; there's even a pier.

I take off my clothes. Standing naked beneath the sky, I am saturated by summer, stoned on the sun, thinking *this must be what photosynthesis feels like*, when a military plane flies low and directly above me, buzzing like a hundred-tonne metal May bug. I watch it disappear over the horizon. Then I slip into the greasy, cold water, and swim.

Floating on the water, facing the cloudless sky, I remember a line from an article in the *Daily Telegraph*: 'Gainsborough's painting of Mr and Mrs Andrews encapsulates many people's ideal of the English countryside.' In fact, it encapsulates the convention of the countryside that is ideal for very few: the orthodoxy of exclusive ownership. The vision we have of England is, like Gainsborough's painting, a highly manipulated illusion of England created by its owners, a self-regarding fantasy, which like the root house on the Duke of Beaufort's land, has weathered into something real. For some scholars, the entire architecture of property law is just as contrived as Gainsborough's painting. Clifford Geertz, American anthropologist and Professor Emeritus of Princeton University, wrote: 'Law is not so much a set of norms, rules, principles, values ... but part of a distinctive manner of imagining the real. Nowhere is this more true than in the realm of real property laws. Property law has in effect, helped us to re-imagine and reinvent what we understand to be the real world.'

I leave the lake, swipe the water off my body with my hands and put on my clothes. I follow the track and find my way to a corner of a fallow field, by a patch of derelict land, fenced and hedged off by barbed wire and large sprawling thickets of bramble – rabbits dart between hiding places, the ground is dry and netted, the earth dusty, the flies making thick noise. I find a gap in a row of hawthorns, and, careful not to spike myself on their feathered spears, I inch through the tree on to the road. Here now, under one strict proviso, is a place where I can be: just so long as I keep moving.

DOG

Fixity, footpaths, gypsies and vagabonds

'The malefactor is first disobedient to God, and afterward
injurious to himself,
and last of all, a wolf and an enemy to the commonwealth'
                                        – Thomas Beccon (1563)

There are no curtains on the window, so when I wake and
my eyes open I see the room filled with the deep violet of
outside. It is a bright darkness, just before dawn, and a car alarm
is sounding somewhere in the trees. Sunk deep in the pillows,
I'm guarding my slumber, but the noise is so irregular it snags
me. It's not an alarm, it's a song thrush, and every phrase that
pours out of him is different, a crazed raga. He's loud, manic
and randy as hell, and I assume by the background silence that
every other living creature is willing him to stick a sock in it.

When I wake again, it is the dog. He's standing on the bed, circling and whining, doling his eyes, cocking his head, doing everything he can to urge me up and out. We're late: he needs me to focus and hit the ground running. But I put the coffee on and he circles the kitchen in sheer disbelief. I stuff some toast into my mouth, an apple into my pocket and, as experience has taught me, only pick up the lead at the very last minute.

I open the door and he darts through, runs ahead of me, and I whistle him back to clip on his leash. He is beside himself with excitement, all aquiver, straining at his collar, but when we turn onto the common his muscles relax, his body transforms. And he runs, head low to the ground, whipping through the grass, his nose planing the trail, scanning for scent. The urgency is cast aside, the business has begun.

The dog sniffs piss like a doctor listens to a heartbeat. He savours it like a sommelier. He might take several short sharp inhalations, turning his head to smell under the thatch of grass, where the piss has pooled and concentrated, or he might take long drafts from the root, drinking its scent with relish. Every now and then, and never wantonly, he will piss on top of the smell: a judicious squirt. It is a widely held fallacy that dogs do this to mark their territory, but the action seems less like hammering in a sign that says *mine* and altogether more like commenting on a friend's Facebook status. In fact, the whole song and dance of it up and down the hedgerow seems a lot like checking your phone in the morning before work. A friend of mine calls it checking his weemails. It's an information exchange.

So with the dog online, busy streaming last night's piss bulletin, I have a moment to wake up. Mellis Common rolls out before me, 150 acres of common land, unchanged for centuries, an inland lake of long grass blustering in the strong wind, a nature reserve of orchids, clover and fern. It bristles with motion: starlings flit constantly in and out of the scaffold of large clumps of hawthorn, the hedges rustle with rabbits and large squelchy depressions in the clay, fenced off by their own spurge of bulrushes and nettles, are home to newts and mink and snakes. It is Virgil's nostalgic vision of nature, where the only fences are temporary, to keep in the hulking Charolais cattle and the gypsy cob horses.

In 1968, the writer Roger Deakin moved into a deserted farmhouse on the perimeter of this common. Setting up home in a skeleton of a Tudor farmhouse, he rebuilt the house around him as he slept on the floor. His diaries, *Notes from Walnut Tree Farm*, reminisce the moment he and his friends were settling in to the task, camping in the garden and making fires in the evening: 'We were on the margins, *les marginaux*, and we identified with the gypsies in a romantic and starry-eyed way.' Later on in his *Notes* the gypsies appear again, this time stepping out of his imagination and onto the Common: 'We talked about the recent gypsy invasion – visitors from another planet – an alien landing – and what to do about the mess they left behind – Calor-gas cylinders, old boots, clothes, skirts, plastic bags, fag ends, fire sites, drink cans etc.'

These two sketches are resonant of a common bipolar sentiment towards travellers – on the one hand, a resentment of their arrival 'from another planet', on the other, an exoticism, a starry-eyed romanticism, the glamour of the open road. In popular culture, gypsies exist in newspaper reports about squatted patches of wasteland and in romance novels about middle-class sexual repression – and barely anywhere else. With their own voice rarely heard, they are projections of the society that labels them, of a suspicion that runs past them to a deep seam of othering. It is a simultaneous fear and fascination of un-rootedness, the danger of a class of person defined entirely by their motion both through, and outside of, the fixity of property: the vagabond.

With the dog at my heels, I turn off the common. The byway is worn and uneven: it undulates as much as it twists, roping alongside the paddocks belonging to the farm. The greenery either side of it is the remnant of ancient woodland, the forests that carpeted Britain after the Ice Age. Thick bands of dog rose hang like vines from the trees whose branches intersect over the path like the folded fingers of a chess player. The sky is rumbling, thunder is approaching and the light is bright in puddles among the tiger stripes of shadows that lace the path. A gust runs through the length of the tunnel, tugs my hair, and, at the mouth of it, the slatted wood gate of the railway line burns white.

I cross the railway line with the dog yanking on the leash. With the gate shut behind me, I let the leash extend to its full length and watch the dog hustle into the field like a boxer from his corner. The path crosses the wide field, exposed to the miles of farmland around it, and the wind is roaring in my ears, snatching at my jumper like a slack sail. The sky is spitting. There's an iron-hued anvil of cloud above us and the dark columns of rain on the horizon suggest the storm is about to break.

We duck into the wooded area of the path which runs for a mile further to the main road, a nice walk lined with fields and private woodland. The path is our right of way, neatly signposted for our convenience, but to step off it, to follow the deep tyre tracks of tractors sweeping into the fields or to slip through the blackthorn into a glade, is to break the law. *But this is where the magic is.* So just before the pink-washed house with a pond and the massive weeping willow, there's a turning into a field. The sign that said KEEP OUT has long been buried in the bramble so we take the more direct route to the trees, to Lady Henniker Woods.

The Hennikers are a family of merchants, politicians and military men, who once owned 30,000 acres in East Anglia. Their estate has now shrunk to a tenth of that, but still includes their ancestral seat, the manor house to the west and all the woods and farmland within walking distance. They are well liked, and have opened up their land to public use: they sold the common of Mellis to the local wildlife trust and the majority of paths that cross their land, though not public Rights of Way, are permissive paths, ones they have opened up to the public – but this could be reversed the moment the property changes hands.

We cross the fallow field to the woods and the dog, snaking about in front of me, disturbs a large hare, which rockets off in front of us with a wide arc into the space of the field, a forest of wild carrot and dock. The magic has begun.

These are shooting woods, all ferns, nettles and wind-felled trees, with rides cut through the flora for beating the birds up into the sky. But their perimeters are dug with ditches, to keep the larger fauna in, and every now and then you come across wide wooden ladders with seats at the top, a plinth for a better shot at a deer. The dog knows these woods better than I do, and when he's crossed the ditch into the green light of the woods, he pauses, sits, turns his nose up to the trees, and inhales their atmosphere.

Simultaneously, I ponder where to go. These woods roll out for miles, broken by fields whose corners I have sketched many times before. If we head due south, there's the deserted chapel and walled garden, while, if we bear west, there's that deer seat in the lightning-cracked oak that I still haven't sketched. And then, right on the limits of my mind map, there are those long lines of coppiced hazel, whose ground is netted with honeysuckle. Every now and then you can find a hazel pole that has been strangled by the creep of these honeysuckles, twining around the branch, spiralling to the light. After several years, the honeysuckle is so tight that the girth of the pole spills out over its bonds, a muffin top of wood that corkscrews up the length of the pole. If you find such a specimen, and the stick either side of it is long and relatively straight, you've just found a walking stick worth about seventy quid in a country show. Cut it down, unfurl the honeysuckle, and you have a wizard's staff that can be taken home, straightened with a damp cloth and paint stripper, capped and varnished.

But that's a three-hour walk, minimum, and the sky is still specking with rain. We'll stick to these woods. We'll follow tyre tracks between the ditches of the wood and the perimeter of the fields. We'll trace a circle around these woods and then cut through the tall nettles of a ride, back to where we are now. We'll take in the badgers' sett, and then that doleful pond, wide and shallow, with a fallen tree that forms a bridge from its perimeter to thirty foot above its centre. You can sit there, high above the sticky water, with the dog whinging at the brim, and watch the hawks that nest in the large ash. The whine of mosquitoes and the low hum of hornets. A stillness that feels endless.

We head west, through a gateway of two oaks that lean towards each other. This pair were saplings when the last great wave of vagrants had flooded England, the survivors of the Napoleonic Wars. In *Discipline and Punish*, Foucault wrote about their French counterparts who had experienced a hostile reception in France, and how they were viewed through the lens of the judiciary system: 'the myth of a barbaric, immoral and outlaw class ... haunted the discourse of legislators, philanthropists and investigators into working class life.'

To find a tree in Suffolk that is as old as this myth, you will have to trespass. Most of England's grandest trees can only be found on private estates, saved from the saws of the Royal Navy by virtue of their aesthetic value to the recently enclosed deer parks. The closest to me is possibly the oldest of them all: the Thurston Oak.

It was the *East Anglian Daily Times* that alerted me to its existence. The article begins: 'MIGHTY oaks from little acorns grow – and this tree has certainly lived up to the fourteenth-century proverb! With a girth so big it would take seven grown men to hug round its massive frame, it can lay claim to being the biggest recorded living tree in East Anglia.'

It was identified by a 'volunteer verifier' a decade ago, as part of the Ancient Tree Hunt, a scheme initiated by the Woodland Trust. You have to go and stand beneath this tree, touch its old gnarly bark, to see the true strength of a myth, how firmly it has rooted itself into the land.

Before this oak was seeded, England viewed its poor, destitute and homeless as useful tools for celestial self-improvement. The writings of St Francis taught that charity was next to godliness, and donations to poor relief helped you climb the ladder to heaven. When the Thurston Oak was a century old, the Black Death came to England and particularly affected the area of East Anglia, the front line of trade with the Continent. Between a third and a half of the population of England died, a tragedy on such a scale that it upended the order of Norman rule: the feudal ties that tethered peasants to the land they worked began to unravel, and, because there were so few labourers, workers were able to demand much higher pay. For the first time in the history of the working class, and maybe the only time, the poor had power – the power to choose to work and to travel to where conditions were better for them. This, of course, was deeply alarming for the hierarchy and required swift action: only a year after the outbreak of plague Edward III enacted the Ordinance of Labourers, which sought to cap wage increases and curb this new-found mobility. With its extra stipulation that any beggar who was deemed able to work should be refused charity, it is also the first time in English law that we see the distinction between the deserving and undeserving poor, a pathological obsession of the English that lasts to this day.

In 1388, the Statute of Cambridge placed yet more restrictions on the movement of people, both labourers and beggars alike – it prohibited anyone from leaving the district where they were living, unless they had a written testimonial issued by the Justices of the Peace for the area – an early passport for internal migration. For this, they had to prove 'reasonable cause', which was an official-sounding euphemism for the whim of the Justices. There was a central paradox to these new regulations that seems like an early, medieval draft of *Catch-22*: if you owned land, you could move; if you were landless, you had to stay where you were, where, without a master, you weren't allowed to be.

The law applied to a broad church of people: itinerant labourers, tinkers, pedlars, unlicensed healers, craftsmen, entertainers, prostitutes, soldiers and mariners. They were freelancers whose jobs did not require them to be tethered to one place or another. They were called 'masterless men', and they roamed as lone wolves or packs of wild dogs, haunting the countryside, towns and minds of their betters. The most significant aspect to these various laws was that they criminalised nothing specific. Vagrancy was vague – it sought to criminalise not anti-social actions but, rather, a state of being, a social and economic status, a type of person.

In the corner of a field I see one of the larger oaks has come crashing down. On the ground beneath it are piles of soggy sawdust, evidence that some of the branches and thinner boughs have been cleared, but most of the tree remains, crushed against the earth and blocking our route. The dog leaps through its broken boughs and I follow awkwardly, untangling the leash, climbing through a canopy that has previously, all the while I've known it, been high above my head. The ragged mess of its trunk has been carved flat by chainsaws and sits like a kitchen table, almost two metres in diameter. According to the Woodland Trust, who have a handy matrix linking the diameter of a tree to its age, this tree was seeded in the late Tudor period, when paranoia about mobility stepped up a gear.

In the sixteenth century, the population of England almost doubled, rising from 2.3 million in 1521 to 3.9 million in 1591. According to *The Land* magazine, an infrequent periodical about local and global land rights issues, 'by the mid-1500s, anything up to one-third of the population of England were living in poverty as homeless nomads on the fringes of an increasingly bourgeois society, in which they had no part'.

The rampant, unchecked enclosure of land had inevitably led to vast numbers of people being robbed of their homes and natural resources that now lay within the fences of the new lords of the manor. When the communities were cleared, they had to go somewhere, so they took to the roads. In a number of vagrancy acts passed in the mid-1500s, the punishments for people found out of their hometowns, whether unemployed, begging or just simply walking, ranged from three days in the stocks, to a branding of the letter S for Slave on the forehead or a V for Vagabond on the chest. You could be tied to a cart and whipped, you could have a hole of an inch diameter bored into the cartilage of your ear, and, if you were caught twice, you could face execution.

This emphasis on the persecution of the body tells us something about the Tudor perspective on vagrancy: it was the outward expression of an inner failing. People wandered and roamed the country because they had strayed from the path of righteousness – and this path was no longer mapped just by God, but by the state as well. To John Gore, writing in the early 1600s, vagrants were 'children of Belial, without God, without magistrate, without minister'. But playwright Robert Greene, writing in 1591, expressed an even deeper Tudor obsession with the body: 'these coney-catchers [rabbit hunters] ... putrefy with their infections this flourishing state of England.' As the moral failings of these vagrants had infected their bodies, causing them to act out of line, so too the vagrants infected the body politic of the land, threatening the health of the state itself.

The Tudor era was notable for intense civil unrest, with Kett's Rebellion and the Pilgrimage of Grace being two of the larger rebellions and riots that occurred throughout the period. Having already enclosed a vast number of disparate people within the same legal definition, the Tudors began to talk of vagrants as an organised collective of seditious intent, a corporation working directly against the state. A popular legend of the day told how beggars and wanderers would meet annually at the Gloucester Fair to vote in new officials – a leader and an entourage of commanders and officers. Elizabethan dramatist Thomas Dekker wrote that a new recruit to this band of brigands had to 'learn the orders of our house' and to recognise there are 'degrees of superiority and inferiority in our society'. The mythical Cock Lorel was one such leader of this tribe of dissolutes, his name meaning literally Leader Vagabond. He was credited with creating the Twenty-Five Orders of Knaves and meeting with a famous gypsy leader in a cave in Derbyshire, on the Devil's Arse Peak, where the two of them supposedly sat down and devised an entire language that was to be rolled out across the vagabond community, called 'Thieves' Cant'. Jenkin Cowdiddle, Puff Dick, Bluebeard and Kit Callot were the men and women who led this army of vagabonds; but, again, there is no evidence that they existed anywhere but in the plays, books and fertile imaginations of the Tudor dramatists.

But these romanticised imaginings had a real effect. Government officials were paid by the head to round up vagrants and enclose them within 'houses of reform'; since idleness was at the core of their withering souls, they would be forced to work for their moral improvement. When this didn't work, they were shipped abroad, transported to the colonies of Virginia and the Caribbean to work as feudal serfs, tied to the farmsteads that would eventually drop all pretence of moral improvement for the cheaper alternative: African slaves.

But just as this bad blood was being piped out of the body politic, it was free movement on a global level that transfused another threat into the health of the land: the gypsies. In 1531 Henry VIII passed the Egyptian Act, whose very title expressed how misconstrued its statutes were. It described:

> an outlandish people, calling themselves Egyptians, using no craft nor feat of merchandise, who have come into this realm, and gone from shire to shire, and place to place, in great company; and used great subtlety and crafty means to deceive the people – bearing them in hand that they, by palmistry, could tell men's and women's fortunes; and so, many times, by craft and subtlety, have deceived the people for their money; and also have committed many heinous felonies and robberies, to the great hurt and deceit of the people that they have come among.

This group of migrants had in fact originated in the Punjab region of northern India, a nomadic people called Roma who had entered Eastern Europe between the eighth and tenth centuries. They were accused of bewitching the English – their sleight-of-hand magic and their palm-reading fed into darker tales of blood drinking in Eastern Europe, werewolf mythology and that recurring nightmare of the wolf at your door. The notion of the glamour of the open road is itself sourced from the Romani word *glamouyre*, which was a spell the gypsies cast to free you of your hard-earned money and allow them access to your land.

Henry VIII's phrase 'calling themselves Egyptians' speaks volumes about the mechanism of state projection – they were defined not by themselves or their actions, but by a panic that drew on the myth of barbarism, the fear of outsiders; by popular repetition, Egyptians was shortened to *gypcyons* which became *gypsies*, and a new scapegoat was born. Unlike the native vagabonds of the past centuries, the Roma people did not need to be branded with letters that marked their depravity – the colour of their skin was enough. And in a typical tactic of state propaganda, the myth of the gypsy was used to seduce the population into supporting legislation that restricted their own freedoms. In 1554, having just executed her sixteen-year-old half-sister Jane, Queen Mary passed another Egyptians Act which sought to legislate against this tribe of people plying their 'devilish and naughty practices'. The statute forbade any further Roma people from entering the land and gave those already living in England sixteen days to leave. If they did not, and they were discovered, they would be hanged. Any possessions they had were to be divided between the state and the arresting officer, effectively co-opting people into paid vigilantism. However, in a detail that expresses the real root of the fear, the legislation allowed for them to escape prosecution as long as they abandoned their nomadic lifestyle or, as the Act put it, their 'naughty, idle and ungodly life and company'. It was not their race, origin or palm-reading that upset the order of the state, it was their mobility.

Because geographic mobility was social mobility, or at least the slightest chance of it. During feudal times the working class were linked to the land in the same way as they were tied to their lord. To move away from the land was to move out of the lord's jurisdiction, and, without any tied contract, it was to move out of any jurisdiction at all. The lords of the land were the lords of the law, and the lines of their property were the limits of their jurisdiction. By moving through the land, these men and women had snapped the leash that bound them to their masters. But there is another element to the perception of vagabonds that is impossible to ignore. It emerges not from the law books, but from the literature and folklore, or, in Freudian terms, not from the superego, but from the id: the eroticism of the gypsy.

D. H. Lawrence loved it. Emily Brontë loved it. It's the oldest trick in the book of Orientalism, to demonise a group while simultaneously wanting to shag them. That way, when you do, it's their fault and not yours: the Devil has had his way with you. And it goes back long before swarthy Heathcliff ever traipsed across the Yorkshire moors, to what is perhaps the oldest folk song in the English tradition. Sung by the Carter family, Woody Guthrie, Bob Dylan, the White Stripes, Planxty, Lankum and hundreds more, under the various titles of Raggle Taggle Gypsy, Seven Yellow Gypsies, Gypsy Davy, Gypsie Laddie, its legend is alive to this day.

Three gypsies cam' tae oor ha' door,
An' O! but they sang bonnie, O,
They sang sae sweet and sae complete,
That they stole the heart of a lady, O.

It is said to have been written about a real gypsy by the name of Johnnie Faa, who in 1540 has been declared King of the Gypsies by James V of Scotland. As the story goes, he ran off with the Countess of Cassillis, who lived on the coast with her earl forty miles south of Glasgow. The earl comes home to find his property has been stolen and he gallops off to reclaim her; he catches up with Johnnie, his wife and the band of gypsies, singing songs around a fire. He imprisons his wife for the rest of her life, hangs the men in front of her window and, insult to injury, carves their faces into its mullions. That the story is most likely untrue did not stop the ballad spreading across England, with slightly different details and with several different endings. In all the versions, the lady is charmed away by the gypsies, bewitched by their glamour, and forsakes her comfy feather bed and expensive leather shoes for a rough life on the road.

> The lady she cam doon the stair
> And her twa maidens cam' wi' her, O;
> But when they spied her weel' faured face,
> They cuist the glaumourye o'er her, O.

This song is about the glamour of the open road, and is a working-class hymn where the rich don't always come out on top. But it can also be read as a metaphor for land seizure. At the start of the seventeenth century, during the continued enclosure of England and a new colonial imperative that was seizing land outside of the country, the improvement of wild land and the taming of wild women were concepts in constant conflation. One was a metaphor for the other. On his return from Guiana, Sir Walter Raleigh described it as 'a country that hath yet her maidenhead', meaning that it had never before been penetrated and mastered by any man. Conversely, the crime of rape was not created to protect women from violence but to protect men from a violation of their property rights. In 1707, Lord Chief Justice John Holt described the act of a man who had had sex with the wife of another as 'the highest invasion of property', referring, of course, to the man's property of his wife, and not the woman's property of her own body. Once a man had claimed dominion of his property, and fenced it with marriage, it was his right to enter, and his alone – it, or she, became impregnable.

In the Tudor era the cult of exclusion was so strong that it entered the psyche and acquired a Freudian fetishisation that had all the power and licentiousness of a sexual taboo. The gypsies, feral, wild and earthy, with their slippery attitude to the boundaries of possession, represented the abomination of this property concept, and were evoked as sexual predators, a threat to the family and state alike. And this interplay between land and sexual taboo, between violation and domination, continues to this day, in the parable of Nicholas Van Hoogstraten.

Hoogstraten has been called many things: slum landlord, the sad Citizen Kane of Sussex and, by one of the many judges he has faced, 'a self-styled emissary of Beelzebub'. He is a B-movie villain, a character whose life story might have been written by Martin Amis in a pique of misanthropy, in a story so far-fetched it could never be published. Early on in his career he spent four years in jail for throwing a live hand grenade at a Jewish cantor and, in 2002, was sentenced to ten years for the manslaughter, or alleged assassination, of Mohammed Raja, another landlord tycoon. He made his money Rachman-style, by buying houses full of sitting tenants and then using a variety of bully-boy tactics to evict them. When they were alive, he referred to his tenants as 'scumbags', 'dog's meat' and 'filth' and when five died in a fire in one of his apartments in Hove, he described them afterwards as 'Lowlife. Drug dealers, drug takers and queers. Scum.'

He is currently in the process of building an enormous palace in Uckfield, East Sussex, started in the 1980s and still unfinished, with rocketing costs estimated at £40 million. To claim the land, he evicted a care home of elderly residents. Built both to emulate and to dwarf Buckingham Palace, it has two gleaming copper domes, covers the entire width of his land and, entirely imprisoned in rusting scaffolding, it is the architectural equivalent of Doug Bradley's character in the Hellraiser films.

I went to visit the estate with two friends: a bike ride, sandwiches in the pub, early summer, a lovely day out. We cut into the estate on a public Right of Way, and then hopped the barbed wire fence into an Eden of nature. Like modern-day

Hiroshima, the almost absolute absence of humans has allowed Mother Earth to thrive in peace: it is a George Monbiot wet dream, entirely rewilded. For an hour or so, I sat in the chest-high grass and drew the house. A fox walked by me, entirely unfazed by my presence and close enough for me to stroke its gorgeous fur. Butterflies bounced low over the earth, insects hummed in the air, I got tan lines.

But, twenty years before, this place was the scene of a real-life pantomime drama, between the Ogre of Uckfield and the rosy-cheeked pastoralists of the Hobbit Activity Guild, otherwise known as the Ramblers' Association. The Right of Way we had taken is labelled on the maps as Framfield Number 9. It is a path that has been featured on maps for 200 years or more, the route villagers took to church every Sunday. Hoogstraten reacted so badly to the sporadic invasion of walkers still using this footpath that he secured his property against the common law rights of the locals by erecting a barn over it and blocking the entrance with a corrugated iron sheet, discarded masonry and a host of refrigeration units. When the Ramblers staged a demonstration outside the obstruction, he went on the BBC to label them 'the scum of the earth'.

In 1999, the Ramblers' president Andrew Bennet MP led a walk along the path and the following day a six-stranded barbed wire fence was erected where the path meets the road. When the ramblers launched a case against Hoogstraten, it was delayed because he had changed the ownership of the land from his name to a shadow identity, a corporation named Rarebargain Ltd. But, with a new Rights of Way Act being discussed at that time in Parliament, the Ramblers were determined to make this case as public as possible: they wanted to highlight the realpolitik of England's Rights of Way network, of which they estimated a quarter was blocked by landowners.

Hoogstraten was incandescent. 'Let them waste their time and money,' he told reporters. 'I'm not going to open up the footpath. Would you have a lot of Herberts in your garden?' Unaccustomed to 1980s slang, or Landlords' Cant, I had to look up 'Herberts' — a Herbert is a creep who befriends your wife so that he can shag her at a later date. He is the incubus of patriarchal possession, an invader of conjugal property. In a later interview with the *Guardian*, Hoogstraten modified this statement saying, 'Herberts wasn't actually my word, it was one of the builder's ... I said perverts, the dirty mac brigade.' Perverts or Herberts, the sexual connotations Hoogstraten has with his land are clear — he owns the land like he owns his bitches (his often-repeated term for his several wives) and any penetration is a direct threat to his dominion, his manhood, a perversion of property law.

The woods around me are a scene of devastation. The foresters have been harvesting them, but have not yet tidied them into stacks, so their long poles lie scattered, strewn like pick-up sticks, as though a dinosaur has swept its tail and felled them by mistake. Their cut ends are bright sticky circles of orange and the air is scented with their sap. I follow the tyre track, picking my way carefully through a mat of crushed branches until I come to the badger sett and sit on a trunk in the vain hope of seeing one: but try as you might, you can't coax the magic.

The dog is tracing scent, head bowed to the ground, drawn by his nose. We're back to where we started, in the young woods planted by the 3rd Lord Henniker when he took over the property in 1821. The Napoleonic Wars had ended, and with it the mass conscription that had dragged so many young men from England. They were back now, wounded, mutilated, unemployed and hungry, regurgitated into a state that had no place for them. They ranged the land, slept in coppices and spilled down the highways, a new cast of characters in the old myth of the deviant wanderer. A new Vagrancy Act was quickly written and passed by the cartel of aristocratic landowners otherwise known as Parliament, to clear them off the land into prison. Its effect was to outlaw homelessness, and it is still in use today. In 2014, three men were arrested and charged under Section 4 of the 1824 Vagrancy Act for taking food that had been thrown away into skips outside an Iceland supermarket in north London. A year later, sixty-two homeless people were arrested in Sussex under the same act, rounded up by plainclothes police officers who walked up and down the seafront, waiting to be asked for a quid.

The Act stipulates that 'every person wandering abroad and lodging in any barn or outhouse, or in any deserted or unoccupied building, or in the open air, or under a tent, or in any cart or wagon … shall be deemed a rogue and vagabond' and later, in provision five: 'an incorrigible rogue'. The sentiment of the Act is as arcane as its language. Even in its day, William Wilberforce objected to it on the grounds that it did not take into consideration the many reasons which might lead to homelessness; again, it was not punishing any particular crime but, rather, the symptom of a social problem. The Act was amended on a number of occasions, making the definition of vagrancy only more vague. In 1838, its scope was widened to include the publication of material deemed to be obscene, reinforcing that notion that vagrancy was a catch-all term for both geographic and moral deviance. In 1898, a further amendment sought to clamp down on street-walking, or prostitution, but was in practice used to imprison homosexual men for their deviant sexuality. Again, it was a law that criminalised not an act, but a type of person.

In 2018 a delegation of thirty Tory backbenchers signed a letter calling for the criminalisation of trespass, a pledge that had already been mooted in their manifesto of 2010. The letter followed the anger of the locals of Thames Ditton in Surrey, when the police refused to evict a gypsy camp from some local common land. There had been reports of tricycles stolen from playgrounds and instances of shoplifting – criminal acts by individuals with a justified legal response. But the locals wanted the whole site cleared, to get rid of the lot of them. When the local Elmbridge police force tweeted, reasonably enough, that they could not make arrests without evidence of wrongdoing, Karen Randolph, a councillor who represented the area said, 'We are all incandescent with rage because of that tweet.' When the site was eventually evicted by the council, the *Daily Telegraph* reported: 'The council also hired a specialist cleaning company to carry out a "cleanse" of the park's playground following their stay.'

'Cleansed' is a potent word, and with respect to gypsies, a little too apposite. In 1927 the 400 or so gypsies camping in Nevi Wesh, the Romani term for the New Forest, were rounded up and herded into seven compounds. Fenced in from their mobile life, they were simultaneously forbidden from building permanent structures and issued with six-month licences for their stay, which could be revoked if their behaviour upset the Forestry Commission.

The gypsies had been living in the Nevi Wesh for centuries, and in the nineteenth century would return each year from harvesting hops in Kent to spend the winter there. The 1920s had seen a surge of incomers into the New Forest area, including Arthur Cecil, the brother of the prime minister, who wrote in his report to the House of Commons Select Committee: 'They are a great nuisance to everybody.' Another local resident was the artist Augustus John, who lived in Fryern Court on the outskirts of the forest, who said later: 'although nobody so far has proposed to liquidate these nomads after the Hitler style,

is it possible that, in his own country, John Bunyan's people have been sentenced to a lingering death?' These incendiary words were echoed by an altogether more sober authority, the Centre for Holocaust and Genocide Studies, who said after the war: 'It is hard to believe that civilised Britons would herd innocent people into compounds because of their race, just as Nazi Germans would a few decades later.'

But it wasn't just their race. Today there are around 300,000 people in the UK who identify as Gypsy, Roma or Traveller. In Europe they number over twelve million and are recognised as the largest ethnic minority in the EU. This statistic alone is indicative of the persistent obsession that rooted society has with gypsies: ethnicity is defined by the UN Office of National Statistics as a concept that 'combines nationality, citizenship, race, colour, language, religion, and customs of dress or eating' – yet not one of these signifiers embraces the entirety of this group. Instead, it is the association and history that these people have with travel that has grouped them out to the margins of society: mobility as ethnicity.

Fixity is the orthodoxy of the modern European age, and the trouble with travellers is that at some point in time, at some point in space, they will lay their camp. Within the tight lines of Tudor property law, there was no room for that and today you are only allowed to stop for forty-eight hours in special council-allocated sites, tarmacked and fenced enclosures with all the romance of a disused motorway service station. Property simply cannot comprehend mobility. Perhaps the glamour of the open road is just another misappropriation by the authorities that defined them. Perhaps the glamour cast by the gypsies is not in fact a spell, but its direct opposite – a jinxing of the spell of private property.

The storm isn't breaking. It might even pass us by. The air is tense with it, but the drizzle is thinning. The sun is pushing through the cloud and the horizon is greasy with light. Me and the dog are picking our way through a tight thicket of thistle and nettles, following the long disused pheasant ride that cuts right through this small section of wood. Either side, dripping trees. Directly in front of us, the light has smeared through the dark clouds, flaring off the thistledown, glaring from the wet leaves. Everything glistens. There is an arc of not one but two rainbows, perfectly placed at the end of the ride, and the scene is so beautiful it's naff, the closing credits of a Disney film. I breathe it in. The dog, not known for his patience, has become inured to this kind of artsy pause, and is now resigned to the dragging moment. He hunkers down onto the ground and rests like a sphinx, drinking in the air with his nose. There is a cracking from the trees, and I glance. It takes me a second to see the dark forms of deer passing, almost silently, through the poles of the wood. The dog is casual, unengaged. I don't move. The deer are heading towards us, a line of maybe ten, about to slip out into our ride. When the first one appears, tentative, it is heavy headed, almost goat-like, pagan. These are not the pretty things I was expecting: they are not roe deer, but red deer, and I've never been this close. A second follows, head, then hoof poised for a long time before it places it and raises the next. They are more than cautious, but the scene is about to explode. Quietly, I let the cord of the dog's leash retract into its canister, and click it locked. The dog and his miraculous sense of smell have failed to register a line of deer directly in front of him, but instinct is about to take over. A third deer is out, this is a convoy, picking its way as a team through the woods. And then, quickly, it happens. The dog's ears prick, his head turns and he bullets off his haunches, yanking my arm taut, yearning against his collar, front paws paddling the air, held back by my weight. The deer swing like wooden puppets on a string and stream seamlessly away through the trunks. The last to turn are two stags, half glimpsed, who trot indignantly after the herd.

This kind of moment is only available off the path. It is an accident, unwilled and unplanned, but it comes dressed as poetry. It is prosaic, but it feels like a miracle, it feels meaningful, and it leaves me with my heart thumping in my throat. The deer were so close they felt dangerous; not aggressive, but wild-eyed and unpredictable. I would swap a hundred nice walks along a pretty Right of Way for this one moment of magic.

And now the heavens have opened. The dog, so focussed a moment ago, appears to have entirely forgotten the incident and is sniffing nonchalantly at my heels. I release the catch on his leash, give him some slack, and together we turn, retrace our steps through the waterlogged field and end up on the path back home.

Behind me, to the south, the Right of Way continues through woodland to a thatched-roof church, whose back door is always open. St Mary's Church of Thornham Parva was built about a century after the Norman invasion and is a tiny treasure trove of history. It's odd to be able to walk into a museum piece, with no red ropes or blue blazers prohibiting your action. In truth, the 800-year-old painted altarpiece is set behind alarmed glass but it's nice to be trusted not to squirt bleach at the half-faded and even older murals that adorn the nave. Perhaps there are no vandals in this part of Suffolk, perhaps the gesture itself inspires a custodial reverence, perhaps the murals are so mashed up it doesn't feel like there is much to desecrate. But you can just about make out their subject: St Edmund, fleeing on horseback from the Great Heathen Army, the Vikings that ravaged East Anglia in the late ninth century. Next wall, he doesn't make it, but someone has redacted the holy martyrdom by installing a window in its place. This is regrettable, because Edmund was tied to a tree, beaten with iron bars, shot with arrows and beheaded, which is a great gig for a Christian artist of any era. The final scene shows Edmund's remains, carried to his shrine in Bury St Edmunds. The path I am walking formed part of that journey, a network of highways that once linked Hoxne with Bury, some twenty-five miles apart. This particular section of the route is called Cowpasture Lane, and it is a superstar path, a literary A-lister.

The lane is described by writer Richard Mabey as 'an aboriginal droveway cut and trod out though wildwood, which survived in marginal strips after the wood beyond had been cleared for agriculture'. He estimates that it was first hewn out of Iron Age forests, making it older than any of the commons or settlements of the area. Roger Deakin also refers to this path in both *Wildwood* and his collection of diary entries, *Notes from Walnut Tree Farm*, claiming it was a trade route leading on to three neighbouring markets.

This part of it, south of the railway line, is almost 100-foot wide in some places. It was then not just a footpath but a highway for various lanes of traffic, wagons, horses, cows, and also offered enough room for the cattle to pasture. The iron shoes dug up along its route point to the fact that these animals were being driven on long journeys (as cattle were only shod for distance) and so would have needed a place to huddle overnight. As Deakin puts it in a letter to the Mid Suffolk council: 'the idea of classifying Cowpasture Lane as a footpath instead of a byway is almost as absurd as the idea that the M11 might one day in the future be accidentally classified as a footpath on a map in the year 3003. I exaggerate of course, but you will appreciate my point.'

It was a busy route. So much so that, if Mabey is to be believed, it didn't just link places, it created them. And the strength of its use determined its longevity. From Thornham all the way to Mellis Common, with the one curious exception of the vast field along the railway line, Cowpasture Lane is an unbroken tunnel of green, with thirteen species of tree that are descendants from the ancient wood now almost entirely obliterated from England. It is another museum piece, entirely unroped. When the path was first forged, it was a refuge through the wilderness, and today, stark against the blank agriculture of Suffolk, it is a refuge for it.

I step out into that open field again, and, at the opposite end, I see the train banshee by. Through the blurred lens of falling water, I wonder if I'm seen. The rain is heavy now, a roar, and even the dog has lost heart. We cross the field, cross the line, and follow the lane until it opens out onto the common. It is like stepping out into a storm-swept beach, the sea of long grass combed into waves by the wind. The trees sway like river reeds and I turn right, and right again, up the track to Walnut Tree Farm, once the home of Roger Deakin.

I came here originally as a pilgrim from his first two books *Waterlog* and *Wildwood*. A mutual friend made the introductions to the current owners of the house and I returned later on in the year, with the words of my first book half written, to live in my imagination for a couple of weeks, bashing away at my book while cats curled around my legs. A year or so later I was introduced to their gorgeous and priapic Rhodesian Ridgeback puppy, and returned intermittently to dog-sit while the family were away on holiday.

I enter the kitchen with trousers clung heavy around my legs. I am drenched. I feed the dog his stinking meatmush, strip naked and pull on some tracksuit bottoms. I take an old towel from the Aga and rub him down as he hofs back his food. I eat and then, barefoot, walk with him out into the rain to the second paddock, where the shepherd's hut stands. I snap some ash twigs from a neighbouring tree, find the key and enter. Shivering, I kneel at the woodstove by the door, and load it up. Little cylinders of wood, branches chopped on the bandsaw, the ash twigs, and some strips from a GCSE exercise book: *There are four main reasons for Macbeth's shame* goes up in smoke, the lid goes on and the stove catches and breathes deeply on the pipe, which starts to ping as it heats up.

The rain is rattling on the corrugated roof, the fire is crackling, the dog has settled in for the long haul and is snoozing on the bed. I hoist a stack of old folders from the floor to the desk by the stove and begin leafing through the papers. Aerial photos of the land, crinkly typewritten letters, photocopies of newspaper clippings, long council reports; these yellowed papers detail the forty-year struggle to save Cowpasture Lane from closure. From Roger's initial letters to the council in the early 1980s, the first volley of gunshots in a battle against a local farmer, to the affidavits, the written testimonies and the newspaper accounts of the showdown at the railway line, the stack is a loose-leaved codex on the war between private and public rights.

For starters, there's the story behind the gap in the woodland tunnel that runs from the railway line across the open field. In 1971, the farmer felled the corridor of trees and grubbed out their roots, levelling two fields into one, so that his plough could move in one unbroken line. He also took down a line of trees heading west from the woodland and you can still see their footprints today, from the satellite image on Google Maps, a pale scar tissue on blank, ploughed earth. It was only through an affidavit from Roger that he had to pay a fine for this vandalism. Then, at the start of 1980, there are letters from other residents to the council arguing that, no shit, the farmer hadn't marked the Right of Way through his new unified field, as was his duty, and after ten months he is ordered to wheel-mark this public passage, Path Number 7 as the paperwork calls it, through his sugar beet.

But the battle was only just beginning. Cowpasture Lane divided Roger's paddocks on the east and one of the farmer's fields on the west; a line in the sand. Somehow, and these are the facts that slip through such papers, Roger caught wind that the farmer was planning to uproot the trees along his side of the lane, and to plough up the lane itself, which covers about 1.6 acres of land, converting an ancient right of passage into an extra 500 quid of annual private profit. So Roger forms a super-group, a Traveling Wilburys of literary and scholarly eminence, who bombard Mid Suffolk council with botanical, historical, archaeological and ecological evidence. Representatives from Friends of the Earth, Open Spaces Society and the Ramblers' Association add their letters to the bombardment, alongside big guns like Oliver Rackham, Richard Mabey and the grandest literary howitzer of them all, Ronald Blythe. BOOM, BANG, CRASH, they get their Tree Preservation Order from the council, and the line of trees along the lane is saved, protected by order of the secretary of state.

But wait: the order is given on the Friday, to come into effect on the following Monday morning. The local paper reports the victory that weekend, the farmer reads it and early Monday morning he's on the lane, with some men and chainsaws. This is where the purple prose of the local newspaper takes over: 'Nightingales no longer nest in Cowpasture Lane. Their song has been silenced by the screech of chainsaws and the hacking bill hooks. A Passchendaele silence reigns ... no birds sing.' Roger's account is more measured: 'On the Monday morning their work was hampered by the presence of myself in the company of reporters and photographers from the *Diss Express* and *East Anglian Daily Times* until the Mid Suffolk district council's landscape officer ... arrived, breathless, at lunchtime, with the TPO.'

What a strange, tense moment that must have been. *Hampered*: how in hell do you 'hamper' men with chainsaws and billhooks? The presence of a photographer or two must have given Roger some courage, some hope that he wasn't about to have his legs sawn off, but to hold the fort until late morning, when the bureaucratic cavalry came huffing up the path, was a sturdy feat. Mellis is a tiny village, and all the men would have almost certainly known each other. In this isolated spot of the railway crossing, the politics of neighbours conflated with the historical conflict of public and private property.

Over the course of the last fifty years, Mellis has lost 50 per cent of its hedgerows. On the land owned by this one particular farmer, only 7 per cent of his original hedgerow remains. When the men stopped work, they had already cut down a large section of the 300-yard path, with the intent of completing their job right up to the common and then filling in the ditch. Many of the trees were now stumps, flat-top stools, their trunks and branches lying devastated on the earth. But because of an obscure ruling from 1978, the Tree Protection Order given by the council still applied. In 1978, a small woodland in Kent was razed by a farmer. In Mabey's words: 'The forest came to be known by locals as the Horizontal wood, and now, protected by the Kent Wildlife Trust, it is thriving. The precedent had been set, and the stumps were preserved. Today, there is no evidence whatsoever of damage, the hazel and the ash have sprung back.'

The life of a wood, as with the path that runs through it, is in its roots. Cowpasture Lane was saved.

It's dark now, the rain is gentle; I stack up the papers and cross the paddock with the dog, past the moat, to the house. I put some leftovers in the bottom tray of the Aga, and go to squat by the enormous Tudor fireplace in the living room, splitting a log into splints for kindling. This time it's maths homework that starts the fire. I pull down Roger's three books from the shelf and settle before the hearth.

I look up an early scene in *Waterlog*: Roger has traced a paragraph from William Cobbett, the Georgian pamphleteer, to Winchester, where the boys' school meets the water meadows. He has been swimming in a reverie of wild watercress and natural springs, thought-streams of the past eddying into the present moment. Out on the shore, his head is swirling with Cobbett's imagery, of fresh cream and milkmaids, and the prose is getting distinctly horny when he is interrupted by two authoritative figures, one 'strawberry-pink with ire': 'You do realise this is private property?' Roger is about to scarper, and save everyone the bother, but he remembers Cobbett and his account of the two poachers hanged in Winchester in 1822, whose crime 'amounted to little more than I had just done'. So, tongue in cheek, he stands his ground: 'I got changed as languidly as possible, then casually leapfrogged the fence and sauntered off along the path, whistling softly to myself, as an Englishman is entitled to do. Excuse me, came a voice, does that fence mean anything to you?'

It's a teacherly, paternalistic question; its sarcasm is rooted in a conviction that is utterly blinkered to any position other than its own. When Roger responds 'sweetly' with a watered-down Woody Guthrie sentiment (a sort of 'this pond was made for you and me'), 'the river keeper practically fell off his bike. The porter flushed a deeper strawberry.' The scene is quaint, utterly devoid of violence, and reminiscent of English 1970s sitcom farces, featuring wily country sorts and stout-bellied authoritarians. Yet to Roger, whistling his Englishman's entitlement, it is of national significance. It springboards into a discussion of the 'Right to Roam', the ideology that opens up certain land to walkers, irrespective of pathways. Roger was writing before the Countryside and Rights of Way (CRoW) Act of 2000, a major piece of legislation which legitimised off-path wandering on mountain, moor, heath, down and common land in England and Wales. That was 150 years of campaigning to gain what to this day amounts to only 8 per cent of the landscape. His words still apply: 'I say "rights" to point up the paradox, that something that was once a natural right has been expropriated and turned into a commodity ... the right to walk freely along river banks or to bathe in rivers, should be no more bought and sold than the right to walk up mountains or to swim in the sea.'

During the Middle Ages, paths formed organically through the practical needs to get from one place to another. As the new notion of private property erected fences to defend its position, new definitions of land brought with them new definitions of rights to them. But these pathways remained necessary for the functioning of the countryside and so were protected by the common law standard, 'once a highway, always a highway'. When enclosure finally emptied the countryside of its workers, many of these paths became disused and most disappeared, churned by the plough, clogged with brambles or deliberately blocked by landowners.

When the Ramblers launched their case against Hoogstraten they succeeded by sheer will and canny politicking. Councillor Skinner of East Sussex council was blunt about the odds. 'He does have an extremely good record in the courts, and English law tends to be biased towards people like him. We don't stand a bloody chance.' But eventually, because the evidence proved a long-standing Right of Way, they did win. Hoogstraten's shadow company, Rarebargain Ltd, were fined £1,600 and ordered to pay the £3,500 costs of the Ramblers' case. But somehow the costs were not paid, and the obstructions remained. Meanwhile, with Parliament discussing the CRoW Act, they petitioned hard for a clause to be added to the Act which would require, by law, such obstructions to be removed. Among ministers this clause became known as the Hoogstraten clause and eventually, when included, became Section 64 of the CRoW Act, defined as the 'Power to order offender to remove obstruction'. The day after this section came into law, Kate Ashbrook, the chair of the Ramblers' Association, returned to the Framfield footpath and served notice to the estate. The case was heard two months later and Rarebargain, who did not appear in court, were fined £1,000 per obstruction, the barbed wire fence, the padlocked gate, the refrigeration units and the barn. From beginning to end, it took the council thirteen years and £100,000 in court costs to open up the path. In February 2003, Ashbrook returned to the path with a gaggle of press and finished the job with a pair of bolt-cutters.

Today there are 117,800 miles of public footpath in England, half that of a hundred years ago. It was only in 1949, in the National Parks and Countryside Act, that procedures were introduced to legitimise these rights of way, to set them in stone. 'Definitive Maps' were drawn up for all counties in England, designating the Rights of Way, securing these passages under protection of the secretary of state, and from the 1970s they were marked on OS maps.

But while these definitive maps enshrine a public right, they simultaneously legitimise the space that is off limits, the private right. Every pathway that is secured by law further strengthens the fence between us and the land either side of it. The Right of Way Review Committee in England, which influenced the Land Access Acts of 1981, 1990 and 2000, was set up in 1979 by the Ramblers' Association, the National Farmers' Union and the Country Landowners' Association, the latter two being dedicated to protecting the rights of landowners. The members of the CLA, just 36,000 of them, own 50 per cent of the rural land in England and Wales, a statistic lifted off their own website. The definition of public rights is in fact a euphemism for the protection of the rights of a very small proportion of the population. Our 'rights' to the land have become streamlined into thin strips of legitimacy, the freedom to toe the line.

Another line is fast approaching – a cut-off line. On 1 January 2026, because of the same Act that returned to us our mountains and moors, any path that has not been registered on these Definitive Maps will automatically be extinguished. To save Cowpasture Lane, just one path, from closure was a relentless struggle, involving at least six different battles over forty years (thirty of those before Roger), each requiring evidence from experts, photocopies of countless maps and aerial photos, an intimate knowledge of the small print of Rights of Way legislation, and, perhaps most importantly, the time and will to bother. To register a path before the cut-off date, there is a 316-page guide which, with all the exuberant charm of a chemistry textbook, will either help you, or break you. You must submit a Modification Order, hard copy, with enough evidence attached to it to support your claim. This evidence could include turnpike records, enclosure records, tithe maps, railway and canals plans, highways records, sales documents and Inland Revenue valuation maps, all of which must be photocopied by visiting the records office, national archive, parliamentary archives, or private records of a particular estate (almost impossible). You are entering a hellish world of box files, permission forms, waiting rooms and impenetrable legalese; it is a process that would, in Hollywood format, be relegated to a pulse-thumping montage, but in real life takes weeks, months and sometimes years. What's more, of course, while every council and government official you meet is paid for their time, you will be a volunteer, unpaid, and must therefore engage all your efforts as an extracurricular activity, squeezed in between your other responsibilities.

And to what end? To secure ourselves a causeway of legitimacy while all around the land has been washed away into a sea of private ownership. The real question is why we allow ourselves to be fenced off in this way. Why do we obey the command of signs and the limits to our freedom silently scrawled across the land in lines of barbed wire? Where does this obedience come from? As Roger says of the interdicted military land of Orford Ness, 'This makes me feel like a schoolboy and want to break bounds.'

The fire is guttering, causing the shadows of the room to lurch up and down the walls. The cigarette has burned itself down to a long cable of ash. Somewhere in the room there is a gloppy sound, wet and insistent, the sound of an old toothless man chewing on cold lasagne. The dog is licking his balls. He's really churning away at them, lapping at them as if they were scoops of vanilla ice cream, entirely untroubled by my gaze. On the page in front of me, the past intersects with the present: just a mile further down the track from where I'm sitting, twenty years ago, Roger Deakin has climbed the fence of Burgate Wood. He has found a patch of land and laid down his head where a decade later his ashes would be scattered. In the light of the fire, his words are alive:

Sleeping one time in Burgate Wood on the moated island of the old hall, I put my cheek against the loam and the cool ground ivy. When I closed my eyes, I saw the iceberg depths of the woods root-world ... this is the part of the wood that only reveals itself occasionally after a big storm, when the trees have keeled over and the roots are suddenly thrown upright, clutching earth and stones. How deep do roots go?

SHEEP

Division, sedition, oppression, obedience

'Your sheep that were wont to be so meek and tame, and so small eaters, now, as I heard say, be become so great devourers and so wild, that they eat up, and swallow down the very men themselves'

— Thomas More, *Utopia*

Hammered into the horizon of Arundel, West Sussex, are the twin stakes of power in old England: the cathedral and the castle, the silhouettes of Church and state.

On Christmas Day 1066, William the Conqueror stood at the head of the table and carved up England like a turkey. Each of the gathered lords had been promised a slice, and to Roger de Montgomery William gave estates in Surrey, Hampshire, Wiltshire, Gloucestershire, Cambridgeshire, Shropshire and the majority of Sussex, an area defined as the Rape of Arundel. Roger's job was to fortify the south flank of England, which was deemed to have had quite enough of French invasions, and so up went castles in Dover, Carisbrooke, Lewes, Bramber and Arundel.

I approach Arundel from the station and watch the turrets of the castle rise high above the rooftops. The town is picture-postcard pretty. With a lazy river, steep winding roads, it's all Narnia lamp-posts, ye olde franchise pub signs, antique shoppes and, when I head up the hill, a large window displaying an oil portrait of Winston Churchill. It is a tourist's vision of England.

At the top of the high street, the road meets the castle walls, twenty foot tall, crenellated and turreted, with a grand gate whose motto reads Sola Virtus Invicta ('Virtue Alone is Unconquered'). Like many of the aristocratic aphorisms plastered onto their buildings, even in translation it is hard to tell what this actually means. I follow the wall west along the street. I pass the priory and then the cathedral, built in 1868 in a style meant to look 400 years older, and soon enough I'm leaving the town behind, following a grass verge alongside the A-road. The wall has shrunk from castle fortification to a more amenable flint wall, low enough for me to stretch my fingers over.

When China opened its gates to the West in 1978, the England football team was too busy to accept their invitation to a three-week tour of the country. So, sort of second best, they sent West Bromwich Albion. The climax of the media circus that accompanied them was the team trip to Changcheng, China's Great Wall, and the televised interview with midfielder John Trewick. When asked for his opinion on the wall, he responded with a flash of socio-political insight that remains to this day the most pithy surmise of all border studies: 'When you've seen one wall, you've seen them all.'

From the nineteenth-century flint wall in front of me to the Israeli West Bank barrier, whose 440-mile-long, eight-metre-high extent combines concrete, razor wire, steel fencing, ditches, tank patrol lanes, an 'Iron Dome' anti-missile air protection, a subterranean extension to block tunnelling attempts plus constant military monitoring from guards, snipers and drones, walls are all the same.

First and foremost, a wall is a technology of division. Its presence alone creates a simplistic binary logic that imposes the idea that one side is separate from the other, and moreover, that both sides are *opposed* to the other. It is both a universally understood command, *do not enter*, and the technology to enforce itself – the wall says no, and backs it up with a blank, stony face that will not engage in dialogue. A wall looks like authority; it implies its own inherent legitimacy. To demolish a wall seems so much more violent than to build one, even though the wall is itself a destruction of the links between societies that existed before its erection.

Walls look like order; but more often than not a wall stands at the precise fulcrum of an imbalance in society. Most walls are only necessary as a means of defending the resources of those that have them from those that lack them. In this way, though they present themselves as mechanisms of security, they are in fact tools of oppression.

But for all their rigid simplicity, the message of walls is rather more fluid and paradoxical. They underline the strength of what lies within while simultaneously reinforcing the perceived threat of what lies without. They *project* power as much as protect it. They guard their territory, conceal it, and at the same time announce its presence, exposing its vulnerability. The longest wall in English history was built by the Romans, not just to defend their territory, but to impose it. Hadrian's Wall allowed the Romans to control and monitor movement either side of the wall, to collect taxes on traders that passed through it, and to announce the constant threat of expansionism. In *The Great Wall*, Julia Lovell discusses the walls that were precursors to China's 13,500-mile monster, swinging far out into the Mongolian steppes, noting that some of these walls 'look less land-protecting than land-grabbing, designed to enable Chinese states to police peoples whose way of life differed from their own, and to control lucrative trade routes.'

As far as their physical properties go, walls just don't work. Most walls are breachable, most fences are broken somewhere. The longer the wall, the harder it is to defend. Think of China's Great Wall, and the image of the Badaling stretch comes to mind, all gleaming local stone and iconic watchtowers. But this section is only eight miles long, a minuscule fraction of the Great Wall's totality. Elsewhere, the wall is made of mud, sticks, grass, sand, and at some points is tacked together with sticky rice. Most of the wall is not a wall, but a scar on the ground surrounded on both sides by a wild, indistinct expanse. But we never hear of this wall; we rarely glimpse it. Because this would breach its most fundamental strength: the Great Metaphor. When the Badaling wall was repaired in the 1950s by Chairman Mao, its purpose was not to defend China against the nomads of Mongolia, but to reinforce a vision of China, both inside and out: he wanted to make China great again. 'I will build a great wall – and nobody builds walls better than me, believe me – and I'll build them very inexpensively. I will build a great, great wall on our southern border, and I will make Mexico pay for that wall. Mark my words.'

When Donald Trump was voted into power, his words were all that counted. The cost of the wall, its colossal impracticability, the vast infrastructure required to support its intent, none of this registered in the light of its one radiant power: the idea. When he came to power he had already built a strong, reliable wall where it counted most: in the heads of his voters.

Kim Jong-un has a similar wall. In 1989, his dad announced that South Korea, in league with the Americans, had erected a concrete wall, twenty-six foot high, twenty foot thick, stretching 160 miles across the border. In North Korea the wall is a widely recognised reflection of the South's reluctance to unify. But Google Maps doesn't register it, even by satellite. And the most intriguing thing about the wall is that it is pure propaganda: it doesn't exist. Or, more accurately: it exists only in the mind.

Following the fall of the 101-mile-long Berlin Wall, the Germans began speaking about a *Mauer im Kopf*, a wall in the head, *a mindwall*. Without the actual presence of the wall, it was still perceived by the residents of Berlin; like a phantom limb, it continued to trigger the brain. A study published in 2005 found that Germans repeatedly overestimated the distance between cities that had been in opposite halves of their once divided country, while those who opposed the reunification exaggerated the distances even further. The wall had gone yet, to this day, its gulf persists.

The road is busy and fast, and I'm dithering about where to climb over the wall running alongside it. With no real path, there are no other pedestrians and I'm already self-conscious, tramping with my rucksack. Even to veer off the road and approach the wall seems like breaching a taboo. There is a moral mindwall, centuries in the making, which prevents me from stepping out of line. But I pick my point, wait for the best moment and duck in. Down the ditch and up to the wall. I toss my bag over, jump, and use the flint to get a foothold. I swing my leg up, hook my heel on the lip of the wall and hoist my waist onto the top. And jump.

The ground is padded with yellowing leaves. I have landed in a strip of woodland that mutes the noise of the road from the castle grounds. I make my way through the trees, break cover and sneak across pastureland that is a time capsule for the largest land grab in English history: the enclosures.

To the north, there are still ruts and rivets in the earth which, from satellite view, are clearly relics of the open field system that would have characterised England in the Middle Ages. Small strips of land farmed communally, on rotating crops, they were surrounded by large areas of tillage, rough pasture for cows and pigs. But by the time Arundel Castle was built, the English landscape already belonged to sheep. The Romans had set up a large wool-processing plant in Winchester around AD 50 and its wool was among the most prized in the empire. In 1275, Edward I introduced the first tax on the export of raw wool and, twenty years later, the barons sitting in Parliament had declared wool 'half the value of the whole land'.

Wool was power and sheep were the reason landlords evicted the smallholding and tenant farmers from their properties. With fields enclosed and the country depopulated, a new mindscape was placed upon the land. 'Enclosure' is the name given to the systematic privatisation of land on which commoners held customary rights of use, a sometimes-legal and sometimes-illegal process that began in the early thirteenth century and reached its zenith in the eighteenth. The first Act of enclosure came in 1235, with the Statute of Merton: under pressure from the barons, Henry III gave the lords of the manor the right to assert private rights of ownership over areas of land that had previously belonged generally to everybody and exclusively to nobody. The land, and the wealth it generated, became a patchwork of privatised interest. Each section of the grid was dedicated not to the interests of the community, but to the most profitable use its owner could find for it.

The English were simultaneously hedged out of their land and hemmed into a new ideology that valued the land and their labour in terms of private profit. But these hedges, walls and fences, so easy to uproot and bypass, were fortified by a moral prohibition that stemmed from the other great shepherds of England, the Church.

Property has always been sacrosanct, and some scholars claim the idea of sacred ground to be the very origin of the property concept. Thomas Nail, Professor of Philosophy at the University of Denver, has written on how property first evolved not with sedentary agriculture, but earlier, when nomads needed a place to bury their dead. Marked by huge stone boulders called megaliths, these boneyards became places to which nomads would return, to pay homage to their ancestors. Palisades went up around the sacred earth, to ward others off, giving birth to the notion of territory as area (a line around land), rather than a vector (a line through land).

Shrines and temples evolved out of these graveyards, and soon they were built without the need for the dead beneath them. They were positioned to root astrological mechanisms to the earth, to mark moments of coalition in time and space, such as the solstice at Stonehenge. With these new temples came a new sense of who this space was for. Their boundary stones marked a division between those who believed and those who didn't, 'unifying the identity of the believers and dividing them from the non-believers'.

Though Christianity arrived in Britain long before Augustine's mission in 597 AD, it took centuries for it to become anything other than a minor sect. It was Alfred the Great, King of Wessex and later King of the Anglo-Saxons, who in the ninth century introduced chapels into the landscape, seeing the pagan invasion of the Vikings as retribution for a slack devotion to God. But it was when William the Conqueror seized England that Christianity truly took hold of the land. William not only built castles, he also built cathedrals, churches and monasteries, using them all to create a new centralised order on the land.

The wall I climbed to get into Arundel Castle's grounds was put up by the 11th Duke of Norfolk, known as the Drunken Duke. But the moral obedience it still commands was engineered by another son of this castle, twenty generations before, who was responsible for strengthening the link between Church and state: His Grace, the Most Reverend Archbishop of Canterbury, Thomas Arundel.

Inspired by John Wycliffe's translation of the Latin Vulgate Bible in 1382, a small band of men and women had been preaching a smorgasbord of heresy. Having read the word of God for themselves, these Biblemen, or Lollards, believed in a number of edicts that challenged the authority of the Church. They believed that the bread held aloft in church services did not turn into Christ's actual living body, but was simply symbolic of it. They believed that the Pope in Rome should have no say over the secular affairs of England. They believed that priests should abstain from all worldly goods, instead placing great emphasis on denying them the property they owned. In short, they believed that every English man and woman had the right to a personal relationship with God, unmediated by the centralised power of the Church.

To a fourteenth-century clergyman, a Lollard was a vagrant in the moral landscape of England. 'Lollard' was a catch-all term that encompassed 'heretics, sceptics, anticlericals, rioters, rebels, felons, eccentrics, lunatics and outsiders of all kinds'. Arundel, like any estate agent who sees himself being written out of a deal, saw them as a direct threat to the relevance of his organisation. His response was to persuade the king to pass his law, unambiguously titled 'On the burning of heretics'. The law gave the Church the power to identify heretics and have the local state authorities arrest them. They were delivered to the Church, which could now handle the torturing, trial and burning of these mendicants themselves, without the red tape of government intervention. Lollard towers, essentially private torture chambers, sprang up beside churches and in abbey grounds, legitimised by this new law. The Church's word was now backed not only by God, but by the state. If the Pope, bishop or clergyman pointed the finger, the sheriff or justice of the peace had to respond. Heresy was redefined as sedition.

No one in England had been burned for two centuries, but Archbishop Arundel now began a spree that was to continue after his death, with twenty-five committed to the smoke in the next eighty years. Unlike many of his followers, Wycliffe escaped the flames but in 1428 his body was exhumed, by order of the Pope, and burned in public. The contemporary chronicler Fuller wrote:

> They burnt his bones to ashes and cast them into the Swift, a neighbouring brook running hard by. Thus the brook hath conveyed his ashes into Avon; Avon into Severn; Severn into the narrow seas; and they into the main ocean. And thus the ashes of Wycliffe are the emblem of his doctrine which now is dispersed the world over.

This may have been the Church's biggest mistake. The Lollards had been a small, disunited band of heretics whose beliefs were only amplified by the paranoid reaction of the authorities. But now the word was out. And a hundred years later its flame was to be rekindled.

At every junction of footpaths, there are *NO RIGHT OF WAY* signs blocking the forested routes. There is no fence, no bear trap, no shotgun tripwires, ditches, moats or army of weaponised men. Just the silent expectation of compliance, and the feeling that someone is watching. As Proverbs 15:3 says, 'The eyes of the Lord are in every place, beholding the evil and the good.' These signs conjure a spell, words that trigger my conscience and change the chemicals in my blood. Out of nowhere I feel as if I'm doing something wrong.

In the Tudor era, obedience to God and the state was taught from a young age. If you didn't learn the Church's catechism by heart, you were excommunicated, which not only served to damn your soul to hell, but, on a more practical level, ostracised you entirely from your community – it was against the law to do business with or even talk to someone excluded from the flock of Christ. You were homeless, hungry and isolated, with hell-fire waiting. The first four commandments of the Bible demand obedience, and the fifth, obedience to one's father and mother, was interpreted rather liberally as 'to honour and obey the king, and all that are put under authority under him; to submit myself to all my governors, teachers, spiritual pastors and masters; to order myself lowly and reverently to all my betters.'

In the late sixteenth century William Perkins' best-selling *The Foundation of Christian Religion Gathered into Six Principles* elaborated on the teaching of the Bible, giving specifics to the lowly multitudes. It said, 'all were admonished to obedience because every higher power was the ordinance of god'. Every higher power: from father, to magistrate, to king, from priest to bishop to pope. Some tracts tackled disobedience directly, such as *A Homily against Disobedience and Wilful Rebellion*, published a year after the Northern Uprising of 1569. Here, the law of the land was expressed in a prayer, sedition recited as heresy.

But these commands to obedience were also imposed outside of the mind. In the sixteenth century London was dominated by the physical presence of the Church. The clergy were the biggest landowners and biggest employers of the city; their power over their parishioners was as practical as it was spiritual. London had more churches than any other city in Europe and more than sixty stocks, whipping posts and cages reminded Londoners of the punishment of overstepping the line. London was resolutely tamed, a flock of 40,000 sheep – with one notable exception.

Aged just twenty-nine, in a small rented room in east London William Tyndale spent a year translating the New Testament into English. Though some English translations were still in circulation, any further translation had been specifically banned in 1408 by Arundel in his Constitutions of Oxford. At the time, the English language was the lowly cousin of the courtly, flamboyant French and legislative Latin, used mainly by the rude oiks of the land. English was coarse Anglo-Saxon, tribal, barbaric, and to recreate the divine scripture into English was to soil it, to rub its nose in the mud. But however offended the clergy were by this debasement, the real threat was to their personal livelihoods: the Bible was the very foundation upon which the Church legitimised its power. To open up the word of God to the commoners was to de-privatise its interpretation and expose the flimsy premise of many of the Church's ordinances.

Neither the Church nor its clergy paid any tax. Instead, like the state, they received it: every common man was required to pay a tithe (one-tenth) of his earnings to the local parish, and work on its lands without wage. Every time the life of a commoner wandered into the Church's domain, it was tapped for cash – fees for masses, dirges, hallowings, indulgences, rent rolls, legacies and penances. At a funeral, priests could demand mortuaries for their services, a part of the dead man's land inheritance. All this, every last coin in the Church's coffers, was based upon a letter that St Paul wrote to the Corinthians, in which he interpreted the laws of Moses for them. He explained, 'Ye ploughman should plow in the hope of sharing in the crop. If we have sown spiritual things amongst you, is it too much if we reap material things from you.' The line of

Moses' legislation he was referring to: 'You shall not muzzle an ox when it treads out grain.'

It's pretty clear, then, why the Church was so anxious not to have this leaked. The entire wealth of the Vatican, its landholdings and power across Europe, was propped up by a wildly creative interpretation of a single sentence written by Moses 3,000 years before Tyndale was born. To cap it all, most scholars now agree that Moses didn't even write these laws.

At the time, Bibles were kept locked in the tabernacle of the local church, behind the altar, on sacred, interdicted ground. Both the Church and state claimed its legitimacy from deep inside this spiritual keep. And the Bible's Latin was the final mystical wall that prohibited access to the common man. The word 'translate' stems from the Latin meaning 'to carry over', an etymology that implies some kind of line. What Tyndale did, however, was not so much carry the word of Christ over the intellectual wall of Latin as to blow the safe.

Working in complete secrecy, alone in his bedsit, Tyndale knew the act of translation alone would be hugely damaging to the authority of the Church. With printing presses now all over Europe, his work would be read by far more people than Wycliffe's. But it was the specific words that Tyndale chose that would be the Church's greatest undoing – and his. Thomas More declared the most seditious changes a mistranslation, saying: 'Tyndale did euyll in translatynge the scripture in to our tongue ... he chaunged comenly this worde chyrche in to this word congregacyon and this worde preste into this word seynour, and cheyte in to loue.'

Wycliffe had made his translation from the Latin Vulgate, which was the standard version used by all churches across Europe since the fourth century. But the author of the Vulgate, St Jerome, had already bastardised the Greek text with some convenient mistranslations that suited his sponsors at the Vatican.

Until Tyndale, the Greek *ἐκκλησία* had been translated into the Latin *ecclesia*, meaning 'church'. Rome's interpretation of this word extended from not only the building of God and all its property, but to all its levels of bureaucracy, from clergy right up to the Pope himself. The English word 'church' itself comes from the Greek word *κυριακός*, a term that specifically denotes property: 'belonging to the Lord'. When Tyndale translated *ἐκκλησία* more accurately as 'congregation', he simply elided the church. With this one change, the entire structure of organised religion was placed on the level of any small gathering of devout followers, reading text from the Bible in a blank room. The hierarchy was smashed; this was anarchy.

But when Tyndale translated the Greek word *ἀγάπη* from the Vulgate's 'charity' to the Germanic 'love', he released Christ's teaching from all its artificial financial matrices, the grid that linked a place in heaven to how much coin you could spare. It removed the Church's right to tithes, legacies and its banks of gold and silver. In what must surely be simultaneously the most romantic and pragmatic use of a word in the history of the English language, Tyndale threw down the walls of intellectual property, levelled the moral ground and proclaimed, 500 years before the Beatles: *all you need is love.*

The sun is low on the horizon, sending long diagonal shadows across the woodland floor. I have come to the end of the duke's property, back on to the Right of Way, to find it blocked by a locked gate. I double back, head south and pass pine plantations, rows of half-grown Christmas trees and stacks of piled timber. Estates of this size almost invariably curtain the industrial endeavours of their interiors with a thin line of deciduous trees, masking the monocultures of their land use with a postcard-pretty veneer; this belies the historic repurposing of the land from common wealth to private profit, and gives their walls an aura of natural order, as if the estates are more private garden than factory floor.

The light is dimming, and the earth is rutted with 4x4 tracks and knotted with lumps of grass and mossy, rotten branches. The forest is alive with the last moments of the day, lines of crows glimpsed through the treetops, three deer pause in the track ahead of me, and then, for a brief moment in the gloom, it seems as if the forest floor is surging away from me, pouring up the steep slopes to the pink stain of the setting sun. My eyes focus, the world quickly rights itself and among the leaves I see it is not the earth streaming from me, but countless camouflaged pheasants.

I come up to a wooden gate, pass through its broken fence posts and see a dot of warm orange light through the black poles of the trees. The track runs uphill alongside a house, which seems to be your archetypal shack in the woods, the setting for an HBO thriller about a guy in a vest with bodies in his freezer. There's a forecourt of dead machinery, drapes of ivy hanging from exposed warehouse girders. I turn on my torch.

It was always the plan to have a small fire before I left the woods, so seeing a shallow dip twenty yards off the path, just like my dell back home, writhing root systems exposed by sub-sidence, I find some kind of cover from the windows of the HBO house. This will be my first fire on a duke's land. In English civil law, this should be no different from my fires on the farmer's land in West Berkshire, or anywhere else, and, as I'm laying the twigs, I'm struck for the first time that I haven't a clue what a duke's power really consists of. But with that mass of castle stone due west of me, hidden behind the valley, I feel a greater sense of trepidation. There seems to be something primal at play, some sort of inherited fear. As the Bible says: 'I will put my laws in their hearts; I shall inscribe them on their minds'.

Tyndale, of course, got what was coming. His translation of the New Testament was arguably the single most dramatic de-privatisation of power in the history of England: he had turned the sheep of the Church's flock into independent, self-determining freethinkers, with their own interpretation of God's will. It was an act that undermined the centralised power of the state as much as the Church. For this, he was chased through Europe, betrayed by an associate who needed the cash and sentenced to death: garrotted, and burned at the stake.

Just three years after Tyndale's execution, the Church relented to public clamour and the Bible was sanctioned into English, a copy sent to every church to be made available to anyone who wanted to read it. Private property was translated into public use. Today, 80 per cent of the standardised James I Bible is Tyndale's work. This includes the Lord's Prayer, which means that we have Tyndale, somewhat tragically, to thank for the words: 'Forgive us our trespasses.'

The wood is silent and I am tense. The crackle of the fire seems excessively loud. Every time something shuffles in the dry leaves, I twitch, and whenever an owl hoots, it feels as though it's snitching on me. I am crouching by the flames, warming my hands, telling myself that I'd hear the crunch and crash of footsteps through the bracken long before they got to me. I look up to the path, and beyond it, to the horizon of trees on the opposite valley slope. It seems unnaturally bright. The sky in winter flashes deep blue before turning to black, but this light is brighter. I stand up, unsure of myself. Slowly, I realise the line is not the horizon, but the crest of the slope I'm on, that the light is not the setting sun but something much closer; with the barely audible tread of tyres on the wet byway, the headlights of a truck pass before me.

I am waiting with my friend on the right-hand side of a stone gateway. We are sitting on the empty plinth, as large as a kitchen table, taking in the view. To our left is the main road and a large field dominated by a massive gnarled oak. Beneath its boughs lie herds of white deer, albino reds, with two stags on their feet, keeping guard. In the far distance, there are more herds, black fallow, slowly passing their muzzles over the grass. Before us there is an expanse of cricket pitch stripes, lines of perspective that lead to a confectionery-box manor house, huge but tiny, snug amid the trees. This is Boughton House, known to its tourists as the English Versailles, and it is the seat of the Dukes of Buccleuch, Britain's largest landowning dynasty.

Before us, not a mile away, beneath two acres of roofing, are masterpieces by El Greco, Van Dyck and Gainsborough; there are pieces by André-Charles Boulle, cabinetmakers of France, there are Mortlake tapestries, a puckle gun, a rare Pettelier sconce and, according to one guide book: 'Ralph's highly important oriental rug collection.' Ralph, the 1st Duke, who from his portrait looks like a chubby glam-rock star, was the self-appointed master of the wardrobe for the royal estates, a seventeenth-century Svengali of haute couture. As such, the palace is a warehouse of luxury goods, a gilded lily, a peculiarly kitsch vision of heaven on earth. And their family motto, with the vapid insouciance of a luxury perfume brand, is simply: *I Love*.

Behind us runs the Right of Way that will lead us into the duke's land and we are sitting on the wall of his 'seat', an 11,000-acre private estate. A few minutes ago, a 4x4 appeared to our right, doing a conspicuously slow crawl of surveillance down one of the tracks, turned and drove resolutely out of view. Now another is driving towards us from inside the estate while the original one, as yet unseen, is creeping up behind us. We are being pincered. A middle-aged woman rolls down the window and asks us what we're doing. She's cheerful and so are we, and she's halfway through telling us that *I'm afraid you're on private property* when she is interrupted by the man behind us. Standing on the footboard of his chugging engine, a man, perhaps sixty, liveried in standard gamekeeper gilet and cords, tweed cap, takes another tone entirely, giving it the *what the hell do you think you're playing at. You can't be up there …*

Perched on the wall, we're caught on a line in between two approaches, a caricature of gendered debate, one aggressive and one calm. The man wins, because he's shouting. We apologise to the woman, as if it's we who interrupted her, turn from the view and get down from the wall. We're right by his side, and he's still shouting. He's very angry, sputtering like his engine, threatening to call the police. He runs out of things to shout, returns to the truck and takes our picture with a digital camera attached to his dashboard. We smile for posterity, and he drives away.

We continue east, to a Right of Way that leads us beyond the wall, 200 yards into the duke's land, then stops, like a jetty. Before us, out of bounds, is a small redirected river that runs towards several artsy water features in front of the main house, and a little hump bridge and a gate whose sign forbids us access. We hop the gate, cross the bridge and walk out into the expanse of grassland, decorated by ancient, thick-trunked, twisting oaks. The sheep lift their heads and stare, indignantly, still chewing, until one turns, runs, and the whole flock follows, streaming up the slope.

In *The Gentle Art of Tramping*, the Edwardian journalist and traveller Stephen Graham describes a 'trespasser's walk':

> You take with you a little compass, decide to go west or east, as fancy favours, and then keep resolutely to the guidance of the magnetic needle. It takes you the most extraordinary way, and shows what an enormous amount of the face of

the earth is kept from the feet of ordinary humanity by the fact of private property.

This estate is over thirty times larger than Hyde Park, and reserved for a single family. We don't have a compass, but we do have a pencil-ruled line on a map printed from the duke's web-site. We're heading north-east to a strange little deserted manor house I want to see, just outside the duke's declared perimeter. The sky is cobalt crystal blue, the leaves on the ground like a children's sponge painting in acid yellows and greens, and, even though it's just past noon, the shadows of the trees are long.

The Dukes of Buccleuch inherited this property through marriage with the Montagus, who had bought it from wealthy Calais wool merchants in 1528. The land was sold to them by St Edmundsbury Abbey, the final destination of the convoy of the martyred St Edmund, the very same route of Roger Deakin's Cowpasture Lane. We are in Northamptonshire, and that the abbey could own land over seventy miles away from its source demonstrates the reach of their interests. Edward Montagu was a lawyer from Hemington, Northants, who bought Boughton Castle, as it was then known, to consolidate his landholdings in the area. But several times through the Tudor dynasty, the family had found themselves on the wrong side of history, with one member doing time in the Tower of London. In 1605, there was another blow to the prestige of the family when Edward's grandson, also an Edward, was stripped of his Lieutenancy and Justiceship of the Peace in the county. The Montagus were hanging on to nobility with their fingernails, so it was little wonder that, when King James called upon them for assistance, they came galloping.

In 1607, two years after the failed gunpowder plot, thousands of commoners took to the fields around us to protest enclosure. In what came to be known as the Midland Revolt, there were eleven uprisings, each with thousands of people, protesting the severe enclosure of the Midlands. The protests were carefully planned, their locations chosen strategically. Each commoner had been expressly urged: 'Not to swear, nor to offer violence to any person, but to ply their business and make fair works.'

The protests may have been peaceful, but the sheer number of people caused alarm to the authorities. Though there was never any explicit statement of intent and complaint, many protesters were arrested carrying cheap prints of the Petition of the Diggers of Warwickshire, which argued against: 'Incroaching tyrants who grind the poor so y they may dwell by themselves in theyr herds of fatt weathers [sheep] … onely for theyre own private gain … they have depopulated and overthrown whole towns and made thereof sheep pastures …'

The Midlands had been ravaged by enclosure. Their communal cornfields had been hedged and stripped to provide pasture for the sheep. The rents on their properties had spiked and their common rights, collecting wood for winter, allowing their pigs and cows to fatten on the pasture, had been removed. With nowhere else to go, many were now squatting on the side of the fields they had lived on a decade earlier. In an enquiry in the August following the revolt, royal commissioners had investigated the scale of illegal enclosure and depopulation in Rockingham Forest alone: 27,000 acres had been enclosed, 350 farms destroyed and almost 150,000 people across eighteen villages had lost their homes.

The protests were led by an enigmatic figure called Captain Pouch who had named himself after the small leather purse he carried with him. The pouch, he claimed, contained a magic substance that gave him the authority to destroy all enclosures from Northampton to the city of York. Alongside his magic charm, the man was well placed to spread sedition: as an itinerant tinker, travelling the length and breadth of the Midlands, he would have had many years before the Revolt to win the trust of locals, unionising the disparate people to one cause.

Pouch was adamant that the commoners were simply doing the king's work for him. In 1593, the Tudor courts had relaxed the laws of enclosure, only to revoke this position four years later: each hedge that went up once again needed the approval of Parliament. Since the landowners in the Midlands were largely ignoring this repeal, the rebels were not protesting the authority of the state, but simply trying to enforce it. They argued that the land was being robbed from the commonwealth of England and fenced into private gain. They were defending England against thieves.

The revolt in Newton was not caused by Montagu, but by his neighbour Sir Thomas Tresham. By all accounts, Tresham was the Hoogstraten of Newton, a 'most odious figure', reviled by the nobility and commoners alike. Sir Thomas had by 1605 overseen the destruction of nine farms and 400 acres had been put to sheep pasture. But he was unable to help quash the revolt, because he had died two years before the Midland Revolt, ruining his remaining relatives with an £11,000 debt and disbanding his army of yeomen.

Edward Montagu was in a tricky position. As an MP, he had already stated the grievances of his Northampton constituency in Parliament, describing: 'the depopulation and the daily excessive conversion of tillage to pasture', a direct reference to his neighbour's crimes. But when the call came from the king to deal with the rebels 'with sharp remedie' he had little choice but to obey. He rustled up a militia and met the rebels in a place called the Brand, in between his house and Tresham's.

This crowd, however, was different from the rest of the revolt: they came primed for violence. The revolt was on its knees: Captain Pouch had already been arrested in Warwickshire, the contents of his pouch found to be nothing more than a lump of green cheese, and the other peaceful crowds around the Midlands had been dispersed with ease. By this time, it seemed that yet another revolt had been swept away, just like the Pilgrimage of Grace or Robert Kett's rebellion earlier that century. But the commoners were desperate, still starving for the corn that had been cleared for pasture to feed to the sheep now occupying their fields. This time they had resolved to 'manfully die' rather than face another winter of starvation. A thousand local men, women and children turned out that day, some armed with weapons, some with tools; all resolved to claim back their land, whatever the cost. A letter from the Earl of Shrewsbury takes up the account:

Sr Anth. Mildmaay and Sr Edw. Montacute repaired to Newton, Mr Thos. Tresham's toune, wheare 1000 of these fellowes who term themselves levellers weare busily digging, but weare furnished with many half pykes, pyked staves, long bills and bowes and arrows and stoanes. These gentlemen, fynding great bakwardness in the trained bandes, weare constrained to use all the horse they could make, and as many foote of their owne servants and fellowe as they could trust; and first read the proclamation twice unto them, using all the best perswasions to them to desist that they could devise; but when nothing would prevaile, they charged them thoroughlie both with their horse and foote. But the first charge they stoode, and fought desperatelie; but at the second charge they ran away, in which there were slaine som 40 or 50 of them, and a very great number hurt.

It is no wonder that the 'trained bandes' were 'bakward'. They were most likely well acquainted with the rebels, who would have been their neighbours from church and alehouse. In the twice-read proclamation, and 'best perswasions', it is perhaps fair to read reluctance in Montagu's final actions. But he did charge his horses and when the captured rebels were tried, hanged and quartered, he saw to it that their limbs were displayed and taken on a macabre tour of the local towns and villages, steeped in vinegar and tarred at their wounds to slow the decay.

My friend and I have reached the north end of the duke's property. The sun has set, and, without it, the air is cold. We had met a man in full camo-gear, high upon his tree seat, stalking deer. With his rifle in hand, he politely redirected us off the duke's estate and out onto the road. We're rushing, because it's a full moon tonight and we want to be off the road to see it rise. We stop off in Brigstock and buy our supper from the Co-op. Sausages for the fire, a cheap cheesecake for the interim.

There are three miles to walk before our destination, Thomas Tresham's abandoned manor house, now owned by the National Trust. With the strange name Lyveden New Bield, no one can be sure why it was built. Tresham's main house is less than ten miles away, due west, and he barely had the finances to keep that going.

The house is faith manifested into architecture. Its footprint is cruciform; its ratios fetishise the trinity. The window that faces due east is a crucifix and meant to catch the light of the rising sun, so that every summer morning Christ's cross shone in gold on the opposite wall. When Francis Tresham was implicated in the plot to murder James I and all his Parliament, the labourers downed tools and scarpered. It has been left, half finished, for over four centuries.

We cross the ring road that runs around the duke's estate and climb a hill in the pitch black, rising to meet the moon, which, round, huge and cheesy yellow, is currently caught in the spindly twigs of the trees. We take the long road that opens out into flat windy countryside, and spot two large bonfires on the airstrip, with not a soul in sight. It is fireworks night, and the sprigs of light that flare and spritz along the long line of the horizon are quiet reminders of the crowds of people, miles away, hustled together for warmth, waving sparklers, drinking mulled wine, ooh-ing and ahh-ing at the display above them. But they are a long way away, and when the flashes are gone we feel as though we're the only two humans in the county.

Everything is still. The expanse of sky has muffled our conversation, and by the time we approach Lyveden New Bield we are already talking in whispers. We're cold, tired and subdued, but the deserted manor is at the end of this gravel path; we're almost there. We pass the shut-up tea shop and pause. There in the near distance is the ghost-house, like a heavy stone cross, fallen from the altar, lying supine on the grass. We approach it wordlessly, circle it and come to rest directly in front of its façade, under the only tree in the field. The moon is high in the sky now, and sends a flickering, silver screen projection onto the world below. It's daylight bright and the shadow beneath the oak tree is as black as the sky above it.

I half remember a line written over a millennium ago by a poet soldier, keeping watch at an outpost on China's Great Wall:

The long wall is propped up on yellow sands and whitened bones
We have inscribed our achievements on the mountains of Mongolia,
But the land lies deserted, the moon shines for no one.

I pull out my sketchbook and try to move my cold hand around the page. My friend sits and eats the cheesecake as if it's a pizza. I abandon the drawing, to fill it in later, and devour my half. It's understood that neither of us wants to get any closer to the house. We want to leave, light the fire, eat something that isn't made entirely of sugar. But we've come all this way. So we get up stiffly, slide down the turfed moat, climb the facing slope and approach slowly. The house is so still it feels like it's about to pounce. It emanates emptiness, the vast blackness of the sky seemingly concentrated within its walls. The windows are holes, gaping open, the roof long since rotted away. We step up onto a stone bench, peer in through the windows, and I feel a cold glass of water pour down my spine.

It's time to go. My plan, hatched in the warmth of my bedroom, was for us to walk back into the duke's land and camp in the ancient woodland of Geddington Chase, four miles away. Clearly, that's not going to happen. We need the fire, its warmth, its light and, most of all, its mirth. So without looking back, we put the New Bield behind us, stumble round a couple of fields and make our way to Lady Wood. We crash through the fallen branches, phone torches on, sweeping the woods for a spot to camp in. We find a circle of trees, with two close enough for my friend's hammock to hang between. We dump our bags and clamber around our spot collecting wood. As I pile the wood in different thicknesses, my friend sparks a tea light and places it in the centre of a circle he's cleared out of the leaf litter. He layers thin wispy twigs on top and slowly I add finger-thick twigs, and then the arms, and then lean in a few legs. We have a fire.

My friend is a physics teacher, which means that even in places like Tresham's half-built ghost-house any loose references to 'energy', especially in its spiritual sense, are strictly prohibited. If I mention energy and I'm not referring to a calculable quantity of kinetic or potential, it's a D- for me, must try harder. We've roasted the sausages, smoked a joint, made a little home for ourselves, and he's currently hanging from his hammock, like a cocooned butterfly, making estimates about how much energy our fire is using. I'm feeding the fire from a pile of collected wood, gently warming the underside of his arse as he swings in the air above me. On the ground, I'm freezing, wearing everything I have and cursing the total ineffectualness of foam roll mats, with every bit of me that touches the ground leaching heat.

We pick over the day. I bring up the moment with the strawberry-pink gamekeeper. His approach seemed so incongruous with our actions, disproportionate to our perceived crime. Was I rude? We were both civil in everything we said, but that wasn't enough: what he seemed to expect was not civility, but servility. We weren't humble enough, and, yes, that antagonised him.

In the aftermath of the Newton slaughter, those commoners who had not been murdered, maimed, arrested and hanged were called back to Boughton House, to make their mark on a register. They were not registering their names, as most couldn't write, but their shame, making it official. In other revolts of the time, mendicants were forced to appear to registration wearing horses' girdles around their necks. Others were branded on their cheeks, a sign for ever more of their moral sin, a scarlet letter burned into their flesh, the mark of Cain.

On a much lesser scale, this gamekeeper wanted us to acknowledge that what we were doing was shameful: eyes lowered, hats off, a sheepish acceptance of his authority. But like the wall we were sitting on, his authority came from a line drawn not by common consensus but by private considerations masquerading as a moral standard.

The Midland Revolt sparked an enquiry into enclosure in the area, which did lead to some landowners, including the Treshams, being hauled before the Star Chamber. They were fined for their excesses, a punishment that became not so much a deterrent to enclosure, but a randomised, sporadic tax on landowners that was rarely enforced.

But enclosure had only just begun. According to Peter Linebaugh, the Gandalf of Commons academia, at the end of the seventeenth century there were still twenty million acres of common ground in England and Wales. But, he writes:

> between 1725 and 1825 nearly four thousand enclosure acts appropriated more than six million acres of land, about a quarter of cultivated acreage, to the politically dominant landowners. The Parliamentary enclosure made the process more documented and more public. It got rid of open field villages and common rights and contributed to the late eighteenth century's crisis of poverty.

In 1621, James I made Edward Montagu a lord, in return for his 'honest and faithful' service to the Crown (plus the customary and unmentioned payment of a ten-grand bung). Six years later he was granted the rights to all the timber in Geddington Woods, and, fifty years later, was granted hunting rights. When the Boughton estate passed to the Buccleuchs, the 2nd Duke, known as Planter John, wanted to convert his entire estate to an extended garden of tree-lined avenues, and petitioned Parliament, saying, 'This proposal is so apparently to the advantage of the commoners that any of them might be glad to embrace it.' Sure. In 1795, the full enclosure of the commons was granted to the Buccleuchs, clearing the commoners from their newly extended estate. Workhouses were built in the surrounding villages to accommodate the commoners whose livelihoods were stripped for the duke's aesthetic vision. Back in Arundel, in 1809, the Drunken Duke was granted full enclosure of his estate, allowing him to chop a third off the high street, and erect the wall I climbed.

The 18th Duke of Norfolk still resides at Arundel Castle, but also counts Framlingham Castle, Bungay Castle, Worksop

Manor, Carlton Towers and Norfolk House in London among his residences. He owns 46,000 acres across the British Isles, which comprise a portfolio of sheep, forestry, shooting and equine recuperation. He's doing all right. The Duke of Buccleuch owns over 270,000 acres of the British Isles, including their holiday homes Bowhill House, Drumlanrig Castle and Dalkeith Palace. The land he owns is more than twice the size of Birmingham, Derby, Nottingham and Leicester put together. The elegant final flourish of this land seizure comes from the Boughton estate which now sells firewood, once a common right, back to the commoners at £95 per cubic metre.

In 1754, the philosopher Jean-Jacques Rousseau wrote: 'The first person who, having enclosed a plot of land, took it into his head to say this is mine and found people simple enough to believe him, was the true founder of civil society.' But Rousseau was wrong. These men, women and children of Rockingham weren't simple. In spite of the staggering, totalitarian assault on their free will, the moral enclosure ratified by the Church, they weren't sheep. They were compelled. Their necks were stretched and broken, their guts were cut from their sides, their limbs were displayed on stakes before their friends and families. They were bled out, garrotted and roasted in man-made hellfire.

In 1963, Stanley Milgram ran a series of experiments testing how far his volunteers would go in administering apparently near-lethal electric shocks to an actor in the next room. The shocks were fake, and no harm was done. In his report of the experiments, *Obedience to Authority*, Milgram had surmised that his subjects were able to abandon their inherent humanity when subordinating their responsibility to a higher institution. However, in 1990, *American Psychologist* published a reinterpretation of Stanley Milgram's experiments, saying, 'what people cannot be counted on is to realise that a seemingly benevolent authority is in fact malevolent, even when they are faced with overwhelming evidence'. Psychologists call this 'conceptual conservatism': the ability to maintain a belief long after it has been discredited by contradictory evidence.

The walls of England's private estates, erected by our richest and most established families, the Arundels, the Buccleuchs, the Beauforts, Grosvenors, Lonsdales and Bedfords possess a grandeur and authority that has somehow overridden the violence and theft, the malevolence they enacted to build them. The wall presents itself as a blank statement of authority, and we obey it because we see it without its context. The mindwall has become so entrenched in our heads that it remains unchallenged and unquestioned. But its power comes not just from what it communicates to us, but from the secrets it conceals, the overwhelming evidence of the dark source of its power, hidden behind its curtains of brick and stone.

COW

Cattle, chattel, property in humans

'The property in slaves which the British parliament sold them is in the rights, the natural — the born rights of the negro — a right to his labour — to all he can acquire, to the possession of him as mere chattel — destitute of will — subject to absolute power. Cruel as this may be, it is the contract between parliament and slave owners'
— Augustus Hardin Beaumont, slave owner, Jamaica

In the slim world of brick-wall fanaticism, one wall is famed above them all. The Great Wall of Dorset is the longest brick wall in England and if you can believe one devotee (its owner), it has cast such a spell on its commoners that during the 2010 general election, in spite of rising house prices and cuts to social benefits, they could talk of little else. The wall is owned by the former army captain, current MP for South Dorset and serial hoarder of syllables, Richard Grosvenor-Plunkett-Ernle-Erle-Drax. Two months after his election, Richard wrote one of his breezy blogs to set the record straight:

During my four years as the Conservative candidate, 'the wall' was a major topic of interest. In fact, I can say with some certainty that it was the most popular topic. The interest came in the form of ridicule, humour and genuine interest. Let me reveal the most popular question: 'Richard, how many bricks are in the wall?' The answer is more than two million. For better or worse, 'the wall' is a Dorset landmark.

Richard goes on to describe how the wall was erected as a money-making venture, creating a new turnpike along the road that eventually became the A31. But there's a little more to it than that. Fifteen years before the wall was built, Richard's ancestor John Sawbridge had married into the Drax dynasty and, in so doing, he had acquired six more syllables, the magnificent Charborough estate and the business that had propelled the Draxes into the premier league of English landowners: their sugar plantations in Barbados. Just before the wall was built in 1841, John Sawbridge had received a handsome dividend from his estates, not from his sugar, but from his slaves.

We climb the wall at dusk. We are at the north-west end of the 14,000-acre estate, just to the left of the three-storey brick archway, with a stag at its pediment. This would once have been the gateway to a long drive leading directly to the great house, but now it is sunk in nettles, blocked with an iron gate and a couple of felled tree trunks. The A31 is a nasty road, loud and fast, but as we drop to the other side of the wall, it is quieter and calmer, muted by the trees. We haven't got long until dark, so we walk quickly along the inside of the wall and, checking the map on our phones, cut into the woods to find a place to sleep. A path leads us to a wide stream that opens out into a lagoon, beautiful in the dimming light. We briefly consider this grove for our camp, but the ground is boggy, the air clouding with mosquitoes, so we press further on into the gloom.

When James Drax arrived on the island of Barbados in 1627, he was eighteen, with barely a syllable to his name. The son of an Anglican vicar in Warwickshire, he had secured a place on a boat skippered by Henry Powell, whose brother John had landed on the island two years earlier. John Powell and his men had finally found the empty Eden long dreamed of by John Locke and his contemporaries. The former inhabitants, 10,000 or so Arawak Indians, had been driven off the island by the vicious combination of a shortage of water and a surfeit of Spanish pirates and for over a century the island had remained deserted. On arrival, John Powell and his men had crossed the white sands to the forests and erected a wooden cross on a tree, inscribed with the words 'James, King of England', the first notice of possession to the only remaining inhabitants of the island, the herds of wild pig. When his brother arrived, he had both the king's blessing and all the tools they needed to set up a colony. They dug wells, built barracks and in no time at all hunted the hogs to extinction.

Their first venture was tobacco. They cleared the trees, grubbed their roots and tilled the soil into arable fields. They sent word to England and received their first consignment of labour: the vagrants that were swelling the workhouses. Between 1645 and 1650, 8,000 men and women were transported to Barbados, strange cargoes of disparate and factional peoples. Alongside the 'sturdy beggars' (vagrants deemed fit enough to work) there were the Irish prisoners of war from Cromwell's military campaigns, the royalist prisoners from the English civil war and, finally, the soldiers of Cromwell's New Model Army, who had been disbanded without pay and left to roam the country in search of work, before being rounded up as vagrants.

We have found our campsite: a small clearing in between three trees from which we can hang our tarp. We are in a thin strip of mixed woodland, 200 yards from the wall and the same distance from Drax's arable fields, which cover the north end of his territory. All day the air has been muggy and thick with the threat of rain, and though the weather forecast says clear skies, we don't want to risk it. We erect the shelter, build a small fire and sit with a couple of beers to dissect the day.

We had arrived late in the morning at the south end of the property, under heavy grey clouds, and spent a good deal of time trying to find a way into the land. Walls and fences are easy, it's the hedges that cause problems: the tangled arms of oak, hawthorn and beech, bill-hooked and pleached into themselves to form living nets of wood and spikes are nearly impenetrable. But, eventually, we follow the fox's lead and on hands and knees we sneak through a smeuse widened through use, one just big enough to allow a human through. We drag the bags after us and walk up the perimeter of a ploughed field to a forest of planted pines.

When James Drax's preparations finally yielded its first crop of tobacco, there was instant disappointment: it wouldn't smoke, it tasted foul and no one wanted it. So within a few years Drax had changed his crop to cotton, a move mirrored by many of the other English farmers who had settled on the island. But though this crop fared better, it was still a cottage industry and a far cry from the industrial ambitions of Drax and his neighbours. It was only in the 1630s that Drax saw an opportunity, borrowed from the Dutch who were shipping hundreds and thousands of tonnes of sugar from their colonies in Brazil. With political unrest in the Dutch colony, Drax thought the time was ripe to rival their industry and brought in the necessary infrastructure, the crushers for the cane, the enormous copper boiling vats for the sugar, and the slaves for the land. Eric Williams, who became the prime minister of Trinidad and Tobago, began his career as a historian with his book *Slavery and Capitalism*, which offered the first counter-narrative to the standardised vision of colonial slavery: 'Here then is the origin of Negro slavery. The reason was economic, not racial. It had to do not with the colour of the labourer, but the cheapness of the labour. Slavery was not born of racism: rather racism was the consequence of slavery.'

Slavery had been dormant in English culture since the 1200s. It had a brief reprise in 1547, when Edward VI brought it back as a punishment for vagrancy, but was repealed three years later after fierce public outcry. In 1772, Judge James Mansfield declared: 'The air of England has long been too pure for a slave, and every man is free who breathes it', expressing a sentiment of blinkered moral sanctimony that pervades England to this day. The enormous hypocrisy of this sentiment was founded on geography. The 15,000 slaves living in England were freed with this single statement, but rules were different in the Caribbean. Barbados and its neighbouring islands were 'beyond the line', an imaginary boundary created by the Europeans that allowed them to operate outside the politics of their home continent. If you were an English businessman operating beyond the line, you could deal and wage war with your Portuguese, French, Dutch and Spanish neighbours without impacting the treaties of your home continent. Similarly, if your countries went to war back home, you were not obliged to follow suit. What goes on tour, stays on tour and the same applied to slavery.

By 1640 James Drax already had several dozen slaves working alongside the white labourers. But the massive scale of the sugar plantations that was required to generate profit required an equally vast resource of labour to 'animate' the estate. The estates absorbed slaves like the sugarcane drank water, and, just as new technologies allowed better irrigation of the plantations, so new trade routes allowed a constant, fast flow of imported slaves. It was finally possible to scale up the enterprise.

In 1663 the Stuart monarchy created the Company of Royal Adventurers who had a licensed monopoly over the trade of Africans for 1,000 years. The company was dissolved nine years later, but was replaced by the Royal African Company which began shipping slaves to the Caribbean at a rate of 5,000 a year. By this time, James Drax had been succeeded by his second son, Henry, who did to sugar what Henry Ford did to the car industry: he turned a small industry into a standardised mechanism of mass production. He itemised every component of sugar production and was the first to bring every element of sugar refinery, the growers, the boilers, the distillers, the refiners, onto one site. The set of instructions he wrote in 1679 for his overseer Richard Harwood came to be seen as the standard textbook for the management of slave plantations. It was a meticulous description of the mechanics of production, where slaves are listed simply as cogs in the system, parts to be repurchased when broken.

We're sweating heavily in the thick humid air. My eyes are stinging with salt. We've covered the long slope of the woodland and are descending into a jungle of lush ferns and sapling trees. We are getting closer to the famous Charborough Tower, a neo-gothic folly thirty metres tall extended by John Sawbridge just before the wall was built. Built on the highest hill on the estate, it can be seen from miles around, and just like John Powell's notice of possession, nailed to a tree in Barbados, it claims the land for itself.

The forest opens up before us, and, though there's still little sunlight from the sky, it's brighter, carpeted with spring-green hart's-tongue ferns splaying out of the ground like open hands. Across the glade there is a wide lawn path cut among the trees, lined with a display of pink budding azaleas. The map says this will lead us up the hill, to the tower.

We're a third of the way up when we see the keeper. He's strolling with a small group of friends and hasn't yet seen us, so we lower our voices and quickly discuss what to do. My friend is a cameraman and has come along to film and photograph the walk – as such, the equipment he's carrying, including the five-foot tripod resting on his shoulder, automatically upgrades the charge to aggravated trespass. But it's too late; the keeper's seen us.

There's a wide, awkward silence as we all make up the ground between us. 'There's no way through here,' he says – it's that old trope of property protection, that classic reframing of reality, the brash denial of the pure bleeding obvious, which in this case is the pathway that ascends behind him. He's very polite and dazzlingly healthy, with an amazing shock of white hair that is half schoolboy, half wizard, and we instantly like him a lot more than he likes us. He's quietly spoken, and so firm in his conviction that we are about to leave that it's impossible to think of an alternative. We thank him for his time, turn on our heels and go back the way we came.

In 1781, the captain of a slave ship called the *Zong* was sailing from Africa with his cargo, hundreds of men and women trapped in a space that infamously gave them each less room than a coffin, when his ship was besieged by a storm. He needed to get rid of some ballast, so ordered his men to throw 133 Africans overboard. His flash of ingenuity worked and the crew survived the tempest, but when he returned safely to England he was hauled before the magistrates. He was tried and convicted, not for the murder of 133 people, but for an insurance claim on the property he had disposed of so wantonly.

If you bought land in the Caribbean, the slaves were almost always part of the deal. They were not defined as real property (the fixed asset of the land itself) but as chattel, the moveable items that were attached to the land, and under property law were subject to the complete dominion of the landowner. The racist epithet 'coon' derives from the Spanish word *barracón*, which was a large building or warehouse constructed to hold merchandise and, from the sixteenth century onwards, it was where slaves were stored for sale. Its meaning hadn't changed or even broadened: it was where you kept your property.

To maintain the illusion that these people were possessions, the white Europeans persistently performed speech-acts to transform them into animals. In Richard Ligon's diaries we see slaves defined 'as near as beasts as may be' and there are repeated references to the field workers as 'dumb brutes' and 'black cattle'. The general slang term for female slaves was 'breeders', which is the dairy industry's term for cows used to supply more stock. Female slaves were repeatedly raped by their owners, not only to sate their sexual urges, not just to stamp their manly power upon their workforce, but as a systematic means of creating new slaves for free – the children of slaves were slaves themselves, they were born owned.

Following our expulsion from the estate, we had biked north to the famous wall and found our campsite. And now we sit, sucking on bottles of West Berkshire ale. The fire crackles, and the sausages sizzle in their tin foil and cave of embers. Barbados under Drax was a sweaty nightmare of rum, yellow fever, Spanish invasion, rape, torture and slave revolts. Beyond the line of civilisation, it was a grotesque masque of the hierarchy back home, master and servant. But, unlike England, the servants could be better controlled by subdividing them by their skin colour, their collective power divided by a line of race. In the words of Eric Williams: 'Racial differences made it easier to justify and rationalise Negro slavery, to exact the mechanical obedience of a plough-ox or a cart horse, to demand that resignation and that complete moral and intellectual subjection which alone makes slave labour possible.'

Owners were far outnumbered by the white servants and slaves, and in constant peril of being overrun. To coerce their African captives into submission they used corporal punishment, and would string up the bodies of murdered slaves around the estate to reinforce their power. They forced into reality the rumours they had heard of their captives' cannibalism by amputating and roasting the limbs of miscreant slaves, then making them eat their own charred flesh. They lashed their slaves and rubbed salt or molasses into their wounds, so that flies and ants would gnaw at the raw flesh. It was a horrifying, physical abuse of the body that Ta-Nehisi Coates discusses in his description of racism in modern-day America: 'But all our phrasing – race relations, racial chasm, racial justice, racial profiling, white privilege, even white supremacy – serve to obscure that racism is a visceral experience, that it dislodges brains, blocks airways, rips muscle, extracts organs, cracks bones, breaks teeth.'

This emphasis of the violent degradation of the body goes beyond the judicial. To the slavers, the inhumanity of these acts was not evidence that *they* were monsters, but the inverse, that their African captives were beasts. Alone in the manor houses, surrounded by thousands of captive African men and women, their culture, their language and song, these slavers were doing everything they could to persuade themselves that these people were their property. Here is the essence of the property principle, *jus abutendi*, because when something is yours entirely, you have the right to destroy it.

To maintain this necessary illusion, they needed allies and skin colour was all they had. The principal difference between the whites and the blacks on the islands was one of hope: when the white servants had served their punishment, usually between five and ten years, they were allowed to return home. Not so for the African slaves, whose entire existence was owned. But while the owners treated the slaves much more barbarically than their servants, both groups of workers saw themselves united by a shared oppressor. For the Irish especially, who had always been treated as savages by their English colonists, the difference of race was nothing in light of the way they were treated, as a sub-species, as a class of human beneath their rulers. White and black, servant and slave, the workers of the plantation lived in close confines with each other; they co-ordinated in uprisings together; they cooked, sang and slept together.

In 1661 the Act of Better Ordering and Governing of Negroes was passed, the first of several attempts to drive a partition between the white and black workers. By banning miscegenation (sex between races) and giving the white workers privileges, it created an imbalance between the white servants and black slaves and linked the white underclass with their white superiors; it gave race a salience it never had before.

The Act didn't work; the Irish and Africans together plotted two major slave uprisings in 1686 and 1692 and to this day there are many Murphys, McDonnoughs and McGanns in the Caribbean phone book. Twenty-five per cent of Jamaicans claim Irish heritage, not least Bob Marley and Marcus Garvey. But the Act had another effect. It was the start of a new era of slavery, one that veered from the economic principle of exploited labour to the quasi-scientific concocted hierarchy of race. The British had just legalised white supremacy.

In the morning we wake early, roll over and snooze for an hour or so. The birdsong plays like a foreign radio talk show, affable, incomprehensible voices gossiping away at each other. As we're packing away everything into our rucksacks, my friend tells me a story. Last night was the first time he'd contravened the 1824 Vagrancy Act and slept out. He'd had that same nightmarish feeling that I'd first experienced in the woods of West Berkshire, that exposure to the cold expanse of night, the fear of what you cannot see. But after the sausages and the beer he'd fallen snugly asleep, newly inaugurated into the coven of incorrigible rogues. After several hours, in the dead of early morning, he had woken. He heard a low, throaty grunting from the bushes, something wild, and, just coming to, heard the heavy gallop of an animal pounding alongside the perimeter wall – suddenly it had veered towards us and before he could wake me it ran directly in front of our camp and disappeared into the dark. My friend hadn't seen a thing, the woods were silent once again, but now his blood was fizzing. The darkness around us had been charged by an untamed spirit, thumping with a heart as large as our own.

When the Drax line had all but expired in Barbados, they began selling up most of their plantations to return home and play politics in England. In 1715, Charles Drax sold 1,000 acres of land to William Beckford, a member of another luminary slaving dynasty in the Caribbean, a family whose English estate is just a marathon away from Charborough House. So once we've removed any trace of our camp, we hop the wall, return to our bikes and head north. My friend's bike is powered by a 100-horsepower engine and mine by a pair of skimpy thighs, so by the time I reach Fonthill he has been sitting in a pub garden for two hours, reading and lubricating the soul.

We follow a public path through a field and down a steep slope to a long glistening lake. We pass a couple of fishermen and stop to chat as one pulls a bucking carp from the water. As we turn the top of the lake, a low wooden gate blocks the path with a sign, more polite than most, saying *Private Woodland, Please Keep*

Out. I climb it and my friend follows, handing over his heavy rucksack of camera equipment and his cumbersome tripod. The Fonthill estate, now owned by the 3rd Baron Margadale, is a 9,000-acre beauty, that comprises residential and commercial letting, industrial farming, forestry and an 80-acre stud farm. It offers pheasant and partridge shooting, angling, deer stalking, holiday retreats and a stunning location for filming. It is what the profits of slavery look like today, laundered in time and land.

By the end of the seventeenth century, Colonel Peter Beckford had 4,000 acres in Jamaica, a share in twenty separate estates and over a thousand slaves. At this time, the sugar magnates had begun to diversify their businesses, branching out into ancillary trades and revenue streams. Colonel Beckford had his fingers in many pies: he began buccaneering; he traded in slaves, alcohol and cattle; he was a moneylender, land speculator and a farmer of livestock and cereal. When Beckford's estate passed to his son, also William, he first increased it by another 3,593 acres, then returned to England and became the Lord Mayor of London and bought the estate in Fonthill. When the Fonthill house burned down some ten years later, Beckford took the opportunity to build a truly magnificent pile in its place, which he called Splendens, a Latin word loosely translated as 'gleaming' or 'distinguished'.

This was par for the course. Many of the slavers were returning home to translate their bloody money into neoclassical architecture. As many as 300 new manor houses were erected in this time, each designed to ingratiate itself within the established order of greatness, the 'old order' designed and presided over by the English aristocracy. Their architecture quoted the Greeks and Romans; they were temples of wealth, pristine, pure and unblemished by the grim stain of the plantations. With their plantations left in the care of their managers, they became known as 'absentee owners', and set about the next steps of power: politics and peerage.

The path has led us through a small woodland of grand chestnuts and oaks. The lake is glinting to our left and to our right is a dense jungle of ferns and laurels that, our map tells us, should open up into the wide landscaped lawns of the manor house, almost a mile away. There is a faint track pressed through the spurge that might be what we're looking for. It leads through nettles and thorn to a tight stone archway, which opens into a dank grove of snaking laurels and moss-laden stone, a circular hermitage sunk in the wet woodland earth. Two empty stone alcoves mark the official entrance to the grotto, its statues long gone, and a third has a large slab of stone for a seat. To its left is the archway we came through, which hides a tight stone tunnel leading to a circular chamber of smoothly cut stone, where the sunlight pours through the small circle atrium above. The stones of its roof are like dinosaur socket bones, smooth and knobbly. Two bats zip past us and, as my eyes accustom to the gloom, I notice a spider in a dark nook, with a teardrop sack of silk, twice the size of her body, hanging from her web. There is a constant, low, priest-like drone, with a slight echo, and I look up to see thick clouds of mosquitoes bouncing in the beam of sunlight. This place is pagan.

We emerge out of the stonework and find a seat away from the dank depression of mulch in the centre of the circle. I pull out my sketchbook and my friend plays with his camera. I am sitting beneath the thick trunk of a yew tree, whose roots clasp the top of a third alcove, as if it is the last thing keeping it from toppling over into the grotto. Its hairy roots are laced with silver threads of slime that lead high up the trunk into the tree's canopy, the trails of countless slugs. There is a strange bird call sounding to my left, one I've never heard before; my eyes follow the sound and see a blackbird, performing a strange ritual dance, bobbing forward and back, waving its tail like a magic wand. Two brown hens watch him, like they're sitting in front of the telly, wondering where the remote is.

This is William Beckford's folly, his refuge from the harsh scorn of society. The great-grandson of Colonel Peter Beckford, he grew up at Fonthill and only visited his family's plantations once or twice in his lifetime. He was nine years old when his father died, the first English commoner to die a millionaire, and when he was eighteen he inherited what was then the largest real estate in Europe at that time, more than a million pounds and a £100,000 annual income from his Caribbean plantations. He inherited paintings by Titian, Bronzino, Rembrandt, Velásquez, Rubens and Canaletto, a large table from the Borghese palace made of the largest single slab of onyx in the world and a museum's hoard of porcelain, bronze, agate, silver and gold. In 1783 he married Lady Margaret Gordon, the daughter of the Earl of Aboyne, and a year later, aged twenty-one, he became MP for Wells. By October of that year he had been made a peer. He was on a roll. But a year later he was spied through the key-hole of a door on a neighbouring estate having sex with the Earl of Devon's son, with whom he had been in love since the age of nineteen. For two years their affair had been kept secret, because homosexual love, or sodomy as the courts then called it, was a capital offence. But when the affair was exposed it became the most salacious scandal of the Georgian era.

William fled the country taking his pregnant wife with him. Not long after, his wife died and he moved his two daughters to boarding school in London while he went to live in Portugal. He returned to England with a young man called Gregorio Franchi, the son of an Italian court singer, and a Spanish dwarf named Perro, and set about walling himself away from

England's prying fantasies. He bought another 1,700 acres for the estate and built the largest complete wall in England at the time, eight miles long, twelve foot high and capped with iron spikes. In 1790 he wrote in a letter, 'I have been raising towers and building grottos', and six years later he began work on his greatest folly, in both senses of the word: an enormous abbey, designed to be larger than Salisbury Cathedral, to house his ever-growing collection of art and manuscripts. It collapsed several times over Beckford's lifetime, yet was rebuilt again and again, becoming not only Beckford's home but a fanatical expression of his eccentricity. William Hazlitt, the essayist and friend of John Keats, described it as 'a desert of magnificence, a glittering waste of laborious idleness, a cathedral turned into a toy shop, an immense museum of all that is most curious and costly and at the same time most worthless. The only proof of taste he has shown in the collection is his getting rid of it.'

He was not alone. Across England the wealth of the sugar plantations was being injected into English society, into buildings and infrastructure that, unlike Fonthill Abbey, remain to this day. Until only recently the exact nature of this wealth and its effect on British landscape and society was locked away in the National Archives. But in 2009 a team of professors from UCL, led by Dr Catherine Hall, began a vast project of mapping the Legacies of Britain's Slave Ownership (whose enormous amounts of research can be found on their website of the same name). Their resource is not just a collected census of slave ownership, but, rather, an encyclopaedia of every owner, attorney, mortgagee and legatee involved with the trade of slaves; and, much more, it charts their wealth and how it was distributed through their descendants, their influence in Parliament, their cultural artefacts and their land.

The team at UCL offer myriad pathways into this dense jungle of information. You can search under the colonies that

were held by Britain, from Antigua to Montserrat and the Virgin Islands, under the specific parish or island; you can search via the crop farmed (not just sugar, but coffee, tobacco, cocoa and indigo), the acreage, or the number of people enslaved. You can search the names of the slave owners, their gender, their occupation, their home address in Britain. You can search any commercial name you can think of for its presence in the archive (try Lloyds, or Barclays, or the Church of England) and you can search under individual names, such as Orwell or Cameron. There are four interactive maps that you can zoom into, of Jamaica, Barbados and Grenada, and of Britain, where you can now zoom into your hometown, your street and see for yourself the footprint of slavery on your doorstep.

These visualisations are hyperlinked to a treasure chest of information about the properties and their owners. You can see the physical legacies of their trade, the country estates built or remodelled, the gardens and statues these men erected in their own honour. You can trace the cultural legacies, the Constables, Gillrays, Gainsboroughs, Blakes and Canalettos they commissioned, bought or bequeathed with their slave interests. You can trace the societies and clubs, the colleges, schools and universities, the asylums, hospitals, charities and golf clubs which benefited from slave wealth and, perhaps most fascinatingly of all, you can trace the letters, pamphlets and newspaper articles associated with the slave trade, and watch the debate of the morality of slave trading sour beneath your eyes, watch as the tide of the conversation turns from the stark inhumanity and logical inconsistency of owning another person to the notion of compensation for the removal of private property.

Because these are the compensation records, the audited accounts of slave owners. They were used as evidence in Parliament for the value of the property the abolitionists were trying to steal from them. And when slavery was finally abolished in 1833, the slavers received a total of £20 million from the British taxpayer, estimated as anything between £87 billion and £500 billion in today's money. The slaves, of course, received nothing, and as part of the deal had to stay exactly where they were and work unpaid 'apprenticeships' for four years after their supposed release.

We leave the grotto through its entrance, stepping over thick swathes of clumped briar. We walk out onto the lawn, dazzling green beneath the clear blue sky. We follow the lawn path along the lake until it emerges from the tree cover to an open space. Four large stone globes are raised on stone plinths, desiccated by time and sprayed with various green and yellow lichens. They are positioned ten foot apart, two on either side of a longer stone jetty, where William Beckford might have alighted from boating around the lake. We take off our clothes and sink into the cool water, watching clumps of foamy green scum float by on the rippling surface. They are a kind of lake plankton, a thick green soup of emergent life, resting on beds of tiny bubbles trapped in the netted hairs of pondweed. The two of us swim, our bare arses shining like jellyfish caught on our spines.

That these men were not indicted for the moral abomination of slavery, and instead rewarded for their losses, is an indication of the power of the anti-abolition lobby groups. They saw the writing on the wall, and, rather than be tried for their innumerable crimes of murder, rape and torture, they deflected the argument. Yet it was a potentially risky move for them, for if one form of property could be de-privatised, why not another? In one petition against compulsory manumission (the release of slaves), the authors argue that they 'will not waste a moment in advancing arguments to establish their right of property in their slaves. To suppose it could be doubted would be to bring into question the title to all property whatsoever.'

Many of the defenders of slavery had no direct interest in the plantations, but as aristocratic landowners they were panicked by this new surge towards de-privatisation. MP and 3rd Baronet of Osmaston Sir Robert Wilmot-Horton wrote in 1830: 'If confiscation is to be the result of guilty wealth why is not the property in England to be confiscated, as well as that of the West Indies?' The rights of private property were so deeply entrenched in the Georgian mindset that comparisons of freed slaves to de-privatised land were being made to underline just how ridiculous the proposition was. Free the slaves, and whatever next?

The Abolition Act was a massive victory for the slavers. They continued their businesses and used their compensation to make new land purchases, build new houses and, thirty miles down south in the Drax estate, raise a new brick wall to keep out the commoners. The bleak irony was that it was only through this eventual abolition act that slaves came to be defined, in British law, as the 'inalienable property of their masters'. Up to this moment the English common law had neither expressly condoned nor forbidden slavery. But when the argument had turned towards compensation, the law had to state explicitly: slaves were the property of their owners. The same law that freed the slaves had ratified their status as inferior humans. Racism had become institutionalised.

We have been drying in the sun: eyes shut, listening to the hum of insects and feeling our skin tighten as the scum from the lake evaporates to a light contracted crust. This is the hottest day of the year so far, but it is a work day and, apart from the fishermen, we haven't seen or heard a single soul. This was precisely the purpose of Beckford's Fonthill: a fortress against society. But when, in one lifetime, William Beckford had managed to drain the largest fortune of Europe, he put his fortress up for sale and headed to Bath to continue his seclusion in more meagre surroundings. The enormous profits from slavery were stemmed by the abolition act but somehow the wealth of England continued to flourish; the West Indies was not its only revenue stream. Fonthill was bought by John Farquhar, an artillery merchant newly returned from the colonies, though this time not from the West, but the East Indies.

A country path is democracy manifested in mud. If the people elect to go one way, then that's the way they go. Its direction is determined by its efficacy for the people, its legitimacy by use and engagement. A wall is the direct opposite of this. It is a dictatorship. A wall not only divides the common ground, but it corrals the people in the direction desired by its builder. The earliest walls in humankind were designed not to defend property, but to compel the self-willed direction of animals into hunting traps. Neolithic corrals, some as old as 7000 BC, were built of wood, stone or raised earth, and are so long that humans had to learn to fly before they saw them for what they were.

The path that runs from my woods in West Berkshire, up past the dell, through the empty woods to join the Right of Way is one such democratic path. That property law pretends it is not a public path is another brash denial of the pure bleeding obvious: the hundreds of thousands of feet that pressed it into being. The properties of the path are entirely contingent on its being the property of the public, in the Lockean sense, by virtue of the work they put into it. However, when the wall was built around Basildon Park, it severed the path, blocked the old route to the river and transformed the function of the land in between. On the will of one man alone, it corralled the commoners of my village like livestock around its newly sanctioned space. This wall was also built on the profits of colonialism.

Francis Sykes bought Basildon Park in the late eighteenth century. A company man through and through, he had started as a 'writer' for the East India Company, a nineteen-year-old clerk who administered the trade of silk in the company's first point of entry, the port of Calcutta. By the time he bought up half my village, he had risen through the ranks to become the Governor of Cossimbazar, the high priest of trade in north-east India. He was on about £25,000 a year, which in today's cash is £1.25 million, about the same amount as the CEO for John Lewis. But like every other member of the Honourable East India Company, the real profits were made on the side: through bribes, gifts, insider trading, personal monopolies, private embezzlement (all of which were actively encouraged by the climate of the company). He was bringing in five times his annual salary, £125,000, in today's money over £6 million a year. The first time he came back, he bought Ackworth Hall in Yorkshire, a small pied-à-terre to get his foot on the ladder. When he returned the second time, he sold that, then bought Basildon Park. He levelled the existing building and raised in its place the house we have today; he then enclosed his land with walls, sealing off my route to the river. He brought back silks, gems, carpets, paintings and, in today's money, a fortune of £35 million. He then set about phase two of the plan – the social ladder, a peerage, Parliament.

So many of the East India Company's men had returned from their expeditions, fingers sticky from the colonial cookie jar, and settled in the South East, that at the time Berkshire was known as the 'English Hindoostan'. It is an area cursed since the Romans by its proximity to London Society. You could frolic around in the country, riding your horses, checking Capability Brown's plans for your garden, and use Brunel's new railway line (built on the profits of Afro-Caribbean slavery) to get you into Paddington for a bit of parliamentary hobnobbing. It remains, to this day, *an ideal location.*

Another of the great elephants of colonial wealth, Warren Hastings, had bought up a little further east of Basildon, in Purley Hall, and the Benyons were due south in Englefield. With the exception of Benyon, whose hereditary wealth had given him leverage into trade, these were self-made businessmen who stormed into the English landscape like lottery winners, Indian gems hanging from their wives' necks, swishing through the halls of Westminster in Indian silk coats, buttoned with pearls. They were not well liked. 'Without connections, without any natural interest in the soil, the importers of foreign gold have forced their way into parliament by such a torrent of corruption as no private hereditary fortune can resist.' So said the Earl of Chatham, the future prime minister, whose own hereditary interest came directly from his grandfather's plundering of a diamond now worth £48 million, with which he bought a rotten borough and his rung on the ladder. The diamond was from Madras.

My lovely mum, who lives a twenty-minute walk from the gates, works shifts at Basildon Park. She is a fancy-dress 1950s housewife who bakes biscuits for the guests, filling Sykes's great halls with the smell of my childhood, shortbread and ginger nuts. The house is now owned by the National Trust, so one morning I get the train from London and head not over the fence, but to the ticket office, so I can meet my mum without her feeling like she's colluding in the dark art of trespass. I pay my fee and wind up the woodland path to the great house. Toddlers are playing on fallen tree trunks, young couples are walking their papooses to sleep and squadrons of active seniors with ski poles and bum bags march ever onwards.

The house shines in the sun. Designed by John Carr, it is a celebration of pure Venetian symmetry. Its four Ionic columns, capped by a shallow pediment, are a temple of silvery Bath stone, raised one storey high on a plinth of utility rooms. It is flanked on either side by two pavilions and linked to the main building with a stone wall, which conceals open-air courtyards. I walk through the archway directly beneath the temple pillars, and am led up the stairs to the grand entrance, an outdoor loggia from which you can observe the parkland of the estate – wide lawns with enormous specimen trees running up a gentle incline to the beech woodland that buffers its walls.

I pass silently through the rooms, the Great Hall, the Library, the Sutherland Room, the Great Staircase, the Octagon drawing room, and the guidebook points me to various textiles and tapestries, the crimson damask hangings, the porcelain urns, the friezes and frescoes. When the East India established their first outpost in Calcutta, India's share in the world economy was 27 per cent, almost a third of all the wealth in the world. It was famed for its textiles, its architecture, its shipbuilding, its spices and its porcelain, which was precisely its attraction. Robert Clive, who as Commander-in-Chief of the British East India Company had one boot in trade and one in war, described his experience as he moved around their newly acquired territories: 'An opulent city lay at my mercy ... I walked through vaults which were thrown open to me alone, piled on either hand with gold and jewels. My chairman, at this moment, I stand astonished at my own moderation!'

In 1930, historian Will Durant published *The Case for India*, in which he describes the Company's methods as a 'conscious and deliberate bleeding of India'. England was the tick on the udder of the world's cash cow, sucking up all it could get, inflating itself in direct proportion to what it took. The British imposed a fast-track Tudor land regime on their new territory, standardising laws of ownership and property with no reference to local custom, geography or climate patterns. They charged rent on the land, not tithes from its produce, so when droughts hit their territory, as they often did, the farmers were broken by unpayable charges and had to forfeit their farms. Britain fenced India off from foreign trade and imposed monopolies on steel, textile and crops. They broke the back of a manufacturing nation and turned the entire country into a *barracón* of stock for export. The railways that Britain 'gave' India were not the standard history book definition of gifted infrastructure, but in fact intravenous tubes lodged deep inside the body, transfusing the blood as efficiently as possible from the heart of India to England. Francis Sykes's own explanation of this gluttony was simple and direct: it was the basic choice of 'whether it should go into a black man's pocket or my own'. And today, here it all is, the opulence of Cossimbazar in my little village in West Berkshire.

I meet my mum for coffee in the tea room and we go and sit in the wisteria-lined courtyard. None of this history is particularly relevant to her day, and certainly by baking gingerbread biscuits she has no intention of supporting the fable of benevolent colonialism. She is recently retired, the place is lovely and it's another activity, like the book group, garden society or art club that twine her tighter to the landscape of our home. Plus, she likes baking. We talk about other things, about her day, how she was buzzing around the rooms I had visited, on tea relief for the other volunteers, not quite remembering the details attached to each display piece, but winging it nevertheless.

The tea room is packing up and the grounds are about to close. We hug goodbye underneath the grand old cedar tree that was here long before the house. She walks to the car and I walk north, to what the map calls the Pheasant Park. I sit beneath a sycamore tree whose branches are hung with baby green helicopters and hear the emphysema wheeze of the Reading road in the distance. A warm breeze makes the long feathered tips of the grass nod in unison, like a parliament in complete accord, and it's as if the day is gently yawning, stretching itself out into dusk. I watch the cars leave along the tarmac section of the old footpath and I wait, letting time trespass for me. My ticket gives me permissive access to the grounds until 5 p.m. and the moment the second hand passes the hour, I am trespassing.

I pull out my sketchbook and gaze for ages before putting pencil to paper. If you think England is beautiful, you should look behind its walls. Without doubt Sykes claimed for himself the finest view in our village. Four hundred acres of classic Chiltern pastoral: rolling valleys of beech and birch and oak that fall away to the gleaming ribbon of the River Thames, with the first billowing vales of Oxfordshire beyond.

With the mansion hidden behind the slope of the valley, with the herds of Aberdeen Angus and Belted Galloways munching in the shade of trees, it's not hard to imagine what it must have felt like when all this was common land. This is the very image of the land of milk and honey, a phrase claimed by the Bible, but which must surely refer to the heavenly splendour of unrestricted common ground, where you grazed your cattle and kept your bees. The parish of Basildon had somehow resisted enclosure right up until the mid-eighteenth century, but then a spate of private acts was passed through government, culminating in the Enclosure Act of 1773, which is when the wall went up and the path was blocked.

The new money from the West and East Indies not only flooded the countryside, but rushed up the river to London and engulfed Westminster. Robert Clive had returned from India with the largest fortune an Englishman had ever made on the continent and now, by right of the land he had bought, he owned three votes in Parliament. Sykes, meanwhile, was made a baronet in 1781 and was MP first for Shaftesbury and then for Wallingford. Down the road, Richard Benyon of Gidea had a seat in the House of Commons and his descendant, also Richard, was, until 2019, the richest MP in Parliament. It is estimated that in 1765 there were forty MPs in Parliament with West Indian connections and, by 1784, twenty-nine MPs with direct East Indian connections. Down in Dorset at least six of Richard Drax's ancestors were MPs and the Beckfords held posts as sheriffs, aldermen, lord mayors and MPs.

As slavery financed more walls around the commons of England, more and more country folk were corralled into the cities, into a new work regime that would spur the industrial revolution. The new money that had flooded England, brought in on the back of African and Indian labour, was the same money that partitioned English commoners from their livelihood and land. And these workers saw the link. Slavery was an extreme version of a time-honoured hierarchy in England: its impetus was profit, its disguise was race, but its mechanism was class. The Anti-Corn Law League was founded five years after slavery was abolished, in opposition to new laws that strove to keep bread prices high, and landowners in charge. They used many of the abolitionist tactics and shared their moral vision: it was the right of every labourer to receive as much recompense for their work as possible; to whatever degree, no one should be exploited.

I have been wandering in and out of the woodland, tracing my way south along the colour-coded National Trust paths. I come out of a dense thicket of wood into a low forest of fern and foxgloves, only just in bloom. There is a circle of grass in among them, under the shade of hawthorns and elder, a grove that has the sense of a druidic altar. The foxgloves are as plentiful as bluebells, and the place hums with a merry congregation of bumblebees, sliding in and out of their bell-jar petals, sipping nectar in a cool violet chamber of shade.

I take off my boots and pull out my sketchbook and crayons. The manor house is directly in front of me, in the far distance, framed by chestnut and oak; the herd of cows have moved into shot, slowly mowing the lawn; the scene is perfect. I lose myself in the sound of the grove, and the rhythmic rubbing of the crayon on paper, when the air around me seems to lighten in a slow flash. I look up and see the sun has slid to such an angle that the lawn ahead of me is glowing lime-green, its rays catching the Bath stone of the manor house, making it gleam like a jewellery box. I think of Beckford's mansion at Fonthill: Splendens. These manor houses of England were always more than just homes: they were PR stunts. They communicated not just power, but *rightful* power, clean and pure. Today, they have become icons of 'Englishness', a tourist-board narrative of a great empire, a proud history, steam engines, top hats and globally acclaimed costume dramas. They have somehow come to represent the great English character, the virtues of freedom of speech and liberty, the nation that freed the slaves. But when the visitors go home, when their rooms are silent and their grounds are empty, this vision of global greatness hollows and implodes under its own sham weight. Without their congregation of believers to sustain the narrative, they become what the Germans call *Mahnmal*, monuments of deep-set national shame. These gleaming, cream-stoned treasure chests, stuffed to the eaves with violent plunder, are in fact radiant monoliths to the myth of white supremacy.

In his opening speech in the impeachment hearings against Warren Hastings, Edmund Burke described how the management of the East India Company was responsible for: 'cruelties unheard of and devastations almost without name ... crimes which have their rise in the wicked dispositions of men in avarice, rapacity, pride, cruelty, malignity, haughtiness and insolence.' When William Pitt the Younger put forward the first abolition bill in 1791, he said: 'Posterity looking back to the history of these enlightened times will scarce believe that it has been suffered to exist so long a disgrace and dishonour to this country.' Pitt was right – we don't believe it, we barely talk of it, and some, from historians to politicians, actively deny it.

When the British left India they had drained its GDP from 27 per cent to 3 per cent. It is estimated that up to twenty-nine million Indians died of famine, murder and organised genocide under the colonial regime. It is estimated that 3.1 million Africans were transported to the British colonies as slaves, of which 400,000 never arrived, lost to malnutrition, disease or the sea. It is therefore not surprising when Dr Catherine Hall says: 'it's been much more comfortable for the British to sit with the history of abolition than the history of slavery.'

In 2014 Reni Eddo-Lodge wrote a blog entitled 'Why I'm No Longer Talking to White People About Race', which in its first paragraph states her reasoning: 'You can see their eyes shut down and harden. It's like treacle is poured into their ears, blocking up their ear canals. It's like they can no longer hear us.' This response is not new. Her words echo those of an unnamed slave quoted in early abolitionist Thomas Tryon's *Friendly Advice* to the planters: 'A false conceit of Interest has blinded their Eyes and stopped their Ears and rendered their Hearts harder than Rocks of Adament.'

When David Cameron refused to apologise for the Amritsar massacre of 1919, in which at least 379 Indian civilians were gunned down by British troops, his reasoning was spurious: 'So I don't think the right thing is to reach back into history and to seek out things you can apologise for.' 'Reach' implies that these episodes might be hard to find; they are not. During the 2010 election, when Richard Drax was repeatedly asked about his family's debt to African slavery he finally snapped and said,

'I can't be held responsible for something that happened three hundred or four hundred years ago. They are using the old class thing and that is not what this election is about, it's not what I stand for, and I ignore it.' He *ignores* it. With a little bit of digging, the truth of Drax's inheritance becomes ever starker. Not only does he still operate within a power and property bequeathed to him by slavery, but he still owns the original sugar plantation in Barbados, and visits his Jacobean manor house there every year. His link to slavery is not tangential, but direct, and current.

Drax's ignorance is a wilful act. He knows the history, he lives within it, but he has hardened his eyes. For most of us, however, the colonial legacy is buried under the false narrative of emancipation; the white saviour complex is built into the architecture of Englishness, the stilts upon which national pride balances. Ignorance is taught in schools. Dean Simon is a vlogger who posts on YouTube under the name of Rants'n'Bants:

A lot of people think that being racist automatically makes them a bad person, but it doesn't. It's a social construct. No one's born racist, it's a learnt behaviour. If you went to school, watch TV, read the newspaper ... if you're white sitting through history class learning white people invented everything, pioneered everything, and discovered everything, and black people... well, we used to own them, then we freed them, and they're still complaining. If you didn't leave school believing in white supremacy, you must have been asleep.

The guidebook that led me round Basildon Park refers only once to Francis Sykes's methods: 'He had amassed a considerable fortune working for the East India Company in Bengal.' In Sykes's former breakfast room, which looks out into the river valley, a sign by the window goes into a little more depth: 'his career however was not unblemished. He was censured for raising an unauthorised tax from which he was alleged to have made considerable gains.' With a bit more digging, we find William Cobbett's slightly fuller description in his *Parliamentary History of England*:

> the Select Committee, in 1765, had begun to levy without any authority, an arbitrary tax called Matoot, under colour of repairing bridges, ways &c. and had diverted it from the public channel to their own private use... Mr Sykes touched of this Matoot 4,000 rupees for his table, 18,000 for his dresses and 18,000 more for other expenses.

It is in equal parts understandable and unforgivable that the guidebook wouldn't want to mention this, or refer to any of the blood, spilt or drained by Sykes and his company. Genocide can really ruin a day out. But while the national institutions and private companies, en masse, neglect to take the responsibility of telling a more complete story of the context of their own splendour, the English are being fed a lie. Ta-Nehisi Coates calls this lie a 'modern invention ... the new idea at the heart of these new people who have been brought up hopelessly, tragically, deceitfully, to believe they are white'. And by white, he takes James Baldwin's definition, that of superior monopolised power.

The superiority of the white race is a story that was shaped on the sugar plantations of the Caribbean. It has neither the moral nor scientific backing that it later claimed for itself, but was invented chiefly for economic ends: to justify the exploitation of free labour. The notion of race is as contrived as the walls it financed in England and, just like the walls, it stands to this day, dividing the land. While we continue to acknowledge the legitimacy of these brick walls, we continue to support the lie of white supremacy, of class superiority, that one type of person deserves a bigger and better share of the world than another. Black people have been the slaves of this lie, but for as long as white people continue to sustain its false narrative, they are its servants.

In 2018 Afrobeat jazz band Sons of Kemet released the album 'Your Queen Is A Reptile'. The promo video for the album mixes clips from the tracks, with a monologue from poet Joshua Idehen. Over a single repetitive note from a breathy sax, he declaims:

> WE the immigrants, we the children of immigrants, we the Diaspora, we the descendants of the colonised, we claim our right to question your obsolete systems, your racist symbols, your monuments of genocide, we who built your palaces, we who paid blood into your banks, we who died in mines so your crown jewels may have the biggest diamonds. We claim our place at the table and we say your history is not pure, your empire is not whole, your conscience is not clean.

So if we finally dig up the bare bones of this colonial guilt, and they lie like open graves on the lawns of our most magnificent estates, what then? When he was prime minister of Trinidad and Tobago, the historian Eric Williams forged an alignment with the prime ministers of Barbados, Guyana and Jamaica. In 1973 these leaders signed the Treaty of Chaguaramas, which created CARICOM: a community of Caribbean islands bound together in one common market and 'functional cooperation'. Part of CARICOM's mission was to define the crime of colonialism and outline specific reparations owed by European governments. They came up with a ten-point plan: from the cancellation of debt to the support of cultural institutions, and the eradication of illiteracy, they are practical directions to repair the damage done to their communities, both economically and psychologically. But right at the top of the list is very simply an apology. And it still hasn't come.

An apology is an acknowledgement of responsibility, a speech-act that changes the story. And it works as much for the speaker as the listener. Instead of dragging a nation out to the stocks for a public shaming, an apology is the moment the addict first looks into the mirror and truly sees themself. It is the first step to recovery. In the twelve-step programme that applies to addicts of all drugs, from alcohol to sugar to white supremacy, item four suggests we 'Make a searching and fearless moral inventory of ourselves'. While the UCL Legacies project is an impressive first step, still nothing of its kind has been attempted with the East Indies.

Shashi Tharoor is a Congress MP in India who worked for the UN for twenty-nine years, culminating as Under-Secretary General. He has argued that India 'should be content with a symbolic reparation of one pound a year, payable for 200 years to atone for 200 years of imperial rule. I felt that atonement was the point – a simple "sorry" would do as well – rather than the cash.' Atonement: at-one-ment. The apology is a spell that, once uttered, changes the story, resets the balance, and (seen in terms of land) it levels the fences, turns division into unity. Atonement, incidentally, was a word first imported into English in 1526 by none other than William Tyndale, who is, in this book at least, the patron saint of speech-acts.

While Britain sustains its false narrative of itself, while it refuses to acknowledge the source of its current status, its land remains riven by racism. Nowhere is this more evident than the countryside. A couple of years ago, Benjamin Zephaniah, Brummie poet and star of the TV series *Peaky Blinders*, was visiting a mate of his in the Essex countryside. They went for a jog before lunch, a jog that was interrupted by two police helicopters and a van responding to reports of 'suspicious men' running across the fields. Were they stopped because they were black, or, same thing but different, because no one else was?

In 2004, Trevor Phillips, the then chairman of the Equality and Human Rights Commission, spoke of a 'passive apartheid' in the British countryside. Figures show that the 9 per cent of Britain's population who are from an ethnic minority constitute only 1 per cent of the visitors to the countryside. Further to this, the stats say that while 10 per cent of the population in towns are from ethnic minorities, only 1 per cent of the rural population are Black and Minority Ethnic. In 2013, Brian True-May stepped down from producing the ITV show *Midsomer Murders* after declaring that 'we just don't have ethnic minorities involved because it wouldn't be the English village with them ... We're the last bastion of Englishness and I want to keep it that way.'

Academics from the University of Leicester in their 2011 report *Rural Racism* found that minority ethnic incomers 'were often treated with suspicion as many white rural residents felt that they belonged only in the city, with all its concomitant "negative" attributes of noise, pollution, crime and, crucially for some, multiculturalism'. In the eyes of rural England, black means urban, but the moment these communities cross the line into the countryside they challenge 'the very idea of Englishness itself'.

The sun has set and I have been watching the cows process slowly from north to south of the grounds. The sky is deep pink, the glow is sensuous. The day is done, it will soon be dark, so I'm shortcutting through the woods out into a sloping field. Swishing through the waist-high grass I am approaching two fallow deer which, though only metres away, still haven't noticed me. It's as though I have spent so long outside, I have absorbed the wide calm of the day; cloaked in the softness of the setting sun, I have lost that human stomp that sends the animal world into panic. It's only when I stop to fiddle with my phone for a photo that the human world comes crashing in, and they scarper.

The English descendants of African immigrants are finally claiming their place at the table, linking their story to the landscape. The play *Black Men Walking*, written by poet-rapper Testament, and based around a real-life Yorkshire walking group, is one such example. One character exclaims:

> It was an African that put the York in Yorkshire! And I'm not even counting the countless others after — all sorts of Africans — black people in England. The Georgians, the Tudors … we were here before the Anglo-Saxons! You see? Generations upon generations. Right down to my dad who worked in the Sheffield steelworks. You see? We've left our imprint on the earth here, in nature. We are here!

Several months after my trespass, while washing up to Radio 4, I hear another voice. Vanessa Kisuule is a poet and burlesque dancer from Bristol and she is being interviewed about the dissonance that exists between the concepts of black and rural:

> It speaks a lot to why perhaps we're not as much in the conversation around all of these big issues, ecology and climate change, because supposedly we're too busy running around getting involved in drive-bys and gun crime and living these urban fairy tales that the media seems to be so obsessed with shoehorning black and brown people into …

But it is her last words in the programme that stick in my head. They resonate with that wedded concept of freedom of speech and freedom on the land. Read her words, and then, with her permission, try swapping the word *story* for *land*: 'For so long it felt like this story, I wasn't entitled to it, it didn't belong to me, it wasn't my place, so I made a decision, a small decision in my head and heart: this story is yours too.'

SPIDER

Wives, Witches, Spells and Protest

'To spin the web and not be caught in it, to create the
world, to create your own life, to rule your fate ... to
draw nets and not just straight lines, to be a maker as well
as a cleaner, to be able to sing and not be silenced'
— Rebecca Solnit, *Men Explain Things to Me*

I shut the heavy door behind me and step into silence. I pad
gently up the aisle, past tall pointed arches and rows of cold
wooden pews, and pause at the chancel. In times past, this would
have been my limit, the space beyond reserved for choir and
clergy, but these days the church is open for tourists and the
transgression has been diffused. I walk into the space before the
altar, packed and stacked with the tombs of the dead lords of
Rutland.

Frozen in stone, there are eagles and lions, peacocks, hunting dogs and unicorns. There are nameless attendant servants, smaller in size and status, on their knees in perpetual prayer. In this small space, there are eight earls and four dukes, with the bones of another fifty lesser family members interred beneath my feet. The men lie in state, some dressed in intricate Tudor ruffs, one in the clothes of a Roman general, another in medieval armour, and their wives lie beside them, faithful, pious and pure. Their lips are pursed and their hands clasped in prayer. All their eyes are open. The alabaster carvings are so delicate it seems like the thinnest veil of white silk has been laid across their faces, which with the slightest draught, might slip off and stir them from their daydream. I barely breathe.

Before me, laid out like corpses on a morgue table, are the life-size effigies of the 1st Earl and Countess of Rutland. Over the sixteen years of their marriage, Eleanor Paston was almost constantly pregnant, bearing the earl eleven children. But, because the first two were female, the couple had to wait for their third child until they had secured the lineage of their estate. By the rule of male primogeniture, their fortune skipped Anne and Gertrude, and landed with their first son, Henry.

The primacy of the first-born male was another of William the Conqueror's imports. Its express aim was to protect the integrity of estates from being particularised into separate holdings, divided by their children; it was a legal wall around the concept of dynasty. The Bible had set the precedent for male inheritance, but Anglo-Saxon custom (as enshrined in the eleventh-century laws of Cnut) provided that the lord's land 'be very justly divided among his wife and children'. Before 1066, Anglo-Saxon women were autonomous individuals, who could own land, run businesses and sign legal contracts. When a marriage was agreed, it was the husband who paid a dowry, the morgengifu, though not to his wife's father, but directly to her.

As a couple, both man and wife handled the finances of the estate and, if they divorced, they halved the holdings between them. But when William imported the cult of exclusion into England, he brought with him another legal fiction: wives became property, too. Under Norman law, a married woman was termed 'feme couvert', a covered woman, and her land, her rights, her 'very being', were entirely subsumed under the protective wing of her husband. In Genesis, woman was created when the Lord took Adam's rib; in Norman England, Adam was taking it back, plus interest. Writing in 1769, William Blackstone described couverture, which after 600 years was alive and well in Georgian England: 'By marriage, the husband and wife are one person in law: that is, the very being or legal existence of the woman is suspended during the marriage, or at least is incorporated and consolidated into that of the husband: under whose wing, protection, and cover, she performs every thing.'

This, of course, was done for her own good. Blackstone continues: 'Even the disabilities which the wife lies under (resulting from coverture) are for the most part intended for her protection and benefit. So great a favourite is the female sex of the laws of England.'

When Eleanor was married in 1523, her value was her womb. Her virginity was a commodity that was bartered to secure a land contract between two men, a guarantee of uncontested lineage. Her cervix was the tunnel that bridged two landed estates and her uterus was the garden in which the earl would plant his seed and cultivate his heir. Had Eleanor not died in 1551, had she lived to a biblical age, she would have had to wait another 319 years to possess her own property, when Parliament passed the Married Women's Property Act, while under care of her husband, she could be raped by him, by law, all the way up to 1991.

As the wife was stifled in law, so there were strict social orthodoxies as to her countenance in public and private spheres.

Gervase Markham summed it up in his influential book *The English Hus-wife* (1661): 'Our English housewife must be ... wise in discourse, but not frequent therein, sharp and quick of speech, but not bitter or talkative.' If a wife flaunted her speech, if she got too saucy by half, she could be branked, that is, have her head encased in a scold's bridle, an iron muzzle that masked her face, with a two-inch bridle extended into her mouth to suppress her tongue. For a wife to speak her mind was deemed inconsistent with her legal status, a trespass outside of the *couvert* placed upon her.

On the south wall of the church, lying parallel to Eleanor and her husband, is the tomb of the 6th Earl, perhaps the grandest of them all. He lies, with his two consecutive wives Frances and Elizabeth, beneath a barrel vault whose pillars and pediment run to the eaves of the church. Behind their heads, their daughter Katherine kneels in prayer, hands clasped, and at their feet are their two boys, frozen for ever in infancy, each carrying a small skull. The inscription at the back of the tomb explains that they 'died in their infancy by wicked practises and sorcerye'. This is the only tomb in England to record death by magic: they were killed by witches.

Leaving the church is like waking up – the noise returns, the real world was there all along. My mind moves from male primogeniture to flapjacks and cheese pasties. I stock up for the night ahead, unlock my bike and head south to Belvoir Castle, the home of the bones in the church. Five miles south of Bottesford, Belvoir is still the principal seat of the Rutland lineage and the core of its 15,000-acre estate. The castle is open for tourists, and the 11th Duke lives in a private wing of the castle.

I see Belvoir Castle at the top of the first slope out of Bottesford. Dark blue against the sky, the castle stands on a lonely wooded outcrop, a heavy stone paperweight on the patchwork quilt farmland of the Vale of Belvoir, the gravitational core of the land. There it is on every turn of the road, getting slowly bigger as I bike towards it. At the foot of the castle car park, I turn right, and ride widdershins around the entire estate, sussing out the best way in. There are no walls around the duke's land, just curtains of trees, occasional loose barbed-wire fencing and the implicit understanding of forbidden ground. I pedal for miles up and down the hills, through various villages that surround the estate, until I arrive at a long, straight road crossing flat plains of cow-cropped grass. The castle is there at the top of the road, on its plinth of wooded stone and beneath me, a small stream cuts underneath a stone bridge, straight into the estate. I decide to enter this way, grateful for the cover of its tunnel of trees. I hide my bike under the bridge, take off my boots and trousers and step in.

The silt sucks at my bare feet and tiny black fish dart like brushstrokes. I find a stick to help me through, and already know this is the single least practical idea I have had all year. Covered by a single line of trees on either side, I follow the meander of the river through alternate pools of gold and green, light and shade. The riverbed is lined in places with slabs of rough concrete, and at others with thick beds of gritty loam that farts and belches at my shins as they sink into it. Between the leaves of the trees, the castle is watching.

When Eleanor married her earl, this castle was in ruins, vacant for a hundred years. Five years after the wedding, the earl began to rebuild the castle, an enterprise that was greatly aided when Henry VIII dissolved the monasteries, allowing him to plunder the stone from both Belvoir Priory and Croxton Abbey. The castle was not just a refurbished house for the newlyweds, but a stark sign to the surrounding countryside that order was being reinstated. Outside of the court the life of women was much freer. When the Elizabethan writer Thomas Harman published his popular discourse on vagabondage in 1566 he described the men as 'wily foxes', in other words cunning thieves. But his description of women reveals that typical gendered fear of freedom: a masterless woman was a 'cow ... that goes to bull every moon, with what bull she cares not'. The men were work-shy, the women were sluts.

The commons were crawling with dissidents, spawning sedition on the plains beneath the watchful, fearful eye of the lords. William Tyndale had been burned the same year that Henry had begun his dissolution of the monasteries and several years later, with his translation of the Bible leaking through the common orders, he had prised open Pandora's box: over the next century a host of sects and cults evolved, spreading alternative interpretations of the word of God. The Family of Love, the Quakers, the Fifth Monarchists, the Seekers and Ranters, Grindletonians and Anabaptists and countless others were creating their own decoctions of sedition and heresy, rejecting the dogma of resurrection, prayer, heaven and hell and principal among them all, rejecting subordination of any kind. Many were sexual revolutionaries, some rejecting monogamy, some rejecting marriage and most proclaiming equal rights across the perceived partition of gender.

Women were central to this sedition. They were core members of most of these new sects and just as active as the men in pulling down the fences and hedges around their commons. The arguments against land and its enclosure were the same arguments for their freedom of will – as the lords of the manor tried to enclose their livelihoods, they sought to extend their dogma on the role and behaviour of women. Strong, self-willed women of the courts were dealt with brutally. Anne Askew was the daughter of a wealthy landowner, and one of the earliest English female poets. She was the first woman on record to ask for a divorce. She converted from Catholicism to Protestantism and was charged with heresy in 1545. Although she was tortured in the Tower of London, she refused to betray the names of other Protestants and was sentenced to death in 1546. Since her broken bones could no longer sustain her weight, she was carried to her pyre on a chair, and when she refused to renounce her beliefs she was burned alive. Similarly, Margaret Cheyney was executed for her part in the Pilgrimage of Grace, for persuading her husband Lord Bulmer to get involved and for conspiring to recruit the locals to, in her words, 'raise the commons'.

But the women of the commons, the working-class women, were harder to control, not least because there were a lot more of them. If the life blood of sedition is communication, these women, labouring in the commons, or spinning and weaving in rooms together, were the beating heart of the problem. The word gossip betrays this fearful link between the older women of the commons, and the spread of seditious counter-narratives. It began its life as a noun, *godsibb*. The godsibbs were the close friends of a woman who attended her in childbirth, and as such had a bond with the child and mother through the hours of labour. Men weren't included. The word came to be associated with the notion of a close confidante and finally, through the Tudor period, evolved into a verb – to exchange closely guarded secrets. In Shakespeare's *Titus Andronicus*, Aaron speaks of 'a long-tongued babbling gossip' who threatens to reveal the truth of his actions and resolves to murder her to keep it quiet. He ends his speech with the lines:

The midwife and the nurse well made away,
Then let the ladies tattle what they please.

But the lords of Tudor England were not content to let the ladies tattle. In 1486, two German Dominican monks had published a work that became incredibly popular with the higher echelons of European society. The *Malleus Maleficarum* (*The Hammer of the Witches*) was the first blow against the working-class women of the commons. Divided into a list of questions, it was a handbook for the paternalism of the Church. Question Ten enquired: 'Whether Witches can by some Glamour Change Men into Beasts'. So powerful were the words of women that they could turn ordered male creatures into feral heretics. The word *glamour* is the giveaway – the men were seeking to link these dissidents with the gypsies that were already spreading through Europe and heading to England. They sought to take integral components of the rural community and ostracise them as outsiders. The following question deals with one of the Church's central paranoias, a woman's control over her own body. Its answer states: 'No one does more harm to the Catholic faith than midwives.' In Catholic Europe it was heresy for a man to ejaculate outside a woman's vagina (a rule that has the distinct hallmark of male authorship). Any interruption to the insemination of holy seed was flaunting the will of God. As such, these 'cunning women' and some men were committing heresy when they advised on various herbs for contraception and especially so when they performed abortions – a woman's womb belonged first to God the Father, and then to the lord her husband. Matilda Joslyn Gage, a nineteenth-century suffragist, activist and author, wrote that 'the superior learning of witches was recognised in the widely extended belief of their ability to work miracles. The witch was in reality the profoundest thinker, the most advanced scientist of those ages . . . as knowledge has ever been power, the church feared its use in women's hands, and levelled its deadliest blows at her.'

Paracelsus, the father of modern medicine, once claimed that he learned everything he knew from a 'cunning woman'. The knowledge these women possessed was accumulated from an oral tradition, passed along a generational thread of storytelling, and the experience of working within nature – many of their 'sorceries' have later been proved by modern science, and privatised by drug companies. A commoner complains of inflamed joints: 'apply willow bark', said the witches. 'Sorcery!' cried the Church. And today salacin, a chemical compound sourced from willow bark, is treated to make salicylic acid, which is now sold as aspirin. In 1540, Henry VIII granted the charter for the Company of Barber-Surgeons which was the beginning of the male-dominated medical profession. By law, women were barred from professional practice and anyone offering medical advice without a licence was operating outside the law. Surgery became the art of the male doctor and the holistic services provided by the cunning women, both psycho-spiritual (therapy) and herbal remedies, were outlawed. The herbs of the common had become weeds, the women of the common were witches.

Of course the Church had something to say about sexuality. As gender scholar Silvia Federici writes:

The witch hunt condemned female sexuality as the source of every evil, but it was also the main vehicle of a broad reconstruction of sexual life that, conforming with the new capitalist work-discipline, criminalised any sexual activity that threatened procreation, the transmission of property within the family, or took time and energy away from work.

Hags and crones were the worst of these: older women, whose bodies had finally liberated them from the consequences of fertility, were able to have sex with whom they pleased, and, worse, get away with it. This was a particular fixation for the Tudor judges. There is barely an account of a witch trial that does not go into lurid detail about an older women's sexual union with the devil, some animal or a whole string of quaking, victimised men seduced by her 'glamour'.

My passage through the river is blocked by a low stone bridge, laced with slack barbed wire. Spider webs lattice the archway, their drag lines extending in diagonals across the semi-circle of space, tethering their nets. The whole space is strung like a mandolin, taut with the report of delicate vibrations that communicate the world to the near-sightless spiders. I can see the swathed cocoons of their young, some still unhatched, and my spine prickles at the thought of hundreds of spiderlings caught in my hair. The Scythian traveller Anacharsis once likened the laws of the land to these webs. Recorded by Plutarch in 75 AD he told Solon: 'These decrees of yours are no different from spiders' webs. They'll restrain anyone weak and insignificant who gets caught in them, but they'll be torn to shreds by people with power and wealth.'

This is the end of the river tunnel: on the other side of the fence, the river opens up to wide fields and sunshine but, on this side, its banks are lined on either side with wire, snagged with little scruffs of sheep wool, and hawthorn trees that make escape through the riverbank impossible. I must pass my rucksack and shoes through the lines of wire and silk and chuck them to a cove beyond. Knee-deep in running water, bent double under the bridge, I feel like a novice troll, perilously close to a drenching. But I make it through and clamber out to bright blue skies, warm earth and the vigilant presence of the castle.

The bridge is in fact a Right of Way into the duke's land, and a famous one at that. In 1893, a man called Harrison took this path into the duke's land to protest the grouse shooting on the estate. As he had done several times before, he waved his brolly and raised his voice to scare away the birds but on this occasion he was 'forcibly detained' (sat on) by the duke's servants. He took them to court for assault. The judge, Lord Esher, found against him, saying: 'on the ground that the plaintiff was on the highway, the soil of which belonged to the Duke of Rutland, not for the purpose of using it in order to pass and repass, or for any reasonable or usual mode of using the highway as a highway, I think he was a trespasser.'

I am following the river across the gnarly, rutted land where the long, open plains of grass meet the river. There are tractor tracks and large squelchy depressions, stippled by heavy hooves, where the cows come to drink. Herds of sheep stare at me as I pass and then suddenly bolt as one across the plains. There is no one in sight for miles around but still I feel a nagging anxiety: the heavy presence of the castle follows me, like Mona Lisa's eyes.

When philosopher Jeremy Bentham returned from Belarus in 1787 he had plans for a new prison he called the Panopticon. Designed around a circular footprint, its revolutionary idea was that prisoners could be seen at all times from a central observation tower. The point, however, was not that they were constantly monitored, but that their behaviour could be controlled by the constant *feeling* of being observed. Two hundred years later, Foucault called this Panopticism, that sense of a higher power constantly surveying the actions of its lower orders. But here, beneath the castle, Panopticism seems to have been a much earlier invention. John Graunt, the Tudor pamphleteer, wrote in 1662: 'Many of the poorer parishioners through neglect do perish, and many vicious persons get liberty to live as they please, for want of some heedful eye to overlook them.' When the duke began his repairs of Belvoir Castle, he was reinstating this heedful eye over the Vale, a lighthouse of control that emitted not light but power.

These common lands, areas as yet ungoverned by the cult of exclusion, were places outside the scope of this heedful eye, places where women and men could live as they pleased. The Tudor courts told stories of Wild Sabbats on the plains and in the forests, great satanic orgies where men and women would come together to spurn the word of God and the order of the lords with sex and booze and dance. The word 'coven', used to describe these meetings, is derived from the same root as 'convention' and 'convent': it means simply a coming together of people. It was another one of Tyndale's legacies: the congregation without the Church. The problem for the lords was that the connections they made on these wild plains, the solidarity they fostered, had constructed an organic, self-governing web of social relations, customs, that risked spilling over into the rigid hierarchal structure of the courts, even toppling them. Claire Askew is a poet and descendant of Anne:

Burn me the same way
you burned her: do it
because we took the plain
thoughts from our own heads
into the square, and spoke.

Anne Askew was burned because she brought her plain thoughts, her direct and unadorned opinions, into the square, the public sphere, the realm controlled by men of power. But perhaps there is a secondary meaning here – these plain thoughts could also refer to the plains on which I'm walking now, the sentiments and sedition of the commons, the only place where the lords of the manor couldn't stifle the voice of women.

I have made my way through the open plains on the foothills of the castle and have come to a tarmac road. On my left is the head of an ornamental lake, which the duke rents out to local fishermen. There are plastic numbers staked into the ground at various intervals and semi-circles of grass cut from the reeds. I follow the road along the lake, passing the Duke of Rutland's kennels, home to his world-famous bloodline of hunting hounds. I head over the bridge to the other side of the lake. I'm searching for a place to spend the night and here, in the flats of the great hill that leads up to the edge of the estate, the grass is up to my thighs, long enough to hide a sleeping bag and its contents. The fishing coves on this side have small fences and gates around their perimeter, and I am drawn to their added sense of seclusion. I shut the gate behind me, dump my bag, remove my boots and dip my feet back into the cold water, putting my t-shirt on the fence to dry. If I keep to the corner I will be snug behind the tall grass, hidden on either side by bulrushes, and the castle will be dead centre in my view.

In 1613 the two young sons of the 6th Earl of Rutland fell seriously and mysteriously ill. Henry, the oldest, died in September of that year and for seven years Francis lay in bed, weakening inexplicably, until he too died. For five years after the first death, rumours circulated that three women who lived in Bottesford had cursed the children in vengeance for having been dismissed by the Countess of Rutland. Joan Flowers and her two daughters, Margaret and Philippa, had all worked as cleaners in the castle but were sacked following accusations by other servants that they were thieving from the pantry.

The women were already suspect. Joan was a widow, which meant that she lived outside the protective *couvert* of a husband. As such her weak mind was susceptible to the lewd advances of the devil. On top of this, she was a 'cunning woman', she knew her roots and herbs, and there were rumours that their house was being used as a brothel. To make matters worse, she never went to church, and had been caught several times swearing on a Sunday. She was, according to one contemporary source: 'a monstrous malicious woman, full of imprecations irreligious and for anything they saw by her, a plaine atheist.'

As Francis Manners took another turn for the worse, his mother decided it was time to act. Just before Christmas 1618 an unnamed person made an accusation against Joan and her daughters, claiming they had cursed the duke's two sons by means of witchcraft. The women were rounded up and taken to prison to await trial.

Only now do I realise how late it is. The day has cooled quickly, and the sun has long since set behind the castle. Bats are beginning to flit above me, and the sky has turned a low violet. I unpack my sleeping bag, lay out the roll mat and cocoon myself from the chilling wind. I remember the fire I had on the Duke of Norfolk's Arundel estate, the truck that had struck the fear of God into me as it rolled by. The driver must simply not have noticed me, but, with the fire blazing behind me, it had felt like a miracle. Tonight I am too exposed for a fire, but, cloaked in darkness, I still feel that same deep sense of unease beneath the squat, stone, heedful eye of the castle.

Today the term 'witch-hunt' evokes an inescapable accusation, a foregone conclusion that seeks only the evidence to corroborate the charge. But with the facts of this actual witch-hunt comes a shuddering realisation just how fenced in these women were. Three working-class women were facing the very essence of the patriarchy. First came the 'examinations' by a group of the most powerful men in the country. Among the men appointed were the Sheriff of Leicester, a Justice of the Peace and the rector of Bottesford. George Manners was there, the duke's brother, MP of Lincolnshire, and a major landowner. And, finally, the duke himself, Francis, who was a Knight of the Garter, the original and most prestigious old boys' club, Lord-Lieutenant of Lincolnshire, member of the privy council, not to mention the father of the 'murdered' child. When two of the women came to trial, they faced an all-male jury, because only property-owning men aged between twenty-one and seventy were deemed of solid enough mind to condemn evil in the face of the devil. The judges, who were handpicked by the king, were Sir Henry Hobart, the former Attorney-General and Lord Chief Justice of the Common Pleas, and Sir Edward Bromley, a baron of the Exchequer who was riding high in the king's estimation having hanged the Pendle witches seven years previously. In Tracey Borman's words: 'The closed incestuous world of the local aristocracy and justice system was not exclusive to Lincolnshire: it was mirrored in every part of the country and underpinned the entire administration of the local and central government.'

Perhaps the word 'patriarchy' is unhelpful. Since the 1970s, it has been used to define power inequalities between the sexes on all levels of the hierarchy. But originally the *rule of the father* was a hierarchy installed by the Church and then borrowed by the state; it was a structure of power relations, from the top to the bottom. A father was the apex of the family power pyramid. Like a king or a pope, he was responsible for their welfare, and also for their discipline – he controlled their couverture. Perhaps *paternalism* is more accurate in describing the system that faced the women of Bottesford. Because what characterised these witch-hunts was not just gender but this particular structure of power. Across Europe, a quarter of witches killed were men (in Iceland, it was 92 per cent). And in England it was a woman, Elizabeth I, who reintroduced the death penalty for witches. The witch-hunts sought to eliminate not women, but what women represented in the minds of the lords: the dangerous disorder of the feminine.

Central to paternalism is the notion of the status quo: that *its* form of government is the only viable option. Through history, the concept of the feminine has been linked by the patriarchy to sedition, protest, any form of questioning this status quo. Sometimes the link was empowering: during the Welsh tax uprisings in the 1840s, known as the Rebecca Riots, men wore women's clothes to tear down the toll booths; during the riots against the Game Acts in the early nineteenth century, men wore dresses to ransack the landed gentry of their deer, a clear symbol of sedition to the established order. But historically, and right up to the present day, most allusions to the feminine are pejorative. When the abolitionists argued against slavery in Parliament, they were feminised by their opponents, criticised for being too sentimental, too emotional to recognise the commercial necessity of free labour. Even in the core of Margaret Thatcher's government, ministers who didn't fully accept her hard-line neo-liberal ethics were labelled 'wets' when they opposed her, that is, effete, feeble-minded, incapable of power. It was Thatcher who coined the famous mantra that turned paternalism into a creed for neo-liberalism: 'There is no alternative.'

I have been trying to sleep, but it's not happening; it's too cold. I hear a hoarse cough from the woods over the lake, a deer or a muntjac perhaps, and, suddenly stirred, the dogs begin baying from the kennels, breaching the eerie silence of the lake, a baleful sound of white-eyed bloodlust, pealing like church bells, which starts the geese off, and then the coots, and now the dark lake is a cacophony of whoops, hoots, screams and howls, a wild sabbat of hidden creatures on the common. I lie like the effigies of the earls in the church, petrified.

Joan Flower never made it to trial. She died on the long winter walk in between Bottesford and the Lincoln court. Somewhat unbelievably, she choked on a piece of holy bread, which in the spirit of the times was proof enough of her witchcraft for her guards not to be accused of malpractice. Her two daughters were tried, however, and the court found them guilty of crimes 'against the peace of the Crown and the dignity of the Lord

King'. They were hanged slowly, to avoid snapping their necks, strangled and suffocated by the noose until their tongues were disgorged from their throats.

I watch the stars fade away and the sky turn from dark blue to grey. I must have slept, but I don't feel it: my head is spinning, my eyes are burning, I'm cold to the bone. I get up stiffly and pack up everything around me, leaving nothing on the ground but a cold dent in the grass. As I turn to leave the enclosure, I hear the dogs again, this time louder, and the bark of a man commanding them. My heart flashes. The dogs are there in front of me, ranging over the hillside, a sprawling pack hungry for exercise, and three figures on horseback galloping them on. I'm too tired to move and so stand, stock still, as they disappear. I wait a while and then follow them cautiously up the valley from the lake, beneath the boughs of huge cedar trees and emerge out onto a common. Cows are gently milling through the scrub, one rubbing her head satisfyingly against a monkey puzzle tree. And at the end of the common, on the top of a steep slope, there is a triangle of sunshine, golden grass, warmth.

I sit on the slope and eat a banana, the entire Vale of Belvoir spread out before my feet, a picture of peace and order beneath the castle. In a 2015 BBC documentary, the current Duchess of Rutland says: 'The building itself is so imposing, it takes people's breath away.' For the three women of Bottesford, this was true in its most literal sense. Today, you can visit the castle at Halloween and 'listen to eerie stories about the Witches of Belvoir and make creepy crafts!' The murder of three women, and their alternative vision of power, has been redefined and reconstituted as anodyne tourism, the weeds of eccentricity ploughed into fields of monoculture. Then, as now, the web of hedges and plough lines that extends over the Vale drains both the yield of the land and the power of the people to one source, the heedful eye of the castle.

Here were the lords of the law because here were the lords of the land. Their control over the commoners came after their control of the commons. Any threat to this order, any alternative distribution of power, was a direct challenge to this order of the land, the order of property. But this order, which masquerades as *the* order, was only ever *their* order.

In 1981, a group of thirty-six women aged between twenty-five and seventy set off on foot from Cardiff City Hall to a patch of common land in Berkshire. With a few men and a few children accompanying them, for ten days they walked along the verges of motorways and A-roads. At the head of their column, the women took turns to hold a sign. On the front it said: 'Why are we walking 120 miles from a nuclear weapons factory in Cardiff to a site for cruise missiles in Berkshire?' On the back were the words 'This is Why' and, below, an enlarged photograph of the corpse of a baby, born dead and deformed in the aftermath of the Hiroshima bomb.

At first, the walk itself was the protest. But their arrival at Greenham Common was something of an anticlimax. The press coverage along the way, national and local, had focused not on the substance of their cause but on something they considered far more remarkable. Helen John, a midwife on the protest, wrote later: 'All they asked about was how our husbands were coping back home, and weren't we irresponsible exposing our children to all that carbon monoxide'.

Above and beyond the threat of nuclear annihilation, the press were astounded that these women had the gall to leave their domestic enclosure and trespass the public sphere, the realm of *men-who-know-better*. When they arrived on the common, they gathered at the gates of the American Air Force base and read out the speech they had co-written, surprising the guard on duty who had assumed they were cleaners. When another guard turned up, he informed them that, since it was a Saturday night, the guys on the inside of the base were hitting the Jack Daniel's and, unless they wanted a good raping they'd better move on. Eventually the US base commander appeared. The women again read out their statement. 'We will not be victims in a war which is not our making. We wish neither to be the initiators nor the targets of a nuclear holocaust.' To which the commander replied he would like to machine-gun the whole damned lot of them. 'As far as I'm concerned,' he said, 'you can stay there as long as you like.' So, for nineteen years, they did.

In 1939, 900 acres of common land was enclosed as a base for the Royal Air Force. Nine miles of barbed-wire fencing went up and the common was tarmacked over. After the war, the MOD bought the site and by the late 1960s it had been leased to the American Air Force. There was room for 2,000–4,000 troops and their wives and children to be stationed there. There was a school, cinema and shopping centre for American personnel and then, a decade later, six trapezoid missile silos, turfed with grass. In 1979, Ronald Regan announced that ninety-six MX ground-launch nuclear missiles would be installed at the site. Just for a laugh, he called his explosives 'The Peacemakers', because there's nothing quite so peaceful as a nuclear winter.

Today at Greenham Common the missiles have gone. The common has been opened up for dog walkers and cyclists and the RAF control tower is a tea shop. Part of the fence still remains, ten foot high, with iron arms angling over its face holding three lines of barbed wire, rusted brown. It now appears to be a car park for a van hire company, policed not by the American Air Force but by two bored-looking men in hi-vis jackets. But forty

miles east, on the outskirts of London, there is another protest camp built on similar principles of the women of Greenham. They are protesting what is perhaps the only thing more dev-astating than nuclear war: the total collapse of the environ-ment, formerly known as climate change. They have squatted a few acres of derelict land in a village called Sipson, just out-side Heathrow Airport, which will be entirely flattened under tarmac if the proposed third runway is built. The Diggers and Dreamers' website describes the camp, which is called 'Grow Heathrow': 'Since 2010 a group of activists, local residents and people living off-grid have worked to develop the site into a self-sustaining low carbon community, and to be a community centre/host for groups, events & activists.'

The site is open to anyone who comes, and so, seeking not the land but the spirit of Greenham, I go to Grow Heathrow, during a cold snap at the start of the new year.

I have come for a ceramics workshop run by Jessica, a woman who lives nearby. I walk up a muddy avenue of makeshift huts, recommissioned sheds raised on foundations of builders' palettes and layered with insulation and rain-proofing. The site is an open-cast rabbit warren of woodchip paths cut through the brambles, leading from one cluster of structures to another. There are tree houses, common rooms, fire pits encircled with cut logs as seats. There is a watchtower at the centre, a con-struction of scaffold and a wind turbine, that turns the stiff wind into hot water for showers below. There are two large boats on stacks at the end of the first avenue, draped in tarp, and the central community hut, which is also the kitchen, where smoke chuffs out of the stove pipe in the roof. One of the residents leads me through a skeleton greenhouse, past raised grow beds made from sawn tree trunks, down into the group space, where people have already begun shaping the clay.

Jessica is several years out of Camberwell College of Arts. She is working on a project to commemorate sites of protests in the history of English land rights, as important as they are unacknowledged. She trespasses the land, digs a chunk of earth, bags it and escapes like a cartoon robber with her swag slung over her shoulder. She has excavated St George's Hill, the site of the Diggers' revolt that was crushed by Cromwell's army — now a golf course — and is in the process of scoping out Mousehold Heath just outside Norwich, where landowner Robert Kett helped 16,000 commoners tear down his own hedge enclosures, and went on to storm Norwich. This is now also a golf course. Today we will be working with clay from Heathrow, dug from a six-foot trench at the corner of the site.

When the Greenham women set up camp that first night, their priority was to build a fire. When more and more people started coming, scores of people, then hundreds, then thousands, they brought tarps and palettes, hay bales, cut wood and food and started erecting benders, traditional gypsy structures made from bent hazel rods. When someone brought a huge cauldron, to cook for the congregation, the witches were finally in place, the coven was created.

Our living room was a fire pit surrounded by straw bales covered in plastic. There was always a kettle perched precariously on the smoking embers and whoever got up first relit the fire each morning. Our office was an old fridge in which we kept the letters to be answered. A chest of drawers contained other handy items like string and paper. Beyond the kitchen and living room, stretching down towards the main road, we'd strung a washing line between two trees and draped plastic over it to form a tunnel. Inside the tunnel we'd laid pallets covered with straw, this was the communal bedroom.

With no leader and no camp hierarchy, the camp evolved organically. Initially men were living alongside the women but, after a year of protest, it became clear that their presence escalated the aggression in clashes with police. A meeting was held, a vote was taken and men were banned from living at the camp. As if to prove the women's point, they kicked off, one taking an axe to the structures he had helped build, but soon they had disappeared, returning only for day visits. And now the press started to take a greater interest. Was this a feminist protest, or an anti-nuclear protest?

> The media have quite consistently and continuously avoided taking up our perspectives on war, racism and sexism ... The confusion has been inside the camp as well as outside because every woman stands for herself and we try to live in a way that is respectful of our differences. Which comes first, disarmament or feminism? It always had to be one or the other – prioritizing. We say you can't have one without the other.

The mass media has always preferred to particularise the concerns of a protest, to find the leader of a group and inter-view them for the single, simple soundbite; their columns are too slim to weave together the many threads of narrative that form the web. To the women of Greenham, however, there were multiple lines that had led them to this camp, and the web was formed of delicate nodes of intersectional concerns, none of which took precedence over the other. Power was arranged not vertically, in the top-down template of paternalism, but hori-zontally, where every thread of the web held the tension of the whole. As the camp grew, more threads were intertwined: the illegal mining of uranium in Namibia that built the bombs, the un-unionised labour that had laid the tarmac and fencing of the airbase. The camp became a howl against the paternalistic hierarchy, that grid of power that compartmentalised oppression and pretended that everything from the exploitation of women and labour to racism, colonialism and nuclear armament was neatly unconnected.

The image of the spider's web emerged from this intrinsic feeling of connectivity to become the symbol of the camp. It expressed the many storylines that had led the women to the camp, the horizontal power share that the women had organised, and, on a practical level, the chain letters and telephone lines that connected the group to outside solidarity. The spider seemed to encapsulate every notion of the protest. For some it drew on that great Freudian *Urangst*, the primeval male fear of the woman as predator, the spider that eats its mate. For some it drew on the Greek myth of Ariadne, the weaver who used her thread to lead Theseus out of the man-made labyrinth, out of the straight corridors of the masculine psyche, into the open plains of the feminine. Some drew on the Native American myths, in which spider webs were woven from thread to catch dreams, to manifest hope, and the great spider mother of the Navajos, who wove strong silk to protect human life. Further south, the Mexican spider grandmother, Teotihuacan, represented the queen of all creation, Mother Earth. The web was a symbol of a protective field, the ability to use arts and creative thinking to create another world, the ability to listen sensitively to the vibrations around oneself, to be attuned to one's environment. It was also a symbol of persistence: the ability to keep remaking the web no matter how many big beasts crash through it.

Fundamental to the Greenham spirit were the spider trickster gods. Like the coyote and the hare, the spider trickster is able to utilise creative vision and cunning to thwart the powerful oppressor, to creep through the cracks of their fortress and come out on top. And so the spider came to represent one of the Greenham women's key strategies: creative, artistic, non-violent direct action. 'I don't see non-violence as just a tactic,' said Rebecca Johnson, one resident of the camp. 'It is part of the accepted lie that violence is more powerful that non-violence and that people can somehow save themselves from violence by taking up arms. Thus non-violence is viewed as less valid, less desperate – a sort of liberal pastime.' In fact, non-violence was itself a threat to the order of things, a refusal to meet the hierarchy on its own terms.

The Greenham women worked tirelessly to find creative ways of protesting the base. They would blockade the base to prevent missile carriers from entering, sitting on the wet ground, arms linked, singing a whole songbook of protest songs they had conceived during the long days under the rain-bashed tarp:

The fragile docile image of our sex must die
Through centuries of silence we are screaming into action.
We're shameless hussies
And we don't give a damn.

Daily they would take their wool to the fences and lamp-posts and barbed wire and appropriate the austere military infrastructure as a canvas for creativity. Keening played a huge part in the camp's sense of solidarity. From the Irish tradition of *caoineadh*, a key component to the pagan wake ceremonies, keening was a loud, long guttural wail, a lament for the children that had died, and would die, in nuclear war. Against the cold silence and blank faces of the military personnel, it was an eerie breach of the peace, an explosion of emotion from a tightly bound nucleus of pain.

In December 1982 they used their telephone lines and chain letters to organise a huge demonstration, the first year with 30,000 women, the next with 50,000. They drove, bussed and walked from across the country to be there, spread out along the nine-mile-long perimeter fence, held hands and enclosed the enclosure with song. They decorated it with woollen webs, drawings, their children's teddy bears, photographs of their babies, bringing the cherished items from the home to the base that threatened its sanctity. It was a poetic, incongruous and deeply unsettling act, bridging the psychological gap between the perpetrators of a possible nuclear war and its future victims. Geographer Tim Cresswell called it 'a type of secular magic', the ability to eradicate the perceptual partition between the clean order of the military base and the ragged mess of burned flesh it threatened.

It was a defining moment in the camp's ideology when the coven decided to cut the fence. Did this count as violence? On Halloween 1983, 2,000 women dressed as witches stormed the fence and tore down five of its nine miles with bolt-cutters. So many were arrested they had to be held at Newbury Racecourse as they were processed through the night. Theresa, another member of the Greenham camp, wrote:

Taking down the fence was, for me, a most powerful celebration, and expression of 'NO'. No to the machine and the barriers it creates, the fence being a visible, physical barrier but no also to those invisible ones that keep us so alienated, east from west, black from white, heterosexual from homosexual, barriers of class, religion, barriers of privilege and deprivation ...

Living day in and day out in front of the base, the women began to see the fence not as the blank, impervious wall of the system, but as a porous membrane, through which they could engage the stony-faced guards and remind them of their own humanity, their own children. On the second Embrace the Base, 50,000 women brought mirrors with them and held them towards the base, reflecting the image back at the soldiers, turning the blank statement of the base back onto itself, interrupting its authoritarian laser glare with its own mask.

As the camp grew organically, it became as much a protest *for* as *against*. It had evolved into a new anarchic society, a bubble both outside and deep within the established order of society. This *no-man-land* was a no-man's-land between two expressions of order – on one side of the fence, the paternalistic inevitability of nuclear armament, the projection of power by threat of violence; on the other side of the fence, the neat English countryside in which women were expected to know their place, a world that had defined and confined women into roles written by men. In the slim space between, the women had woven their own web of relationships that refused to conform to the partitions imposed on them. Theirs was a space where womanhood was self-defined, where womanhood was powerful, where womanhood was no longer ostracised to the margins of public debate. The witches had reclaimed the common.

I have taken a break from the workshop and am making tea for the group in the large shack by the entrance, the common room and kitchen. There is a battered Aga in the corner, alongside a variety of shelves and surfaces built out of reclaimed wood, covered in chipped mugs and coffee grains. Above the sink, someone has written: 'To attain true enlightenment one must learn to do the washing up.' Like Greenham, the horizontal power share of this place gives it a rare quality: no order has been imposed from above, it adheres to no blueprint, homogeny has rotted under a wild spurge of creativity. No one area looks the same as another: everything reflects the mind of its conceiver, bears the handprint of its builders. With the constant flow of protesters and local residents pumping through its veins, with the repurposing of its areas, the constant changing of its skin, the organic development of its structures through the thought and work its residents put into it, the camp grows like a tree in proportion to the resources on offer; it is as close to a living thing as a place might be. I fill the kettle, put it on the stove and turn to split some wood with the axe. I open the door of the Aga and layer up the kindling, and I feel the roar of its fire on my face. I'm looking into the heart of the camp, the nucleus around which everything survives. Home is where the hearth is.

Foucault had a word for places such as these. He called them *heterotopias* – spaces of outsiders forged deep inside society, spaces that reflect the orthodoxy of that society by arranging themselves differently. These spaces are distinct from utopias in that they are real, they actually exist, and they manifest their ideologies in real space. Someone has done the plumbing, set up the solar panels, dug the long-drop compost toilet. They work; there *are* alternatives. This is a message that the Fathers find profoundly threatening.

In Greenham, the media continued as they had begun. Everything was not in its right place. There was an appalled sense of the women's dereliction of duty, that by leaving their appointed geographical identity, their home, they had deserted their very womanhood. As Cresswell writes:

An analysis of the media response reveals the boundaries of assumed, normative geographies. The divisions of mad/sane, good/evil, criminal/law-abiding and normal/ abnormal that appear so frequently in the press discourse all have geographic foundations in the assumed displace- ment of women from the home and family to the all-women environment of the camp.

These women had transgressed their geographic normativity and trespassed into a world that was not for them. The media fixated on the squalor of the camp, and by extension the filth of its women. Auberon Waugh claimed the women smelled of 'fish paste and bad oysters' and the *Daily Mail* reported that local police dreaded 'being ordered to lay hands on women who often deliberately and calculatingly stink'.

What these reports ignored is the fact that the council had banned the use of chemical toilets and were constantly removing the women's standpipe (which they used to access water) in a direct bid to make conditions inhabitable. But there is a deeper, more primal element to this obsession with dirt. The concept of woman in society was then intrinsically associated with perfume adverts and cleaning products, but on the common these mud-spattered women were shattering these sensual projections of men and that centuries-old enclosure of purity. As anthropologist Mary Douglas says: 'Dirt is matter out of place'; out of the home, in front of the clean order of the military base, these women *were* dirt.

Of course, as with the witch trials there was a salacious interest in sexuality. Sarah Bond was a reporter for the *Daily Express* who went undercover in the Greenham camp. She went around counting lesbians: 'Half the women I lived among at Greenham were lesbians, striding the camp with their butch haircuts boots and boiler-suits. They flaunt their sexuality, boast about it, joke about it.'

Here, the homophobia of *flaunt* is married with the misogyny of *boast*, exposing not so much the reporter's bigotry, but her innate sense of territorial orthodoxy: these are things that should be hidden away, they do not belong in the public sphere.

The residents of Newbury also responded viscerally. They formed an alliance called Ratepayers Against the Greenham Encampment (yes, RAGE), which organised constant vigilante attacks on the women. Dog shit was thrown, pig shit and buckets of maggots; the camp was set ablaze on various occasions. Signs went up in pubs, 'No Peacecampers', and the local Little Chef banned Greenham women, an illegal act that was supported by teams of police officers. Three years into the camp, one local resident organised a plane with a banner to fly across the common, breaking innumerable laws and national security measures, not to mention trespassing the airspace, with no complaint from the police or MOD. The banner, in three short words, surmised the central crux of the horror, the geographical dogma these women had broken: GO HOME GIRLS.

The women of Greenham were resented not for the spells they cast, in song and woven nets, but for the spells they were breaking. Before the women arrived, the camp comprised neat tarmac roads, triplicate fencing and rolls of barbed wire. It was a trance of order that blinded England to the base's devastating potential. Within the perimeter fence was the hardware to destroy half of England, each of Reagan's Peacemakers possessing the destructive capability of sixteen Hiroshima bombs. On top of this, the site itself raised the little Berkshire town of Newbury high on the Kremlin's hit list for strategic retaliation – it was a new bull's-eye for Russian rockets. But somehow, the Apollonian order of the camp was more seemly than the earthy, Dionysian protest against it. By constantly decorating the fence, the women called attention to its presence; by constantly perforating it, they tore holes not just in the fence, but in the matrix that justified it. And by simply being there, the women were breaking the spell of couverture, the spatial politics that kept them enclosed within the household. As Foucault says of heterotopias: 'their role is to create a space of illusion that exposes every real space, all the sites inside of which human life is partitioned, as still more illusory.' They were bursting the property bubble.

In Sipson, the village around the Grow Heathrow camp, the land has been almost entirely consumed by this bubble. In preparation for the third runway, and decades before it was given the green light, Heathrow Airport Holdings, a subsidiary of a private multinational firm called Ferrovial, have been buying up the land across the entire village, offering prices that depreciate with every passing year. By 2012, three-quarters of the village had been bought up and the houses it owns are now either vacant or rented to newcomers on short leases. The village has been ghosted away: crime has increased, the empty houses have been left to decay. Gerald Storr, the local butcher, is quoted in the *Guardian*: 'There's an almost tangible feeling of doom and desolation. People have given up and moved away.' Sipson, or Sibbwineston as it is called in Domesday Book, was a community hub for at least a thousand years before the airport was built. With four other villages it shared rights to the local heath: a web of customs linked the villagers to the land and to each other. But when Harmondsworth Moor was enclosed in 1819, the connections between villages were cut by a fence and a new spell bound the land. And when the first airport was built in 1930, the row of cottages along the heath was elided like the space between the words: Heath Row became Heathrow.

By squatting the land, Grow Heathrow have burst the bubble of 200 years of enclosure. Their ethic of 'positive alternatives' has rewilded the rubbish heap, clearing it of thirty tonnes of industrial waste and using permaculture techniques to re-fertilise the soil. Through workshops, tea dances, music events and green-fingered volunteer work, local residents have come together once again; by digging the earth, they have unearthed the old root systems that connected them to the land – and to each other.

For the first two years of the Greenham women's protest camp, the police were almost powerless to stop them. The evictions they ran were at best misnomers – they removed all the necessary infrastructure for survival, but the women remained. They could arrest protesters for breaching the peace, but only when the women lay in front of the missile carriers and obstructed the daily operations of the military. Because the camp was on common land, the women had every right to be there.

So the laws were changed. With the bang of a judge's hammer, the council revoked the deeds of the common land. The *Observer* reported: 'Previous attempts to evict the women have failed but council officials now believe they have found a way of silencing the politically embarrassing camper, by making anyone who walks on the land a trespasser.' And this is the heart of the matter. At Belvoir Castle, Mr Harrison's protest against the Duke of Rutland was deemed illegal, not because of the substance or style of his protest, but because he didn't own the land. Even though he was on a public Right of Way, his ethical protest was silenced with trespass laws. When the council revoked the deeds to Greenham Common, they removed the women's right to protest, a move justified not by ethics, or danger to society, but by property law.

Only recently have our rights to protest been secured in law. Article 10 of the European Convention for Human Rights (1953) ratifies our right for Freedom of Expression and Article 11 gives us a human right for Freedom of Assembly and Association. However, in England, the laws of private property trump our collective human rights, which means on private land neither of these rights apply.

Terra nullia was one of Emperor Justinian's categories of land ownership, meaning land owned by no one. In England, there is no such thing. Public spaces, whether in towns or the countryside, are all owned. If they are owned by the council, then they have a duty to provide for public protest, but the councils across England have been selling off these spaces to private corporations or individuals, for *improvement*. When the Occupy movement went to protest the banking crisis outside the London Stock Exchange in 2011, they were thrown out of Paternoster Square by the private security guards of Mitsubishi Estate Co., who own the land. Signs went up saying: 'Paternoster Square is private land. Any licence to the public to enter or cross this land is revoked forthwith ... There is no implied or express permission to enter the premises or any part. Any such entry will constitute a trespass.'

London's public spaces have been swiftly sold off to private companies, and the same is happening across the country. Go to Canary Wharf or the Bullring in Birmingham, or Liverpool One, now owned by the Duke of Westminster, and pull out a sign (any sign) and see how long it takes for you to be escorted off the premises, on to a public highway. Even there you might be chased up the street: with a 'stopping-up order' the council may have sold the public right of way to a private developer, removing the right of access and turning the road into a private drive. The Duke of Westminster now owns thirty-four streets in Liverpool city centre. You will have broken no law, you will simply be removed by the mobilicorpus of trespass and if you resist you will be breaching the peace, a charge of such wide, billowing parameters that it also hanged the witches of Belvoir.

In 1985, the then secretary of state Michael Heseltine introduced new by-laws for Greenham Common that upgraded the trespass into the camp to a criminal charge. Heseltine warned that the women could now be shot if they crossed the line. Appropriately enough, the new by-law came into effect on 1 April 1985, April Fool's Day, and was instantly and deliberately contravened by the Greenham women, a hundred of whom were arrested that day. Using the trickster spirit of Anansi, that creative, slippery mindset, the women had inverted the power that was used on them: the new criminal trespass laws could aid their attempts to get their message heard. By dealing with the women on simple trespass charges, they were removed from the land and dealt with in civil court, with no jury or assembly of press. But under criminal charges these women had to go to court, where they could offer their plea, where their opinions would go on record. For this reason, to make sure they were arrested they labelled their bolt-cutters with their names. 'In court,' said the longest resident of the camp, Sarah Hipperson, 'we had to be listened to.'

As a window into the scale of civil disobedience, Hansard recorded a total of 812 trespasses in the fifteen months from January 1987, each breach calculated to expose the flaws not just in the fence, but the legal systems that supported it. And it worked. After a four-year legal battle, the courts ruled that Heseltine had pushed aside a legal constraint in his quest to end the protest – he had acted *ultra vires*, beyond his powers, or, more literally, beyond his manhood. In 1992 the courts ruled that the fence itself had not been erected under ministerial consent and Judge Lait ruled 'the perimeter fence at RAF Greenham Common was unlawful at all relevant times'. The fence was the crime, not the crossing of it.

The last of the Greenham women left the camp in the year 2000. Nineteen years in the mud. They were met with almost universal derision, their protest declared a failure. But in December 1987 Ronald Reagan and Mikhail Gorbachev signed the Intermediate-Range Nuclear Forces Treaty and, two years later, the first missiles left Greenham. Of course, despite Gorbachev specifically referring to the role the Greenham women had played, the world was told that this would have happened anyway, that it was entirely unconnected to this coven of woolly-hatted, woolly-minded protesters. *Of course: you wouldn't want the word getting out.*

In 1986, there were over 70,000 active nuclear weapons in the world; today, there are still 9,000 in active service, with 1,800 ready to fire at a moment's notice. The Greenham women's protest did not fully eliminate the danger of nuclear war, but the silk thread of the Greenham web, the line of resistance as persistence, runs through to the present day. As one of the protesters said: 'Greenham was powerful. It taught my generation about collective action, about protest as spectacle, a way of life … Greenham created an alternative world of unstoppable women.'

In June 2010, two women walked into Tate Britain with ten litres of molasses strapped in rubble sacks to their legs. Wearing long, pretty floral dresses, lipstick and mascara, they walked through the security at a prestigious evening annual event, the Tate Summer Party, all smiles and styles. That year, the party was bigger than ever – more politicians, more canapés, more art-world celebrities and more press: they were celebrating twenty years of sponsorship with British Petroleum. At exactly the same time, 5,000 miles away in the Gulf of Mexico, a total of 201 million US gallons of crude oil was pumping through a leak in BP's oil pipes, as it had been doing, uncorked, for the past two months. When the two women had sipped their first flute of champagne, they walked into the middle of the hall, bent down and, with keys, they cut the sacks of molasses beneath their dresses. Onto the white polished floor flowed the thick black liquid, a secular magic trick that brought the filth of an oil spill right into the heart of the spectacle of order. But more than this, as the guests retreated from the mess, the two women had cleared themselves a rotunda, a space for theatre, a new spectacle of disorder. Before the eyes of the guests and the lenses of the national press, they put on BP-branded plastic ponchos and began cleaning up the mess on their hands and knees, smearing the oil over the polished floor. Don't worry, they said, we're handling this.

This was *Licence to Spill*, the inaugural performance of the newly formed Liberate Tate, an arts and performance collective aiming to end the sponsorship between the Tate and Big Oil. In the following years, they created a variety of performances, each strategically designed to make the news, to broadcast their alternative vision of the Tate's marriage with BP. One of the performers, Mel Evans, went on to write a book called *Art Wash*, which details the relationship of Big Oil with art galleries across the world, describing the techniques they use to normalise their imperialist, colonial, ecologically toxic imperatives, by washing their stains in the clean, Apollonian temples of art galleries. The other performer, Anna Feigenbaum, co-authored a book called *Protest Camps*, which analyses, among others, the techniques and tensions of Greenham Common Women's Peace Camp. To say one action directly influenced the other misses the point of this silver thread of protest: the line extends through time, each action is another node that holds the web taut, each strengthens the other. And this thread continues to this day, in the anti-fracking protests in Preston, with Extinction Rebellion, both of whom use the lock-on techniques of the suffragists, the willingness to get arrested and non-violent direct action to burst the orthodoxy of paternalism.

After six years of persistent resistance by Liberate Tate, BP announced they would no longer be sponsoring the Tate Art Galleries. When asked about the efforts of Liberate Tate, a spokesperson said: 'They are free to express their points of view but our decision wasn't influenced by that. It was a business decision.' *Of course* ...

It is vital for the status quo to appear as if it is the natural order of things, to proclaim the absolute lack of alternatives. The systems that create places such as Greenham Airbase or Heathrow Airport rely on the blank statement of inevitability, fused with the sense of futility in opposing it. A *Daily Mail* article on the Greenham peace camp claimed that 'the women never really came to terms with how to respond to the inevitable'. Horizontal power structures, covens, communities that prioritise listening over telling are repeatedly dismissed as woolly, fanciful, feminine and weak. Doomed to fail. And yet they won the abolition of slavery, the right to vote, the right of gay marriage and just about any other human right that was not given by the lords, but taken by the commoners.

Here in Heathrow, in the dilapidated greenhouse, the light is dimming quickly and everyone else has disappeared, their pots and sculptures lined up on a shelf. Our fingers are waxy-white, frozen bloodless by the slip water we have been smoothing into the clay. As we scrape the table of its residue and sponge it down, Jessica is talking me through the alchemy of turning dirt into clay. When she returns from the site, she tips her sack of soil incrementally into a cauldron of water, into which the clay, with steady stirring, dissolves. She pours the solution through a fine sieve and discards the undissolved soil, leaving a thick filmy liquid, which carries the clay. She hangs this liquid in an upturned pillowcase, letting it drain for days, and then wraps it like fresh cheese in a muslin net, or an old t-shirt, and squeezes the remaining water from it. What remains is a glistening wet terracotta, a material which can be shaped and moulded to hold the creative visions of all that work it, which, when baked in the kiln, will harden into something real. Like the protest camp we stand in, she has reclaimed the earth from its title deeds and transformed it into something new.

Grow Heathrow was issued with eviction orders in 2012. The solicitors of the owners of the property stated: 'while no doubt Grow Heathrow have put in a lot of work in clearing up and improving the site, at the end of the day this gives them no legal right to continue trespassing on the land.' The protesters fought the order, and remained where they were for another seven years until the bailiffs appeared again, several weeks after I had visited the camp. This time, they came armed with the heavy heft of the law, with officers from the Met Police and a helicopter present to 'prevent a breach of the peace'. The day of the eviction just so happened to be the hottest February day ever recorded in England. Half the camp was cleared. And though the protesters simply moved to the other half, whose owners had not yet filed for eviction, it began to look like the construction of Heathrow's third runway was indeed inevitable. The power of the castle had again triumphed over the commons: protest silenced by the uncompromising paternalism of property.

But then, something magical: exactly one year later a court of appeal ruled that the plans for the third runway were 'inconsistent' with the government's commitment to the Paris agreement on climate change. With this ruling, Heathrow's plans for 700 more planes per day no longer just flew in the face of a greener future, they were also now illegal. This was the first major ruling to be based on the Paris agreement and its influence extends beyond Sipson, through England and out across the globe. It sets a precedent for the 194 states that signed the agreement, stating plainly that international climate agreements have a direct bearing on domestic decision-making for all future high-carbon projects. The alternative has been baked into law, the Earth has been transformed.

The case was brought by Plan B, a legal charity that represented a web of different vested interests, including environmental charities, volunteer campaigning groups and residents from various boroughs. At the centre of this web was a place where people could gather, the protest manifested into real space, the living embodiment of the alternatives: Grow Heathrow. But had the bailiffs been successful the first time round, or the second, this new world order could have been scuppered by the owners of a small plot of land in Sipson. It is in this way that control of the land turns into dominion of the Earth. The rights of the community of Sipson and the rights of the community of the planet would have been silenced, as they often are, by the most powerful and exiguous elite on earth: the lords of the land, the landlords.

PHEASANT

Peers, parvenus, perquisites and peasants

A buck or doe, believe it so
A pheasant or a hare
Was put on earth for all who know
Quite equal for to share
— Anonymous, nineteenth-century folk song

The scene opens on the back of a golden retriever trotting faithfully at his master's heels. Ahead of them, just out of focus, is an exotic cedar tree and the great, towering castle. We cut to the interior where, as if by magic, the shutters open on an opulent world, the servants' bell, the silverware, the perfume bottle, the artsy falling rose petal, the careful brushing of the glittering glass of the crystal chandelier. Surging, insistent strings, the welling of irrepressible emotion, underpin a resolute piano motif, a sound that says there's business to be done. The strings poise and the scene resolves into the programme's masthead: the screen is split horizontally, the blue sky and celestial castle above, and below, its reflection, in negative, swathed in blackness. It is a strange, binary vision of heaven and hell, and it reads: Downton Abbey.

Running for six seasons, the television series *Downton Abbey* won a string of prestigious awards and glowed with critical acclaim. Sold to over 220 territories, by 2013 its estimated audience was 120 million. *Downton Abbey* is the newest in a long line of costumed melodrama that reflects the global demand for England's foremost export and principal delusion: class.

The real Downton Abbey is Highclere Castle, in Hampshire, several miles south of Greenham Common. My friend and I enter like guests, through a smart driveway at the north end of the estate. Before it sweeps us round to the London Lodge, we cut off the tarmac onto a grass path through a dark green maze of tightly packed azaleas. The path opens up to a broad lake: 'How scenical! How scenical!' said Benjamin Disraeli when he first came here.

Highclere belongs to the 8th Earl of Carnarvon, George Reginald Oliver Molyneux Herbert. Its 6,500 acres have been in the Carnarvon family for almost 350 years but was first enclosed during medieval times as the official residence for the Bishops of Winchester. When William of Wykeham became bishop in 1366 he created two more deer parks, set up five more fishponds and enclosed the rabbit warrens from the pilfering nets of the local commoners. Confiscated by the Crown, the estate then fell into private hands, and eventually, in 1679, was bought by a wealthy lawyer, Robert Sawyer, the current earl's ancestor. It is now a classic aristocratic estate, with farmland, forestry, a deer park, pheasant runs and an ornate castle at its heart. But for all its ancient heritage, its solid stone structures, it is a mercurial place, where fact dissolves into fiction, and fiction resolves into fact.

The script of *Downton Abbey* reflects much of Highclere's actual history. Both Highclere and Downton were used as a hospital for officers wounded in the First World War. Downton's earl married an American heiress to inject the estate with her fortune. In real life, the Highclere estate was saved from financial ruin by the 5th Earl's marriage to Lady Almina, the illegitimate daughter of Alfred de Rothschild of the American banking dynasty. The banker finally paid off his indiscretion with a $200,000 gift to cover the earl's debts and an $800,000 dowry, much of which the earl took to Egypt to finance the excavation of Tutankhamun's tomb.

In Season 3, Downton Abbey is shocked by a sudden death in the family, forcing them to pay an enormous death tax which threatens to break up the estate. Similarly, in 1923, when the 5th Earl died suddenly of the curse placed on him by the young Egyptian king (or from sepsis from a shaving cut) the increased estate duty imposed by Lloyd George in 1909 almost broke the Highclere estate in two. They were faced with a tax that today would amount to £30 million and, rather than selling land, the biggest taboo in aristocratic estate management, they managed to dig around in the attic and organised a yard sale at Christie's, where they sold a few paintings by Gainsborough and Leonardo.

One of the great themes of *Downton Abbey* is the restrictions and burdens imposed on those with great wealth. Lord Grantham is the paterfamilias and is seen forever wandering the corridors of his castle in a state of pained concern – even when fondling a housemaid in his dressing room, he has a stately anguish to him, constantly exasperated by the bonds of his own innate nobility. On the lord's shoulders lie not just the prosperity of the present, but the twin weight of his lineage: his ancestors and his heirs.

The real Earl of Carnarvon mirrors the sentiment: 'As Julian Fellowes has said in the *Downton* script, you don't want to be the Earl that lets the whole thing down and it all collapses – and that's the thing that really sort of hangs over one a bit.'

Here at Highclere the fantasy of *Downton* has seeped through the veil of fiction and hardened into something real. Before the success of the show, Highclere Castle faced £12 million worth of damage restoration, the roofs, the follies, the relentless pressures of the elements on old stone architecture. Luckily for Lord Carnarvon, the writer of *Downton* sends his kids to the same school as the Carnarvons, and is also one of the club: Julian Fellowes is properly addressed as Lord Fellowes, and even more properly addressed as Baron Fellowes of West Stafford, lord of the manor of Tattershall, Deputy Lieutenant of Dorset. From his head came not only a phenomenally successful TV show, but also a gambit that earns the Highclere estate a reported £1 million per season, and 60,000 tourists a year. Highclere survives on the vision of itself.

The maze of azaleas opens out into long, sloping fields, with large fallen oaks like ossified squids trailing their tentacles across the grass. The fields are bound with low pheasant fences, grids of intersecting wires held taut beneath waist-high wooden struts, a pleasure to climb. We follow the dried ruts of tyre tracks across the fields, following a young fallow deer, which is bolting around trying desperately to find a way through the fences. She leads us up the slope where she butts against the boundary and finally finds some loosely slung barbed wire to scrape through, where she disappears into the beechwoods. The top of the slope is the perimeter of the standard-issue Capability Brown landscaped parkland, those famous Lebanon cedar trees, and there, rising above the treetops, is our first sight of Downton Abbey.

Highclere Castle is the twin of the Houses of Parliament. It has the same Bath stone and decorative ashlar flourishes and was designed by the same architect, Charles Barry, three years into his commission to rebuild the seat of government. Like all the great houses so far in this book, like Badminton, Boughton, Belvoir, Basildon, Charborough, Fonthill and Arundel, its design communicates both classical splendour, the touch of God, and also, very clearly, an aristocratic authority upon the land it controls. Lady Carnarvon talks with fondness of the tourists that come to the estate: 'They turn up here, and get so excited there's a real Earl and Countess.' But what exactly is real about the aristocracy?

On the surface, the aristocracy seems to be a form of cosplay for hereditary landowners, a subculture of adults titillated by their own fancy dress. It is obsessed with fashion. The monarch doesn't invent new hereditary titles, she 'fashions' them; likewise, you are not made a lord, you are 'styled'. At the queen's coronation in 1953, the moment the archbishop placed the crown on her head, the dukes, and the dukes alone, were also allowed to put on their hats – their coronets. They were wearing robes with four bands of ermine stitched in diagonals down their front, while, further away, the earls remained hatless, with only three ermine bands on their chest. The earls have coronets, too, and on them they are entitled to eight strawberry leaf motifs and eight silver balls. But this sartorial peacockery is the foliage of a much deeper rooted ideology, one that encapsulates everything from knightly honour codes to the later Victorian regulations of cutlery spacing. In Season 4 of *Downton Abbey*, Julian Fellowes coins a beautiful phrase to describe it: 'conforming to the fitness of things'. *Vanity Fair*, in describing the *Downton* series, puts it just as neatly: 'we are whisked into a world that is distinctly based upon the sanctity of the done thing.' The nobility operates on a system of manners.

The concept of a superior class of human predated William the Conqueror. The Anglo-Saxons had their eorls, ceorls, gesiths and thegns, each elevated above the other in proportion to the land they owned. A set of status regulations from the early eleventh century, the *Textus Roffensis*, states that if a ceorl prospered and he 'possessed fully five hides of land of his own, a bell and a castle-gate, a seat and special office in the King's hall', then he was entitled to the rights of a thegn.

But when William invaded England, the 4,000 or so thegns were wiped from power and replaced by 180 of William's closest mercenary allies, the barons. A new hierarchy of French nouns was imposed: the barons, then the viscounts, the marquises and the dukes. The only remaining Germanic title was earl, which was kept to divert the crass minds of the English, and is a lasting legacy that the English were not always so bewitched by their betters. Geoffrey Hughes, Professor of the History of the English Language in Johannesburg, explains: 'It is a likely speculation that the Norman French title "count" was abandoned in England in favour of the Germanic "earl" ... precisely because of the uncomfortable phonetic proximity to cunt.'

The numbers of nobility swelled as successive kings bought new allegiances. The land that now belonged entirely to the Crown was parcelled off and attached to titles that the kings plucked (fashioned) from their heads. When the barons forced King John to sign Magna Carta, they secured more power and autonomy than anyone before them. They had continued in the spirit of the *Textus Roffensis*, as self-anointed fathers of their flock, and with their church bell and castle gate they offered both spiritual and protective *couvert* to their tenants. In exchange, they expected a tithe of the land's produce and military allegiance to their own private army. England became a collection of principalities, like the Roman concept of Latifundia, private estates run by slaves (in England, serfs) that were entirely self-sufficient. Against the king's orders, some even minted their own currency.

Just as Highclere survives on its own illusion, so the nobility of the Middle Ages based their hierarchies on fairy tales. Chivalry was the governing ideology of French romance literature and when Edward III set up the Order of the Knights of the Garter, he did so to emulate the bedtime stories he had heard of Arthur and his knights. This feedback loop between real and unreal continues to this day: when the queen's third son married, he was honoured with an earlship and decided to 'style' himself Earl of Wessex, a region that no longer exists but that was inspired by his admiration for a character invented by Tom Stoppard for the film *Shakespeare in Love*.

Amid this make-believe there were some real-life perks. Up until 1949, a peer of the realm could only be tried by a jury of his peers, that is, other peers – no commoner was allowed to pass judgment on his actions. A peer could not be arrested for debt and bankruptcy and, up until 1711, nor could his servants. They alone had the right to sue against slander and, like a special offer coupon cut from junk mail, they got free postage.

We have hopped the fence of the private park and found our way to a road leading past the castle and on to the chapel. William Cobbett galloped through this estate in 1821 and praised it as 'the prettiest park that I have ever seen. A great variety of hill and dell. The house I did not care about, though it appears to be large enough to hold half a village.' This is a sly, Cobbetty reference to the village of Highclere which was uprooted and forcibly cleared in 1774 to make way for the earl's house and private gardens. This old style of power, the landlord as warlord, has waned with the relatively recent fad for human rights. Aristocrats no longer get free postage, and all other real-life privileges have been abolished – but still the aristocracy, like a phantom limb, triggers the nervous system of the English. And still the question remains: what does it all mean?

I found the answer in the bookshop of another aristocratic estate, Hatfield House, the seat of Lord Salisbury. Optimistically titled *Democracy Needs Aristocracy*, the book was written by *Daily Telegraph* journalist, and quasi-aristocrat, Peregrine Worsthorne, and is a defence of aristocratic values in the modern age. The book is a masterclass of self-delusion: like a papier-mâché balloon made from wet newspaper, it pastes reams of words around a concept that is nothing more than hot air. But as Andrew Marr says on the front cover: *it is compelling*.

The key to the aristocracy is in its name. From the Greek *ἄριστος* and *κράτος*, it means 'rule by the best' and the twinned concepts are crucial to comprehending the vision. The aristocracy is a governing class that emerged out of military conquest of other nations (including England) and has been deeply embedded in the judicial framework of the land since the Middle Ages. The House of Lords evolved from the king's closest advisers, the Magnum Concilium, the consigliere to their mob boss. For Worsthorne, the principal justification for their influence on the laws of the land was their experience of managing their own personal fiefdoms. Second to this were the trappings of privilege – by being subjected to the best education they were better suited to high-minded thinking. In the absence of having to work for a living, they were able to spend their days leafing through ancient tracts or walking their estates engaged in blithe philosophical thought. The third justification is a French term: *noblesse oblige*. The aristocrat is brought up in an atmosphere that makes him profoundly aware of his own social responsibility, both towards his estate and by extension his nation. Worsthorne quotes Viscount de Tocqueville, the nineteenth-century social historian and descendant of Norman nobility: 'He willingly imposes duties on himself towards the former and the latter, and he will frequently sacrifice his own personal gratifications to those who went before and to those who will come after him.'

This is the reason Lord Grantham paces the corridors of Downton with knitted brow, and the same thing 'that sort of really hangs' over the Earl of Carnarvon. Heavy lies the head that wears the coronet. *Noblesse oblige* is the core concept of the aristocracy, which sees the hereditary lineage of power as its own justification. However, Worsthorne is aware of the dissonance this has with the concept of suffrage:

Most certainly it was not the most democratic way to fashion a governing class. For by linking the widespread desire to acquire local status to the performance of public duties and the upholding of professional values, it almost guaranteed and legitimised the continuation of hierarchy and social inequality. So if equality of access is to be regarded as essential for any morally acceptable system of recruitment into the political elite, this old way definitely does not pass that test. But judged by whether it serves the public interest by producing a regular supply of top rank politicians, public servants and professionals, did it pass that test?

He's being serious. Worsthorne's phrase 'equality of access' is the bridge between the concepts of privilege of class and rights to the land. He goes on to discuss the philosophy of public schools such as Eton and, just down the road from Highclere, Winchester: 'They went on being taught to regard the governance of England as their personal responsibility and to believe that if they did not set an example of civilised standards of behaviour, then the country would go to pot … the ethics of public service bred into the marrow of their bones.'

Eton was originally established in 1440 as a charity school to provide free education to seventy poor boys. Its founder Henry VI based it on Winchester School, which was set up by Highclere's own William of Wykeham fifty years earlier. Again, it was constructed to provide education for seventy poor boys, hand-selected because of their aptitude. Today, fees at Eton are now almost £13,000 per term, and at Winchester £400 more. But with the phrase 'bred into the marrow of their bones' the aristocracy suddenly lurches from a quaint daydream to something altogether more chilling. This is eugenics, in top hat and tails.

The aristocratic vision of England is a system of layered supremacy: provided each order defers to its superior tier, England remains in perfect harmony. And just as with the witch trials in Rutland or the slave colonies in Barbados, the deepest roots of this self-deception lie in the pretence of the greater good. Worsthorne speaks of 'the bonds of mutual sympathy and respect that should naturally exist between rich and poor, governors and governed' – that devotion of the faithful hound, trotting at his master's heels at the start of every *Downton* episode. Subordination to the higher class of person is as essential as it is natural. One of the mechanisms of this system is nostalgia, a harking back to when times were more peaceful, that Grand Olde Englande where people knew their place. Lord Fellowes again: 'I love that faith in the institutions. And I don't think we really have that any more. We don't think our leaders shine in that way.'

But did we ever? This notion of the acquiescent nation is a self-regarding fantasy, a vision in the mirror the aristocracy hold to themselves that blocks from their view the entire landscape of working-class history. And here on the borders of Berkshire and Hampshire, this seems particularly short-sighted.

We are trawling our way through long grass beside dark coniferous timber forests and long sweeping cornfields. We pass blue plastic bins raised on stilts, feeders for the pheasants, and wide metal ladders that lead up trees to the sighting perches. The place is teeming with pheasants; they stream along the paths before us and every so often one suddenly flusters out of the bushes like an adulterous duke, escaping the paparazzi with his trousers round his ankles.

The shooting here is about as prestigious as it gets. It's a social occasion, with luxurious accommodation, grand dinners and a liberal approach to daytime boozing, but its core ethic remains the noisy elimination of pheasants, with each day judged according to the amount of bodies in the bag. A photograph still stands in the Highclere shooting office of King Edward VII who visited the estate in 1904: he shot 1,600 pheasant in just fifteen minutes. But just like the fox of horseback hunting, the pheasant has symbolic meaning. As Harry Hopkins states in his account of the poaching wars in England: 'The gentry in many parts of England began to look jealously upon their pheasant as the very essence of that property principle upon which the political philosopher John Locke had shown English liberty to be founded.'

The pheasant represented the rights of a landowner because by rearing the birds, and feeding them, they were symbols of the work he put into his estate. But to the commoners, the pheasant represented nothing more than a full belly. As with the fox in the Pierson v. Post case, the pheasant had come to represent a wider battle of property rights, a debate whose fulcrum lay, like trespass, precisely on the line of the fence.

Hunting was the original source of the cult of exclusion. As soon as William the Conqueror forested the lands, the ancient tradition of working-class hunting became redefined as poaching. Simultaneously, the food the working class relied on was redefined as 'game', the objects of a moneyed pastime. The Game Acts of the Middle Ages commanded the 'lawing' of the peasants' hunting dogs, the wolfhounds and lurchers. 'Lawing' was the term given to chiselling off the front toes of the dog, turning a machine of working-class subsistence into a lame pet. Following the Game Act passed by Richard II, game became the property of the owner of the land. But when Charles II returned to England, resolved to install law and order onto the population that had chopped off his father's head, he passed another Game Act in 1671 that redefined the 'qualification' to hunt. To shoot a pheasant you now had to be an owner of land worth £100 per year, or hold a ninety-nine-year lease on land worth £150. You needed fifty times more land to shoot a pheasant than to vote in local elections.

Property had now developed into what lawyers call a 'bundle of rights' – when you bought land, you bought a collection of rights connected to it, the rights to mine its minerals, lop its trees and hunt its game, which were called its 'perquisites'. Perquisites were the perks of property, the itemised benefits of land ownership, and, because the law had now categorised them as separate entities from the land, they could be sold or rented as individual commodities. By the early seventeenth century, these rights were being leased, as they are today, to City types: merchants, bankers, lawyers and army officers, the squirearchy who would bring down fashionable sporting parties to hunt at the weekends. The majority of tenant farmers who were forbidden by law to shoot a rabbit for their supper now had to watch as the squires came onto the land they worked to kill hundreds of them for sport. But, contrary to Lord Fellowes' vision of a harmonious England, their resentment was never far from the surface.

By the end of the seventeenth century, the forest wardens of the Middle Ages had mutated into gamekeepers, employed in great numbers as private security guards to patrol their masters' fences. Poaching had become a quiet, moonlit occupation. Poachers sneaked into estates and with a variety of techniques, netting, coursing, baiting, shooting with crossbows or longbows, they bagged the pheasants in silence. They slid them into deep jacket pockets and took them home, either for the pot or to sell at the local public houses, which had become a marketplace for the black economy.

But at the start of the eighteenth century, fuelled by the civil unrest of commoners across Hampshire and Berkshire, the silence of poaching transformed into a brash, violent protest for equal rights. In broad daylight, hordes of men and women would cross the fences, on horseback or on foot, and devastate the deer stock of local manor parks, taking some home, but leaving, like foxes in the henhouse, most of the carcasses strewn in blood on the plains. Some men wore women's clothes during the attacks, and because many smudged their faces with charcoal, they were known as 'the Blacks'.

At long last the aristocracy had what they had always feared: an organised network of sedition. All around Highclere, Enfield Chase, Waltham Chase, Caversham Park, Bagshot Heath, groups of working-class men and women swore oaths of allegiance upon the stag horns of the chimney of the local pubs. They were led by a fictitious character named King John, whose name would underscore the threats and notices they left for the gentry, nailed to the trees of the estates. They branched out from poaching to hijacking and freeing wrongly accused men on the way to the gallows, destroying fishponds, reacting to any breach of their self-construed notion of liberty. When John Trelawney became the Bishop of Winchester in 1707, he began his tenure by auditing his land: he found his woodland coppiced by the commoners, his farms undervalued and his deer stock depleted. When he announced he would restore the 'Bishopric's lost rights', sixteen Blacks invaded the episcopal deer park at Farnham, took three deer and left behind several carcasses — including that of a keeper.

In a justice system dominated by the power of property, where the right to vote was restricted to those with property, where the right to represent was determined by property, where the justice establishments, from the common courts right up to the House of Lords, were governed by men of property, the Blacks were fighting fire with fire. They brought their own philosophy of ownership, the shared rights of the commons, up against the aristocratic, hereditary cult of exclusion, which had reified these rights into the sources of personal profit. Both sides were willing to kill for their rights. But while the Blacks used longbows, the aristocrats used the law.

The Black Act of 1723 introduced fifty new capital offences across the land. For though they were concentrated in only two counties, the Blacks were labelled a national emergency. The land they invaded was owned by royalty and prominent members of the Whig government and, as such, their protests were judged not just as a threat to private hereditary landowners, but to the order of the nation. They were described as Jacobites, terrorist cells seeking to topple the king. The Act was supposed to be a temporary measure, but lasted for another century: the law had stepped resolutely over the fence to defend the interests of a tiny elite over the majority of people outside the enclosure. And there it has stayed.

We have come out of the pheasant rides onto a tarmac road. A ruined folly stands at the foot of a steep wooded slope and to our left are fields of scattered sheep, the tops of trees and the turrets of Highclere. We begin climbing the slope, heading diagonally across the steep hill to the tree line when we hear the low engine of a 4x4 approaching. The cover of the woods is only fifty yards away so we scramble, running on all fours up the hill, to enter the woods and sit, hearts thumping, as the truck rolls by. We continue up through the woods and come to a crest of chest-high feathery grass, glowing gold in the sun. A path has been mown through the long grass and, as we progress up it, we see the triangle pinnacle of Highclere's most imposing folly: Heaven's Gate, another of Capability Brown's concoctions. Either side of us the pheasants rustle the undergrowth, occasionally and needlessly exploding into the air with wild, terrified eyes.

The three-storey brick folly, a large arch with two smaller flanking arches, and two urns either side of its pediment, emerges through the tops of the trees. We walk towards it, stand beneath it and turn to survey the view. From our toes to the horizon, Hampshire is laid out before us, a sea of woodland with the castle deep at its centre. The air is light and crisp. The sky is pinky peach; the sun has just set. We breathe deeply from the climb, inhaling the peace of the scene, drinking in its calm. I am reminded of philosopher Edmund Burke's definition of the aristocracy:

> To be bred in a place of estimation; to see nothing low and sordid from one's infancy ... to stand upon such elevated ground as to be enabled to take a large view of the widespread and infinitely diversified combinations of men and affairs in a large society; to have leisure to read, to reflect, to converse; to be enabled to draw on the attention of the wise and learned, wherever they are to be found ... these are the circumstances of men that form what I call a natural aristocracy, without which there is no nation.

Beneath the arches of Heaven's Gate, bathed in soft light, this is the aristocracy's vision of England: glorious and empty. To the west and east of the estate, we can see the roads choked with traffic, the lower orders crawling home from work. They are the modern-day descendants of the communities that were cleared from the land, the commoners forced from self-subsistence into the workhouse. They are reminders of the other side of the aristocratic myth, the black inverse of the *Downton* masthead: the classification of the lower orders that reaches its most extreme bigotry in the myth of the undeserving poor.

Those who share the aristocratic empty workless day are labelled not aesthetes, but idle benefit scroungers, who bleed England of its wealth. It is a fiction as old as enclosure and stands, like its walls, to this day. In 2012 the former Archbishop of Canterbury, Lord Carey, described the welfare system as: 'an industry of gargantuan proportions which is fuelling those very vices [Want, Disease, Ignorance, Squalor and Idleness] and impoverishing us all. In the worst-case scenario it traps people into dependency and rewards fecklessness and irresponsibility.'

The land beneath me is what England's welfare system used to look like. With its old community-based customs, it offered a winter fuel allowance and food banks without the stigma of social shame. When these lands were enclosed, self-subsistence was criminalised into poaching, and common ground, like the welfare state today, was presented as a nursery of idleness. The words of an Elizabethan surveyor in Rockingham, just before the outbreak of the Midland Revolt, echo Lord Carey's sentiments, and predate them by half a millennium: 'So long as they may be permitted to live in such idleness upon their stock of cattle they will bend themselves to no kind of labour.'

'You must work for a living,' proclaim the nobility (from the chaise longue). In the Middle Ages, under a French concept of *dérogeance* the nobility were actively punished, demoted, for taking part in any kind of labour, and the idea that work dirtied one's day, which was better spent in contemplation, or sport, lasted well into the nineteenth century. As they avoided work, they also compulsively avoided tax, as John Wade wrote in 1820, in an exposé of the aristocracy called the *Black Book*,

Or, Corruption Unmasked: 'Instead of bearing the burthen of tax-ation, which in fact is the original tenure on which they acquired their territorial possessions, have laid it on the people.'

The aristocracy have always lobbied hard against taxation, from demanding lower window tax to actively stifling progressive taxation on the nation. When Chancellor Lloyd George presented the People's Budget of 1909, with the stated intent of redistrib-uting wealth through the nation, the House of Lords bucked 200 years of tradition and blocked it. The Liberals had sought, for the first time, to introduce a tax on the value of the land. They reasoned that, so long after enclosure, it was too late to redis-tribute the actual plots of land, but that they could instead redis-tribute the wealth that had been enclosed with it; as their official pamphlet that began the campaign stated, this was 'the best use of the land in the interests of the community'. The initial proposal for the tax represented just 0.3 per cent of the total tax burden, but for the Lords it was a trespass on the cult of exclusion, a step too far. They rejected the budget by 350 votes to 75.

Today, many large country houses, including Highclere, have negotiated tax deals with HMRC, swapping hidden inheritance tax breaks for limited, or 'reasonable', rights of access to the land they stole. It is unfortunate for HMRC that their arrangement with Highclere even reads like a deal with the devil: *Unique ID: 666* details the arrangement between the tax office and the castle, including the opening of Path 3, between Easter and the end of August, from the Wayfarers Walk up to Heaven's Gate. The public are granted access, but the taxpayer foots the bill. On top of this, aristocrats, like many other landowners, have registered their land to businesses based offshore: today, Lord Salisbury has 2,000 acres of his land in Hatfield registered in Jersey-based companies.

But still the aura of magnificence wreaths their world. And sitting beneath the folly, on Lord Carnarvon's hill, the

magic trick is unveiled. In a study of the landscape architecture of Capability Brown, John Phibbs uses Heaven's Gate as
an example of what he calls 'transumption'. This is the effect
of magical architecture: to infiltrate one site with the aura of
another, to be Greece, or Rome, or Heaven itself, and yet still to
be in Hampshire. 'Brown's early work can create this dream-like
state of dissociation, his park wall confining not just deer but a
vision, like a precious gas, more dense around the house, and
steadily diffusing as it spreads, but likely to burn off against the
touch of reality.'

These follies, the sculpted parkland, the crate-imported
pheasants, the near-empty houses, are props in theatre sets
constructed to create the aura of natural supremacy. *Downton
Abbey*, with all its awards and fine acting, is another perfumed
spritz of precious gas that sedates the nation into acquiescence.
The aristocrats who tread the boards of this stage, dressed in
costumes of ermine, enact a pantomime drama based on a fairy
tale. As the nineteenth-century essayist Walter Bagehot said in
support of the monarchy: 'Its mystery is its life. We must not
let in daylight upon magic.' Decorative pomp and verbose
flummery is all that disguises the bare basics of the aristocratic
wealth system – land enclosed, resources monopolised and rights
of use sold back to those that can afford them. Let the daylight in
on the magic, and you have nothing but basic rentier capitalism.

Today, a third of Britain is still owned by the aristocracy.
The twenty-four remaining non-royal dukes own almost four
million acres between them. There are 191 earls, 115 viscounts
and 435 barons, and most are still significant landowners. In 2016
the fourteen marquises received just over £3.5 million worth of
farm subsidies for their 100,000 acres while seventeen of the
dukes who received farm subsidies got £8.4 million between
them. Unlike the welfare benefits to those most in need, these
farm subsidies are neither means-tested nor capped. Today the

perquisites of land ownership have multiplied from basic rent of rights into tax avoidance and subsidies from the state. The Common Agricultural Policy (CAP) costs UK taxpayers around £3.8 billion per year and, with these subsidies linked to the number of acres owned, it is often the richest landowners who receive the largest benefits. The writer and activist George Monbiot suggests that the reason these benefits are considered more acceptable than the welfare benefits given to the poorest of our community is because, 'After being brutally evicted from the land through centuries of enclosure, we have learned not to go there – even in our minds. To engage in this question feels like trespass, though we have handed over so much of our money that we could have bought all the land in Britain several times over.'

Travelling in England after the First World War, the German bishop Dr Dibelius wrote: 'the English gentleman will always rule because he has captured the soul of the people.' But this is precious gas. It was never the soul of the people he had captured but simply the value of their land.

We're sitting in the Packhorse Inn, just north of Hebden Bridge in Yorkshire. There's a dark moor outside, a full moon shining through the window, a coal fire in the hearth and I'm telling my friend the story of the Rufford Park poachers, the folk song that starts this chapter.

All among the gorse to settle scores
These forty gathered stones
To make a fight for poor men's rights
And break those keepers' bones.

In 1851, a group of forty men trespassed onto Rufford Park estate, 18,500 acres of Nottinghamshire owned by John Lumley-Savile, 8th Earl of Scarbrough. The estate was so large it incorporated thirteen parishes and thousands of villagers, none of whom were able to hunt anywhere in the vicinity. From the large number in their group, it's safe to assume they were not there for poaching, but for payback: they went looking for a fight. Ten keepers blocked their path. There was a violent battle, during which one of the keepers had his skull shattered and died. Four of the ringleaders were arrested, tried and transported overseas for fourteen years' hard labour.

By the middle of the eighteenth century, the Blacks had all been hanged or transported. But over the following century the violence of working-class protest and the urgency of their predicament only intensified. Between 1750 and 1860, over 4,000 individual applications of enclosure were passed by government and, according to historian J. M. Neeson, this accounted for a third of the English agricultural land now in private hands. In 1773, a year before the village of Highclere was cleared by Lord Carnarvon, George III had passed a new enclosure act that simultaneously hastened the procedure of enclosure and criminalised the rights of commoners. In 1811, the Luddites had begun smashing up the new automated looms, in 1815 there were riots against the new Corn Laws, four years later came the Peterloo Massacre and, in 1830, the Swing Riots were spreading across the south and east of England, with groups of men and women scuppering the threshing machines that had stolen their jobs. It was not just enclosure being protested, but its effects – the mechanisation of industry, the monopoly of the corn trade, the funnelling of the working class into factories and workhouses, the hollowing of the countryside, the decimation of community.

Since the sixteenth century, the earls of Scarbrough were also in possession of much of Calderdale, which by the nineteenth century included the moor outside the Packhorse Inn. By this time, the aristocracy had been swamped by a new breed of land-owner, the mercantile classes, the parvenus, whose industry and colonial trade had amassed them fortunes to rival the old families of England. The moor outside the Packhorse Inn, Walshaw Moor, managed to keep its noble bloodline unblemished until 2002, when it was bought by a local retail tycoon called Richard Bannister. Three years later, he bought the adjoining Lancashire Moor, establishing his sole domain over 16,000 acres of the Calder Valley. He immediately set about improving the land, upping the yield of grouse from 100 brace to 3,000, industrialising the land as he had done the trouser industry. In doing so, Walshaw Moor became the new centre of an ancient debate: how should land be used, and whose decision is it?

It's closing time, and suddenly we're out in the cold car park, facing the moor. It is vast and dark. We feel as if we're standing on the shore of an ocean. We stock up on extra layers, cheese sandwiches and whisky, lock the car, hope very much we'll see it again and head out.

Every year, thirty-five million partridge and pheasant are released into the estates of England, twice the biomass of the nation's wild birds. Of those, Defra estimate that half are bred like factory-farmed chickens, trapped in colony cages of about sixty to eighty birds, giving them less room than a sheet of A4 paper. While basic welfare regulations exist for farmed birds, they do not apply to any bird reared for 'use in competitions, shows, cultural or sporting events or activities'. Pheasant shooting is the English equivalent of the South African 'canned shooting' where big game is kept in cages until the day of the hunt, when it staggers out into the plains to be shot by big-barrelled money men. Pheasants are decorative supermarket chickens slaughtered by firing squad.

Grouse shooting, however, is billed as the 'Formula One of game sports', drenched in adrenaline and machismo. It's *wild*. The red grouse is native to the uplands, used to the weather, and goes like shit off a shovel. In flight the grouse can reach speeds of 70mph: they fly low and turn fast, and because they offer the best shooting they are hailed as the king of gamebirds. But their wildness is a fantasy.

The record for the most grouse bagged in a single day is 2,929 birds; they were shot in 1915 on the Abbeystead estate, now owned by the Duke of Grosvenor. More typically, in the present day, you might expect to bring down between 75 and 150 brace (a duo of grouse) from a day's shooting. As with pheasants, a good grouse moor is judged by the quantity of corpses in the bag. As such, these wild and remote lands have become a production line for live quarry. England has just 15 per cent of the total landmass of Britain devoted to grouse shooting, but still manages to account for almost half of the 450,000 grouse exterminated each year. So, since the Victorian age, the rough heather of the moors has become home to a host of intensive farming techniques, designed to improve its yield.

The grouse are bred in such numbers that their colonies are vulnerable to infection: parasites in their gut often wipe out swathes of the population, so the moors are littered with birdfeeders containing grey pellets of levamisole hydrochloride, a short-term fix that lasts forty-eight hours. Other estates prefer a more direct approach and keepers drive onto the moor at nights, daze the birds in powerful spotlights, net them and force the medication down their throats with syringes.

We have entered the moor through an old iron gate that has the same haunted-house atmosphere as the gates in the first shot of *Citizen Kane*, with the slow pan over the 'No Trespassing' signs.

But for the last two decades the spell of trespass has been lifted from these moors. Since the Countryside Rights of Way Act of 2000, all moorland in England has been opened to a right of access. You cannot camp here, but you can walk wherever and whenever you like. But our right to roam was only one of the common rights that was extinguished by enclosure. For when the fences went up around common land, commoners lost not only their access but their rights to contribute to a collective decision on how it was used.

The wind is like thunder up here and bullies us relentlessly. We veer for cover and cut off the tarmac path, heading up a steep path of green cut between the heather. Our feet bounce on the ground making our steps elastic and exaggerated, as if we haven't quite found our sea legs. We are walking on a specific formation of sphagnum moss known as blanket bog, layers of hairy green sponge that have felted into peat beneath the surface. A third of all grouse moors in England, about 250,000 acres, is covered in this rarest of habitats, which is protected by the highest level of stewardship in the EU. Professor Joseph Holden, an expert in peat bogs, states: 'In the UK we have 13 per cent of the world's blanket bogs. Globally, peatlands are more important than tropical rainforest in terms of taking carbon out of the atmosphere.'

These bogs have blanketed the moors since the end of the Ice Age, when the trees there had been cleared for grazing by Bronze Age settlers. Over millennia they have absorbed the carbon in the atmosphere, which now lies densely packed beneath our feet in 'carbon sinks'. However, every year, these moors are systematically burned to increase the yield of new green shoots on the heather. Grouse can eat up to 50 grams of heather shoots a day, and to keep up with the prodigious productivity of these moors the growth of heather must be maximised in its efficiency. But the burning destroys the sphagnum moss and dries out the peat, turning the carbon sinks into a carbon source: the damage done to these peatlands in England releases 260,000 tonnes of carbon back into the atmosphere every year, the equivalent emissions of 88,000 average-sized saloon cars.

The government's environmental agency Natural England first launched a case against Richard Bannister and Walshaw Moor in 2010. Burning this rare eco habitat is somehow still perfectly legal, but Natural England judged Bannister's 'improvements' to be far more extensive than was permitted by their previous Notice of Consent to Lord Savile. They sought to modify the Notice of Consent and simultaneously launched a case against him for his adaptations to the moor. It wasn't just the burning. In total there were forty-three listed claims, mainly referring to damage done to the wildlife by installing illegal infrastructure – gripping (digging drainage), and the installation of five new car parks and five new tracks, to better facilitate Mr Bannister's guests as they are driven around the moors. This is called *moorland management*.

Walshaw Moor fought back. Richard Bannister sent Natural England a claim for £31.8 million compensation if the modification order was found to be unjust. He was supported by the Moorland Association, a pin-striped iteration of the Knights of the Garter, who were anxious that this might serve as a test case for the other areas of blanket bog that cover grouse moors: it was a threat to productivity. Selections of their lobbying emails and details of their dinners with the then Defra under-secretary MP Richard Benyon were published in Mark Avery's book *Inglorious*: 'Suggestions of readdressing the basis of existing agri-environmental schemes and whether heather burning should be allowed on blanket bog and wet heath has the potential to destroy two thirds of heather moorland in

England and with it, all the mammoth economic and environmental benefits!!'

Then, out of nowhere, Natural England dropped its claim
against Walshaw Moor. Before the scientific evidence had been
presented, they settled out of court with Walshaw Estates Ltd.
Over a period of the next ten years, the taxpayer will now pay
Richard Bannister a total of £2.5 million to keep to agreements
that we know nothing about. This is called *higher level stewardship*.

All around us, the moor seethes and bristles with wind. The
sky is overcast, but the wind is so strong it moves the cloud like
smoke from a burning stack – it lathers over the moon, masking
and revealing it so that down below the earth flashes and strobes
and seems to surge like the heavy swell of the ocean. We find a
broad slab of rock and clamber up onto it to sit like shipwreck
survivors, floating on the swaying wrath of heather. The air is
thick with moisture, beading on our jackets, and beneath us the
moor is a sea of woven roots, thatched tendrils and spongy wet
woollen moss that is laden with water. The whole landscape
heaves with hydraulic power.

George Winn-Darley is the head contact for the North York
Moors sector of the Moorland Association. He inherited a 7,000-
acre grouse moor in 1986 and is as integrated into the powerful
cabal of land ownership as a man might be. He has sat on Defra's
Best Practice Burning Group, was chairman and vice-chairman
of the CLA's (Country Landowners' Association) Yorkshire
branch, and is currently trustee/director of Yorkshire Esk Rivers
Trust – we met him before in chapter two kicking a hunt sabo-
teur in the chest. He has declared moors to be 'the only unsubsidised upland land use on offer'. It is unclear what he means by
unsubsidised. In 2014, then chancellor George Osborne raised
the subsidy given to moorland by 84 per cent, from £30 per hec-
tare to £56, while, two years earlier, the total annual subsidies

awarded to land used for grouse shooting was £17.3 million. Winn-Darley goes on to say:

> It's all dependent on the moors' amazing attraction to men with money. Rich men have always fallen in love with them, be they nineteenth century industrialists or modern City types. They bring their wealth to these wild places and it trickles down the valleys like rain, supporting jobs in hotels, garages and helping keep the culture of the moorlands alive.

Grouse shooting is presented by the lobby groups as the only commercially viable means of maintaining a grouse moor, a rhetorical hall of mirrors, which is like saying golf is the only way of keeping a golf course running. This is the old Tudor justification of land improvement, the idea that by privatising land you can better serve the community through the increased production and distribution of wealth. It trickles down from on high.

But Hebden Bridge sees very little of the wealth of the Walshaw estate. Richard Bannister doesn't charge for shooting, but keeps his moor for friends and business associates. They are wined, dined and boarded at the lodge on the estate and, other than the seven full-time keepers, day rates for beaters and a bit of diesel at the petrol station, it's hard to see where the wealth is distributed, not to mention what value the taxpayer receives from its subsidies. Here in Hebden, what descends from the moors is not money but rain, and it doesn't trickle, it gushes. In the last twenty years, Hebden has been engulfed in six serious floods. On Boxing Day 2015, more than 3,000 homes were flooded: cars were submerged, people evacuated by helicopter and rescuers kayaked down the streets.

The residents of Hebden link the floods to the management of the moors above them. The Moorland Association disagree, claiming to be 'fully engaged with doing all that can be done through consensus and innovation to help flood alleviation, but even with every inch restored to active blanket bog (which may or may not be possible and will take a long time), the help this will add to the needed suite of flood mitigation in the North of England is limited'.

No one rejects the notion that burning the bog reduces its capability to hold water, but the arguments flare over how much it affects the scale of the flooding. A 2016 study found a direct correlation between the burning of blanket bogs and an increase in the peak flow of water down in Hebden. Any arrangement of burn patches on Walshaw increased the peak flow by 2.5–5 per cent, enough to tip the surge over the floodgates. Rather than limiting the burning, the findings of this study showed that all burning should be categorically banned.

In 2016 Walshaw Moor Ltd resumed its burning. Damages paid to the residents for flood repair totalled about a fifth of the money promised to Richard Bannister in the out-of-court settlement for his Higher Stewardship of the moor. A further £8 million of taxpayers' money has been allocated to build defences across the Calder Valley, building walls that protect the houses of Hebden from flooding, and obscure Mr Bannister's role in its cause.

The community at Hebden Bridge has been fighting the moor for years. When Mark Avery's petition to ban grouse hunting reached 100,000 signatures, forcing a debate in Parliament, the single largest area of signatures came from Hebden. They have set up a community group called 'Ban the Burn', which has taken its complaints direct to the EU to launch another case against Walshaw Moor, for burning land protected under their directives. And they are not just fighting, they are planting. Twenty-five years ago they launched a group called 'Treesponsibility', initially a pub-table group to discuss concerns about the environment. In the following two decades, its members began to focus on tree planting in the area, a direct move to thwart climate change and to mitigate the effects of flooding. Hundreds of people gather to plant twelve acres of woodland every year, binding the ground with roots to intercept the rainwater, and connecting the community in activities that have visible outcomes.

Yet no matter how hard they campaign, and how many trees they plant, they are constantly thwarted by the cult of exclusion and its central hallucination: dominion. The laws of property pretend that whatever lies within the fence line is entirely unconnected to the land and communities outside it, as if ecology can be partitioned with a neat line. Floodwater doesn't obey these legal fictions. Nor does the wind that in the early nineteenth century carried the pollution from the coal-burning Lancashire mills and dropped it, as acid rain, on the uplands of Calderdale, scouring it into bare peatland. Like the communities in Hampshire and Berkshire, fenced off from the wealth of the land, the community of Hebden is directly affected by the total dominion of the property owners. And like the community of Hebden, the entire global community is affected by the burning of peat and the release of carbon into the atmosphere.

The British taxpayer finances this destruction to enable the pastime of a select few. Avery estimates that the 147 moors across England, which occupy over half a million acres, are used by just 5,000 individuals – under 0.01 per cent of the population. The law defends the rights of the few over the many, by right of property alone.

It's about four in the morning. The lights of Hebden are bleeding from the horizon into new swathes of fog that seem to be spreading our way. Sitting on our lifeboat rock, we've grown cold. We creak to our feet and jump around for a bit, and, though we're exhausted from the ceaseless battering of the wind, we press on. There is a ruined farmhouse on the highest point of this moor that the guidebooks claim was inspiration for Heathcliff's house in *Wuthering Heights*, and a path of stone slabs laid by Lord Savile's men to take us there.

The path winds us east towards the edge of the moor. The hills are not steep, but the buffeting wind and the roll of the valley instil a weird sense of vertigo, like being up in the eaves of a theatre, with the roof blown off. Far beneath us, we can see the streetlights of Oxenhope and Haworth, and we imagine the villagers asleep in their beds, the silence blanketing their streets. The whole land is dreaming.

For centuries, England has been lulled by the aristocratic myth that land is better off in the hands of *men-who-know-better* and, even more spuriously, that its value belongs only to those that own it. Just as the fence lines of property pretend that the surrounding community is not affected by the management techniques within, they also create the illusion that the value of the land is unconnected to the community around it. The opposite is true.

While a landowner can improve the property, or capital, on their land, by building new and better houses, the value of the land itself (on average, 70 per cent of its total price) is only increased in direct correlation to the services provided by the community that surrounds it. Land banking proves this. When a property firm buys land as an asset, they hold it as it accrues in value. The buddleia takes root, the place is fly-tipped and the owners do nothing to increase its worth. Instead, they wait, while improvements in infrastructure (the roads, rail links and hospitals financed by the taxpayer) and the value of local amenities (the theatres, bars, shops and mechanics' yards) do the work for them. Society generates the value of the land.

When the Liberals proposed their Land Value Tax in 1909, they sought to separate the value of the property (its capital) from the value of the land beneath it. They reasoned that because land values are financial reflections of the interconnectedness of society, they should belong to the communities that have created them. For this reason, Land Value Tax, or Site Valuation Tax, is seen by some not even as a tax at all, but simply the recovery of the economic rent owed to the community that created its value. The idea that landowners should pay a tax to the community that has generated the wealth they enjoy is such an inversion of the accepted orthodoxy that it has always been presented as an upheaval of the order of the land. But it is nothing more than waking out of the spell that has bound the land for so long. Let the daylight in on the magic and the paradigm of private property inverts: the landlords pay a rent to the people.

Top Withens is everything a gothic farm cottage should be. Built into the bank of the moor, in the shade of two trees, it is roofless, squat and ruined. It's Brontë-bleak. But it also has a sense of humour: attached to the wall, engraved in stone, knowing full well how far visitors have walked to reach it, is a sign that tells us it's all make-believe: 'The buildings, even when complete, bore no resemblance to the house she described but the situation may have been in her mind when she wrote of the moorland setting of the heights.'

Well, thanks for your honesty. As we sit and eat our sandwiches, my mind is stuck on Heaven's Gate at Highclere: another architectural illusion celebrating another famous fiction, the heavenly splendour of the aristocratic class. Like the folly, the illusion is crumbling. Either side of the earls of Carnarvon, the parvenus are encroaching on the aristocracy. To the west, Stowell Park, a 5,500-acre estate, belongs to the Vesteys who made their money through beef. And to the east is Sydmonton estate, whose 400 years of noble bloodline was cut short in 1978, when it was bought by musical impresario Andrew Lloyd Webber. In 2010, just before the Downton cash cow, Lloyd Webber offered to buy Highclere Castle, to alleviate the earl of the cost of upkeep. The Carnarvons refused his offer, quoted in the *Daily Telegraph*: 'We are not selling up to some rich man.' *Ouch*. It seems that the earl has been intoxicated by his own precious gas, bewitched by the idea that his class distinguishes him from any other type of landowner. But as historian David Cannadine says, class has always been an illusion: 'classes never actually existed as recognisable historical phenomena, still less as the prime motor of historical change. They were nothing more than rhetorical constructions, the inner imaginative worlds of everyman and everywoman, seeking as best they could to explain their social universe to themselves.'

The myth of the aristocracy is that they were ever anything more than rent collectors. All old money was new money at some point. The motto of Lord Salisbury, commissioned when he was styled an earl in 1605, is *sero sed serio*, late but serious. When he was given his lands, he was well aware he was the parvenu, and now 500 years in, he's taken off the plastic wrapping and become part of the furniture.

Professor of Law Joel Bakan describes the modern-day corporation in words that could equally apply to the aristocratic family. 'The corporation's legally defined mandate is to pursue, relentlessly and without exception, its own self-interest, regardless of the often harmful consequences it might cause to others.' The similarities between corporations and aristocratic families are prevalent. Aristocratic escutcheons, their shields and mottos, are early prototypes of corporate brands and slogans. The noble lineages, sustained by primogeniture and biased tax relief, employ the same techniques of trusts and offshore estates used by corporations to keep the taxman away. *Noblesse oblige* is no more than paternalism dressed in tinsel: the idea that the elite have a better sense of the world than their lessers. The chivalric codes of *chevisance*, *largesse* and *valiance* have mutated into the modern corporate jargon: environmental stewardship, land management, estate conservation, best practice, engagement, innovation, progress.

The aristocrats of England made their money by monopolising the land and using their elite definition of property rights to line their own pockets. Whenever they have been in need of money, they have suspended their 'higher stewardship' of the land and squeezed it until the coins came out. To raise money for the repair of Highclere Castle, the earl applied for planning permission to build new houses on forty acres of the estate. While the locals called it ecological vandalism, the aristocracy call it 'Enabling Development', a loophole in planning legislation that allows for development, otherwise viewed as harmful, if it pays for restoration of heritage assets. In *Downton Abbey*, when the Granthams are faced with their huge inheritance bill, the dowager countess exclaims: 'The point is, have we overlooked something, some source of revenue, previously untapped ... if only we had some coal, or gravel, or tin!'

To this day, if it's not gold, coal, oil or silver, if you own the mineral rights you can hollow the land of its resources and pocket the value. The Dukes of Norfolk and Rutland mined the land they owned in Sheffield for its iron ore, likewise the Dukes of Buccleuch, Hamilton and Portland. A hundred years after the Rufford Park poachers, Lord Savile leased the manor of Ollerton to a coal-mining company. The surrounding area is still known as the Dukeries, because of the enormous swathes of land (around 88,000 acres) in Nottingham that were owned by just four men, the Dukes of Norfolk, Portland, Kingston and Newcastle – they, too, enclosed the land, and leased it to mining companies, transferring its wealth from the people that once used the common lands, into their own pockets.

Mining was just one means of extracting wealth from the land. Enclosure was the means of extracting this wealth from society. Land as a resource is naturally scarce; as Mark Twain said, 'they're not making it any more'. To enclose the land is to monopolise its value, to privatise community wealth, a process summed up by geographer David Harvey with the phrase 'accumulation by dispossession'. In land, private wealth comes only at the expense of the public treasury.

When taxpayers' money finances infrastructure projects such as Crossrail or HS2, money is taken out of the common purse to provide infrastructure for all to use. However, when the value of the land around these new stations increases dramatically, under the current laws of property it goes directly to the property owner. The extension of the Jubilee underground line in London cost the taxpayer £3.4 billion. Eleven stations were added to the line, increasing the connectivity of these sites and raising the value of the land. An independent survey estimated the increase in value of land 1,000 yards from each station to have been £13 billion, all of which went into the hands of landowners, who contributed nothing to its gain. A Land Value Tax could have entirely paid for the new infrastructure and left the communities affected by the new line significantly better off.

In the era of the Blacks and the Rufford Park poachers, the wealth of the land was expressed by a buck or a doe, a pheasant or a hare. Today, wild animals are no longer the currency of a common treasury; tax represents the value of the land that, in the words of the Rufford Park poacher, should be 'quite equal for to share'. Since 1995, land values in this country have risen by 412 per cent, with land now accounting for over 50 per cent of the wealth of the UK. But, under the current laws of property, the nation sees none of it.

The fence lines around private property are the dotted lines around the map that say *cut-out-and-keep* to any owner, blue-blooded or otherwise. Gradually, year by year, England is beginning to recognise the systematic draining of resources and wealth that occurred in colonial exploitation, when Englishmen took the wealth of foreign nations and claimed it as their own. But we are still a long way from recognising the deeper truth: that it was practised first on their own soil, when the landlords colonised the commons.

As moneyed men drew lines around common land and swallowed up its resources, their fences redefined the purpose of the land: what was acceptable within it and who had rights to it. As more and more of the land was enclosed, the cult of exclusion came to define not just local land, but extended across the country as a whole. They defined the nation.

COCKROACH

Nouns, nations, values

'Make no mistake, these migrants are like cockroaches'
— Katie Hopkins

'Rescue Boats? I'd use Gunships to Stop Migrants.' So
began the article by 'media personality' Katie Hopkins
published in the *Sun* in April 2015. In just under 600 words,
Hopkins compared the people fleeing the Libyan civil war to
cockroaches, the virulence of norovirus and a plague of feral
humans. 'I don't care,' she wrote, 'show me pictures of coffins,
show me bodies floating in the water, play violins and show me
skinny people looking sad. I still don't care.' The very next day,
another boat sank off the shores of Sicily, taking the lives of
almost 900 men, women and children.

The piece was a light-hearted take on mass drowning. It called for the Italians to stop singing opera and drinking espressos and sort out the situation like the Australians, 'throwing cans of Castlemaine in an Aussie version of sharia stoning'. Katie Hopkins is not troubled by coherence. The article was written in her trademark style of staccato non-sequitur paragraphs, firing off sentences like a child with an Uzi: short, sharp spurts of invective, with no control over the power in her hands. She is indiscriminate in her targets, veering from fat people to dementia sufferers, to breast-feeding mothers, maybe because she means it, and maybe because sensation sells, vitriol pays her cheques; either way, for Hopkins this was just another day at the office.

But not for everyone. The Independent Press Standards Organisation (IPSO) received 300 complaints, their largest to date, and a petition was launched calling for her dismissal, which attracted over 310,000 signatures. Though Hopkins was subsequently sacked by the *Sun*, not long after a silver lining came in the form of a golden handshake: her article had doubled as a cover letter for a promotion to the *Daily Mail*, then edited by Britain's sorcerer of sensation: Paul Dacre.

I turn off the main road and follow a dirt track up past horse boxes and an oval running paddock to a gorge of nettles and thorn in the corner of the field. An old map I found suggests this was once a Right of Way that led through this field into the next, and so I scramble down the trench, into the clumps of bramble whose berries are just ripening, and find a delicate old gate made of rotting wood, sunk in tangled thorn. I step over it, barge backwards through another thicket of nettles and emerge into the field beyond, a gentle slope of waist-high grass, hissing with grasshoppers. East Sussex unfolds before me, the very picture of Middle England, paddocks and bristling woodland. Between me and the oast houses on the horizon is the private estate of Paul Dacre.

Dacre retired in 2018, but for twenty-six years he was the wizard behind the curtain of Britain's most widely read newspaper. As former editor-in-chief of the *Daily Mail*, *Mail on Sunday*, MailOnline and the *Metro*, plus executive director of the parent company, Daily Mail and General Trust, his peculiar perspective on the world reached, in 2014, almost 200 million users online and twenty-nine million readers of its paper.

The *Mail* presents itself as a newspaper, and calls its employees reporters, but for its entire existence it has occupied the grey ground between fact and fiction. In February 2017, Wikipedia banned the use of the *Daily Mail* for references on account of it being 'generally unreliable'. Wikipedia explained that the decision was based on the *Daily Mail*'s reputation for 'poor fact checking, sensationalism and flat-out fabrication'. Originally, the *Mail*'s priority was never anything more than entertainment, presenting stories that bent the news into a format summarised by the son of its founder, Sunny Harmsworth: 'the British people relish a good hero and a good hate.' The *Daily Mail* specialises in the translation of reality into fairy tale, turning complexity into simplicity, the sober into the sensational. Or as Dacre himself said: 'Dull doesn't sell newspapers. Boring doesn't pay the mortgage.'

And, for Dacre, newspaper sales have paid for several large mortgages. He has converted the glamour of sensation into a 17,000-acre grouse farm near Ullapool in Scotland, a house in Bloomsbury, a house in the British Virgin Islands and an estate in Sussex. For the middle-class kid from Arnos Grove, who won a scholarship to a private school in Hampstead, the fuel behind Dacre's personal rise was the very values he promoted in his paper: aspiration and self-reliance. In a rare interview he summed up his life succinctly: 'the idea of the self-made man: it had worked, I'd got there.'

I step over the electric fence at the foot of the hill and into a wide paddock of grass. I follow some tyre tracks through an opening in the field, towards a long line of trees that snakes across the estate. In spite of the record number of complaints, it turned out that Katie Hopkins' cockroach article had broken none of the regulator's rules. IPSO monitor the press for discrimination against race, gender and ethnicity, but since migrating people are a mix of all these categories and not classed as one single group, she hadn't put a foot wrong. It was the very lack of substance in her argument that saved Katie Hopkins from prosecution. But her words were like a spell cast across England: they unlocked a seam of resentment and casual disregard for humanity that spread through the media and political class. 2015 was the year of the insect migrant.

In July of that year, David Cameron referred to 'a swarm of people coming across the Mediterranean' and was criticised later that day on Radio 4's *Today* programme by the then leader of UKIP, Nigel Farage, for trying to sound 'tough on immigration'. Mr Farage had used the same word just an hour before on ITV's *Good Morning Britain*, recounting his personal experience of driving through Calais, 'surrounded by swarms of potential migrants to Britain'. The next day, the *Daily Mail* ran with the headline: 'The "Swarm" On Our Streets', describing hordes of migrants storming and massing on the roads towards the Eurotunnel and warning: 'this tidal wave of migrants could be the biggest threat to Europe since the war' (for the *Mail* there was really only ever one war). And in August the foreign secretary Philip Hammond reached for the arcane word 'marauding' to describe the 'millions of Africans with the economic motivation to try to get to Europe'.

Marauding is one of a select group of words that only ever seems to be used as a present participle. I don't *maraud*, you don't *maraud*, no one ever *marauded*, and, as such, the word is not so much a conveyor of meaning, but simply of bias – it is an adjective that contaminates its object. It exemplifies the kind of sly rhetoric that turns waiting into loitering, and walking into trespassing, fusing a moral judgement of the act into the act itself. Whether Hammond knew it or not, he was once again drawing on that historic vein of paranoia of the propertied class, because maraud derives from the Old French *marault*, meaning vagabond. From Hopkins to Hammond, the words they used were a modern-day version of the Vagrancy Acts of the Tudors, grouping disparate people by virtue of their movement across borders.

Just as the plays and broadsheets of the Tudor era presented vagrants as a single, co-ordinated unit, the politicians and news-paper editors of the new millennium presented the refugees as a threat to the sanctity and order of the nation. The migration crisis is an international iteration of the cult of exclusion, div-iding those with rights to land from those without, rights which are defined by the line of a border.

The line of trees has been mown flush to the fence, and the thick gauze of its hawthorn spears and branches is almost impene-trable. I follow the fence to its corner: with a foot on its diagonal strut and one hand on a branch above, I climb over. Scraping backwards through the sharp branches, I find a dank winding stream cut deep into the earth, starved of light by the wall of trees either side of it. It is the ghost of the River Limden that cuts from west to east across Dacre's estate and by its side is the ghost of a path, a depression in the ground worn by years of use, and now concealed by the trees, unregistered and lost to the public.

Just as the vagabonds infected the body of England, so the insects of the migration myth penetrate the sanctity of the nation. You don't invite insects to stay: they come in through the open window, or emerge out of cracks in the floorboards. And of all the insects, the cockroach has particular resonance with the concept of eugenics, of filth and purity. A cockroach in the kitchen is a wild, dirty intrusion on the cleanliness of a space, the order of a nation state. In the Rwandan genocide, the Tutsis were repeatedly called Inyenzi (cockroaches) by the Hutus, who used the word to trigger a subconscious acceptance of the need to crush and kill them. You don't murder an insect, you exterminate it, a far cleaner concept, devoid of moral complexity.

Words can change how we see the world. In Ken Burns and Lynn Novick's documentary about the Vietnam War, a soldier named John Musgrave describes his first kill, and the trauma it caused him. From that moment on, he vowed never to kill another human being: 'However, I will waste as many gooks as I can find, I'll wax as many dinks as I can find. I'll smoke as many zips as I can find ... Turn a subject into an object, racism 101, turns out to be a very necessary tool ...'

Right-wing journalists often attack the left for trying to silence their words. Sticks and stones may break your bones, but words are just vessels: they transmit opinions that their writers have every right to hold. But as John Musgrave's experience shows, words are more than conveyors of meaning – when used enough, when repeated like a mantra, when held by consensus, they can create cognitive boundaries between subjects and their objects. They can wall off the human from the humane.

Words can form not only partitions, but enclosures as well. A year after England's summer of swarms, a team of researchers from Kent, Warsaw and New York released a paper, 'On the Grammar of Politics, or Why Conservatives Prefer Nouns'. Building on proof that grammatical forms can shape 'social-cognitative processes' (in other words, influence the way we think about each other) the team published evidence demonstrating that people's voting habits could be predicted by observing the words they used to describe others. The evidence demonstrated that people who gravitate towards conservative ideologies have a preference for using nouns to describe other people. This, they concluded, was because: 'Nouns convey greater permanence, stability of subjects and objects, as well as categorical perceptions of social actors and the world at large. As such, they are likely to address conservatives' greater needs for order, certainty, and predictability.'

Nouns provide cognitive closure; they seal their objects off from the mutability that comes with time and context. To use an example from the study, participants were presented with the sentence *Magda had no doubts about the success of her business* and asked to choose between two subsequent descriptions: first, *Magda is an optimist* and, second, *Magda is optimistic*. The latter description, using an adjective to describe Magda, allows for the idea that Magda may not always feel this way; it allows for cognitive mobility. However, the former statement, which uses a noun, implies that optimism is for Magda an essential, inherent trait; it denies any freedom of movement from this one authoritative enclosure. The noun 'optimist' carries with it largely positive associations, but when the noun in question is migrant, or cockroach, the implications become more serious.

In a process that linguists call 'reification', a noun abstracts its object in much the same way as a fence line abstracts the area within it from the land surrounding it. A word can enclose vast numbers of people within one definition, obliterating the specifics of their lives, the myriad contexts of their situation, into the parameters set by the speaker. There is a link between words and fence lines that can be found in the origin of the word define. 'Define' comes from the fourteenth-century English *deffinen*, meaning 'to fix or establish authoritatively', which in turn comes from the Latin word *finis*, meaning boundary. To define a group of people is an operation of power – whether by fence or by noun, a definition asserts control over what lies within.

I have followed the lost path east and the tunnel of trees eventually opens up into a track that passes through a thick jungle of deciduous trees on my left, and the tall poles of a pine plantation on my right. The sun is filtered by the needles into heavenly shards of light, and the thinner branches shine silver like spider silk. Finally, I reach an old steel gate, wrapped in barbed wire and the blank backside of a sign. I climb the gate and step back to read its declaration: *Private Woodland*.

In 2015 the words of the migrant crisis – cockroach, marauding, swarm – shaped our response to the needs of the people they defined; they confined our perception of these people and set a limit on their rights to the land. With their constant repetition, such words create a mindset of partition and enclosure that can manifest out of the conceptual and into the material world. Divisive rhetoric endorses divisive architecture. Words incite walls. In 2015, one such enclosure became central to the migration debate in England: the unofficial migrant camp in Calais, nicknamed 'the Jungle'.

I'm not quite sure what country I'm in. I'm shuffling through the passport queue at St Pancras station, in a stretch of land between the British and French checkpoints, ten foot apart. By the rules of the Dublin Regulation, if a migrant sets foot on British soil then Britain is responsible for their asylum, so in May 2000 a legal fiction was invented called 'juxtaposed controls', which brought the border of France to St Pancras. Three years later, the Le Touquet border agreement was passed for cross-Channel ferry routes, which brought the border of France to Kent, and the border of England to Calais and Dunkirk. '*Merci*,' I say as I'm handed back my passport and I pass through the French borders to sit on a train parked in London, lost in a legal fiction.

It's been three years since I last visited Calais, when I took the ferry with some friends, a caravan hitched to our car and a boot stuffed with second-hand clothes in bin liners. I remember the choppy winter sea, the confetti of ketchup wrappers that blew in the air every time a smoker came in from the windy deck. This time round, sitting on a plush leather seat, I'm reading George Orwell's *Notes on Nationalism*, and keep coming back to a couple of lines: 'Indifference to objective truth is encouraged by the sealing-off of one part of the world from another, which makes it harder and harder to discover what is actually happening.'

Orwell wrote these lines in the final year of the Second World War, which saw the greatest number of people displaced in history. In 2014, this record was broken, with 59.5 million people uprooted from their homes and set in motion across the globe. Crossing the Channel in 2015, I had the distinct feeling of slipping through the lines of newspaper print, the gauze of words that sealed off my world from the other.

I arrive in Calais on a blustery, drizzling, cold spring day. I take the train into the town centre and see a new militarised zone speed past the window. Rolls of razor wire stretch across miles of grass verges, trapped in between two fences, one green and one white. The white fence is 'the Great Wall of Calais', thirteen foot high, capped with rolls of razor wire, which stretches around miles of motorway right up to the Jungle camp. This fence cost the British taxpayer £2.3 million, just a fraction of the

£316 million we have paid to police our new British border in France. Construction started in September 2016, weeks before the camp was finally cleared, then burned down. It still stands today, a monument to shutting the stable door long after the horse has been evicted.

A taxi drops me off at the gates of the warehouse and a volunteer lets me in. Three years ago, this was the hub of the volunteer force in Calais. People of all ages and many nationalities would come here, for days, weeks or months, and help out with sorting clothing donations and food supplies and with preparing food in the kitchen. Since the Jungle was officially closed in 2016, the migrants in Calais have slipped out of the news and disappeared from our consciousness. But the crisis is ongoing, and the warehouse still cooks for the 500 people currently living in the woods around the Jungle site and the other 1,000 or so near Dunkirk. The kitchen is larger now, decked in stainless steel, a much more professional operation than before. I wander round to the muddy yard, which links the clothing and food warehouse to the back, where the carpenters worked all hours preparing prefab boards to be trucked to the Jungle and turned into chipboard huts to house families. But since I was last here, the roof has blown off the warehouse, and now it is used simply to cut and stack the kindling that is distributed nightly to the people in the forest.

The car park is about an acre of mud, carved up with deep tyre ruts that are filled with rainwater and the reflected sky. It's empty now, but when we arrived to donate our caravan it was a miserable facsimile of a holiday park from the 1970s, packed with ancient caravans, ex-army jeeps and the converted vans of the long-timers, with smoke chugging from their wood stove flues. I remember the dark wintry mornings in this place, woken by the hail on the caravan roof, a constant sluice of ball bearings on thin metal, putting the kettle on the gas hob, looking out through the window at the wind roaring through the line of poplars, thrashing at loose corners of tarpaulin, whipping white wavelets across the deep puddles. We'd pull on damp socks and layers of rain-proofing, go to load the food van and hitch a lift to the camp.

The winter storms would devastate the Jungle. Even before we entered the camp, we would see collapsed tents, poles broken by the wind, flapping like ragged flags, people dressed head to toe in bin bags, and all manner of litter swept up and snagged in bramble and rowan bushes. We'd pass the Welcome Caravan at the entrance, staffed twenty-four hours a day and stuffed full of cheap donated tents and bulging bin liners prepared at the warehouse with scarves, gloves, hats, blankets, roll mats, wind-up torches, packets of biscuits and high-energy yoghurt drinks. Those who arrived through the night were directed to the big geodesic dome at the centre of the camp, to sleep in commune until they could find a place to pitch their tent the next day.

Quietly, we would unload the van, unlock the storage container in the Ashram kitchen, light the two Calor gas canisters and begin swabbing the floor for breakfast. The camp woke up slowly, as many of its inhabitants had been out during the night, walking miles to find trucks to hide in or under, so the hours between breakfast and lunch were the quietest, when people were trying to sleep. We would boil great vats of chai, and serve whatever we had, from beans and eggs to dry Rice Krispies, and, for two or three hours, 500 or so people, mostly men, would line up, take whatever we offered them, eyes red raw with a grim, compacted tiredness.

I leave the warehouse and walk my old shortcut to the Jungle. This part of Calais is all factories and warehouses, a zone of flat tarmac and business parks. The air shudders as trucks pass by and my jacket is already drenched from the heavy spit in the air. I pass through a sports centre and find a new pebble-dashed wall, two humans high, between the path and the bank of the motorway. It has long metal arms leaning in arcs over it, laced with barbed wire, and of all the walls erected in Calais, this seems the hardest to scale.

In the last decade or two walls like this have spawned across the globe. In 1990, only fifteen states across the globe had a border fence; today the number is over seventy. The increasing military presence on borders, and the simultaneous privatisation of migrant detention facilities, has led to a criminalisation of migration that has somehow justified the violence at these borders. Fortress Europe has become the most dangerous border in the world, with over half the deaths on border zones occurring while crossing into EU territory.

I pass by wet farmland, riven with deep dykes almost full, turn the corner by the motorway and, for the first time in three years, I see what remains of the Jungle camp. Without its make-shift architecture of wood and tarp, it seems much smaller, a flat, bleak wasteland about a mile long. On the far side is the motorway, with its white fence and barbed wire, and, beyond that, the chemical factory, still chugging white smoke into the grey sky. I walk up the verge and look over what was once the family and children's camp, right beside the road. A large red sign says *ACCÈSS INTERDIT* and though there is no fence around it, and no apparent reason, the land is still charged with exclusion.

I walk around the verge, past the graffitied pill box, and turn left onto the Chemin des Dunes. The entrance is all that I recognise of the camp, a steel gate wedged open into blocks of concrete and mud on the verge, with four red hearts still painted on one of its posts. I'm about to walk in when a large van, crammed with CRS security guards, passes by me. It slows as it approaches, and in perfect unison the guards' heads turn to eyeball me as they pass, like soldiers in a fascist rally, saluting their great leader. They're scowling theatrically and I'm reminded instantly of the tactics of abuse they employed when I was here, the French translation of Theresa May's 'Hostile Environment'.

The CRS are a civilian reserve corps of the French police, a modern yeomen militia, trained in anti-insurrection techniques. They have been used to suppress French riots since 1944 and have constantly been accused of racial profiling and excessive force. Every night during the Jungle they would line up, shoulder to shoulder with the police and vigilante fascist groups, forming a roadblock to the shortcut back to the warehouse. They would enter the camp in helmets and riot shields to perform arbitrary searches of tents but, more generally, their job was to glare at anyone who walked by them.

Together with the vigilantes their presence was a constant, unspecified threat to anyone who left the camp. They would slow their vans alongside migrants or volunteers, create roadblocks to delay the delivery of hot food and today they still work on the remaining migrants in Calais, systematically destroying their tents, confiscating their shoes and blankets, sometimes kidnapping them, driving them hours out of town, leaving them on the roadside to walk back to the woods. Today, they are the heavily armed gamekeepers of this land. I stand motionless as they pass, let the van disappear over the motorway bridge and then walk into the camp.

Only the topography of the ground is the same. I walk up the sloping path, to where the Ashram kitchen would have been, and all around me are piles of rotten carpets, discarded shoes, tampon dispensers, broken wind-up torches, lying in clumps among the marsh grass. Various patches of the earth are still scorched from the fires that obliterated the camp and, occasionally, I see an empty tear-gas canister. I walk up along the main avenue and come to the central courtyard where the Eritrean church was built, two storeys of wood and tarp with a wooden cross at the top. Here was the camp library, the shack for the Jungle radio station, and here, every day for a month, I helped distribute the lunchtime delivery of food.

By midday, the Jungle would be buzzing with life. The restaurants that lined the gravel path would be hissing with hot oil, and their plastic windowpanes foggy with breath. People would sit in them, shoes off, and wait for their phones to charge, while Bollywood DVDs played on loop, stout authoritarians being thwarted by tight t-shirted, good-looking heroes in fake moustaches. No one would watch them, but instead sat, eyes cataracted with exhaustion and hopelessness, waiting for some-thing, anything, to happen.

In 2002, the Sangatte Red Cross asylum was closed in order to stop 'encouraging' migrants to come to Calais. It had housed up to 1,500 people, and, when it was shut, they had simply moved to this area of land. By 2015, when about 5,000 people had massed here, the French government still refused to declare this site an official migrant camp, which meant that no aid agencies were allowed access to the site. Food, hygiene and safety were compromised by this stubborn refusal to accept the bleeding obvious, and as aid agencies lobbied for this speech-act, the simple declaration of recognition, untrained volunteers, amateurs like myself, were left to supply the aid that was needed.

Every day, in the shadow of the camp's church, I would open up the chipboard hut and wait as the hot food delivery negotiated roadblocks and arrived, sometimes hours late, to deliver lunch for the queues of several hundred people. It was our job to keep the queue orderly, but with around fifteen different nationalities in the camp, with the tiredness and tension of constant sleepless nights, the harassment and vitriol of the CRS, not to mention the severe effects of PTSD from the wars they were fleeing in

Sudan, Syria, Afghanistan, Iraq, the persecution of Christians in Iran and the forced military conscription in Eritrea, the queue was tense with anticipated violence. People would jump the queue, and others would shout out *LINE! LINE!* and if neither the migrants nor the volunteers could resolve the situation there would be fist fights, nothing like the movies, arms swinging wherever they could land a blow, tears in each man's eyes. Sitting here now, I still feel the sickening shame, that sense of inadequacy to the task, the deep frustration that someone better qualified wasn't sorting this out.

I move on to the grove of trees where the Iraqis lived, just beside the motorway bridge, where Banksy painted his mural of the son of a Syrian migrant called Abdul Lateef Jandali. The mural depicts a man carrying his possessions in a bag, and a small first-generation Macintosh computer, because this man was adopted, aged two, by an American family, and renamed Steve Jobs. This is where the police vans would line up, in phalanxes of helmets and riot shields, and enter the camp. And as dusk descended, this large crossroads in the camp would host the black market, where you could buy anything from dry socks to mobile phones. The lights would come on overhead and restaurants would play the call to prayer on sound systems, with various routes blocked by the Muslims of the camp, wearing miraculously clean tunics, performing the Salat al-maghrib on palettes laid out on the mud.

I remember wandering round here in the first few weeks of my stay and being caught between two lines of riot police. I was trapped in a tight knot of people, entirely unaware of what was happening, as walls of helmets and riot shields advanced towards us. Suddenly, I was up against the line of shields, an inch from their batons, panicking, and to my shame I yelled out '*Je suis Anglais, je suis Anglais*', as if the walls would suddenly part and let me through. It was then that I learned that you can't negotiate with walls. Made of men or made of bricks, walls don't listen; they face you with a blank expression and compel you to their will. We were herded to another part of the camp, someone was arrested and the enclosure of riot police dissolved back into the night.

Sitting here now, under the drizzle and hollow cries of the gulls, I think of the Midland Revolt, and the camps of villagers, forced from their homes and the common lands they worked, to squat on wasteland in makeshift colonies just like the Jungle. In his book *Violent Borders*, Reece Jones describes how national borders were the direct extrapolation of the enclosure of common land, the expansion of the logic of private property on to a global scale:

> The factors that led to the Midland Revolt in 1607 illustrate how the power to control the land was captured through the imposition of boundaries, and how this transformed the relationship between humans and their environment. This relationship continued to transform in the centuries after the revolt as states claimed the land of the earth as sovereign territories.

As quiet and peaceful as the Duke of Buccleuch's land was when I visited it, it just takes a history book to exhume the ghosts of the violence that was committed to claim the territory. All borders, from the fence lines around fields to the militarised zones around countries, are scars on the earth caused by some kind of contention, at some point in history. It is not enough to draw a map, or put up a sign, or lay some hedges – the border must be defended. And whether it falls to Simon Montague's Nottingham Yeomanry or the CRS, this almost always boils down to physical violence.

A 2015 report into living conditions in the Calais migrant camp noted:

> Qualitative data suggests that the atmosphere in the camp changes during the hours of darkness, with concerns about safety and security during the night. There were reports of residents living adjacent to the road being beaten in the night by unknown persons, who arrive and depart by car. Others reported being beaten and sprayed with gas by local police.

In the evening, the restaurants smelled of stewed beef and the pop music blared out from the Eritrean bar. The public spaces were filled with the overlapping rhythms of French, Farsi, Dutch, English, Pashtou, German and Arabic and there were brief moments when the Jungle seemed convivial, a common ground for different nationalities – without interference from the state, people got along. But buried deep in the clothing of the volunteers was something that nobody acknowledged, something that totally undermined any feeling of parity we might have had among the migrants: our passports. We were never without them, because they saved our jaws from being broken by the CRS and allowed us safe passage out of here whenever we'd had enough.

One night I had just finished scrubbing the floor of the Ashram kitchen. Dinner was over hours ago, but, having chopped and washed all day, both the migrant and European volunteers in the kitchen were lingering under the one bulb, sharing tins of beer. I was invited back to the chipboard hut of a young Iranian woman, to spend the last hours of the evening with her mother and brother. We took off our boots, slippery with mud, and entered through the drape that covered the door. They had lined their box room with blankets, for insulation, and though the space was small it had been compartmentalised into sleeping, cooking and living areas. The gas stove was burning and my friend's brother lit a small shisha bong. Together, we smoked apple tobacco as she slid me through photographs on her phone, photos of her home, the mountains, a wedding in the wine region of Shiraz: she had plucked, Kim Kardashian eyebrows, hot pressed curls in her hair, a shimmery pashmina, and I realised then that the person I worked with every day, in second-hand dungarees and cast-off floral wellies, the migrant, bore little resemblance to the woman she was just months ago.

Just after midnight, with her brother asleep in the corner, I thanked her mother and left. I stepped out of the door, put on my soggy boots and entered a strange atmosphere. Silhouettes were running through the chipboard huts, stumbling over guy ropes; there was shouting in the distance. As I picked my way through the shanty town of tents and joined the main street, crowds of young men were rushing towards the exit. Orange sparks were trailing through the air and then, just ten foot away, a plastic canister dropped with a clud from the sky. Thick white fog gushed from one end, and some of the young men, masking their faces with scarves, kicked it into the ditch. More followed.

Banned in war, but somehow acceptable to use on civilians, this was tear gas. Unsure of my next move, breathing through my jumper, my eyes and nostrils already beginning to sting, I joined the rush of youngsters to the entrance, and saw maybe a hundred young men, faces wrapped in scarves, thronging around the Chemin des Dunes. The air was acrid, clouding with poison, and through the tears in my eyes I gradually made out what was happening. Lines of police and CRS security vans were backed up down the road, their blue lights flashing out of sync, and a small army of black and blue helmets had lined up behind shields. Behind them, officers with cannons were inter-mittently firing canisters, not just at the crowd, but into the sleeping camp. The young men, screaming in croaking teenage voices, were scrabbling for rocks to throw at them.

I turned back: there were other ways out of the camp. I passed through the tents again, and everywhere young men were running, frenzied, slapping on the huts, trying to wake the people inside who had no intention of joining them. These were the lost boys of the Jungle, a fraction of the thousand or so unaccompanied minors, the most vulnerable inhabitants of the camp. Even then, amid the chaos, it occurred to me that I was inside tomorrow's news. You could tell this story one way, and report how migrants had clashed with officers of the law, swallowing the 5,000 or so other inhabitants who wanted nothing to do with the riot into one group definition. Or you could write it another way, and sketch lonely children with stones in their hands, fighting adults with batons, shields and tear-gas cannons. It would depend on how you framed it.

Tear gas is used for riot control, to create exclusion zones by limiting the breath of its victims; but here it is the gas that incites the riot. With the plumes of white fog flashing blue in the police lights, forming a seething ceiling over the camp, with the men running headlong through the night, here was a hellish sense of chaos. I was beginning to panic. The exit under the motorway bridge was blocked by another phalanx of CRS and the same, too, by the dunes. I was enclosed. The gas had entered my chest and my lungs were beginning to sting. I could barely see, it hurt to breathe, and suddenly I felt a desperate sense of disorientation. Still the canisters kept falling. The restaurants were still going but the doors were locked shut; the men inside too long in the tooth, or too tired, to get involved. Lost, with no home of my own to protect me, half blind with tears, there was only one place for me to go.

I banged on the door. And again, and again, and eventually it opened and the brother ushered me in. I was given a wet flannel for my eyes and swapped the poison in my lungs for apple shisha, grateful beyond words for the security and calm of this feeble hut, for a family who, 4,000 miles from their birthplace, had done for me what England wouldn't do for them.

Hours later I still hadn't slept, but the noise had died down outside. I pulled my boots back on, left the hut and made my way back to the warehouse, to my caravan. The sky was light with dawn, but the ground was still dark. An air of menace lingered, and I could see groups of French vigilantes stalking the line of the motorway and groups of young migrant men, in hoods, in the distance. The land was still fizzing with aggression.

Too scared to take my chance on the path, I slid down the gully of a dyke, sloshed through the muddy water and made my way up to the motorway. Bright lights turned on ahead of me, and five or six French police officers, big bruisers, hauled themselves out of the van and circled me. '*Passeport*,' they demanded, and I handed them my faux-leather maroon booklet so they could check my credentials. Were it not for this little booklet, I had only the stories of other migrants to suggest what might happen to me. I thought of the man in the Jungle whose mouth was fixed shut with metal struts, letting his jawbone fuse after a similar meeting with officials and their batons. Since he was unable to eat solids, for the past month I had been stealing baby food from the warehouse to give to him to squeeze through his broken teeth. But inside my passport is a terse bit of text from Her Britannic Majesty's Secretary of State, which 'requests and requires' officials to give me safe passage, without let or hindrance. And since Her Majesty's treasury also happens to pay their wages, the officers handed the book back to me and stepped aside. I got back to my caravan, turned on the battery-operated Christmas lights, and, shaking with exhaustion, hollow and suddenly very cold, I cried so hard that the snot bubbled from my nose.

I wander up to the northern end of the camp, once the Sudanese and Syrian sectors, which has now been smartly fenced off. The space has been repurposed as a nature reserve, with grim irony, for migrating birds. Already there is a plush new wooden-slatted bird hide on a peak of the verge, and I climb the steps to enter it and escape from the relentless wind and drizzle. It's quiet in here, a place of calm, with rectangles cut from the walls at varying heights forming postcard views of the land; the scene changes depending on which frame you choose to look through.

I remember another of Orwell's lines: 'By "nationalism" I mean first of all the habit of assuming that human beings can be classified like insects and that whole blocks of millions or tens of millions of people can be confidently labelled "good" or "bad".' The ability to treat people with such hostility, to poison their lungs, beat them and herd them like animals is the gift of nationalism. Its binary class system, good versus bad, is an ideology that organises the world along an innate need for simplicity, that necessarily ignores complexity, context and nuance. Orwell went on to list the symptoms of a nationalist fever, obsession, instability and an 'indifference to reality', describing its effects as a waking hallucination: 'some nationalists are not far from schizophrenia, living quite happily amid dreams of power and conquest which have no connection with the physical world.'

In 1973 the sociologist Erich Fromm expanded on Sigmund Freud's idea of 'collective narcissism', describing nationalist tendencies in the terms of psychological neurosis. Collective narcissism involves an inherent self-belief in one group's unique superiority. Like individual narcissism, the belief is intrinsically linked to a deep self-doubt, a fear of inferiority that is almost psychopathic in its inability to see any perspective other than its own. The collective narcissist sees every situation polarised by the innate excellence of their nation and the subsequent assumption that other nationalities want a piece of it.

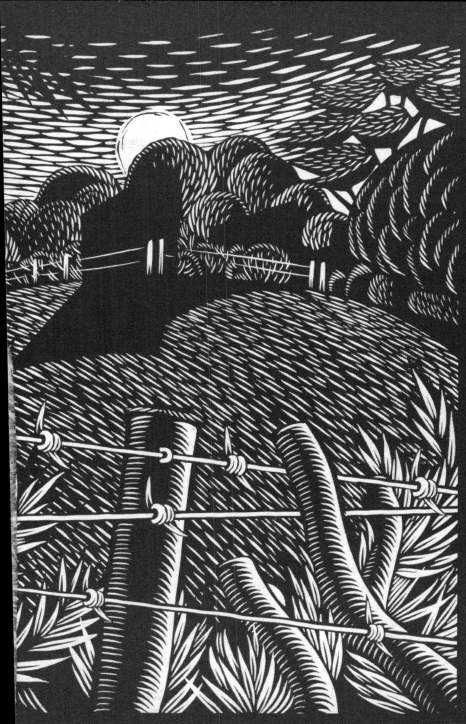

During the tear-gas attack in the Jungle, I banged on the door of the Iranian family's hut because I had nowhere else to go. Had they been collective narcissists, they would have assumed I wanted entry to their hut because it was superior to mine, redefining the situation from an evasion of the danger outside to an invasion of their property, from my perspective to theirs.

France's refusal to 'encourage' migrants to Calais by designating the Jungle camp as an official refugee camp is another example of collective narcissism: it foregrounds the belief that the pull of a muddy camp in Europe was a stronger force on migrants than the push of the bombed cities they were leaving behind. Even the phrase 'migrant crisis' carries the fingerprint of narcissism. To refugees and aid workers, the migration of millions of people from their homes is more accurately defined as a humanitarian crisis, in that barrel bombs and gassing are a systematic contravention of human rights. However, to the right-wing British media, the devastation of war is redefined by a more self-centred perspective – the threat of the migrant at the border, the nation under siege. When David Cameron described the migrants as 'swarms' he went on to explain their motives in a burst of textbook collective narcissism. To Cameron, these people were not running for their lives, but: 'because Britain has got jobs, it's got a growing economy, it's an incredible place to live.' This distortion of priorities is not indifference to reality, but its bare-faced denial.

When Jean-Claude Juncker, president of the European Commission, declared in 2016 that 'borders are the worst invention ever made by politicians', the then prime minister Theresa May instantly dismissed the comment. The notion that borders were bad wasn't quite so hard to stomach as the idea that they were invented. Nationalism needs to believe in the inherent legitimacy of borders because, with such a binary perspective, you need some certainty as to where your loyalties end. But the fixed borders of nation states have always been plastic contrivances, echoes of the ebb and flow of the politics that creates them.

Historically, tribes and religions, empires and principalities ruled the earth long before nation states. Their influence was projected from centralised citadels, and borders were rarely definitive lines, but zones through which cultures merged. Nations were only formally recognised after the Thirty Years War, in the 1648 peace treaties of Westphalia. From then on, borders became the flashpoints between cultures, the tripwire that could cause wars when breached. Today, geographers refer to the 'territorial trap' of nationalism, which leads people to believe that culture is directly contiguous with a line on a map, as if in England, Cumbria has more in common with London than it does with Dumfriesshire, just over the border in Scotland. Nationalism is a dream of simplicity, an anaesthetic to the complexities of a fluid world.

So if the idea of a nation is not determined by fixed territorial borders, how is it defined? The historian Benedict Anderson suggests that the concept of nation took on a new strength with the proliferation of the printing press. The printed word led to a standardisation of language that grouped people together under the pretence that a shared language represented a shared ideology. National newspapers became the principal conveyors of this ideology, a daily affirmation of nationhood: 'The newspaper reader ... is continually reassured that the imagined world is visibly rooted in everyday life ... Fiction seeps quietly and continuously into reality, creating that remarkable confidence of community in anonymity which is the hallmark of modern nations.'

For the philosopher Hegel the ritual of reading the morning newspapers was comparable to prayer. Though the act is solitary, it is in fact an alignment with a community of like minds. Through prayer or the papers, he wrote, 'one orients one's attitude toward the world': we reaffirm our allegiance to a system of values, we recite the creed of a congregation. But who writes this creed?

The power of the media is its role in fixing the basic principles and dominant ideologies of a nation. Through repetition of a consistent perspective on world news, they create what sociologists call doxa. Originating from the Greek δοκεῖν, meaning to seem or to appear, a doxa is a belief so widely held in society that it becomes seemingly self-evident: it requires no explanation and receives no scrutiny. While orthodoxies proclaim themselves as the correct opinion among a host of alternatives, a doxa is so deeply fixed in the mindset that it becomes the foundation of all other debates. When Jean-Claude Juncker suggested that borders were bad, he was challenging the orthodoxy that they were good. When he called them an invention, he was attacking the more deeply rooted mindset, the doxa, that they are mechanisms of a natural order and not simply man-made, political contrivances.

To establish a doxa, the key tactic is repetition. In the twenty-three weekdays running up to the EU referendum, the *Daily Mail* led with the narrative of migration on all but six days. They claimed ownership of the debate, by repeatedly defining its terms. This tactic is fundamental to propaganda. 'It would not be impossible to prove with sufficient repetition,' wrote Joseph Goebbels, Reich Minister of Propaganda for Nazi Germany, 'that a square is in fact a circle. They are mere words, and words can be moulded until they clothe ideas and disguise.'

From its earliest days, the mass media has always been an effective tool to corral the public debate of an issue. In her book on the Belvoir witch trials, Tracey Borman discusses the role of the popular pamphlets reproduced as 'reports' of witch trials. Through the repetition of certain principles, 'these small works were devastatingly effective in whipping up popular fear, anger and hatred towards the women accused of witchcraft'. That the reports were so similar to each other only added to the sense of a collective conspiracy, but was in fact the result of them being lifted, almost in their entirety, from a fanciful treatise on witchcraft by James I. *Daemonologie* was a work of misogynistic make-believe from the troubled mind of one powerful man, a string of subjective assertions that became objective fact by their constant repetition.

During the Rwandan genocide, the Hutus used both their magazine *Kangura* and the national radio station Radio Milles Collines to spread the notion that the Tutsis were cockroaches, or sub-human. The bi-pronged media onslaught was considered so integral to the subsequent slaughter of Tutsis that both the editor of *Kangura* and the chairman of the Radio Milles Collines were later convicted of inciting genocide by the International Criminal Tribunal for Rwanda.

Both cases illustrate the efficacy of the media to amplify a highly personal, select bias into a shared ideology, a consensus held by many. Subjectivity is cloaked as objectivity, propaganda disguised as news, baseless opinions step forward as undisputed facts. And when private considerations masquerade as moral standards, when the parameters of a national debate are defined by individual bias, the morality of the nation becomes a kind of property. Not unlike the former common ground beneath Belvoir Castle, it is controlled by a centralised power, restricting the rights of those that operate within it; its people are partitioned not by walls but by values.

I have left the shelter of the bird hide and wandered south along the Chemin des Dunes. I sit on the verge and make a quick sketch of the land before me. Spring is irresistible. The cotton-wool buds of the pussy willow are transforming into soft, feathery cones of green. The land is sprouting in clover and dock, and, soon, the footprint of the Jungle will have disappeared entirely beneath lush vegetative growth.

In 2016, 5,000 people were trapped here because of a single lie: England. The noun, like the nation, has meaning, but the lie is that its definition is anything other than porous and mutable. The lie is proved by the Le Touquet agreement, which demonstrates that the definition of England can extend to the ports of Calais and Dunkirk, if the shifting of borders so suits the legislators. The lie is also proved by the 2018 World Cup English football team. The team that took their nation all the way to the semi-finals was celebrated as true representatives of a modern England. But remove the first- and second-generation immigrants from the team and England would have fielded just five players. Even in 1966, the most successful team England has ever put forward, the reserve goalkeeper Peter Bonetti was the son of Swiss-Italian immigrants who fled the alpine lakes a year after Mussolini sided with Hitler. England, and Englishness, has meaning, but it is not fixed.

On the way back home, at Calais-Fréthun, forty minutes before the train pulls in to take me back to London, the barrel of a gun appears before my face. I have been filling in the sketch I made of the camp, to pass the time in the dreary waiting room. But suddenly, with an overhead tannoy announcement that the train is due and the passport checkpoints are now open, heavily armed soldiers have entered the station, posted at various points for a better shot at any migrant chancers. One such position is right next to my table, and the muzzle of the soldier's gun is hanging just centimetres from my head. I want to reach out and use my index finger to push it away. Instead, I pack up my stuff, go through two checkpoints, and, having passed through the border of England, I sit in the waiting room in Calais.

The soldiers are the sharp point of the terrible delusion of nationalism, the obsessive denial of reality. Walls and militarised border zones will not stop migration, but only increase the violence at the gates. A report from the EU policy lab studying the future of migration in 2030 predicts with near certainty not only increased migration flows due to floods, droughts, food and water shortages brought on by climate change, but also a desperate need for migration into Europe. With an ageing population and decreasing labour force, the free movement of people will be vital to secure Europe's economy and population. Here the paradigm of walls inverts: open borders and increased freedom of movement are the key to a nation's security and prosperity. The report suggests that only by an increased dialogue and collaboration between nations can migration be handled adequately. Central to this, the report says, is the role played internally by the arbiters of a nation's ideology, its media. The real barrier to migration is not walls, but the technology that legitimises them: words.

Back in Paul Dacre's estate in Sussex, the sun has sunk beneath the canopy of trees, and now shines through the pine poles whose shadows splay like dark rays across the ground. I pack away my crayons and head north along the perimeter of large, empty fields. Every gate I climb is wrapped in barbed wire, a curious expression of paranoia that means even the farmers can't lean on them.

During a debate on immigration in the House of Commons in 2012, MP for South Dorset Richard Drax took to his feet to declare: 'I believe, as do many of my constituents, that this country is full.' It was a standard declaration of right-wing nationalism, and utterly empty of meaning. Like Philip Hammond's 'marauding', the word 'full' is less a conveyor of fact and more a trigger to the limbic system of the brain, the area that governs our emotions. In what way is the country full? In England, the urban landscape accounts for almost 11 per cent of the landmass, and most of that is open space – roads and parks. Of the 2.27 per cent of urban zones that are actually built on, many homes are themselves empty. In England there are 216,000 empty houses, enough to accommodate the inhabitants of the Calais Jungle forty-three times over. And, if we're honest, both Mr Drax and I know for a fact where we can find eleven square miles of empty land: behind his slave wall in Dorset.

But this isn't where asylum seekers are being housed, nor is it likely they will ever be. Instead, 57 per cent of all asylum seekers are housed in the poorest third of the country. When the Conservatives privatised the contracts for housing asylum seekers in 2012, the companies sought housing where land was the cheapest – in deprived areas, places already suffering from neglect and the stranglehold of austerity. In 2016, in Middlesbrough, one in every 152 people was an asylum seeker; in Rochdale, one in every 204 and in Bolton, one in 271. Perhaps unsurprisingly, these towns all voted to leave the EU in the 2016 referendum. While the feeling of being swamped was blamed on an external threat, it was in fact caused by internal inequality, organised from deep within the system of England: the price of land.

The greatest lie of nationalism is that it defends the interests of its nationals. The people it defends, however, are not those it defines, but those who define it. Englishness has always been defined by the landed lords of England and fed in columns of hot air to the landless: you might not have land, but at least you have England.

This point was especially clear to the soldiers returning to England after the Second World War. Having laid their lives on the line to protect the nation, they came back home wanting more for their sacrifice than just words. The Attlee government knew they had to respond to the calls for a country that provided for more than just the captains, colonels and generals that owned it. And so, alongside the nationalisation of healthcare and the provision of social security benefits, the newly conceived welfare state had initially planned 'a people's charter for the open air'.

The Hobhouse report of 1947 proposed a fundamental change to the access laws of the countryside – it envisaged a full right to roam over all uncultivated land in England, so that people could actually experience the land for which they had fought. It was proposed as a corollary to the NHS, providing health and recreation, the prevention of illness before the need for a cure. But landowners, many of them in the Houses of Commons and Lords, lobbied hard against this proposal, and so when the Bill was transitioned into law, a full right to roam was deemed a step too far. The compromise that followed was called the National Parks Act, and though it was still hailed as a people's charter it was in fact a major success for the landowning establishment.

The National Parks Act initially set up ten areas of recreation for the public, including the Lake District, the Peak District, Snowdonia and Dartmoor, and created a structure in which to register and maintain footpaths, but any notion of full access to the countryside was redacted from the debate. From then on, the prevailing philosophy was that the public constituted a threat to the countryside and must therefore be corralled away from its woodland, lakes and plains into areas specifically designated for recreation. By the 1960s, with more people owning cars, better rail and bus infrastructure, the landowners, the planners and the legislators began to talk of an invasion of the land. This time, the threat came not from outside England, but from within it; day-trippers to the countryside were described not as cockroaches, but, in Michael Dower's influential book on tourism, as 'ants, scurrying from coast to coast, on holiday, swarming out of cities in July and August'. The solution was to create more designated spots, which are known to this day as 'honey pots', areas to which swarms of holidaymakers could be directed without disturbing the old order of land ownership.

Nationalism suits the landowning classes because it gives people a sense of ownership without their actually owning anything at all. But if we reread Edmund Burke's quote from the last chapter, where he describes a natural aristocracy ('without which there is no nation') we begin to see how nationalism has its roots in the aristocratic mindset. The nationalist's rights in a nation are founded on the aristocratic fantasy of their inherent and exclusive right to land. It is a notion of legitimised superiority by virtue of inherited property, birth and land, blood and earth, a concept which translates directly into the fascist ideology of 1930s Germany: *Blut und Boden*. By introducing a lower level of human, nationalism raises its lowest members higher than anyone else in the world and, in so doing, it ratifies the aristocratic story of class hierarchy, the story that some people deserve a bigger share of the world than others. Nationalism presents the orthodoxy of class supremacy as a national doxa, and, just like Cannadine's definition of class, it is nothing more than a 'rhetorical construction', whose walls are built with words alone.

In the *Daily Mail* these words paper over striking double standards. Its owner, Viscount Rothermere, has a fluid allegiance to nationality – he is himself a kind of migrant, at least as far as the Inland Revenue are concerned. Though he lives with his family in Ferne Park, Wiltshire, his father's registered home was in France; he is considered to be a non-domicile. This enables him to pay no tax on his offshore income and capital gains unless the money is brought into the UK. Luckily for him, much isn't, because, according to *Private Eye*, the Daily Mail Group Trust's parent company is also registered offshore in Bermuda. Similarly, Paul Dacre, the nation's firmest opponent of the something-for-nothing culture of the welfare state, is himself the recipient of taxpayer handouts: between 2011 and 2016, Dacre's estates in Scotland and Sussex received a minimum of £460,000 of CAP payments. Per year, that's the same as the maximum limit of welfare for four households in Britain.

But the two men have forged a propaganda machine that defends their interests through a process of what Noam Chomsky calls 'dichotomisation'. Dichotomisation presents the world in binary form, dividing the worthy from the unworthy. Through relentless repetition of this narrative, Dacre and Rothermere have sidestepped the need to explain their definition and created a consensus in their readership that presents issues in terms that serve their ideology. Rothermere is the right sort of migrant, and Dacre receives the right sort of handouts.

I'm approaching the northern edge of the estate, following the perimeter of a field to a small, dark hole in the hedge. It's an overgrown entrance, tangled willow falling and framing the clear blue sky, with another ancient wooden gate wrapped in barbed wire. Like the first gate into Dacre's estate, it is wedged shut by foliage, but it is thigh-high and can be scaled with a simple scissor-step. But through the gap in the hedge, my eyes catch something that my brain can't compute. At the crest of a long slope of cow-cropped grass is a ten-foot shard of black, cut like a hole from the sky.

As I approach it, climbing the slope, it sinks slowly into the tree line behind it, which blocks the sun and allows the shape some colour. It turns from a thin onyx monolith into the foreshortened face of a single brick wall, like an obstacle to be scaled on a soldier's training ground. As I get closer I see to its right another wall. In between them is a chest-high thicket of thistle, thorn and nettles, which stretches back to the tree line. The entire area is wrapped in taut lines of barbed wire.

National boundaries are presented as defence systems against the invading swarms. But from a field to a nation, the first effect of a wall is to claim an area of absolute control within the boundary. Historically, as people who cross the boundaries of a territory are increasingly controlled, so too are the freedoms of people within it. Central to the idea of nationalism is a single, fixed definition of what the nation consists of; any deviance from this narrow criterion is presented as a threat. As the meaning of *England* becomes defined by its hard borders, so the meaning of *Englishness* becomes increasingly confined. In the three months following the Brexit result, when Britain voted to partition itself from the European Union, homophobic hate crimes, though ostensibly unconnected, rose by 147 per cent. A border might seem as if it protects the land, but, really, it buttresses a mono-lithic control over it, it dichotomises the land.

Standing before this strange sculpture, I realise it is a ruined, single-storey cottage and these are its only two remaining walls. The grass up to the fence has been chewed to its roots by cows, but behind the fence it has been left to grow wild, for years. I didn't expect this estate to be so riddled with metaphors for paranoid nationalism, but here it is, the heart of Paul Dacre's England: a crumbled old house, wrapped in barbed wire, an inhospitable jungle of thorns and spikes. I sit down, take out my sketchbook and begin to draw. Looking up at the cottage, and back to the paper, the cockroach crawls back into mind.

The cockroach is primarily understood as an invader not of nations, but of homes. But the reason nationalism manages to trigger such deep-set emotions is because it has always drawn on the implicit understanding of family, the blood ties of kin. Motherland, Fatherland, Homeland – your nation is where you were born, the home that you are brought up in. And while right-wing newspapers and politicians are usually adept at avoiding overt nationalist sentiment, they can't help themselves when it comes to that dog-whistle phrase for nation: *family values*.

HARE

Commons, carnival, space and rave

'What the fuck do you think an English forest is for?'
— Johnny 'Rooster' Byron, *Jerusalem*, Jez Butterworth

The city is a spell cast in steel, stone, tarmac and glass. It is a network of ideologies concreted into architecture, buildings and roads that direct our actions and organise our thoughts. Each building is a box built not just of bricks and mortar, but of a series of practices, associations and taboos, the designation of what is acceptable, the design of normality. Block by block, line by line, the city constructs reality.

I'm boiling the kettle for my thermos, gazing from my window on the eleventh floor, watching the building site opposite me. The temporary fence went up a few months ago, declaring not first possession of the land, but a repossession of its purpose.

Today, lorries arrive with heavy stacks of steel, and, to a background of clanking and high-whining metal saws, cranes turn and lift prefabricated blocks onto hollow houses: the air is claimed by concrete, space turns into place.

The shape of this building site is a microcosm of the shaping of the city as a whole. As new places are created, new boundaries are established, and with concrete margins come social taboos and legal frameworks, which either include or exclude certain sectors of society. Power is organised through space.

The kettle boils and I pour the steaming water onto a brown nest of organic matter at the bottom of the thermos, screw on the cap and head out. Down at street level I join the exodus from work, walking down the Bethnal Green Road to the Tube. The market is dismantling, corrugated metal casing is being pulled over the shop fronts, burly men and women in boiler jackets, with ID tags wrapped around their biceps, guard the doorways to pubs. The streets are battening down the hatches. Because squeezed between the rock of one week and the hard place of another, the weekend here has a seismic pressure: it goes off like an earthquake.

When I return home tonight the armies of weekenders will have cried havoc to the streets. The roadsides will be littered with the bullet casings of nitrous oxide gas, a drug you inhale through party balloons, sold on the kerb when the police aren't looking. The pavements will be sticky with the sugary melodrama of drink; bodies cored of their consciousness will lurch and sway and stumble and fall, there will be shouting, arguments and fights. The air will be thumping with the turboed bass of expensive cars speeding up and down the road, and, here and there, the people will be pressed, arms behind their backs, against the walls and billboards, lit by the flashing blue rave lights of the police. This is normality; but because we have neither the money, nor the inclination, nor the correct shoes, we're off to the woods.

Passage clogs as we enter the Tube: we pass into the city's intestines like a mudslide. As one, we mass forward through the stone pipes until we pan out onto the platform, slowly filling up the space. A train arrives and we pack ourselves against the wall of strangers, the doors shut and we lurch forwards through black tunnels.

Tightly insulated by other humans, encased in steel, buried by concrete and earth, I consider the nature of space. Space is the arena of action and interaction; it is where our lives play out. But after sociologist Henri Lefebvre's book *The Production of Space* was published in 1974, a new wave of academics began to view space not just as an impassive backdrop to the theatre of society but as a protagonist in the play. They were interested in how the organisation of space affected its inhabitants, how space created a paradigm for power: '[Social] space is a [social] product ... the space thus produced also serves as a tool of thought and of action ... a means of control, and hence of domination, of power.'

The way space is divided (or, in other words, the way place is constructed) has a direct influence on the people who operate within it – it affects their habits, customs and ideologies. The decision of who and what space is for directly shapes the structure of the society within it: what is allowed, what is encouraged and what is forbidden. Lefebvre created the term 'Third Space' to discuss this interaction between how places were conceived (mapped and designed) and how they were perceived (how they affected the lives of those that lived within them); Third Space is the place where real life occurs amid its theoretical design. His theories were influenced by philosopher Michel Foucault, who had developed the notion of *heterotopia* five years before. For Foucault, 'spatial politics', the interaction of societies with the places they created, was the 'central theme of modernity'.

Foucault spent his life studying the history of how centralised power achieves control of the masses through the compartmentalisation of society. He believed that social constructs, or values, were both reflected and directed by the built environment, creating moral vagrancy by building walls of acceptable behaviour. His phrase 'carceral archipelago' referred to the city as a network of insulated institutions, which created a general architecture of prison-like control. In London and all other major cities today, the CCTV, the gated communities and the spikes that councils attach to pavements to ward off homeless people are prominent examples of the architecture of a carceral archipelago. Foucault's thinking moved from the exterior 'architectonics' of control to the interiorisation of their methods, which he called the 'technologies of the self'. Margins and boundaries are established in the minds of citizens through advertising, media and education, which assert the dominant ideologies of society. In the carceral archipelago, 'the judges of normality are everywhere'.

After half an hour of being pressed into the personal space of strangers, light fills the Tube, the underground has gone overground and we stream past the gardens of terraced houses towards Loughton, three stops from the end of the line. Just over the boundary into Essex, Loughton is the place where the fields start, where urban architectonics fall away into wide space, where you can spot the totem spirit of the plains: the brown hare.

Only ten minutes' walk away, they will be gathering for dusk and performing the strange ritual of spring, the magnificent bouncing dance where the females choose an eligible mate by punching the various bachelors in the face. The hare is a weird, slippery animal and has bewitched the lore of the countryside for centuries. With its smeuses and smoots, it is a trespasser of fields, and it is as hard to define as it is to confine. *Old big-gum, aunt sally, old bouchart, the swift-as-wind, the cat of the wood, the stag of the stubble, wee brown cow, the turpin, the trickster*, the hare is almost always described by reference to what it is not. Bugs

Bunny, who is not a bunny but a jack rabbit, the North American brown hare, is the most famous of hare tricksters, a folkloric archetype who leads the powerful members of society in a wild chase before it slips through the net to freedom. In folklore, the hare permeates the partition of gender – the Welsh thought that it was male one year and female the next, and in the Tudor era the bucks were widely believed to give birth to young. In every way, the hare defies enclosure.

But as we gather provisions for the night in the local supermarket, we see squadrons of sentinel hares lined up on the shelves, cast in palm oil and cocoa and wrapped in foil. Dressed as bunny rabbits, the hare's pagan wildness is watered down for the consumer of Easter treats, tamed into product. As we head down the high street, we pass the Lopping Hall, with its frieze of woodsmen, reminding us that Loughton is not just our gateway into Epping Forest, it is the reason there is a forest at all.

In 1864, William Whittaker Maitland, the High Sheriff of Essex, inherited Woodford Hall and with it the property rights of 1,120 acres of Loughton, including much of the common ground of Epping Forest. He had plans to develop the land, to *improve* it by building or farming on it, so up went the fences around five square kilometres of woodland, activating the cult of exclusion. The space was redefined by the fence line, and commoners who had previously had rights to lop wood on the land were now excluded. Two years later, Thomas Willingale and his two sons were caught in Epping Forest, lopping branches as their ancestors had done since time immemorial. Arrested and convicted under the 1820 Malicious Trespass Act, all three were sentenced to two months' hard labour, during which one of the sons died of pneumonia.

Perhaps because of the death, perhaps because of how recently the land had been enclosed, the case became a cause célèbre among the champagne socialists of London society. Back in the city, the chattering classes had become increasingly interested in the concept of space and how it was used. London was densely populated and much of the squalor and disease prevalent in working-class areas such as Bethnal Green was blamed on the density of living conditions, the lack of space. These were the aesthetes of London society, and included artist and writer John Ruskin, philosopher John Stuart Mill and Arts and Crafts supremo William Morris. With a quaint sincerity that would be crushed under the boot of today's neo-liberalism, their arguments were built around the concept of beauty – as William Morris wrote in the magazine *Justice*: 'The grip of the land grabber is over us all; and commons and heaths of unmatched beauty and wildness have been enclosed for farmers or jerry-built upon by speculators in order to swell the ill-gotten revenues of some covetous aristocrat or greedy money-bag.'

Octavia Hill was a central member of this group. As a young artist, her talents had been spotted by Ruskin who offered to train her as a copyist; they spent long afternoons in the National Gallery, copying the masters and talking politics. To Hill, space was an external dimension that had a direct influence on the interior wellbeing of a person: on mood, on self-esteem and on health. In a working-class world of heavy drinking, hard labour and domestic squalor, she saw that the provision of space could alleviate the pressures on the self: 'But to me it brings sad thought of the fair and quiet places far away, where it [light] is falling softly on tree, and hill, and cloud, and I feel as if that quiet, that beauty, that space, would be more powerful to calm the wild excess about me than all my frantic striving with it.'

Amid the soot and smog of the working-class districts, Hill was insistent that the poor should have places where they could catch a breath of fresh air. In 1865, she set up the Commons Preservation Society, still running today as the Open Spaces

Society. A year later, they offered Thomas Willingale their support and raised £1,000 to contest the case, fighting to maintain common rights over the land. Willingale died four years into the case, ostracised and unable to find work among a community who were Lord Maitland's tenants. But his case was taken up by the Corporation of the City of London and in 1879 Parliament finally passed the Epping Forest Act, which stipulated that the forest would always remain 'unenclosed and unbuilt on as an open space for the recreation and enjoyment of the people'.

The Commons Preservation Society went on to save Hampstead Heath from gravel extraction, Wimbledon Common from building development and, without their campaigning, the public would not have been granted access to Hampton Court Park, Regent's Park or Kew Gardens. As perhaps her crowning achievement, in 1895 Octavia Hill co-founded the National Trust.

At the crossroads, we meet the line of the forest. In early spring, the new leaves of the beech trees are lime-green, furry and translucent. They seem to hold light as well as filter it and, with the sun slowly setting, the trees are lit like Chinese lanterns and our faces are washed in a green glow. Fallen trees lie like sunken whales, drenched in luminous pools, and the air that streams through our noses is cool and refreshing. Breathing seems like drinking and the effect is psychotropic: it drugs us. The Japanese practice of *shinrin-yoku*, forest bathing, has recently arrived on our shores, backed by peer-reviewed science journals that have proved that trees, through their essential oils, release chemicals called phytoncides which boost the immune system for up to thirty days after immersion. In the woods, you thrive on the essence of trees.

We follow a meandering brook to the main path and then cut left up a hill. The trees around us are the record of centuries of common rights; they have been copparded six foot in the air, so that more poles could spring from the trunk and provide firewood for the locals. The scars of constant cutting have formed great gnarly, knobbled basins of wood, from which long, snaking brontosaur necks stretch up to the sky. At the rotten birch, we take a faint pathway through briar and thorn and arrive at the fire pit. We stumbled upon this space a decade ago, a patch of earth blackened by previous fires, and when we'd pulled some cut logs around it, it became a place we returned to. Over the years, we've found evidence of other use: beer bottles and spliff ends, and once a coronet of roses left in the centre, with gold ribbons streaming from the holly bushes, a wedding perhaps.

Though we didn't know it when we first sat down here, the circle is on the border of an Iron Age camp, a large tract of woodland barricaded by steep earthworks, now sunk into the topography of the wood. Here, Iron Age men and women kept their cattle, and 500 years later, as the story goes, Boudicca and her allied Iceni and Trinovantes tribes gathered here before devastating Londinium, only twenty years old, in AD 61. The space is broad and, with the canopy of the trees so high above us, walking through it feels like being inside an organic acropolis: it is a space inside, and a place aside, from the woods.

The architectonics of the wood, the structures and how they operate on the mind, are entirely different from those of the city. Nothing tries to sell you anything, nothing forbids access, no spaces have been designed or designated. Here, the mind unbelts. The grid has been replaced with a calm chaos, the straight lines of roads and rationalism are sunk in the smooth curves of beech boughs, wooden flights of fancy and the dazzling spray of bright green, free-flowing thought.

In 1989 the philosopher Edward Soja published the first in a series of books and essays that advanced the concept of Henri Lefebvre's Third Space. For Soja, 'Thirdspace' is a conversation between ideology and architecture open to all who inhabit it. It is both imagined and real, both abstract and concrete, and builds a space where the borders of society can be constantly challenged. In Soja's Thirdspace, groups who are marginalised by the ideologies imposed by place can interact on an equal footing with the centres of power that created them. Thirdspace can become an area of: 'radical openness, a context from which to build communities of resistance and renewal that cross the boundaries and double-cross the binaries of race, gender, class and all oppressively Othering categories'.

Thirdspace is not imposed from above, but created from within. Its central concept is its slipperiness, its openness to change, the permeability of its borders of definition. It is in constant flux, an 'open-ended set of defining moments'.

It is a theme picked up by bell hooks in her book *Yearning: Race, Gender and Cultural Politics*, where she talks of 'heterotopic marginality' as a place, and mindset, of resistance against unequal power distribution. Is there a place on earth where a white, middle-class, straight, cisgendered, able-bodied man like myself can stand before any member of a marginalised group, and be truly equal? Is there a place outside of the histories and politics that have given me power and privilege, simply by taking it from others? Inside the structure of the carceral archipelago, whose grid has been fashioned by men of power and constructed along lines that serve their ideologies, certainly not. But outside of this grid, with none of the signage and architecture of power, perhaps spaces can exist that reflect the needs of all those that use them. For all this radical thinking, Thirdspace sounds a lot like the oldest use of space in history: the commons.

We have been clambering through the woodland, gathering fallen branches. Bit by bit, we return to the circle, where a friend has already laid a nest of twigs over a tealight. We arrange the night's firewood in loose piles and roll the sawn birch logs a little closer to the centre, a circle drawn in proportion to its members. As the night draws in, the tealight will rise to a furnace and forge a temporary place out of space. Its margins will be dictated not by stone but by light, creating a place that is permeable to any who come its way.

Over the years we have met many people who have simply stepped out of the darkness, drawn by the dance of the fire. Homeless people have appeared at the bushes, streams of night-time joggers, middle-class hippies practising *ayahuasca* ceremonies, an impossibly young traveller from Russia, local Loughton lads. We have no property here, no right to exclude, and so the circle simply widens and the ambience changes according to the sum of its parts. With no signage, no directives to appropriate, proper behaviour, there is no normality here, no baseline to conform to.

This is a place for every occasion and every mood. This is the place you can come to when your best mate's dad dies, when your friend announces the baby in her womb, when you don't want to pay sixty quid to get into a club on New Year's Eve, where can you howl and whoop and sing your throat raw without offending your neighbours, and where you can get profoundly and marvellously high.

I unscrew the thermos and breathe in the dank steam. The water is brown, infused with the psychoactive capacity of psilocybin. All mushrooms are magic: more animal than plant, theirs is a weird kingdom that sprouts from the damp darkness of the underworld. They are transformative: some can turn oil spills and plastics into digestible material, some can absorb heavy metals and remove radioactive isotopes from the soil, and at least 200 species of them can tear down the fences of the self, and open the mind to new space. And like the phytoncides of trees, their effects have been shown to outlive the trip.

They have been used in couple-counselling and to mitigate the psychological effects of PTSD and a growing body of evidence suggests that 'micro-dosing' could help alleviate the symptoms of anxiety and depression. They have been shown to open the mind to new experiences, wider understanding, a feeling of inherent unity and sacredness to life that pervades experience long after the rush has died down. They are, of course, *extremely* illegal: as of 18 July 2005, Section 21 of the Drugs Act outlawed possession of magic mushrooms. Today, if caught, your newly liberated soul can be reincarcerated for seven years, two years longer than the minimum sentence for possession of an illegal firearm.

Magic mushrooms, however, are tricky to police. They are a commons drug, what philosopher Ivan Illich would call 'vernacular', referencing a legal term from ancient Roman law, *vernaculum*, that designated anything that was not a commodity. You can farm them and sell them, you can go on the dark web and buy them, but you can also just go for a walk and pick them: they grow free and wild, often on the estates of the most powerful men of society. And for this reason there are certain sections of the Act that provide for property owners – if you are caught in possession of magic mushrooms on land that you own you can claim to be disposing of them safely, which (in medical terms at least) would certainly include digesting them: to this day there is no evidence of harm from the occasional use of magic mushrooms, either short or long term.

We sit and pass round the tea, taking small sips until it disappears. The fire is crackling and no longer needs our nurture. It turns on the blacklight of the woods: old stories, half-remembered childhood legends and folktales that lie dormant in the light of the day now shine brightly in the firelight. Rationalism is a long way away and when night falls there are no concrete walls or electric lights to protect you from the atavistic – the boggarts, changelings, giants, ghosts and monsters step out from behind the line of fiction, and dance in the dark space around us.

Because of the work of Octavia Hill and the Commons Preservation Society, we still have about one million acres of common land in England. They are green and pleasant spaces, where people walk their dogs and where some still take their cows to pasture. But their true value, the social structure they embodied, the philosophy of 'commoning', has largely disappeared.

The commons are physical, but 'the Commons' is metaphysical. In practice, before enclosure, the Commons were a paradigm of social ties and community values that were used to regulate a particular local resource. Their terms and conditions, rights and responsibilities were determined by the people who used them, and every year they would vote in 'reeves' to oversee these values. The laws were not imposed by distant landowners, but, like Soja's Thirdspace, they were the sum of the people involved.

Though modern commons can still include areas of land or water whose rights and duties belong to the locals, their core philosophy has now transferred to the virtual world of the internet, to online operating systems, networks and platforms whose rights and duties belong to a global community. Wikipedia is one site that follows an open-source philosophy, encouraging users to contribute content; and, just as the old commons were organised by reeves, so Wikipedia is managed by experts to improve the quality of the resource. Wikipedia has signed up to the Creative

Commons licence, one of several public copyright licences that enable the free distribution of intellectual or creative resources – on their website today, they have over 1.1 billion works on offer, from photography, to art, to writing, educational resources, software, music and scientific journals and they belong, right now, to you. To attach a creative commons licence to a piece of work turns it from commodity to *vernaculum*.

The philosophy of commoning has thrived on the internet just as it has died on the land. It encourages a system of social interaction that foregrounds co-operative, inclusive values, sharing, over the ideology of privatised profiteering. The social platform Twitter is just one example of the modern commons. In 2013, when an American police officer was acquitted for shooting the teenager Trayvon Martin, a community organiser called Alicia Garza wrote an open letter on Facebook stating: 'our lives matter, black lives matter'. A year later, this phrase had become a hashtag and migrated to Twitter. During a march in Ferguson, Missouri, the police confronted protesters with tear gas, rubber bullets and assault weapons; they created free-speech zones, gag zones and press pens; and they utilised a spurious rule allowing them to arrest anyone loitering for more than five seconds (later declared unconstitutional by a Federal judge). But they could do nothing about the solidarity expressed on Twitter: the message that Black Lives Matter was projected without filter to a global audience. Likewise, the historic attempts to silence women, from physical violence to the Non-Disclosure Agreements of the modern age, have been seriously weakened by the collective vocalisation of the #MeToo campaign on Twitter: plain thoughts are broadcast loud and clear in the public sphere. Twitter, for all its drawbacks, has taken the marginalised, subjugated sectors of society and brought them, by *commons* consensus, to the centre of society. It is Thirdspace.

Something that feels like fear is hollowing my stomach. The light of the fire is starting to kaleidoscope. Its sparks slow and seem to float upwards with red dragon-tails tracing their motion. Form blurs, vision echoes, distinction slips and slides. The textbooks call this derealisation, the phase the mind slips into before an epileptic attack, as if the world is seen through a foggy pane of glass. But what mushrooms offer is the opposite of derealisation; they seem to lift the veil. When mushrooms take hold of your perception, you enter a transitory moment that can last up to six hours, that presents the world as a series of realisations, or epiphanies.

Something shifts behind my eyes to change the scene before them: like an optical illusion, when the background suddenly flips to the fore, the image remains the same, but a new form leaps forward. Overlooked in the humdrum drone of normality, it has been there all along, but now it is unmistakable and unforgettable. The hectic patterning of the woods has clarified into something sacred, sentient and slightly scary: I see the grimacing face of Pan.

My gut churns, my bowels turn, my blood is rushing like an electric kettle coming to the boil, except someone left the lid off and so it just goes and goes and goes. I'm on my feet and away from the group. I have wandered into Boudicca's acropolis, that hangar of beeches that now stand above me with the heavy presence of humans. Their canopies sway like the arms of festival crowds, thick streams of invisible wind combing through them, animating them. The light of the fire is behind me, but I see, or perceive, its light flying like burning arrows through the trees, warp-speeding through the darkness. The world has become intensely vivid.

I sense the ferns unfurling around me, the ivy writhing up the trees, their leaves ruffling like the feathers of a waking bird. Around my bare feet, the earth is moving; I feel the shield

bugs clambering through the leaf litter, the clumps of har-
vestmen arachnids skittering in tangled webs across the earth.
Beneath them, the wet soil is squirming with worms, woodlice
and millipedes and, suddenly very still, I sense the presence of
the insects asleep beneath me, the hibernating nymphs, larvae,
pupae, the unsprung embryonic stag beetles, encased for six
years in the Epping loam, which will soon crawl out of their
grave-cradles and fly drunkenly around the woods. I sense the
seeds, the tiny dots of energy with the unrealised space of trees
contained inside them and the white webs of mushroom roots
that net like neurons through the soil, that can *feel* my footsteps
on the earth, and as the kettle finally comes to a boil, the blood
beneath my skin fizzing like champagne, the bottle bursts, the
cork flies out and I am drenched in a frothing foam of laughter,
because finally I can comprehend with my whole body and soul
the words that William Morris once wrote beneath an elm tree
in Uffington in 1890: 'And all, or let us say most things, are brilliantly alive.'

I awake, several months later, in a grove of green light.
Somewhere in the distance I can hear the thump of heavy bass
and the shrieks and screams of a funfair. Long grass towers over
me, ferns over them, and, high up in the sky, the swaying tops of
the trees. I am lost in time and space, idling in the Wychwood.

Wychwood is *Hwiccewudu*, the old realm of the Anglo-Saxon
Hwicce tribe, which once stretched from Bath to Stoke-on-Trent,
through Birmingham and down to West Oxfordshire, to what
is now called Cornbury Park. When William the Conqueror
snatched up England, he forested about 120,000 acres of this
region as a deer park and from then on it proved very popular

with the hunting tribes of England. Henry III hunted here, Edward IV, James I (who hunted everywhere) and then from 1770 onwards, the Duke of Beaufort, having just discovered his love of chasing foxes, moved his retinue sixty miles from Badminton every year, to perform the selfless act of pest control in his neighbour's woods.

These woods form some of the most ancient tree cover in England, and are these days protected under the designation of a SSSI (Site of Special Scientific Interest). However, before its protection, under a succession of owners the forest had been cleared to make way for arable fields, to raise money for various building ventures and aristocratic debt relief, and now only about 0.5 per cent of its original extent survives. On the fascia of the cornice in the chapel, under the pediment of the Clarendon wing, is a quotation from Virgil, *deus nobis haec otia fecit*: 'a god has made this place of leisure for us'.

The Royal Forest was officially out of bounds for commoners, but they had used it nevertheless, to graze their pigs and cattle and poach venison. But every Palm Sunday they were allowed legitimate entry into the woods to perform the age-old cere-mony of 'Spanish water'. They would seek out a magical well deep in the woods and mix the wild liquorice that grew around it with the healing water to take back to their ailing relatives. The well flows with chalybeate waters which are so rich with iron that it is rimmed with a reddish-orange scum, as the salts build around its mouth. These days it is fenced and the tradition has died, but its name lives on in the festival that takes place here annually, and the reason for my visit: Wilderness.

Wilderness is a four-day music and cultural festival held every year in Cornbury Park since 2010. The year I arrive, 30,000 people are camping and raving behind the miles of temporary metal fencing. It is the absolute cream of English festivals and marketed towards the fat cats of society. It isn't just music on offer, but lakeside spas, yoga and mindfulness, theatre, comedy, debates, TED-style lectures, wild swimming, a champagne garden, a Rioja terrace and banqueting halls with celebrity chefs; it is the apotheosis of what has become known as a boutique festival and is to the festival scene what glamping is to camping: it's gorgeous. David and Samantha Cameron are regular visitors, Mark Carney, the former Governor of the Bank of England, has been spotted amid the crowds, and for all its chinos, pink shirts and Ferraris on the lawn, it has been christened *Poshstock* by the press.

I have finally risen from my druid dell in the Wychwoods, and have been walking the long hunting chases that run through the forest, towards Newell Plain. The plain is a vast hole cut out from the forest and today is a mixture of rough grassland and ploughed earth. In 1790, a group of Methodists from a neighbouring village came here for a picnic. They returned the next year, and the next, with more and more picnickers, and by the early 1800s the picnic had turned into a fair. It is impossible to say when and how this happened, but it says something about how people saw their common ground – though officially the property of the Crown, it was poorly policed and since it belonged to no one exclusively, like the firepit in Epping Forest, no one had the right to exclude any other. A combination of word of mouth and an intrinsic sense of right to the land led people to this plain, ready to lose themselves in a carnival spirit.

The scant descriptions that remain of the fair are enough to set the scene: 500 coloured lanterns were erected, the Duke of Marlborough's yeomanry band played, the Vauxhall Dancing School were there, there were freak shows, jugglers, and George Wombwell was a regular, with his menagerie of exotic beasts that included elephants, giraffes, leopards, panthers and 'the real unicorn of scripture', a rhinoceros.

Because the fair was free, it was open to members of all stations of the Georgian hierarchy, from the navvies working on the railway line, the commoners of Cornbury, to the gentry and the Duke and Duchess of Marlborough themselves, who lived down the road in Blenheim Palace and had recently purchased the neighbouring estate of Cornbury. They made their appearances at the fair in a wagon with attendant coachmen and footmen dressed in scarlet liveries, white stockings and plush cockades, no strangers to the joy of fancy dress. Yet by the 1830s the forest rangers had become increasingly exasperated by the fair 'bringing the neighbourhood vast numbers of idle and disorderly characters' and on 25 September 1830, it was announced that the fair 'shall be DISCONTINUED'.

The fair was banned until 1833 but returned for another decade, when it was banned again. But people kept coming back. The very last fair, in 1855, saw a dozen special excursion trains offloading revellers from London on the newly built railway line, who would crowd through the forest, ramble up past the great manor house and return at the end of the day, soaked in gin. When the 7th Duke of Marlborough, Winston Churchill's grandfather, finally bought the rights of Newell Plain in 1856, *Jackson's Oxford Journal* reported: 'It is understood that his Lordship will allow the fair, under certain restrictions, to be held another year, although the spot is now assigned as private property.'

But he didn't. By the following year he had fortified the commons against incursion, dug deep trenches through the approach roads to stop the wagons and policed the woods with his own gamekeepers, who had been sworn in as special constables. He was, of course, the local magistrate, so anyone caught on this former common ground went before his judgment on the bench. The fair was finally dead.

Today, the Wilderness website proclaims: 'for four days this August, no one belongs here more than you' (providing, of course, that you have purchased a wristband). Since 2010, Wilderness festival has resurrected the site for carnival, selling the perquisite of wildness back to those that can afford it. On top of the minimum ticket price of £180, you can choose the boutique camping, which offers a hierarchy of comfort, from bell-tents to gypsy wagons. Prices here start at £829 and rise to around £2,499 for a cute little gypsy wagon with a double bed.

This weekend, within the compound, a friend of mine is interviewing a hero of mine, the writer Jay Griffiths, and has sourced me a wristband for a day's entry. So I leave Newell Plain, follow the perimeter fence round to the entrance of the festival, join the queue, collect my wristband – and gain my legitimacy.

The festival is a riot of colour and wonderment. Brass bands are processing in full pageant regalia, teams of mad scientists in oversized spectacles run around with clipboards talking theatrical gibberish, there are people on stilts, acrobats, jugglers and fire-breathers. Everywhere you turn, the world is a kaleidoscope of micro-experiences, palmistry, theatre, operatics, tiny tents of quiet wonder amid the noise of carnival.

This is the fingerprint of the organisers of Wilderness, the 'boutique festival' experience, first perfected at Secret Garden Party, the grungier, druggier, hardcore-ravier older sister of Wilderness. It still places music and theatre at the heart of the entertainment, but fills the interstices of the main stages with a jumble of hare-brained eccentricity.

It is a fairy-tale vision: far beyond fancy dress, everyone seems to be in some state of anthropomorphic metamorphosis. People in long dress-coats turn to reveal plush fox tails, people in top hats have the ears of hares poking through the rim, there are peacock feathers, pheasant feathers, owl masks, there are badgers wearing skin-tight fuchsia jumpsuits and wildcats in Edwardian bodices and fishnet tights.

This is therianthropy, the ancient practice of becoming animal, a shamanic shape-shifting that stretches through the mythology of werewolves and satyrs and fauns, past the Egyptian hieroglyphs, to cave paintings and amulets tens of thousands of years old. Ever since humans ceased to be animals, we have been ritualising our link with them, bridging the gap between human and non-human. Even in today's format, with synthetic feathers or a papier-mâché crown of antlers, by dressing up in animal form we strip ourselves of our habitual human veneer, and reconnect to something wild.

I duck into the literary tent and pick a deck chair far back enough so that Jay Griffiths won't pick up on my saucer-eyed love for her. The tent fills and the talk begins, and it's quiet and interesting and nothing like my experiences of being on stage at such events. As a writer of the lower order (graphic novels) I have always been put on after peak hours, which usually means when the sun has set, and when the raving has started. At that time of night, people use the literary tent like a saline drip: from the stage, you can see people stagger in from the chaos, and sit in the corner, skinning up, coming down, grateful for the low drone of literary murmur, as if sobriety can be transfused through the ears.

But these guys are pros and the tent is packed, attentive and moderately sober. After the talk, while a long queue forms for the book signing, I mill around the bookshop, scanning the titles. One table is piled high with the twenty-first century's answer to the self-help book, the 'Mindfulness' literature that has master-fully appropriated the experience of existence. In a world dominated by work and productivity, mindfulness reminds us how to appreciate the passing moment. But mindfulness is just idleness without the social stigma, repackaged with a barcode and brand. Idleness, from the Germanic word *Idla*, meaning worthless, has historically been a term given to any use of time not dedicated to turning profit; it is a slur on a vernacular use of time. It is the bane of the authorities and used to this day to describe anyone who is not doing what they ought to be doing. And since the industrial revolution, with the work ethic firmly installed into our modern minds, the final victory of commercialism has been to sell idleness back to us. This is rentier capitalism of the mind – access to experience is enclosed, monopolised and rented out as a commodity.

The most recent example of this is forest bathing, or *shinrin-yoku*. As soon as the health benefits of being immersed in woodland became evident in England, what is in fact nothing more than a stroll in the woods became rebranded under the exoticised cloak of Japanese culture, swallowed into corporate consumerism, and is now sold by various companies as a luxurious retreat from the working world. Of course, trees release their essential oils whether you've paid for it or not, but here in Oxfordshire, where the public are barred from 90 per cent of woodlands, even a walk in the woods is now something to be sold.

I duck out of the literature tent and take a walk. Beneath its veneer of unfettered freedom, this festival is no less stratified than the city it offers you escape from. You can bathe in the lakes, but only as far as the line policed by stewards in kayaks. Nakedness is prohibited, which feels unnecessarily restrictive since in 2012 it was here that the world's skinny-dip record was broken. The path along the lake is partitioned with a banner that says 'Live your Freedom', but the banner hides a metal fence that blocks the route to a separate enclosure of hot tubs and leisure facilities, for a more exclusive experience of the lake. The Veuve Clicquot tent serves champagne at £16 per glass and

THE BOOK OF TRESPASS

£90 per bottle, and in the evening, the banquet costs £85. The open plain has been enclosed into little boxes of space, segregated by the blandest, least carnivalesque notion going: how much coin you have in your pocket.

Originally, the word 'wilderness' was a compound of wild and deer; it was any place where wild animals roamed free. But wild-deer-ness was always more than just a place; it was a state of mind. Frances Zaunmiller, the mountain woman who spent forty-five years living along Salmon River in the Idaho outback, defined wilderness as the psychological expanse where 'a man can walk without trespassing'. In her fierce and phenomenal book *Pip Pip*, Jay Griffiths goes several steps further:

> wilderness is a ferocious intoxication which sweeps over your senses with rinsing vitality, leaving you stripped to the vivid, your senses rubbed until they shine. It is an untouched place which touches you deeply and its after-math – when landscape becomes innerscape – leaves you elated, awed and changed utterly. Forget the lullaby balm of nature tame as a well-fed lawn, here nature has a lean and violent *waking* grandeur which will not let you sleep ... It is an aphrodisiac; it is a place of furious fecundity ... not virginal but erupting with the unenclosable passion at the volcanic heart of life.

Boom! That's why she gets the afternoon gigs. But at this festival, Wilderness is a brand, and wildness is its product. Wildness means *self-willedness* and is the state of being undir-ected, uncultivated, free from the template of someone else's design. It links us with the non-human world; it connects us to the animal within. Because wildness is feral, it is sexy and therefore it sells well. But when wildness turns to commodity it is hollowed of its core meaning and becomes only its shell, a facsimile of itself. True wildness is unpredictable, and can lead people to question their position in society.

The Swing Riots of 1830 broke out across the South West only a week after the Gaelic harvesting festival of Samhain. Likewise, the Midland Revolt of 1607 began straight after the spring festivities on the commons. People met up in their hundreds and thousands, got drunk, talked, and, like an analogue Twitter, exchanged like-minded views which led to an uprising. Fifty years earlier, Kett's Rebellion, which saw 16,000 people storm the city of Norwich in protest at enclosure of their common land, began at the annual feast of Thomas Beckett. The authorities, as ever, labelled the feast a gathering of 'idle and disordered people', and perhaps this was the case. But perhaps it wasn't the inherent nature of the people themselves, but simply the autonomous act of coming together, the sharing of solidarity, that triggered the people to rise against the system that was starving them.

Free festivals, organic gatherings of people on common land, have always been a threat to the status quo. But organised, sanctioned festivals, the bread and circuses of ancient Rome, were seen as a way of allowing people to vent their frustrations in a manner contained by local authorities. An article from the *London Magazine* in 1738 sums up this paternalism neatly: 'Dancing on the Green at Wakes and merry Tides should not only be indulg'd but incourag'd: and little Prizes being allotted for the Maids who excel in a Jig or a Hornpipe would make them return to their daily Labour with a light Heart and grateful Obedience to their Superiors.'

They just don't say it like they used to. These days, such bald honesty has been smothered by a more brand-conscious commercialism, and local authorities have been replaced by global corporations. Wilderness Festival is a subsidiary of Secret Productions Ltd, who are a subsidiary of Mama Festivals who are a subsidiary of Mama and Company Ltd. Among other festivals such as Somersault, Global Gathering and God's Kitchen, they run venues such as the Garage in Islington, the Institute in Birmingham, the Ritz in Manchester and the Arts Club in Liverpool. They are themselves a subsidiary of Live Nation Entertainment Inc. who have their central offices in Beverly Hills, and whose total assets amount to $7.5 billion. In the words of their own website, somewhere in the world, every eighteen minutes, is a Live Nation event. What we have here is not culture, but monoculture.

Wilderness is, without doubt, a slick festival experience: it's very well run, the entertainment is second to none, there's always bog roll in the toilets (no small thing). In itself, there is no harm in a multi-national corporation providing entertainment to people, whatever their financial income; rich people need somewhere to get high, too. But if there is no place for people to come together on their own terms, no space (conceptual or literal) for an alternative, vernacular culture, then this prism of corporate control encloses our landscape and constructs our experience of nature. Here the wild, weird hare of carnival, the totem of the commons, has been tamed into palm oil, foil-wrapped bunny rabbits, reified into product.

I meet up with a couple of friends. They're at the festival already, legitimate with their wristbands, but they are keen for the trespass outside. So, dodging the security guards, we plot an inverse trespass, and break out of the festival, over a wall in one of the car parks. For the last hours of the afternoon, we roam free through the ancient Wychwood, dabbing at a small bag of MDMA. When sold as grey crystalline powder, the drug is called MDMA, when sold in pills, it is Ecstasy. But originally, before its commercial value was tested, it was called *empathy*. Invented in 1912, used extensively as a therapeutic drug to disinhibit patients, it first migrated to England from the disco scene of 1970s New York, where it went on to fuel the rave revolution of the late 1980s and early 1990s. Again, it is *extremely* illegal.

In an editorial he wrote for the *Journal of Psychopharmacology*, Professor David Nutt criticised the current designation of Ecstasy as a class A drug. He compared its dangers to those of horse-riding: while one in 350 people harm themselves through horse-riding, only one in 10,000 people experience adverse effects of Ecstasy. For bringing these plain facts into the public sphere, he was instantly dismissed from the Advisory Council on the Misuse of Drugs. The orthodoxy of drug legislation will permit no alternatives to its perspective, even if they are peer-reviewed and based on clear scientific evidence.

We come again to Newell Plain. We climb a fallen tree and lounge like leopards on its boughs, staring across the plain, absolutely up to our necks in idleness. Ecstasy makes you unambiguously tactile, and I find that I've been stroking my friend like a cat, running my fingers through his hair, massaging his neck. It feels like Sunday morning in my flat, but it is Sunday evening in a field. This is what Octavia Hill was talking about when she wanted to turn the cemeteries and waste ground of inner-city London into 'open-aired sitting room' – very simply: to be at home in nature.

I can hear the muted roar of the festival through the Cornbury woods. Carried on the wind, it reaches my ears like a faint ghost of the fair on Newell Plain. My imagination fills this empty space with the anarchy of the long-gone, half-cut crowds, the place lit up by lanterns, the elephants and rhinoceroses of George Wombwell's travelling circus. Before enclosure, this space was Thirdspace. It was a place outside the matrix of commerce and, for several days a year, it upended the hierarchy of power that governed the lives of the revellers. It was anarchy in its purest sense: the culture of this carnival was not designed in an office in Beverly Hills, but by the people who turned up to it. But all that is gone.

These days, multiculturalism takes the blame for watering down the culture of England. The persistent myth of Winterval, the story of how councils are forced to rebrand their Christmas festivities for fear of offending Muslims, is emblematic of how immigrant communities are scapegoated for diluting the culture of England. Though entirely fabricated, the myth was repeated forty-four times by the *Daily Mail* between 1998 and 2011, forever keen to blame systemic, inherent problems on new arrivals.

The eccentric melee of folk customs, localised fêtes and seasonal carnivals was stamped out long before multiculturalism was even a word. Lammas festival, Oak Apple Day, Jack in the Green, Hocktide, Imbolc, Bealtaine, Lughnasadh and Samhain, any number of forgotten festivals were cut from the culture when the people were excluded from the land.

Hundreds of years of private property laws have morphed into a strict orthodoxy in English society, an unquestioned consensus as to what can and can't happen in the countryside. If it's not a walk along a Right of Way, or a picnic in a designated area, if you haven't paid for it then you're almost certainly not allowed to do it. This has led to a peculiar and hugely distorted vision of the English countryside: its brand. Watch TV, read the papers, walk into a camping shop and you'd think the countryside is custom-built for enthusiastic middle-class white people in Thinsulate hats and sensible walking shoes. This is the land as it is sold to us, because, today, even leisure is an industry.

But when 'Rooster' Byron, the hero of Jez Butterworth's play *Jerusalem*, asks 'what the fuck do you think an English forest is for', he's not talking about a nice walk with a thermos of mint tea. He's referring to a much deeper, historic use of the countryside, one that predates the cult of exclusion. He's talking about the wild sabbats on the open plains, the world outside the heedful eye of the patriarchs, an alternative, vernacular life-style that operates beyond the matrix of commerce. He's talking about a place where wildness doesn't come with a price tag, where freedom is free.

In the tragedy of 'Rooster' Byron, it is not the gods who govern his fate, but the bureaucrats at Kennet and Avon Council. The entire play takes place on a small clearing of land in front of his caravan; outside the village, it is also outside its conventions. Byron uses his little circle of land just as Shakespeare uses the Forest of Arden in *As You Like It*. It is a place of fairies and giants, of magical thinking, where characters can slip off their usual roles and metamorphose into something new. It is a place where myth and folk culture, the stories of the commons, permeate the real world. There is a drum somewhere in the clearing that Byron says was a gift from a pylon-sized giant who claimed to have built Stonehenge. But Byron has no rights to the land, and thus has no rights to his activities on it, so along come the Kennet and Avon Council to evict him.

In the real world, the final nail in the coffin for freedom in the countryside was the Criminal Justice and Public Order Act of 1994. Like the Tudor and Georgian Vagrancy Acts, it targeted specific types of people, grouped them together and defined them as a threat to the state. It outlawed alternative lifestyles and ideologies, by removing people's rights to express them in real space. Its trigger was the largest rave in English history, on Castlemorton Common, but its roots stretched into the early 1980s, to Margaret Thatcher's attempts to obliterate what she called the 'permissive society', to a long-established battle-ground in the fight for space: Stonehenge.

In the early 1900s Stonehenge 'belonged' to Edmund Antrobus, because he owned the land it sat on. He had objected several times to the mass initiation ceremonies conducted there by the Ancient Order of the Druids (which was in fact not very ancient, and set up only a century or so before). When he began charging the druids for entry to his land, they objected, and brought a case in which they claimed they could not be charged for admission into their own temple. They won. They didn't own Stonehenge, but it was theirs to use. When Sir Edmund and his heirs died in the First World War, the land was put up for auction and bought by Cecil Chubb, who then gifted it to the nation (in exchange for a knighthood). In the deeds of the gift was Sir Cecil's express directive that there must be 'free access for all'.

In the 1920s, 20,000 visitors came to experience the stones. In the fifties it was 124,000 and, by the 1980s, 800,000 tourists were visiting the stones each year. The fence went up in spring 1978. By the time Ecstasy hit the shores of England, a large society of travelling hippies, called the Peace Convoy, were settling at Stonehenge for solstice celebrations, free festivals of mysticism, drugs and rave. But this was the wrong use of the countryside, by the wrong type of people.

The National Trust and English Heritage, who by this point co-owned the site, obtained an injunction for eighty-three named people, banning them by law of trespass. But on 1 June 1985, a group of 600 hippies and New Age travellers were driving along the A303 to set up another festival at the stones. They were met seven miles away from the site by 1,300 police officers and a roadblock made out of three trucks' worth of dumped gravel. The police, in full riot gear, shields and batons, went up and down the stalled convoy, smashing windows, arresting the drivers. Their primary objective was to find the ringleaders of the festival, whose names were displayed on the Peace Convoy's posters and marketing material: 'Boris and Doris proudly present ...' But in spite of checking each and every person in the convoy, they couldn't find them, because Boris and Doris were geese.

Trapped in their line of convoy, under attack from the state, the hippies tore down the fences on one side of the road and escaped into an arable field, followed by lines of police vans, who could now do them for criminal damage and breach of the peace. So began the Battle of the Beanfield.

Eight policemen and sixteen travellers were hospitalised. There is footage, filmed by an ITV camera crew, but not shown at the time, that is dizzying to watch. Brightly coloured buses and lorries doughnut around the field, as armies of helmeted officers run in squadrons, bashing their sticks through the windscreens, showering the families inside with glass, before hauling the drivers out through the jagged windows. Shields are used to flatten prostrate hippies; truncheons are jabbed into their stomachs. The whole melee was an act of state-sanctioned hooliganism, the wanton destruction not just of motor vehicles, but of homes, which to the Peace Convoy were one and the same thing. Eventually 537 travellers were arrested, one of the largest mass arrests in English legal history, and Operation Solstice was deemed a success: Stonehenge remained empty. The *Daily Mail* ran with the headline 'A New Generation of Vagabonds', that same, tired projection, as old as the Thurston Oak in Suffolk.

The sociologist Howard S. Becker wrote about moral deviance in such a way that the word can easily be swapped for trespass: 'social groups create deviance by making rules whose infraction constitutes deviance, and by applying those rules to particular people and labelling them as outsiders. From this point of view, deviance is not a quality of the act the person commits, but rather a consequence of the application by others of rules and sanctions to an offender.' The hippies and their alternative, unsanctioned use of the land, had been turned into moral vagrants. By pouring three trucks' worth of gravel onto the A303, the police had turned a temple into an exclusion zone, drawn an ideological line in real space that excluded an alternative way of life. They weren't responding to a crime, they were creating one.

Twice a year the hippies are now allowed to gather at Stonehenge, to watch the sun rise on the solstice. But Cecil Chubb's demand for free access remains unacknowledged. Today, £20 will buy you a seat on a bus that will shuttle you to a fence set ten yards from the stones. However, if, like the festival-goers at Wilderness, you can afford a little more, you can book months in advance and pay £140 for an exclusive Special Access Tour, which will take you inside the fence. It has never been clear why 'Rooster' Byron's giant built Stonehenge, but the new designation of place, for tourism and not worship, is indicative of how space is now sanctified across the land: it is a commodity. By restricting access to land, and then charging for entry, whether it be Stonehenge or Cornbury Park, sectors of society unable to afford the cost have become marginalised and cut off from experience. Experience must be sold to grant it a licence. This is the leisure industry, because leisure shares its roots with the word licence, from the Latin *licere*: to be allowed.

We have cut through the woods and arrived at the highest point of the estate, the peak of a hill of long swaying grass, on the perimeter of the Wychwood. The festival is laid out in a bowl beneath us and we can hear the hubbub of the crowds and the heavy thump of the music. We find a large flattening in the grass, the long stems bent to the ground to form a living straw mat, like the scrape of earth that a hare sleeps in, its 'form'. The stars come out quickly, the satellites glide through space and the planes soar silently, scoring lines of vapour across a violet canvas. Then someone turns the lasers on.

The verb 'to rave' is from the French *rêver*: 'to dream, to wander, to behave madly', an etymology that, just like trespass, implies some sort of given line. In the eighteenth century, raving led you to incarceration in the workhouse; these days it leads to expulsion from the land. Illegal raves are still held throughout the country, in deserted quarries, old industrial sites, the holy Brecon Beacons, because no law of trespass will ever quench the human need to dream, or behave madly. But the power of the police to close down raves has little to do with morality, noise pollution or community disruption; it is decided by property alone.

A few years ago, the 3rd Baron Margadale, the current owner of William Beckford's Fonthill estate, threw a twenty-first-birthday bash for his daughter. The sound system went on until 8.30 in the morning and could be heard for miles around. After local residents complained about the noise, the Warminster police turned up on site and then wrote on Twitter: 'Complaint of loud music in Tisbury ... area checked, private party on private land. No criminal offences.'

Property decides what is proper. It decides what land is for and who land is for. If you can't afford to pay for access to city clubs or country festivals, or if you don't own property spacious enough to create your own community gathering, if no landlord will give you their permission, there is simply nowhere for you to commune. As long as what happens on the land is governed by a select few there will never be a society that reflects the values of its constituents, there will never be an England that reflects the values of anything but a tiny minority of its citizens. If we are truly to discover what we have in common, we must be allowed to gather on common ground.

Both my friends are gently snoring. Octavia Hill's outdoor living room has become our open-aired bedroom. Fizzing with Ecstasy, warm and snug in our form, I don't want to shut my eyes, or lose consciousness. The sky before me is a paradox of time laid out in space. To my left, the crescent moon shines in pitch darkness, to my right, the rising sun shines in a blaze of blue; small clusters of birds fly from night into morning. The lasers are still slicing the sky, but the festival ground is empty. There is a low thrum of noise, which I take to be the sound of some giant generator still feeding the place with electricity. But it isn't. It's the sound of heavy, thumping techno sunk in a tight gorge of the valley, where the last dancers are still raving to the beat of a drum.

We need space for the mind to rave, to wander and to dream. Access to land is access to experience and access to nature is access to our own wild, spiritual mind. And while the current logic of property forbids our experience of land unless it is sold, we are expected to buy weekend tickets to access our own wild creativity. Twenty miles due south of us, 130 years behind us, William Morris is still sitting beneath that elm tree in Uffington. His words apply as much to our minds as to our land: 'The beauty of the landscape will be exploited and artificialised for the sake of the villa-dwellers' purses where it is striking enough to touch their jaded appetites; but in quiet places like this it will vanish year by year (as indeed it is now doing) under the attacks of the most grovelling commercialism.'

TOAD

Fluidity, transparency, binary opposition

'I should like to say one word about our kind host, Mr. Toad.
We all know Toad! (great laughter) –
Good Toad, modest Toad, *honest* Toad' –
(shrieks of merriment)'
– Kenneth Grahame, *The Wind in the Willows*

Water is the ultimate element of trespass. Dam-buster, ditch-leveller and hydraulic digger, it has no respect for borders. It slips through cracks and gushes down hillsides; it falls from the sky and seeps up through the ground. As it reflects, it distorts: it dissolves definition, blurs distinction and spurns division.

It is a nightmare for property lawyers. In his *Commentaries*, William Blackstone refers to it as 'a movable, wandering thing' and has to redefine its property to make it property: 'It is observable that water is here mentioned as a species of land, which may seem a kind of solecism; but such is the language of the law.'

Water makes a mockery of legal fictions. As a river, it takes acres of land from one estate and attaches it to another as it bends, leaving lawyers to fight over the question: who owns the silt deposits? Often, it marks the boundaries of estates, and, just as often, it moves them so that the lines on a map rarely conform to its line on the land. It is neither on one side of property, nor the other: while it creates the moat that blocks the trespasser, it also provides the anti-gravitational capacity to cross it, with a lot more grace than a wall. That is, if you don't mind getting wet.

There's a flash, like a spark from a struck match, and the moment I see the kingfisher it's gone. Everything else is still; the blanket of mist above the river, still in the windless air and a half-moon, still in the sky. It is cold because it is early, but today will be a scorcher.

I unzip the kayak from its rucksack, unfold it and pump air into its various compartments. Two dogs run by, and then a jogger. I slide its plastic fin into the bottom, plop it onto the water, tether it to a barge pin and load it with food, a sleeping bag, roll matt, several layers of warm clothing, a camera, sketchbook and crayons. I grab the paddle, slide in, and push off.

The River Kennet starts on Silbury Hill in Wiltshire and runs through Marlborough and Hungerford to arrive here in Aldermaston, West Berkshire. It flows another ten miles as far as Reading when it fuses with the Thames, which takes you all the way to London, where, barring extreme weather events and a potential breach of the inflatable, I hope to be in three days' time. With the wide sky above me, and its reflection below me, and the long unbroken expanse of water before me, I feel a childish excitement, as if my whole life is ahead of me.

The river is where time flows gently, a world of soft green light where idleness is the only option. Unlike the seas, its gift is not the magisterial contemplation of infinity, but the parochial contentment of a quiet life. When Mole first meets Ratty in the opening pages of *The Wind in the Willows*, the fuss and bother of busyness meets the calming influence of the river. Having spent his entire life underground, Ratty's boat is the first Mole has been in and he can't quite trust his own excitement. So Ratty assures him with the book's most famous words: 'Believe me, my young friend, there is nothing – absolutely nothing – half so much worth doing as simply messing about in boats.'

But that's easy for Ratty to say. He lives on the banks of the Thames, where right of access has, since 1623, been secured under a Navigation Act. But I'm four miles south of Ratty's home, on the River Kennet, which, if you can believe the Fishing Officer on the Reading and District Angling Association's forum: 'is most defenatly [sic] NON-NAVIGABLE'. Like the vast majority of rivers of England, it seems the River Kennet is subject to a different ideology – the most extreme expression of the cult of exclusion. Of the 42,700 miles of river in England, we have a right of access to 1,400 miles, just 3 per cent. In England, if you're by a river, on a river or in a river, there's a 97 per cent chance that you're not allowed to be there.

Rivers and their banks are subject to a category of legislation called Riparian Rights. While the Crown is said to own the water that flows through a river, the landowner holds the rights to the riverbank which extends across its bed towards an imaginary line drawn halfway through the river. To kayak or swim along a stretch of river, you must have permission from each and every one of the property owners on the banks, meaning the long stretch of open water is actually (or, rather, legally) divided up into an invisible grid of lines, each under the control of the lord of that section of land.

The ownership of a river has been particularised into its various components so that they can be rented and sold as separate entities. When the Liberty Stadium was built in Swansea, the home of both the football and the rugby club, a seventy-foot bridge was erected over the River Tawe so that people could actually get to it. For the privilege of building this city amenity, the council had to pay the Duke of Beaufort, who lives ninety miles away, £280,000 for an 'easement' (a Right of Way over private property) because for the last 400 years his family has owned the riverbed. But it is the fishing rights, usually but not always conjoined with the ownership of the bank and the bed, that cause the most friction.

I have slipped past various small villages and am now surrounded by open fields. I have entered the Englefield estate, owned by the former richest MP in Parliament, Richard Benyon. To my left, a mile north, is his manor house and on my right are tall iron fences, which gauze my view to the private fishing ponds beyond. Mr Benyon's rights over this section allow him to rent the river and its ponds to angling associations whose members pay annual subscriptions to fish the bream, tench, carp and pike that live in the lagoon. These rented rights have created a fierce, ongoing enmity between fishermen and other users of the river. Principal among these are the kayakers, and the battles that flare between them and the fishermen are the modern expression of the old poacher/gamekeeper dynamic.

Kayaking turns a river from a boundary into a highway through boundaries and, in so doing, it undermines the total dominion of modern riparian rights. It calls attention to the absurdity of a legal fiction that pretends the river is segmented into private domains, partitioned by invisible lines that cannot be crossed. Fishing on rivers is by and large a fixed pastime, rooted to one spot, and property is comfortable with that notion: if you

vant this spot, it belongs to me, but you can access it *for a price.*
ut kayakers and swimmers slide through boundaries and are
o slippery for property rights to get a grip on. Without a toll
..oth on every boundary line, property has not yet found a way
of profiting from kayakers; kayaking is a vernacular sport.

The Angling Trust, who represent the interests of fishermen
across England and Wales, see it differently. In the words of
their National Campaigns' Coordinator:

> The Angling Trust has been challenging the claims being
> made by militant canoeists that they should have a right
> to paddle up every river, stream or brook in Britain irre-
> spective of ownership or the impact this has on wildlife
> or other people's enjoyment. The rights of navigation are
> clear in law and there are thousands of miles of navigable
> rivers and waterways to which canoeists have legal access.

Even down to the 's' at the end of 'thousands', everything
about this statement is disingenuous. The high-octane rhetoric
of 'militant' is typical of the fishing lobby groups, and is incongruous to the point of surrealism. The reference to wildlife is
also typical, and sly, and in spite of being repeatedly proven
otherwise, it remains a dominant tactic of the fisher-kings. In
2000, the Environment Agency produced a report that stated
conclusively: 'there is no empirical evidence linking canoeing
with damage to fish spawning grounds or damage to fish stocks
... there is unlikely to be any significant impact on or lasting dis-
turbance to wildlife from the passage of canoes.'

The Angling Trust borrow this tactic from the owners of
agricultural land, who persistently defend their exclusive use
of their land with the claim that they are protecting it from the
ignorant masses. This claim rests on a conflation of land ownership with land-stewardship, a story invented by landowners that

conveniently overlooks the element of scale. While the inconsiderate rambler may occasionally stumble into the eggs of a ground-nesting bird, their effect on the wildlife of England is nothing compared to that of industrial agriculture. In the fifty years after the Second World War, the destruction of 121,000 kilometres of hedgerow (and the consequent decline in sparrow, linnet and thrush) was not the work of vandal ramblers but landowners, often using dynamite to blow the roots from their soil, seeking to increase the financial yield of their property.

The owner of this stretch of the River Kennet, Richard Benyon, has been a staunch defender of the rights of fishing. As the former Under Secretary of State for Fisheries and Natural Environment, Benyon has come under fire for what some perceive to be a vested interest in supporting fishermen over other users of rivers. In an interview with the *Angling Times*, he said: 'While we want more people to get out and enjoy activities in the countryside they must be complementary. There are plenty of places to canoe where it is appropriate and others where it is not. There will be no change to our policy of supporting voluntary access agreements as the only way forward.'

These are silky words. Once again, what is deemed 'appropriate' is determined by what is deemed property. Once again, the construct that 'voluntary access' is the 'only way forward' smacks of obstinate paternalism. And the notion that access to 3 per cent of rivers is 'plenty' has such rhetorical gall to it that it can only be described as Politicians' Cant.

The open fields have morphed into the back gardens of the terraced housing on the outskirts of Reading. Something about rivers draws out the eccentricity of the English, and each plot here is decorated in a ramshackle, water-weathered style. There are stone owls, plastic herons, driftwood sheds, old rusted benches and bunting, blanched by the sun and rain, all sunk in glorious profusions of bindweed and buddleia. As I get closer to the heart of the town, the shallows are clogged with Lucozade bottles, discarded shopping trolleys, Walkers' crisp packets bleached and leached of their colour, and along the scrubby banks, every twenty yards or so, the fishermen. Their long trail lines extend, almost invisible, out in the river, and I have to manoeuvre my kayak to avoid their hooks. I try a cheery Enid Blyton-style 'hallo!' to the various characters attached to the rods, and am met with stony silence. Further down the river I change gear to a gruffer, more macho 'how do', the kind of surly non-invasive tone appropriate to pub urinals, but this is equally fruitless.

I get the distinct impression that I'm intruding. The fishermen have bought an exclusive right to sit on this riverbank, and here I am, with no licence in my pocket, bursting their bubble of dominion. Their purchased right of property has created a division between us where none is necessary: across the country, kayakers report stones and lead weights thrown at them, threats hurled, and some are still paying off thousands of pounds of court costs for cases they have lost against fishermen. The peaceful river has become a tetchy battleground, an incongruous world of binary opposition, imposed by the idea that one right supersedes all others because it has been purchased. But of all the people on the river today, surely we have the most in common: we're here for the stillness, the gentle passing of time, the simple pleasure of being enveloped by nature.

As the Kennet winds through Reading town, its banks turn to concrete, foliage disappears and the sounds of police sirens and traffic smother the birdsong. Before meeting the Thames, it cuts through the Oracle shopping centre, which has a loud, sticky grot to it. I slide past barges, boats and packed public houses, under the railway bridge and out into the dizzying breadth of the Thames.

In 2004, the Reverend Dr Doug Caffyn wrote a master's thesis entitled 'The Right of Navigation on Non-tidal Rivers and the Common Law' which claimed that, between 1189 and 1600, there had been a right of public access to all rivers. This, he claims, is confirmed by Clause 33 of Magna Carta and again in the 1472 Act for Wears and Fishgarths. Caffyn's dissertation sparked England's newest bout of Ownership Anxiety and was refuted in no uncertain terms by the fisher-kings. Interviewed on the BBC in 2013, the then CEO of the Angling Trust, Mark Lloyd, said: 'The law of the land is absolutely clear – there is no universal right for people to canoe on non-tidal waters.' He had commissioned his own report by QC David Hart, who followed the footsteps of the judges in the Pierson and Post case, and trawled through the ancient legal texts, Glanville, de Bracton, Britton and Callis, to refute Caffyn's claim.

According to Hart, the crux of a claim for Public Right of Navigation (PRN) comes down to two points: first, whether the river is navigable and, second, whether it has been used as such for 'time immemorial' (a romantic phrase that is actually very specific: in English law, the reach of memory goes back to 6 July 1189, the accession of Richard I). Both aspects need to be proven 'before navigation rights can be acquired against riparian owners'. The last four words show how the cards are stacked against the public. Just as trespass can reframe a walk in the countryside as an attack on the rights of property owners, so, too, public rights along rivers are described as being 'acquired' and 'against' the private rights of owners. Yet the only thing kayaking takes from fishing is its exclusivity.

Nigel Saul, a Professor of Medieval History at the University of London, delivered a lecture to Parliament in 2013 arguing that Clause 33 of Magna Carta 'was to be of enormous significance in the history of navigation in this country, because it established the principle of free passage along England's rivers, so laying the foundations for transport development in the Industrial Revolution'. This position starts from the opposite of the Angling Trust, that rivers were always open access until they were privatised – in other words, in line with the entire history of land enclosure, private rights were acquired against those of the public. But Clause 33 is actually very vague. It demands that all fish-weirs should be removed across the inland waterways of England, essentially providing that there should be no blockages, or tolls, to impede free passage on the waters. It leans on an implicit understanding that waterways are free and therefore should not be blocked, and the fact that not one toll receipt has been found in the history of river navigation does seem to support this. However, as QC Hart argued, nowhere is this explicitly stated in law.

The same cannot be said of the River Kennet. The 1715 Kennet Navigation Act includes the emphatic declaration that 'all the King's Liege people whatsoever may have and Lawfully enjoy their free passage'. It turns out that public right of access to the River Kennet has for 300 years been specifically enshrined in law, which means my trespass on the waterway was in fact no such thing. But unlike with earthbound public Rights of Way, there was not a single sign along the river to indicate a right of access. In the absence of any clarity, the fishermen on the RDAA's forum have, reasonably enough, assumed that, like the lion's share of rivers in the country, I have no right to be there. And because I neglected to bring a laminated copy of the 1715 Navigation Act with me, the consensus remains that my quiet paddle along the river was an act 'acquired against' their rights as fishermen.

This leaves me with the predicament that nowhere in this chapter have I committed a trespass. Luckily, I have a plan. Deeply embedded within the common laws of trespass is the notion that an action of trespass is recoverable even if no harm has been caused to the land. The breach of the fence is itself the harm. The exact wording of this ancient code is as follows: 'a person who enters upon the land of another without leave ... and who breaks off a blade of grass in so doing, commits a trespass.' This is excellent news. The extreme nature of this ruling allows me to save enormous amounts of time, and, if I wish, trespass every property along sixty miles of the Thames by simply plucking a blade of grass from the bank. I can maximise my trespass efficiency, and in one sweep more than double the amount of trespasses in this book. My inaugural blade of grass is plucked from the mown lawns of Shiplake College and stashed safely in my pencil case.

I paddle up through Sonning; I spot herons half hidden in the reeds and cormorants sunning their wings on the bare limbs of fallen trees, looking like black crucifixes on cragged, decaying shrines. The sun is beating down, sun cream and sweat is stinging my eyes, but it feels exhilarating to have come all this way. At Wargrave, squeezed in between two mansions and their football-pitch lawns, seven or eight teenage boys are messing about in the shallows of the river bend. They are shrieking and giggling, and seem like young otter cubs, playing rough, loving the living of life. Whatever the legal status of the river, they are protected from accusations of trespass by the dirt track behind them: the law states that whenever a Right of Way meets the watercourse, it continues to be a Right of Way, though in the slippery world of water no one knows exactly where this right ends. The scene is a picture of the public/private dynamic imposed on rivers – on either side, the private mansions have claimed acres of the riverbank for themselves, while the rest of the town must make do with a dirt track the width of a car.

The Angling Trust make out like they're the reasonable ones. They have written to the canoeing governing bodies, offering the possibility of limited voluntary access, with various demands whose paternalism is rank even on their own website. They 'demand', among other things, that the canoe organisations:

Recognise and accept the law as it is (rather than as they would prefer it to be); Stop (wrongfully) asserting that the law is unclear; Stop discouraging paddlers from considering or entering into voluntary access agreements or arrangements; Stop encouraging paddlers to ignore the legal rights of others, commit trespass, and obstruct water bailiffs, anglers, fishery owners and riparian owners.

This hardly sounds like compromise. And it's not just kayaking: any sort of walker, wild swimmer and general hot-day toe-dangler is banned from our rivers, by order of the fisher-kings. Their demands come from an interpretation of common law that assumes priority by right of property. Yet Australia, which has the same common law as England, interprets it differently: 'while there is no public right to fish in non-tidal rivers, there is a public right to navigate a navigable river for all that can navigate it'. In America, following the Revolution, the Founding Fathers were quick to enshrine public access to all navigable rivers and streams, calling them 'common highways, and forever free'. Norway, Finland, Sweden, Bulgaria, France, Hungary and Belgium all allow public access to their rivers and in Scotland (following the Land Reform Act of 2003) people have a general right of recreational access to all inland waterways. In these countries, the right of access to rivers is a common right, and the right to fish, or deplete the resources of a common wealth, must be bought. Perhaps most importantly, under this system, there is no cause for enmity.

I'm passing through Henley, crossing the large, slow bend of the river, and a mile downstream I see my bed for the night. Temple Island is a long, slim spearhead of land whose foliage spills across its perimeter over the water. The southern half of the island, pointing towards me, was cleared many years ago of its trees, carpeted with a plush lawn, and in 1771 a mock temple

THE BOOK OF TRESPASS

was erected, a fishing lodge for the MP of Pontefract, owner of Fawley Court and lord of the manors of Henley and Remenham, Sambrooke Freeman. It was leased in 1987 to the organisers of Henley Regatta, and is where the races start. For 999 years, they have the right to lease it out for weddings, corporate events, and as an exclusive enclosure for VIPs (or VRichPs), for five days a year during the Regatta. Offering champagne receptions, truffles and canapés, tickets start at £474 per person, rising to £599 on the Saturday.

Until the contention between the canoeists and anglers is tested in court, stalemate means status quo, and the fisher-kings remain in possession of 97 per cent of our rivers. If British Canoeing, the national body representing paddlesports, agree to the fisher-kings' terms of voluntary access, they will be ceding the moral argument of public rights for a limited prag-matic gain. They will have ratified an unequal system, to be paid off by a licence to paddle in limited stretches of limited rivers, under limited conditions at limited times which don't interrupt the fishing. And because this permissive access can be removed as quickly as it is given, the imbalance of private power over public access will remain intact.

As I approach the island, the temple rises like a paper-cut pop-up from the open book of valleys that fan out behind it. It is colder now, the sun has gone down and the banks are empty of people. The water seems to have thickened to mercury, and as boats pass their wake shines like silver cut with the black knife blades of the waves. There is a small, neat fence around the grass lawn of the island, so I paddle into the trees, where I find a sandy cove to disembark. The water, which I have barely touched all day, is warm. I haul my supplies onto land and tether the kayak to a tree. The small forest has a path that leads to the lawn, and I follow it to inspect the temple.

The statue under the cupola is not the original. In 1952, following their failure in the Regatta, a team of Irish rowers got drunk and tried to kidnap the statue. Misjudging its weight, they dropped it into the river and broke off its arm. But the replica is beautiful, and depicts a bacchante, a priestess of Bacchus, the god of getting high. I roll a joint, sit at her feet and watch the geese honk up the river. The sky turns from blue to violet to black. When I lie down to sleep that night, I feel the rolling wash of the water in my blood. And when I shut my eyes, my mind opens up to the wideness of the waterway, an expansiveness that feels just like peace.

The next day I wake just before dawn and go to eat my breakfast by the temple. Coming out of the curtain of trees, I see the morning suspended in an eerie dream, the whole river sunk in thick mist. The banks of the river are the only sign of the land around me, and their trees are dark silhouettes against ghostly veils of white. The fog conceals the land but in so doing it exposes its hidden truth: in terms of tax, it's not there at all.

On the west bank of the river is Fawley Court Farm, said to be one of the inspirations for Kenneth Grahame's Toad Hall, which was sold for £4.3 million to Fawley Court Inc., a company registered in the British Virgin Islands (BVI). Further south, the land is owned by Cherrilow Ltd, a company registered in Jersey. Over the river are 300 acres in the village of Remenham bought for £120 million by the exiled president of the Bank of Moscow, Andrey Borodin. The land was bought under the name Durio Ltd, which is also registered in BVI. On the east, there is a small strip of land owned by a family of turkey farmers from the local area, but, beyond that, land bought for almost £33 million by Culham Court Inc., who are also registered in BVI. Just a mile north of me is the backdrop for ITV's *Midsomer Murders* (that 'last bastion of Englishness'), the village of Hambleden, whose 1,600-acre estate and forty houses, pub and village shops are all owned by Swiss foreign-exchange dealer Urs Schwarzenbach. The village was bought in 2007 under the name Hambleden Estates Ltd, who are also registered in the British Virgin Islands. Though it might not look like it now, this place is the Caribbean-on-Thames.

In 2015, *Private Eye* published an interactive map revealing the 490,000 acres of England and Wales owned by offshore companies, a glitch in the law that allows an area of land larger than Greater London to avoid stamp duty and inheritance tax. The magazine identified £170 billion-worth of properties acquired by offshore companies in just ten years, and described how such companies are used by property developers such as the Candy brothers to avoid stamp duty, by aristocrats such as Lord Rothermere to escape inheritance tax and by 'any number of arms dealers and oligarchs covering up properties they'd rather nobody knew too much about'.

The largest swathe of English land hidden behind offshore companies is the grouse moor Gunnerside estate, whose 27,258 acres of the North Yorkshire moors is registered in the British Virgin Islands and which, over the last decade or so, received €430,000 of handouts from the taxpayer, in the form of agricultural subsidies. Lord Salisbury is mentioned, the descendant of Elizabeth I's spymaster-general Lord Cecil, whose 2,000 acres of land are registered in Jersey. Before the map was created, these tax-avoidance schemes were largely unacknowledged, manifested as occasional news reports, obscured behind consensus. However, with their visualisation on an interactive map, they are harder to miss. You can see how they speckle and cluster around cities, how towns like Newmarket and Marlborough are disproportionately affected, and you can zoom into your own town and see exactly where the tax is drained from the land.

I go back into the woods to change into my swimming trunks, which are hanging from a tree, still wet. I am shivering. I step into the water, load up the kayak and push off into the river. There is no sound but the occasional plip of a fish's lips and the slosh of my paddle. The sun has risen and, since the river leads me east, I paddle into a mirrored infinity of blazing sky, dazzled as much by the beauty as the light.

As the sun burns off the mist, it remains in curious lines of smoke rising from the water, ghost weeds on a long fallow field, little wispy strands that blur into a low blanket in the distance. Either side of me the bank is shaggy with jungle-lush greenery, great willow trees like the heads of river gods, just emerged, dreadlocked hair draping over their faces and woody spines. With no road or field visible behind the trees, floating on the mirrored glass of the river, with the whole sky trapped beneath me, I feel as if the world has flooded and I am the only soul left alive.

Joggers ruin the illusion. They are the first sign of the suburbs and soon I am passing through some of the most expensive land in England, Hurley, Marlowe and Cookham, where almost every house has a vast garden lawn dressed in the uniform of wealth. Red carnations spill over fake Grecian urns, there are ubiquitous small wooden outhouses, flat-packed follies for the nouveau riche, and acres of clipped, lush turf. Some houses are built into the bank, their post-modern aesthetic fusing fairy-tale turrets and steel-framed glass veneers, an architecture built around the value of a view.

The beauty of river life is another perquisite of property, sold in the brochures as a 'feature', and no one but the super-paranoid builds a wall between their house and its river view. For this reason, the kayaker gets a rare glimpse into private property, an accidental understanding of what it really looks like. And just as so much of England is hoarded behind brick walls, so the information about the land, and its ownership, is secreted behind paywalls and bureaucracy. What happens to the land is of immense public significance, but in England it has always been categorised as private information. There have only ever been five attempts to create a census of English land ownership: the first was in 1086 with Domesday Book, followed by a 700-year breather until the next four attempts between 1830 and 1941.

The obstinate resistance to opening up data on land use is an indication of the power of both land and knowledge, which, since the Tudor surveyors, have been for ever fused. It was in this era that knowledge of the land itself became a kind of property: as the land was enclosed, so, too, were the exact specifications of its acreage, use and ownership fenced off from public access. But to peer over these walls of secrecy is not just an act of nosiness; it is essential to both the economy and democracy of England. Without openly accessible data, the market of land sale operates sluggishly and inefficiently: infrastructure is harder to implement, long conveyancy chains are retarded and the market is biased against new house builders who struggle to find the information on land they have interests in (today only eight companies build half the houses in Britain). How land is used in England has far-reaching implications for the whole of our society – it determines where we build our homes, how we grow our food, what our taxes are used for, how many bees, badgers and birds we make space for. Without the full facts of how land ownership operates in England, we forget how much it matters.

In France, you can walk into any town hall and request to see the maps of ownership for that part of the country. In the US,

Montana's land registry is online for all to access. New Zealand opened up its land registry in 2015, and now has a minister for Land Information whose job it is to oversee the transparency and accessibility of this data for the public. In England, when Companies House went online in 2015, it opened up data including registered office addresses, filing history, annual returns and shareholder details: the world kept turning and companies were subject to a greater scrutiny of fair practice. In spite of these successful alternatives, the resistance to opening up the Land Registry continues to this day, because when you put up a fence around land it becomes your business and yours alone.

So it falls to the trespassers of the digital domain to expose the truth. Anna Powell-Smith is a computer programmer and data analyst who worked with *Private Eye* to construct their map of offshore ownership. In 2004 she volunteered with a civic hacking movement that began constructing various websites aimed at opening up the secret keep of parliamentary democracy. They built the website faxyourmp.com, which allows you to contact your MP securely and directly; they opened up Hansard, the verbatim minutes of all parliamentary debates, to the public; and they set up theyworkforyou.com, where you can cross-reference every MP with their voting record. In 2008, she spent a month of evenings after work transferring the data of the 1087 Domesday Book online. She has made maps and matrices for everything from house prices in the UK to algorithms that translate the multitude of dress sizes across the world into comprehensible, relevant data for the consumer. Not unlike William Tyndale, she takes large swathes of dense, incomprehensible information and translates them into a language the public can use.

Following her work on the *Private Eye* offshore map, Powell-Smith met writer and activist Guy Shrubsole, who was beginning to compile information for his blog, and subsequent book,

Who Owns England?. Together, they sourced information from environmental maps from Natural England, OS Open Data downloads, valuation maps and freedom of information requests to local councils.

One set of maps proved particularly useful: following the Highways Act of 1980, all landowners who wanted to protect their land from claims for additional Rights of Way through their acreage had to deposit a statement and a map to their local authority, which also showed the boundaries of their estate. To protect their land from public access, they had to expose its parameters. Bit by bit, estate by estate, Shrubsole and Powell-Smith began compiling a map of England that is available online at their blog, an anarchist iteration of the map owned by the Land Registry. The map is not so much a levelling of the walls of secrecy, but holes drilled into it, shining sporadic light on the truth of land ownership.

I have turned a bend in the river and come to an immense unswerving corridor of trees, a liquid avenue that extends five miles due south before me, before it curves towards Windsor Castle. I am suddenly very hungry and stop at a tier of ancient stone steps that lead from the water's edge up into an estate hidden by the flush canopies of the trees. This is Cliveden, one of the grandest estates in England, the residence of a long line of English nobility, including three dukes, an earl, a prince, several countesses and, most recently, the Viscounts Astor.

These steps, and the summerhouse they lead to, was where Christine Keeler first met the secretary of state for war, John Profumo, where the two embarked upon an affair that would eventually bring down the Macmillan government. They are fraught with the tension between private and personal spheres: here, the private world of politicians leaked into the public life of politics; here also is the line where the public commons of the Thames turns into the private domain of the landowner. With my feet dangling in the water, I munch my sandwich, and think again of William Beckford's estate at Fonthill, how he used his estate to construct a personal haven that walled out the homophobia of Georgian society. Home, for everyone, is a bastion of privacy, an essential personal space where one can live according to one's own parameters. But when these parameters extend over thousands of acres of land, the binary line between public and private becomes more contentious.

As I'm packing up my rucksack, two keepers descend the steps from the estate and pretend to fuss over a tree leaning out into the river. They're ten foot away and are hoping their presence alone will send me on my way. I say 'hello' as I climb into the kayak, and now they have to turn, and descend the steps to me: one is in his sixties, the other in his mid-thirties, my age. I ask them how they're doing. '*We're* fine,' says the older, and in the simple inflection of the first word he manages to convey the entire dynamic of property rights since William the Conqueror. I'm floating on a Right of Way, but with my fingertips still touching the steps I fall under their jurisdiction.

I'm reluctant to push off just yet: I want to see if we can get past the usual enmity, to a place where we can exchange a few pleasant words with each other. The younger keeper asks me where I'm going, and I say that I hope to be in Runnymede tonight. The older one scoffs: 'that's four hours in the skiff'. I tell him that I'm in no rush. There's a long pause. He asks where I'm coming from, and I tell him Henley and after another lengthy beat he replies: 'Well, you're a long way from home.' This is starting to sound like an artless pastiche of a Harold Pinter play, every word a threat that is somehow both veiled and explicit. They're evidently better at this game than me, and privately, as the older keeper's 'four hours' estimate sinks in, I'm starting to wonder if

I probably should be in some kind of rush. I lift my fingertips off the land, take the paddle and push off down the river.

In all my trespasses, I've never met the actual owner of the land. It is always their gamekeeper or ground staff that approaches me, and, secondary to their actual job of caring for the land, it falls to them to protect it from invasion. I have a huge respect for the ground staff, gardeners and keepers of these properties: they spend much more time than me outside, they know the area better than I ever will and they don't need a Google search to identify one wildflower from another. Yet in the binary dynamic of property, we are always cast against each other.

Sarcastic, sardonic or point-blank rude, the approach of a gamekeeper often rests on a kind of masculine aggression that is fuelled with indignation, as if they are justly retaliating to the first act of violence, the trespass. And the civil law that governs trespass, known as tort law, encourages this notion. Tort governs a vast scope of civil law, seeking to standardise the civil responsibilities we have to each other, any interaction we have that is not governed by a contract. It covers physical assault, battery, defamation, libel, negligence, and aims to assess what damage has occurred, where the responsibility lies, and thus who is liable. The word 'tort' derives from the Middle English meaning 'injury' and operates under the assumption that a person's property is an extension of their self. To step over the line into private property is, in the eyes of the law, not an act of digression but of aggression, and makes the landowner the victim.

The same law of private property projects such an extreme perspective on reality, one so entirely lacking in nuance, that it fails to acknowledge the factors of scale, proportion and context. By denying any difference between a private patio in a suburban street and a dense woodland on an 11,000-acre estate, it turns a stroll in the woods into a home invasion. It refuses to accept the point-blank bleeding obvious: that in terms of harm, they are worlds apart.

There is a defensive paranoia to private property, to the extremity of its position, to the absoluteness of its demands of dominion, that, with the barbs on its wire and spikes on its walls, looks something like fear. In mid-nineteenth-century Nottinghamshire, when the 5th Duke of Portland sought to close the public roads that ran across his vast estate of Welbeck Abbey, the government had to intervene to stop him. The duke was a recluse, and hated the notion of bumping into other people, so instead commissioned a vast network of underground passages to be built beneath his estate, where he could live without the threat of human interaction.

Many of these estates have that same sense of seclusion. It's hard to comprehend fully the silence and emptiness of their grounds until you hop back over the wall and land in the busy clatter of the streets, the chaos of other people. The walls of these estates don't just exclude the outside world, they buttress a misanthropy and fear of what lies outside them. In the words of Donald Trump, referring to the most isolated magnate in the world of cinema, Citizen Kane: 'in real life I believe that wealth does in fact isolate you from other people – it's a protective mechanism, you have your guard up.'

The river becomes busier as I leave the Cliveden corridor, turn the bend and see Windsor Castle before me. By the time I have passed the abandoned Bray Film Studios and Eton College, the river has become a commons once again, buzzing with the wide variety of life. There are eccentric elderly gentlemen, with handlebar moustaches and straw hats, chugging around in antique paddle boats; there are tanned, portly executives in river cruisers with their grandchildren; there are towering three-tiered tourist paddle boats, whose guests wave happily at anything that passes, lovers on hired pedal-boats and several other kayakers. Toddlers are throwing bits of bread at ducks, seagulls swooping at chip butties and the river is a kaleidoscope of noise and action. I look up to the windows of Windsor Castle, and imagine the view from there, the silence of separation from the masses. The monarchy, of all institutions, knows what it is like to have your guard up – at the top of the pile of the English hierarchy, only a few families have walked the castle's corridors: the houses of Normandy, Blois, Anjou, Plantagenet, Lancaster, York, Tudor, Stuart, Hanover, Saxe-Coburg and Windsor, all constantly threatened by a host of royals, lords and peasants who have wanted, more than anything else, to cuckoo them from their feathered nests.

I pass Windsor town, and follow the curve of the river to the quieter back garden of the castle, Home Park. This area of land, formerly a common, then cleared for a deer park, then walled to create the private gardens of Queen Victoria, has to be the loneliest park in England. It is one of the sixteen areas of land, largely associated with the monarchy, that since Aaron Barschak raised his smock to reveal his pubic 'heir apparent', have been upgraded to the charge of criminal trespass. I paddle up to its raised bank and float alongside the clipped green lawns. Neat signs stuck at intervals along the bank show the silhouette of a person enclosed in a red circle, with a red line dashed diagonally across their body: 'This is a protected site under section 128 of the Serious Organised Crime and Police Act 2005. Trespass on this site is a criminal offence.'

Somewhere inside this park is the Herne Oak, a tree that commemorates Berkshire's greatest pagan deity, Herne the Hunter, referenced by William Shakespeare in *The Merry Wives of Windsor*. There's no one around, not a soul in sight, and I'm tempted to moor up, ignore the signs and see what happens. Instead, I lean over and pluck a blade of grass from its bank.

The sun has set by the time I reach Runnymede. The geese are honking up the river, drawing in the darkness, and I'm wondering where I'm going to stay tonight. Runnymede is where Magna Carta was signed, but because of the capricious oscillation of the river no one can be sure whether it was on this side of the bank or that. Some say it was signed under a 2,500-year-old tree called the Ankerwycke Yew, and others claim it was on a thin spar of land that juts into the river, called Magna Carta Island. On this island is a stone upon which the great charter was supposedly signed, but this foundation stone of English liberty is enclosed in an oak-panelled room, which is enclosed in a Grade II listed mansion, which was sold to a private family by Sotheby's in 2014 for £4 million. Not for me, then.

Eventually I find a sandy cove on a small turn of the river, co-owned by the National Trust and a small, irritable robin, who bounces indignantly about the place as I disembark. The boughs of a chestnut tree reach over the cove, out into the river, draping down to the lip of the water, forming a perfect camouflage net from the park and busy road opposite. As I shut my eyes that night, my mind sparkles with iridescence of the river water, the fluid, ever-changing shapes of the colours and the dazzle-dance of light.

I wake up late, stiff and cold. Beyond my chestnut leaf camo-net, the day is grey. My body feels racked by the kayak, stretched and raw. I pack up my litter and float out to deposit it in a bin beside the wan smile of Queen Elizabeth II, a statue erected in

2015 to mark the 800th anniversary of Magna Carta. On the very day that the queen and Prime Minister David Cameron assembled to honour this great charter of Liberty, a group of thirty or forty squatters were at a High Court trial, being evicted from waste land just beyond Her Majesty's shoulders, across the water meadows, up in the woods.

Following the eviction of the Occupy demonstration in 2012, a group of protesters walked out of London to pursue their protest elsewhere. They had discovered a sixty-five-acre site, formerly a campus for Brunel University, in the valley overlooking Runnymede. The land had been bought five years earlier by an offshore property investment company called the Royalton Group, who were looking to develop it into 600 luxury apartments, a high-end gated community they called Magna Carta Park. But for years nothing had happened, and the land was used for illegal fly-tipping, strewn with broken fridges and car tyres. The group of squatters called themselves Diggers 2012, after the occupation of St George's Hill by Gerrard Winstanley and a smaller group of land reformers in 1649. Like Grow Heathrow just across the river, their ambition was not just to protest against the unequal division of land in England, against the hoarding of empty buildings, against the worst tenant rights in Europe, but to culture its alternative, to grow food and live in low-impact, eco-friendly fashion.

They built a geodesic dome for community meetings, a longhouse kitchen and about forty homes from scrap, salvaged and recyclable materials. They dug a well to access water from a natural spring and, just like Winstanley's Diggers, they began planting crops. This was the living re-enactment of John Locke's justification for private property: they were improving the waste ground, making it theirs through their own labour. But 300 years after Locke, the logic of property had taken on its own momentum. Private property was no longer justified by use and improvement, but by itself alone.

There was a nuance to John Locke's argument about private property that has, from the moment it was written, been conveniently overlooked – for Locke, the enclosure of common land was only justifiable so long as there was 'enough and as good left in common'. Nicknamed the 'Lockean Proviso', this small addition shines an altogether more egalitarian light on the logic of Locke's *Two Treatises of Government*. But it has been buried under almost 500 years of capitalist ideology, meaning that the Diggers 2012, who were not only protesting homelessness, but providing actual homes, had no rights to the land. The Royalton Group sent in the bailiffs twice, destroying their buildings and tearing up their crops, and on the eighth centenary of Magna Carta, the High Court issued the Diggers with an injunction. Finally, in September 2015, the land was cleared.

I pass beneath a great concrete bridge of the M25, a huge cavern of concrete that hums with the tyres rolling above it. I yell *BOLLOCKS* at the top of my voice, and it returns back to me, satisfying, round with reverb. Since Locke's time, the power of private property has swelled into a gargantuan monster that trumps freedom of expression, the need to subsist and the right to shelter. But while it primarily secures the rights of a tiny elite over the public rights of the many, its secondary effect is to establish a two-way dynamic of enmity, a binary polarisation between the haves and the have-nots.

On one side of the fence the *have-nots* are criminalised in their attempts to use land, and, on the other, the *haves* are simultaneously vilified, turned into fairy-tale ogres as if their own personalities are to blame for the current system of private property. E. P. Thompson quotes a smuggler from Dorset in the eighteenth century who justified the murder of an excise man by saying 'the smugglers swore they did no more matter to kill him than they would a toad'.

Such a dehumanising attitude was understandable in a time when a poacher could have his neck broken for feeding his family. But the sentiment lasts to this day in a tired, robotic resentment that allows men of power to dismiss political dissent as personal financial envy. When he was implicated in the parliamentary expenses scandal in 2009, MP Anthony Steen responded: 'I've done nothing criminal ... and do you know what it's about? Jealousy. I've got a very *very* large house, some people say it looks like Balmoral ... what right does the public have to inter-fere with my private life?'

The answer, of course, is that the public paid the £87,000 of his expenses for his 'very *very* large' second home, which made the issue very, *very* public indeed. But the story is emblematic of how a stream of specific allegations can divert into that stagnant pool of loosely defined resentment that England keeps for its wealthy. It's a pool that we wallow in.

I have marched alongside protesters in all manner of demonstrations, walking shoulder to shoulder with people carrying signs that declare: 'Fuck the Rich', or, more humor-ously, 'Eat the Rich'. But such a focus on the character of the rich is simply an inversion of the coin that declared the aristocracy a superior breed of human and fails to examine the basic inequality of the system that makes their actions legal. It imagines a world where the line of morality can be drawn as simply as the line of a fence; rich is bad, poor is good. It reinforces the partisan belief that richness is itself a sign of moral failing. Worse, it engenders a kind of orientalisation of the working class, that old biblical trope that there is nobility in poverty. And, worse still, it internalises the central fiction of the fence – the lie of binary thinking.

A fence is first and foremost a method of division. When the line is drawn in an argument, it implicitly creates the illusion that, according to its logic, one side represents the direct opposite of the other. The notion of common ground, the idea of shared values, is entirely obliterated by the dualist command of the fence. It divides the value judgement from all context and polarises the debate into an absolutist, partisan mindset of good versus bad. The partisan is a servant of partition.

Life is more complicated. Thomas Beckford was the richest man in Europe as a direct result of the African people his father enslaved. To the binary judgement of the fence, he was a villain. But lift that definition from his life and you can see a more complex picture: in the gay community, he is celebrated as a hero, an icon. Like Ludwig II of Bavaria, or Oscar Wilde, he was a gay man harangued by a fiercely judgemental, hypocritical society, a man who refused to capitulate to the bigotry of his era. Similarly, John Bentinck, the 5th Duke of Portland, was, on one side of the fence, a mad recluse, nicknamed 'the Mole' for his obsessive tunnelling projects that led him as far away as possible from society. But remove the fence line and you find that local historians also view him as a benevolent landowner, creating employment opportunities for the people in his manor, who were living in abject poverty. His schemes cost him £100,000 per year, and provided a living for 15,000 workmen and women, for eighteen years. So was he a hero or a villain? The answer, along with the question, is meaningless.

In the words of the great trespasser of partisan politics Christopher Hitchens, 'the truth seldom lies, but if it does, it lies somewhere in between'. Truth lies in the free movement of ideas, in other words, discussion, where either side is on equal footing with the other. The need to turn characters into cartoons of good or bad is something that drives newspaper sales, structures the narrative of Hollywood movies and keeps Twitter twittering, but it doesn't help the land debate. Winston Churchill, who himself crossed and re-crossed the fence line of partisan politics, said much the same thing: 'It is not the individual I attack; it is the system. It is not the man who is bad; it is the law which is bad. It is not the man who is blameworthy for doing what the law allows and what other men do; it is the state which would be blameworthy if it were not to endeavour to reform the law and correct the practice.'

In some ways landowners are just as trapped within their walls as we are outside them. In the early 1700s, an eccentric aristocratic landowner called Richard Norton died. Warden of Bere Forest, he lived at Southwick Park in Hampshire and possessed estates worth at least £60,000. When he died in 1732, with no children or direct heirs, he left a detailed and unambiguous will bequeathing his entire estate to the poor of that district. Inevitably, with so much money at stake, his distant relatives contested the will and, seven years later, a special jury of Hampshire gentlemen declared the will null and void: so great was the consensus of private property that Norton was deemed, by law, to be mad to give it away. The land was eventually given to Norton's nephew, Francis Thistlethwayte, whose family still own the 7,000-acre estate and take rent from the seventeen farms, various commercial industries and 164 houses.

On top of the legal system, the social network of wealth, its customs, responsibilities and shared ideologies exert tight restrictions on its bearers. When the Duke of Westminster inherited the Grosvenor estate from his father, he became the richest man under thirty in the world, with over 130,000 acres to his name. But with interests in sixty-two international cities, with almost 11,000 employees worldwide and total assets of almost £50 billion, can he really be expected to give it all away? With respect to his employees, does he even have the right?

Similarly, the Earl of Carnarvon has already been quoted describing the pressures of managing an ancestral estate: 'you don't want to be the Earl that lets the whole thing down ... and that's the thing that really sort of hangs over one a bit'. And why not take him at his word? For the earl, the expectation for him to maintain his estate literally hangs over him: he can barely go for a piss at Highclere without the eyes of his ancestors following him from their gilt frames. With their glare comes the expectation of heritage, the silent command to maintain privilege at all costs.

The most popular caricature of the landowning class is Toad of Toad Hall. He is vain and narcissistic, imbued with an ugly sense of entitlement and entirely unqualified to wield the power in his possession, symbolised by the new motorcar that he is forever crashing into country verges. Typical of the English, we love him. Or love to hate him: he makes us feel secure in the simplistic enclosure of values. But the truth behind Toad is more complex.

The inspiration for Toad Hall was Hardwick House, then owned by the Baronet Sir Charles Rose. He was friends with Kenneth Grahame and entertained the author on several occasions. His house is a Grade I listed Tudor building, which once played host to Charles I. It sits on a straight run of the Thames just before Mapledurham Lock and its 900-acre estate stretches out over the steep hills of woods and wildflower meadows behind it. I grew up roaming his estate.

Its current owner is the 4th Baronet Sir Julian Rose. Like many of the other Toads in this book, he inherited his wealth and his titles: he is a paragon of privilege. But even the most hard-bitten, anti-rich 'militant' would be hard pressed to criticise how he has managed his fortune: his estate embodies almost every ideal of the land movement.

His farm on the estate is resolutely free of genetic modification. He is a pioneer of ecologically sound farming techniques, beginning the conversion of his farm to organic in the mid-1970s, joining the Soil Association Board in the 1980s and writing several books that promote what he calls 'the proximity principle', an ethic that fuses food growing with local community interaction. He refuses to sell to supermarkets, distributing his food locally instead, and various low-impact growing schemes and businesses have been given space on his land: there is a renewable energy company that supplies biomass boilers, an organic veg box scheme and a non-profit organisation that offers outdoor activities for younger children. They specialise in working with children with autism, anxiety and other issues that they believe can be managed by exposure to an outdoor environment. Every spring, locals are encouraged to come and help out the toads in their mating rituals, by carrying them in buckets across the main road.

Over the course of writing this book I found myself increasingly keen to speak with a landowner, to offer a right to reply, to hear a perspective from the other side of the fence. With his openness to so many of the core ethics of the land movement, Sir Julian had always seemed the most likely candidate. But Sir Julian's Hardwick estate is on the other side of the Thames from where I grew up, meaning he resides in Oxfordshire and not West Berkshire. He is not the lord of my manor.

Guy Shrubsole, author of *Who Owns England?*, is, like me, a West Berkshire boy, and one of the posts on his blog was a detailed investigation into who owns the land we both grew up on. He discovered that over half of the county is the private property of just thirty landowners. The Ministry of Defence is listed, with its acres at Greenham Common, Aldermaston and Burghfield, there are various industrial farming corporations, offshore corporations and the Iliffes, a family of newspaper and media tycoons, who restored Basildon Park to its former colonial 'glory'. But principal among these is a landowner who controls 12,332 acres across West Berkshire. In my home county, the real Toad of Toad Hall is former MP Richard Benyon.

Richard Benyon is a controversial figure, the fulcrum (or fence) between partisan opposition. With a net worth of an estimated £130 million, he was for fifteen years the richest MP in Parliament. He was Defra under-secretary during Natural England's prosecution of Walshaw Moor, and, himself the owner of a substantial grouse moor in Scotland, he was suspected by some newspapers of a vested interest, of being at the heart of the decision to drop the case. He launched an enquiry into the link between buzzards and pheasant populations which led to a trial licence for keepers to kill this otherwise protected species. The campaign drew so much criticism that David Cameron was forced to withdraw it almost instantly and, when asked if it had failed, Mr Benyon replied, in marvellous Politicians' Cant, that it had 'hit a wall of credibility'. In 2014 he criticised the welfare state as a 'something for nothing culture' and yet the year before, as the largest landlord in West Berkshire, received £119,237 in housing benefit. Turner Prize-winning artist Jeremy Deller has painted a picture of him prostrate on his grouse moor, being eviscerated by buzzards, one on his chest, pulling out the strings of his intestines. To the left-wing environmental lobbyists, Benyon is simply a Toad.

On the other side of the fence, however, he is well liked by many of his constituents, including my own parents. He was named by the *Daily Telegraph* as one of the 'saints' of the MP expenses scandal. 'There are two things people often say having met Richard Benyon MP,' wrote fellow Conservative MP Robert Wilson in an online profile on Benyon. 'First, "What a bloody nice bloke" he is, and second, "Is he really 52?" He can disarm even the most lunatic of left-wing opponents, with a few well-chosen words, and, when coupled with his boyish looks, it's difficult to find someone more earnest and likeable.'

Mr Benyon is the landowner whose holdings, by being closest to my childhood home, are closest to my heart. I have trespassed many of his 14,000 acres, in both Hampshire and West Berkshire, including his ancestral seat at Englefield and its gorgeous undulating deer park. I did this not in opposition to anything, least of all Mr Benyon himself, but because it is full of hills, dells, streams, glades, meadows, rivers and kingfishers. I lived in the area, and wanted to see it, to draw it, to know it.

But to the orthodoxy of land ownership we are sworn enemies. The trespasser is the bogey man of property, the personification of the threat to the cult of exclusion. By refusing to accept the rules of what Locke called 'the foundation of all democracy', the trespasser is the antithesis of natural order, a lunatic, left-wing opponent to common sense. Likewise, to the trespasser, the landowner is the mysterious, unseen puppet master, the power behind the curtain, the hand that pulls the invisible string that yanks us from the land. Mr Benyon and I may have grown up only five miles away from each other, but we live in different worlds.

It is this schism between us that allows either side to be caricatured into a lunatic or a toad. But if the mantle of lunatic didn't seem to fit my quiet rambles over the countryside, then why should the figure of Toad apply to Mr Benyon? I wanted to see if an abstract trespass was possible, if I could engineer an encounter with him that would lead us both over the lines of partisan politics, to a pun that no land rights activist can resist: common ground.

A few months before my paddle along his stretch of the Kennet, I figured out a way that we could meet. I discovered a rule that allows people with more than one home to choose where they cast their local votes, which meant, with my parents' permission, I could re-register my voting address from London to their home in West Berkshire. In doing so, I was suddenly eligible to attend one of his Friday afternoon open surgeries. So I booked my place.

I'm down a side street in Newbury, waiting for the Conservative office door to open. I have in mind the famous scene in Michael Mann's film *Heat*, where the two enemies, Al Pacino and Robert De Niro, meet for the first time. They've been playing cat and mouse all through the film, and when they meet in a diner it is a tense, quietly aggressive display of machismo that forges an unspoken mutual respect between the two. There is a moment where the two meet each other's eyes, share a lingering look, and almost smile. This is the Holmes and Moriarty moment, the loving connection shared only by nemeses, the moment they realise they are the yang to each other's ying.

I'm wondering if something similar will happen here when a man steps out of a side door into the street, in a suit and white shirt, and I realise it's Mr Benyon himself. Very graciously he approaches me, we introduce ourselves, and he offers to forgo his errand. The description was right: with his ice-blue eyes, his boyish looks, I am dazzled and disarmed. 'That's *very* kind,' I say (a little too emphatically) and we step inside.

The office has two or three people working on computers, and immediately to my right is a small, bare cubicle, with just a table and a chair either side of it, that looks like a police interview room. I am, annoyingly, nervous. I have never spoken to a man of such power and wealth before, and already the furniture has placed us in opposition. This is my one opportunity to speak to someone outside my coven of left-wing lunatics, to test the ideologies of land reform that, from my side of the fence, seem so clearly beneficial to all of society and, from his, so abhorrent to natural order.

I have eight questions in my sketchbook that I hope will lead us from a discussion about public rights along the River Kennet, through public rights to all rivers, through public rights to the value of land, and eventually to a place where we can talk about the right to roam. I'm hoping that we can be civil, discuss the issues of public access without retreating to our partisan trenches. There are many other issues that put us on the same side of the fence: from Britain's position in the EU to the importance of localised fisheries for the reduction of discarded fish stock, we agree on many things. We even have shared interests, namely the land he owns. I'm hoping we'll get on.

But that's not how it goes. In the next fifteen minutes the scene descends from formal politeness to a horrible awkward tension. Our session ends with him on his feet, with the door open, declaiming to both myself and the volunteer Conservatives in the next office how the fiasco of the New Era Estate had damaged his family, how he never wants to revisit that period of his life again, 'impeaching' me not to believe everything I read in the papers.

But I hadn't asked about the New Era Estate. I knew that the intricacies of this saga, which included ninety-three residents facing eviction from their Hackney flats on land that the Benyons own, and also included comedian Russell Brand dressing as a chimney sweep, stapling an eviction notice to the door of the Benyons' London office, would occupy too much of our limited time together. I had only mentioned it towards the end of the interview because I live five minutes' walk away in London. There was something performative to his speech, something rehearsed, something disproportionate to the questions I was asking. It felt histrionic.

We had started gently. With reference to his earlier quote, I asked how access to only 3 per cent of rivers in England and Wales could ever be regarded as 'plenty'. He appeared not to know the exact percentage, and when I said it had been confirmed by the CEO of the Angling Trust, his reply marked my inaugural live exposure to the phenomenon of Politicians' Cant: 'I don't want to get tied down in percentages.' Tied down? I'd seen this on the television and heard it on the radio: politicians live in an extraordinary unreality where questions can be deflected with scripted sentences. Words as walls. I wondered how many landowners know the statistics, how many of the earls and dukes in this book know the exact histories of how they had come to gain the land. One of the perks of privilege is that you rarely need to stop to question how you got it. When I suggested that the privatisation of rivers could be the source of the enmity between fishermen and other users of the rivers, he echoed Julian Fellowes' vision of a harmonious stratified England, twice wondering: 'Look, why can't people just get along?'

It was the moment I asked about the extraction of shale from Benyon's Inclosure that the smile fell from his face and the atmosphere turned. This Inclosure, with its nineteenth-century spelling, was the area of common land that was fenced off and enclosed by his ancestor in 1829. Mr Benyon is currently mining 350 acres of his Inclosure for 200,000 tonnes of sand and gravel, employing the same rights to the land as the commoners held for centuries, but on an industrial scale, and for his profit alone. I wanted to use this as an example of how the community that lives around land might benefit from a share in its worth. They might even, I suggested, have a right to it.

The notion of commoning, the shared regulation of resources along the principles of anarchism, community decision-making, where every member of a community has equal rights to the value of the land, appeared so detestably ideological to Mr Benyon that by simply raising the point I had automatically disqualified myself from the debate. Oh, I *see*, he said, as if I had just dropped my cards and revealed my hand. He refused to speak about philosophical or ideological issues, as if they could be partitioned from their pragmatic effects on the ground. We both ploughed on with our argument, steadily getting nowhere. We were both framing the issue differently: for me, Benyon's Inclosure was emblematic of a wider discussion of how the value of land could benefit all society while, for Mr Benyon, it was quite simply, in both senses of the word, his own private business.

Impasse. Brick wall. A line in the sand. Any step further would be treated as an act of aggression. Be it common land or conversation, when the wall goes up, dialogue is blocked. While the issue of land ownership continues to be defined as a private interest, even the discussion itself seems to be off limits. When public land is enclosed, it becomes the private business of its owner alone, and just like the issue of transparency of data, or the argument between the anglers and the kayakers, it is the landowners who define the terms of the discussion: to own the land is to own the debate.

As our meeting came to an end, Richard Benyon rose to his feet, opened the door and began his monologue about the New Era Estate. Then, with a flourish of an imaginary velvet cape, he exited stage right to the silent, but impassioned, applause of his office workers. I was left alone in the office, stunned. No handshake, no farewell. I had promised my mother I would be polite to her MP and now I was heading home for dinner to tell her I had virtually chased him out of his office. From a distance, this time-encrusted system of private property in land is a rock-solid castle keep. But get anywhere near it, it is just a house of cards – one prod, and all the kings and queens come fluttering down.

This scene passes through my head all the while that I'm paddling into London and my chest still tightens as I think about it. It was horribly tense. The issue of land use is such an emotive subject that, when raised, it seems impossible to meet in the no man's land between trenches. But without the discussion, without the dialogue, I was unable to understand the view from the other side of the fence. I was left wondering if perhaps the true source of the paranoia of the cult of exclusion, the roots of

Ownership Anxiety, the obsessive evasion of scrutiny, is that it simply cannot be justified.

An hour or so after the M25 tunnel, the river loses its wildness. I pass through the uniform green lawns of business parks in Chertsey, and just before the neat flats of Walton-on-Thames I come to the strangest space of land in this book, D'Oyly Carte Island. It is a small eyot, whose foliage grows wild into the river around a mown lawn and Swiss-style wooden chalet. Bought for £2 million by Eyot House Ltd, a company registered in Hong Kong, it is now inhabited solely by a pack of semi-feral guard dogs which live in the house and roam free through its open door. The dogs, fed daily by a local employed by the absentee owners, protect the property from invasion and keep it empty while the land it is built on appreciates in value. This strange, vacant isle is the manifestation of how far the property concept has come since Locke's justification: land is no longer valued for its use, but for its worth as an investment. Empty, bewitched and worthless to all but its owners, this is England.

STAG

Stories, rights and crimes

'They've got Gandalf in a chokehold'
                    — Anonymous Sheffield tree protester

Early evening, Windsor Forest, sometime in the late four-teenth century. The hunt horns are blasting, echoing through the trees, and a group of horsemen led by King Richard II have chased a stag within sprinting distance of the River Thames.

Richard and a gamekeeper called Herne have broken away from the pack, and are closing in on the beast when it turns and stands its ground. It lowers its antlers, charges, and gores the king's horse, toppling the monarch into the mud. The stag disengages himself and charges the king, who is helpless beneath the weight of his horse. But Herne leaps between the two, takes the full thrust of the antlers and somehow manages to place a dagger's blade deep into the heart of the stag. The beast dies instantly, and beneath him, impaled, Herne lies bleeding out on royal turf.

Herne's two black lurchers whimper around their master, licking his face. The king, hauled to his feet, leans over Herne and proclaims that if only he can stay alive, he shall be made head keeper of Windsor Forest. The other keepers, huddled around the body, bristle at this. And just then, on a black horse, a figure appears. The keepers recognise him as Philip Urswick, a poacher, hermit and infamous witch who lives in the scrub of Bagshot Heath. He offers a cure and, grudgingly, the circle widens to let him in. He packs Herne's throbbing wounds with earth, cuts the antlers from the dead stag and attaches them to the crown of Herne's head. As the king returns to the castle, the keepers carry Herne's drained body to the hermit's hut on an improvised stretcher of bracken and bramble.

On their way to Urswick's hut, the keepers surround the hermit and force a deal. If Herne recovers, he must lose his famed woodcraft and hunting skills and become useless to the king. Urswick agrees, but only on condition that the keepers must obey the next demand he makes of them, whatever it might be.

Months pass and Herne recovers, the antlers still fused to his head. He returns to the court at Windsor and claims his title of head keeper, but it doesn't last long. Urswick, a witch of his word, had ensured that none of Herne's woodcraft powers returned with him from the underworld. The king finally dismisses Herne and, distraught, slipping into madness, Herne wanders south from the castle, into Home Park. Later that night, during a vicious thunderstorm, a pedlar finds him with a noose around his neck, hanging from the bough of an oak tree.

Hearing the news, the keepers wait until dawn to cut Herne down, but when they arrive at the tree the body is gone. The weeks pass, the atmosphere is tense and the keepers find that they too have lost all their woodcraft powers. They summon Urswick who tells them the only way to remove Herne's curse is to take all their hunting equipment, dogs, horns and horses, and head back to the oak tree by the light of the full moon. Gathered there under the oak, Herne appears, spectral, antlered, and leads the keepers on a wild hunt through Home Park to Bagshot Heath, where Urswick again steps out of the night to finally claim his part of the deal: the keepers must ride with Herne for as long as he sees fit. For nights on end they gallop and shoot, depleting the king's deer stock, leaving the bloodied corpses on the ground. At the king's command the keepers are eventually caught and hanged from the Herne Oak and the spectre of Herne is laid to rest. To this day, Herne's wild hunt is said to return at times of national crisis, haunting Home Park, horns echoing through the trees, hooves thundering on the royal land of Windsor.

Not really sure what to make of all this, I get off the train at Datchet, just over the river from Home Park. With my sleeping bag, sketchbook and kayak on my back, I find the diverted section of the Thames Path and head north along the riverbank. It is late spring, the air is sparkling with birdsong and either side of the path billows with wild mustard, cow parsley and sticky willy. I wander up and down the path, looking for a place to set up camp, to spend the day and its night in an open-eyed vigil for Herne. Various coves offer themselves, but are either too exposed or too entrenched in nettles for a comfortable night. Eventually, just before Victoria Bridge, opposite the north-ernmost perimeter of the park, I find a small path through the undergrowth which leads to a perfect inlet on the river's edge, a semi-circle of land strewn with beer bottles, with a small patch of burned earth where someone has laid a fire. It's perfect.

I unpack my stuff, unfold the kayak from its bag and begin pumping it up. Across the river, a dark blue form on the horizon, framed by the willows and poplars of the park, is Windsor Castle. Founded by William the Conqueror in 1070, it has been the residence of thirty-nine monarchs and is today the weekend home of the largest landowner in the world, the Duke of Normandy, the Duke of Lancaster, the Lord of Mann, the Defender of the Faith, Her Britannic Majesty, the right royal Queen of England.

If you include Northern Ireland, Canada, Australia and the Falkland Islands (which she does), the queen owns 6.6 billion acres of land across the globe. As the largest landowner in the world, she has 12,000 times more than her nearest runner-up, King Abdullah of Saudi Arabia (who owns a paltry 550 million acres). But the majority of this is just paperwork and branding, and the land that she profits directly from falls to about half a million acres, divided up into three distinct holdings.

The Duchy of Lancaster comprises 45,600 acres, whose portfolio of assets is valued at around £534 million, including commercial, residential and agricultural properties across Lancashire, Yorkshire, Cheshire, Staffordshire and Lincolnshire, not to mention a tasty slice of London in the form of the Savoy precinct. In 2017 the queen creamed £20.18 million profit from the surplus of this estate. The Duchy of Cornwall is a significantly larger property holding, comprising 130,000 acres across Cornwall, Devon, Herefordshire, Somerset and almost all the Isles of Scilly and is again classed as a private estate, though, like the Duchy of Lancaster, it pays no corporation tax. In 2017–18, it generated an income of £21.7 million that paid for most of the official duties of Charles, Camilla, William, Kate, Harry and Meghan.

The third asset belonging to the monarchy is called the Crown Estate and, at 336,000 acres of land, it is their most significant holding. It consists of some of the finest farmland across England, fourteen retail parks, almost all of London's Regent Street and in 2016 was valued at just over £13 billion. Under the rules of the sovereign grant, the monarchy receives 15 per cent of its surplus profit, raised recently for the next decade to 25 per cent to pay for repairs to Buckingham Palace. The land surrounding Windsor Castle, including Home Park opposite me, is Crown Land.

Firm and plump, my kayak is ready, bobbing on the river, its rope wrapped round an elder tree that juts out over the water. Clouds of mayflies are yoyoing up and down above my head, birds flit and dart from the willows, ducks and geese honk like horns in a traffic jam, and the world is thrumming, buzzing, humming with late spring. My legs are nettle-stung, shins torn with tiny scratches from the brambles, and the sun is baking the sweat into salt rims across my shoulders. After six months chained to a desk, writing this book, I am finally outside again. I slip into the water, cold, silky on the skin, and swim hard across the river to the indicted bank, and skull back again, on my back, eyes drawing in the wide sky. Time dissolves in water, seconds slip slowly into minutes. It's good to be back.

I haul myself into the kayak, cast off and paddle along the perimeter of Home Park, following the river downstream to Queen Elizabeth's Walk. Cursed not just by Herne, but by its proximity to the castle, this was always destined to be private ground, the buffer zone to the heart of the English monarchy. But somehow it resisted the cult of exclusion right up until 1848. It was once a common ground in the Manor of Orton, held by the powerful Walter FitzOther who was tenant-in-chief of twenty other manors, and was later converted to a deer park, or frith, a sanctuary for animals. Under Henry IV, the park was a mere

fifty acres, a pleasure park for the monarch's philosophical contemplation, but when Edward IV came to the throne he enclosed
a further 200 acres, no doubt for a broader outlook on life.

I glide past a small bridge that arcs over a stream leading off
the Thames into Home Park. There is no gate over this stretch
of water, and it is tempting to let the current carry me gently
into the forbidden land, where it will lead all the way up to the
foothills of Windsor Castle. A little further down is a house that
marks the gatepost of an old, now dismantled, bridge. Directly
opposite, on the Datchet side, is the London road, which once
linked Old Windsor to the village.

Since the thirteenth century this was a ferry crossing, and
an ancient public footpath led from the south-east of the castle,
through Home Park, to cross the river here. When Queen
Anne came to the throne in 1702, the route had become popular
enough for the ferry to be replaced by a bridge. Over the next
hundred years, the responsibility for the bridge's upkeep fell
to both Berkshire council, on the castle side of the river, and
Buckinghamshire, on the Datchet side. This shared responsibility caused a fierce argument between the two shires that led
to the deterioration of the bridge and culminated in an almost
unbelievable manifestation of dispute: the Divided Bridge.

By 1836, relations between the two shires were so contentious
that the lord chancellor was called in to proclaim that they should
both 'proceed in such a manner as not to impede each other'.
Like a parable authored by Lewis Carroll, who was four at the
time, both shires decided to build two half-bridges spanning out
into the river, designed to meet in the middle. Berkshire built
theirs out of iron, Buckinghamshire built theirs out of wood,
but because they couldn't resolve who would pay for the final
connecting link, or what material it should be made of, neither structure touched the other. For twelve years the Divided
Bridge had a gap at its apex, one large enough for an elephant

from George Wombwell's travelling menagerie, on its way to
Cornbury, to fall through and almost drown in the river below.

The cult of exclusion finally closed its grip around Home
Park in 1848. Prince Albert was accustomed to bathing naked in
the Thames, and required a greater degree of privacy from the
prying eyes of his subjects. The Windsor Improvement Act was
passed by Parliament in August that year and determined the
present extent of the park. The Divided Bridge was demolished,
and the road and public footpath from Windsor Castle to Datchet
redirected north over the newly built Victoria Bridge. For the
first time in history, the park's perimeter was drawn out to the
lip of the Thames, and the 655 acres became part of the Royal
Domain of Crown Land. All public paths and Rights of Way
were blocked and the Hope Inn, once situated along Frogmore
Green, was absorbed into the grounds of Frogmore House,
which was briefly the residence of Prince Harry, Meghan and
their son.

But the cult took time to take hold in the minds and actions of
the commoners and sever them from their rights to the land. In
1850, a park keeper wrote to Sir Charles Phipps with that time-
honoured paranoia: 'Windsor Park is trespassed by all sorts
of Ruffians, they form themselves like a regiment of soldiers.'
Walking had been redefined as invasion, rights as crimes.

I have paddled my way alongside the enormous London
plane trees on the bank of Home Park. I arrive at the end of
Queen Elizabeth's Walk, a path of lime trees that leads into the
park, and eventually, towards its very end, the famous Herne
Oak. I am alone on the river, no one passes by boat and no one is
in the park. Behind me, the private gardens of Buckinghamshire
are empty. Every minute or so the silence is broken by a distant
roar of pressurised air, which slowly crescendos and peaks as
a plane, low and loud, flies along the line of the trees, over my
head to Heathrow. I follow its belly over me and am hit with

a sudden sense of reverse vertigo, as if I might fall out of my kayak and be drawn up to the monster above me.

> There is an old tale goes, that Herne the hunter,
> Sometime a keeper here in Windsor forest,
> Doth all the winter time at still midnight,
> Walk around about an oak, with great ragg'd horns;
> And there he blasts the tree, and takes the cattle;
> And makes milch-kine yield blood, and shakes a chain
> In a most hideous and dreadful manner.
> – William Shakespeare, *The Merry Wives of Windsor*,
> IV.iv.24

When *The Merry Wives of Windsor* was first performed in 1602 it made a celebrity of the Herne Oak. People flocked from London to visit the tree, paying homage both to Shakespeare and to this fantastical horror story of spectral sedition. The legend was still strong in Queen Victoria's reign, transmitted across national borders on the wings of Shakespeare's fame, and five years after the park had been privatised the King of Prussia came to Windsor, at the invitation of Her Majesty, to pay homage to their new son. The morning after he had arrived, he and his large consort asked to be shown the tree. As a contemporary chronicler described the visit and the spell cast by the Bard: 'The splendours of the castle, its pictures, the noble scenery surrounding it and the many historical facts connected with it, were objects of inferior interest compared to a single time-destroyed, withered tree yet rich with recollections of the genius of our immortal Shakespeare.'

Decades ago I remember wandering the streets of Verona with sketchbook in hand. I chanced upon a long queue to a small house, I made enquiries, and discovered that this was Juliet's house. When eventually I paid my fee and entered, there before me was the balcony that Romeo knelt beneath, and in Juliet's room, lit by candles, the lovers' tomb. Wandering with the many other tourists through this tiny space, it took me a clear fifteen minutes to realise it was all a sham, a scam even. Juliet never lived here, because Juliet never lived at all; she was invented by Shakespeare. But it took just a minute more for me to realise how wrong I was. Like the gothic farmhouse on the top of Walshaw Moor these tourists had come not for authenticity, but for magic. By wandering the poky corridors we were connecting not to the characters of the play, but to what they represented: art and love and tragedy and hope. Churches, synagogues, mosques, groves, graves, woods and trees: places are sacred because of the stories we tell about them.

Herne was a legend long before Shakespeare. He is a small branch of a great tree of folklore that links him with a multitude of other Celtic myths. He is one of a long succession of horned gods whose storylines lead to one central horned god, the god of everything from life, to death, to fertility, and the inexorable power of nature: Cernunnos.

Though depictions of the great horned god are ubiquitous across northern European traditions, only once is his name mentioned: found buried within the foundations of Notre-Dame cathedral in the eighteenth century, the Pillar of the Boatman, from the first century AD, depicts a man with short stag horns and a beard, with the name Cernunnos etched above him. Another famous depiction of Cernunnos is on the Gundestrup cauldron, a beaten silver vessel found in Denmark made sometime between 150 BC and 1 BC, uncovered from a peat bog in Jutland. On one of the interior plates sits Cernunnos, this time with large antlers, surrounded by wild animals, cross-legged like the Buddha.

As the god of nature, of wild growth, of untameable passions, Herne is the close cousin, or ancestor, of the Green Man,

Bacchus from Italy and Dionysus from Greece. He is linked to Herlechin (harlequin) from France, Cernach from Ireland and, when the Christians began meddling with the pagan myths, the Devil himself. Herian (Herne with a flourish) is a name used for Woden, the god of the Anglo-Saxons, who derives from Odin, the Viking god. Here there are deeper parallels with Herne's story, because Odin also hanged himself from a tree, though not from an oak but an ash tree called Yggdrasil. These ancient tales of death and resurrection, found across the globe, and later in Christianity, are all expressions of the great turn of the seasons, when nature dies for winter and is reborn for spring.

And though there is no documented evidence of this, the legend of Herne seems to have influenced the spirit of sedition in Berkshire. It is no great leap to see the echoes of Herne's devastation of King Richard's deer stock in the practice of the eighteenth-century Blacks, who trespassed the private deer parks of Berkshire and Hampshire, especially concentrated around Windsor, leaving the deer carcasses, as Herne did, bloodied on the ground. Perhaps also Herne lends significance to the oath that these Blacks swore before the horns of a stag in the local pub. Herne might be an iteration of a wider myth, but his story is rooted in its location, in Berkshire, whose county emblem consists of a stag and an oak.

In short, Herne is wild, untameable, terrifying, inspiring and seriously cool; he is literally a legend. I want to see the tree. I want to touch it, to connect to this long thread of storytelling that worships the unruliness of the wild wood over the order of the mown lawn. But since Aaron Barschak's stunt at Prince William's party, a single foot on this turf will land me in jail for a year, with an unlimited fine. I'm wondering, if I'm caught, if I can play the same card as the druids at Stonehenge and claim religious rite of access; maybe I can sit in the police interview room, spout some of this paganism into their tape recorder and be reclassified from a criminal to a kook.

I'm sitting in the kayak, dead centre of the avenue of limes, aware that the tree is about a mile ahead of me. Several months ago, I was disappointed to learn that the original tree no longer exists. It was either felled in 1796 at the unwitting order of George III, who had ordered a cull of the dead trees in the park, or it was blown down in a storm in 1863, while Queen Victoria was on holiday in Germany. The oak was so important to the queen that she ordered it to be placed under twenty-four-hour watch until she returned, and then for it to be turned into a variety of furniture, including a bust of Shakespeare now on display in the local museum.

Either way, the old tree is gone. However, in 1906 Edward VII planted a new tree, enclosed it with a small picket fence and set a plaque commemorating the original oak. Now over a century old, it has become the Herne Oak. Somewhat pointlessly, since no one is allowed to see it, it is even labelled on Google Maps. The site of the pilgrimage, the space sanctified by the story, is still there, and it is tantalisingly close. But, still, a year in prison.

As I'm weighing it up in my mind, I watch a middle-aged woman walk along the bank of Home Park, taking her dog for an early evening stroll. As she turns up the avenues of limes, towards the new Herne Oak, we lock eyes and nod silently. Now is not the time; if I do go, I'll go at dawn.

The sun has sunk beneath the trees, the day has greyed. I kayak back up the river, against the stream, and find my little nook in the spurge of the bank. I change into warm clothes and face the castle and park with a sketchbook for the last moments of the day. There is busy preparation for some kind of plush event: tractors are hauling trailers of fencing along Prince Albert's Walk, temporary stables are being erected and there is a large marquee and a line of ten or so Kawasaki MULEs, the moon buggies used by well-financed gamekeepers. They have parked up for the day, and I watch as Home Park empties of its ground staff, then settles and stills for night.

The mayflies have changed shift with the midges, which smoke in columns above my head, crazy moving notches on a blue scatter-graph. As the wind passes through the poplar trees opposite me, the fretting leaves sound like dry rice pouring into a metal pan. I find two willow spears and pierce them through a few Polish sausages so I can grill them over the fire later on in the night. I pull out my sleeping bag, drag the kayak so I can lean against it, unfurl the roll mat and settle in for a long night. The world around me turns from green to deep blue, the bats come out for spring's easy pickings and I feel the anticipation of the crime I'm about to commit flitting in my chest.

I'm thinking of Gandalf. Not Tolkien's Gandalf, but the sixty-seven-year-old retired head teacher from Sheffield who now works as a suicide liaison counsellor in Rotherham. He's a beekeeper, a keen cyclist, and, like many men of his age across the world who sport a similarly impressive beard, he has been nicknamed Gandalf by his friends. Not long ago, he, too, stepped over the line to become a criminal.

There is a video online of Gandalf on a street in Sheffield. Five or six of his friends are sitting with arms linked around a lime tree on Rivelin Road. Arboriculturalists in hi-vis jackets and white helmets have paused their work while private security contractors are called into the temporary fence enclosure around the tree to forcibly remove the protesters. Gandalf, white beard and bike helmet, appears in shot when trying to slip through the fences to replace one of his friends. Then someone shouts: 'they've got Gandalf in a chokehold' and the camera phones swing towards the scene where we see Gandalf has been caught around the neck by a young police officer.

Suddenly, there is a wall of police blocking the videographers, officers avoiding eye contact with the protesters as they push them away from the fence, and all the while Gandalf is shouting, 'you're hurting me, you're strangling me', the policeman's arm still clamped around his throat, trying to pry him from the fence. The atmosphere is boiling, no one knows what's going on, least of all the police officer, who has now released Gandalf, or, rather, clamped him by the arm and not the neck. He's ordering Gandalf to calm down, but Gandalf's having none of it, telling the police officer to let go of him, saying, 'you look pumped up, you look really wild'.

Gandalf is eventually escorted to a police van. His bag is checked and then he is hauled into a claustrophobic metal cage at the back of a police van, an enclosure suitable for Hannibal Lecter, but a little overbearing for a beekeeping tree-hugger. He is driven away, and the healthy, hundred-year-old lime tree is felled.

Two months earlier, Gandalf was on his bike, riding for twenty-four hours straight, raising money for the Sheffield Tree campaign. He raised over £2,000 to pay for legal costs and court charges for those arrested while trying to stop their street trees being carved to stumps. The felling is part of a private finance initiative contract between Sheffield council and Amey contractors, a firm that was, at the time, owned by Ferrovial, the company responsible for the Heathrow expansion. They call the felling their 'Streets Ahead Initiative'; the residents of Sheffield call it vandalism.

In 2012, Sheffield council signed a £2.2 billion-per-year contract with Amey for highway, pavement and street-light renewal, a twenty-five-year commitment to improving the city streets. Part of the contract included dealing with dangerous, diseased, dying or dead trees that line the roads of the Sheffield suburbs, four criteria with which the residents had no argument. It was the other two that caused the contention: 'damaging or discriminatory'. Any trees that were considered to have root systems that disrupted the straight line of the kerb, or interrupted the passage of the street, were also felled. In this case, the trees themselves were defined as trespassing, and were killed for their crime.

In an independent survey, paid for by the Sheffield residents, 84 per cent of the trees earmarked for felling were deemed perfectly healthy. Felling is always supposed to be the last resort. Root pruning, kerb thinning and the implementation of Flexi™-Pave, a material which adjusts as roots grow or shrink, are just three of the fourteen alternatives used as standard by local authorities across the UK. Because these alternatives are already written into the Streets Ahead contract of 2012, they wouldn't cost the people of Sheffield a penny more. The cost, however, would be incurred by the contractors. By 2017, over 5,500 of the 36,000 Sheffield trees had been felled, with another 200 projected per year, totalling, at the end of the initiative, 17,500: half of the previous urban forest of Sheffield. The chainsaws were being used to cut costs.

It didn't take long for the people of Sheffield to respond. In 2014, when the initiative began work, it was the felling of the 450-year-old Melbourne oak that set the hare running. Despite local protests and an expert survey showing that the tree was 'uncompromised', the tree was cut down. Felling notices began to appear in laminate folders, stapled to the trees all over the city. Street by street, neighbours started to talk to each other, sharing their grief and outrage as the trees, their canopies and the ecosystems they sustained, the buzzing and the birdsong, disappeared from their world.

By spring the next year, various groups had formed to represent the streets that were targeted by the contractors: Save Our Rustlings Trees, Save our Nether Edge Trees, Save Gleadless Valley Trees, Save Ecclesall Road Trees. These groups began by compiling petitions and letters and commissioning independent surveys to present to the council. But when the various isolated groups began to exchange information, tactics and ideas, to connect with each other, they quickly unionised into one single umbrella organisation, the Sheffield Tree Action Groups, or STAG.

Having tried to block the fellings with words, they now progressed into action. They cross-referenced Amey's published plans with the trees around the Sheffield streets, and wrapped yellow ribbons around the targeted trees. They began camping out beneath some of these trees, in the parks where they couldn't be removed for obstructing public highways. Art groups began drawing the trees en masse, there were street festivals, performances of music and theatre to raise both money and awareness of the alternatives to the felling.

Swelling WhatsApp groups linked the disparate members of STAG across the city, and buzzed with reports from members positioned outside the Amey base in the early hours of the morning, watching the lorries and cutting machines leave the depot. As the vans arrived on the streets, messages would be sent from behind the twitching curtains of the houses and the protesters would mobilise almost instantly, gathering around the trees, locking arms, putting their bodies between the chainsaws and the trees.

The authorities reacted with a predictably heavy hand. First of all, Amey hired private security guards. Fences went up around the trees and security strengthened the perimeters of the newly indicted space with the broad-shouldered, implicit threat of thuggery. When this didn't work, entire streets were fenced off, with residents banned from walking up them by signs that said: 'You have no right to enter this area. Any entry of this area will be a trespass.' And then the police started supervising the felling sites, to protect the fence – and its spell – with the force of the law, a move that STAG called 'legal bullying'. The signs and fences were a temporary re-enactment of the entire dynamic of enclosure in England – put up a fence, declare the space inside it off limits, then arrest people for exercising their rights in it. Once again, the fence creates the crime.

There were smear campaigns that veered from the outrageous to the hysterical. Of these, 'Teagate' became the most famous, reported as far away as the *New York Times*. When three Amey workers fell ill while felling a tree outside the home of Dr John and Sue Unwin, it was alleged that they had been given tea and soft drinks laced with laxatives. In spite of South Yorkshire police confirming that the investigation, which included forensic tests on the Unwins' kitchen utensils, was 'no longer live', Amey persisted in accusing this retired couple of poisoning their staff. Sue Unwin responded with dignity and wit in the *Yorkshire Post*: 'we don't have laxatives, we are vegetarians and don't have any problems in that department.'

By spring 2017, Amey had begun photographing the protesters and, by the summer, seventeen individuals, including Green councillor Alison Teal, had received documents warning them of an impending injunction, with a large array of photographs and screenshots revealing an extensive campaign of surveillance against the protesters, who throughout had been acting both peacefully and lawfully. The letters demanded that these seventeen promise never to attend or even to encourage protests against felling, with the threat of imprisonment and extreme financial penalties if they did. The letters effectively vetoed their recipients from protection under Articles 10 and 11 of the European Convention on Human Rights, and turned their rights into crimes.

As a member of the STAG campaign told me, 'everyone involved had stepped into unknown territory'. Because when these fences were set up around the trees, spelled with their legal force field, they became a moral line that each member of STAG had to negotiate: should they cross into criminality? If they did so, the repercussions would be pragmatic as well as moral. Just as those who were excommunicated from the Church in the Middle Ages were banned from receiving work in their parish, so, too, the lives of the modern commoners of Sheffield would be impacted in real terms. Being arrested would harm their credit rating, damage their chances of a new mortgage, and, through the Disclose Barring Service, some would risk losing the chance of further employment. There were lots of educators in STAG, from university academics to secondary and primary school teachers, and a criminal record would seriously hamper their chances of remaining in their position. On top of all this, the court cases and legal fines could break people; one member of STAG is currently faced with a £16,000 bill.

But STAG won. Of course they did. They saved individual trees such as the Chelsea elm and the Vernon oak, which has its own Twitter account with more than 2,000 followers. They won a £24,000 out-of-court settlement for wrongful arrest and they won a six-month pause in felling while the council organised mediated negotiations between Amey and STAG. The national and international outcry prompted government intervention, with Michael Gove, the secretary of state for the environment, visiting Sheffield and calling the plans 'bonkers'. A year later, Gove announced the Urban Tree Challenge Fund, which has now made £10 million available for 130 million new trees to be planted across England's cities and towns.

The mediated talks were themselves a victory: with representatives from STAG finally being called in to discuss the future of the streets that they lived on, residents finally had a say in the future of their community. Just as the residents of Hebden were refused any say in the management of the land that affected their lives so integrally, so, too, the residents of Sheffield had been denied any say in the contract negotiated, behind closed doors, between the council and the contractors.

In 1968, Henri Lefebvre published a book called *Right to the City*. It was a call to action for people to reclaim the city as a 'co-created space'. He urged readers to 'rescue the citizen as main element and protagonist of the city that he himself had built' and to transform urban space into 'a meeting point for building collective life'. For five years, the members of STAG relentlessly badgered Sheffield council. They campaigned, marched, protested, they risked their livelihoods and homes, they stepped over the line into criminality. They claimed their right to the city and achieved what should have been theirs in the first place: the right of a community to have a say in the land they live on.

Gandalf is doing well. Like most modern wizards, he now has a Facebook account, so I wrote to him to ask a few questions. After his arrest, he had returned from the police station to snatch a thin slice of the tree that he had tried to protect. He took it home, scrawled onto it '110 year old Sheffield tree – you killed it' in chalk and later delivered it to the Amey offices in Oxford. His email, which describes the 'visceral pain' he felt when he saw the healthy trees come crashing down, ends with the lines: 'I am now engaged in protesting the imminent felling of trees in Barnsley and using what I learned in Sheffield to inform my actions.' Gandalf has been radicalised.

And this word is key. The term 'radical' is often conflated with more threatening words, such as extremist and fundamentalist, and is used as a slur by media organisations seeking to present such politics as a threat to law and order. But originally the word radical refers not to the style of change, but its location. Radical politics is not about pruning the structure, lopping off the occasional unsightly bough or branch. Instead it seeks to modify the *radix*, the root of the system, the source of systemic inequality. Inevitably this leads you to where the roots lie, deeply embedded in the compacted strata of social and natural history that we call *the land*.

The sky stays bright for a long time. Everything at ground level sinks into darkness. Cocooned in my warm mummy sleeping bag, with everything I need a reach away, I feel like a baby in a womb, or a pig in shit, deeply, comfortably ensconced in nature. The ground keeps surging and swaying, like the surface of the river, and it takes a while for me to realise that the moon is rising behind me, shining magic light through the swaying fronds of the willow trees, making the shadows seethe.

The authoritarian tactics of the police in Sheffield was a standard response to a protest that refused to accept the boundaries they had imposed. STAG were prepared to cross the line, to ignore the temporary fences which created the crime and defined them as criminals, and instead to operate within their own self-construed paradigm of peaceful protest. But by crossing this line, what they were really doing was bursting the bubble of consent, challenging the consensus of established order by pushing at its limits.

There's a word for that. Coined by Erving Goffman, whose work was to influence Stanley Milgram's prison experiments, 'breaching' is a technique in social psychology which seeks to highlight commonly accepted societal norms by violating them. The technique is also known as 'garfinkeling', after Harold Garfinkel, who used the technique to demonstrate how much of social interaction operates along the unquestioned, accepted norms (doxa) that are deeply riven into the psyche of societies. By breaching the lines of what was considered appropriate, by acting out of line, Garfinkel shone a light on what it is that constructs this social reality, what binds the spell of consensus. There is no better description of trespass than this.

Trespass is an act that breaches a societal norm rooted deep in English culture, that the value of the land should belong exclusively to those who own it, and not to the communities that so badly need it. But to climb the walls that were built around our common land is to garfinkel an even deeper consensus: it questions the legitimacy of the castle that built these barriers in the first place, the laws that were constructed to defend them and the entire dynamic of elite power that defines and confines the freedoms of the wider community. Trespass shines a light on the unequal share of wealth and power in England, it threatens to unlock a new mindset of our community's rights to the land, and, most radical of all, it jinxes the spell of an old, paternalistic order that tell us everything is just as it should be.

And when this spell is shattered, the first response is often anger, and sometimes violence. When Extinction Rebellion took to the streets to blockade bridges, they were seeking to disrupt not just the flow of traffic, but the current that sustains this spell. The system can absorb a march or a petition and carry on as blithely as before. But Extinction Rebellion recognised that what was needed was a breaching of the code of conduct, something to wake us from our reverie. As the wheels kept turning on the London tarmac, the spell of capitalism kept generating its precious gas, blocking our minds from the brutal truth that we are killing the planet. So Extinction Rebellion blocked the roads, turned the bridges into podiums for protest and reclaimed the city. And for bringing these plain truths into the public sphere, they were derided: they were called middle-class narcissists and uncooperative crusties, they were accused of disrupting local businesses, they were defined as radicals hell-bent on anarchy. Such hysteria is the sound of the spell breaking.

The response was similarly shrill when Guy Shrubsole's *Who Owns England?* was published. The book was a breaching of the lines of propriety, it punctured the illusion that property works for everyone. Presenting its evidence empirically in graphs, tables and footnotes, supported by a blog with interactive maps showing the extent, value and ownership of land, the book is unequivocal in the data it presents. Not one of its critics has come forward to challenge its facts. However, a reviewer from the *Daily Telegraph* called it 'pie-in-the-sky', while Owen Paterson, the former minister for the environment, accused Shrubsole of seeing 'conspiracy at every turn'. A reviewer writing for *The Times* said: 'A more rigorous editor would have told him firmly to focus on the important and interesting question of who owns the country, rather than carping about who runs it.' *Carping*, he says, completely ignoring the vital message of the book that who owns England is, and always has been, who runs it. Alongside the sword and the horse, property is power in its rawest form.

The threat of the alternative story is that it downgrades a doxa to an orthodoxy; it suggests that what appears to be the natural order of things is in fact a construct, with its roots in private interest. The cult of exclusion that holds England in its thrall is at once the most established of its form, and the most fragile in its consistency; it is brittle. Because the alternatives are all around us. In the Nordic countries of Finland, Iceland, Norway and Sweden, the Baltic countries of Estonia, Latvia and Lithuania and the Central European countries of Austria, Czech Republic and Switzerland, the freedom of individuals to roam and camp in the countryside is a time-honoured common right that has in some countries been codified into law. The lines of property still exist, but they are porous.

In Finland, the freedom to roam is called *jokamiehenoikeus*; in Sweden it is *allemansrätten*, in Norway *allemannsrett* and in Austria *Wegefreiheit*. In all instances, these rights existed in the country long before there was a nation or a language to define them. In a recent campaign by the Swedish tourist board, the advertisers chose simply to register the land of Sweden

on Airbnb. The move was an inspired piece of free publicity, but also expressed one of the key concepts of the Swedish psyche: the land is your home. In the words of the Visit Sweden website: 'Sweden has no Eiffel Towers. No Niagara Falls or Big Bens. Not even a little Sphinx. Sweden has something else – the freedom to roam. This is our monument.'

The closest threat to England's cult of exclusion is the system found just over the border of the River Tweed in Scotland. Since 2003, the Scottish Land Reform Act has opened up the vast majority of land in Scotland that isn't designated for schools, industry or national monuments and access rights now apply to any non-motorised activities, including walking, cycling, horse-riding and wild camping, canoeing, rowing, sailing and swimming.

Yet far from crying havoc to order, fundamental to the Scottish Outdoor Access Code is that ancient understanding of the commons, that rights come with responsibilities, both to other people and to the land itself. Many of the nuanced responsibilities are laid out in law. Littering is a contravention of the Environmental Protection Act of 1990, and there is even a set limit on how far away you should piss from a river (thirty metres). Even in England and Wales, when the Countryside Rights of Way (CRoW) Act came into force in 2000, opening up 10 per cent of our land to walking (but not camping), it came with a more clearly defined set of responsibilities, not to mention higher penalties for their infraction. The safeguarding of nature conservation was crucial to the architecture of this new right to roam and the maximum penalty for threatening the balance of the ecology was upped from a fine to a term of imprisonment. The secretary of state was given new powers to designate 'wildlife inspectors' and offences such as disturbing various animals have now been extended to cover both intentional and reckless acts.

Scotland's access code is reasonable. First and foremost in its ethic is the protection of private property and personal space, a feature found across Europe in the various forms of *allemannsrett*. There is an understanding that the 'curtiledge' of a private dwelling, the extent of its garden and drive, are personal sanctuaries and should not be invaded. In Sweden this zone is known as the *hemfridszon's size* and is codified at seventy metres away from the boundary of a property. In Norway it is 150 metres, and in Scotland it is looser, defined simply as a 'reasonable distance'. You are required to camp far enough away 'to enable those living there to have reasonable measures of privacy and to ensure that their enjoyment of that house or place is not unreasonably disturbed'. Written into the code are various exceptions to the right to roam – no one is allowed to walk or camp on land where crops are growing, on school grounds, golf courses, building sites and a variety of other sites where damage could be caused.

The code is very specific about what it considers responsible behaviour. In England, one of the greatest bugbears of landowners is the dog walker, and the threat they pose to livestock. For dog walkers, the Scottish code advises against entering a field where there are young animals, or ground-nesting birds, and keeping the dog on a leash during the breeding season. If a dog does end up worrying the livestock, then the owner will be found guilty of an offence under the Dogs Act of 1953. If the dog owner leaves dog faeces in any open space, they can be prosecuted under the Dog Fouling Act of 2003. The fifty-page document detailing the rights and responsibilities of dog owners (magnificently titled 'Taking the Lead') suggests that public awareness, rather than wilful malignity, is the central issue, and that signs, and even conversations, will settle the problem. Key to this approach is that walkers are prohibited from causing actual harm and not pre-emptively punished with exclusion for the walk itself.

And yet in England, the cult of exclusion translates our desire to access land into a criminal, violent, threatening, and in the case of Nicholas Van Hoogstraten, perverted impulse. The land lobby groups use the same technique as nationalists to charm the nation: they make it personal. Throughout history, homeowners have been co-opted into the cult of exclusion by the deliberate and spurious conflation of enormous estates with the notion of the English garden. When the Labour manifesto of 2017 proposed to replace council tax and business rates with a new Land Value Tax, the *Daily Mail* renamed it a 'Marxist Garden Tax', redefining the issue not in terms of the millions of acres of England in single private ownership, but in terms of their favourite fabrication: 'normal people'. The laws of trespass, structured around the legal fiction of personal harm, feed into this myth that redefines a walk through woodland into an attack on the sanctity of a home. That this interpretation of walking can be so radically different north of the border suggests either that Scottish law directly encourages home invasion, or that the harm is not in the act itself, but simply in how it is defined.

To illustrate precisely this point, I made a rule at the start of this book, a small personal commitment that I have kept hidden in my pockets throughout. Every single one of the trespasses in this book was carried out in precise accordance with the Scottish Outdoor Access Code. In other words, under Scottish law none of the trips in this book was a trespass. Though I ignored England's cult of exclusion, though I climbed every wall and locked gate that blocked my way, I went nowhere near the garden, let alone the house of an estate. This was not difficult. I simply followed my heart, rambling, adventuring, and took whatever route seemed most enjoyable – to walk into someone's back garden would have ruined my day almost as much as theirs. More often than not, I and whichever friend I could per-suade to join me met not one other soul on our trip. We walked,

sat around, talked, took in the day, lit a fire, slept, cleared away
our rubbish, and left. And the most striking discovery of all this
rambling was just how wide the world is, how many hills, lakes,
woods and dells there are to this land. If England is full, it is full
of space. And the walls that hide it.

It is some time after midnight, and the chill has set in. Earlier
on in the day, I had gone exploring around the base of Victoria
Bridge, whose final archway extends not over water, but wasteland hidden in the greenery beneath the road. Under this arch,
among discarded shoes and a broken buggy, I found enough dry
wood to keep a fire going through the night. I had been nervous
about lighting it at nightfall, unsure how many teams of security
would be prowling Home Park, but now, after several hours of
stillness, it feels safe enough to give it a go.

The fire crackles and brings a new life to my cove, a warm-
heartedness that feels like home. It reminds me of Octavia
Hill's vision of nature as an outdoor living room, and that the
Countryside Rights of Way Act is not enough. It is nowhere
near enough. The CRoW access maps on Natural England's
website, or on individual council sites, show Open Access areas
of England shaded in a yellow wash, dribbled over England
like small puddles of piss-all. There are even occasional areas
marked out that have no Rights of Way linking them to public
access, small islands of freedom walled off by a simple lack of
planning. There are larger areas in the moors and the coastal
paths, but while they remain as they are, where they are, they are
inaccessible to the large proportion of the nation. When you add
the factors of cost included in rail fares or petrol, not to mention
the need to stay somewhere overnight, access to land is both a
postcode lottery and biased against those that can't afford it.

The CRoW Act needs expanding, not just in the area it covers,
but in its scope. Just like our European neighbours, we need the

full right to roam; we need the right to camp and we need the right to make a fire. Without this, we are treating the natural world like a museum, isolated exhibits of a culture long gone, something to be observed behind a red rope. How can we care about the life outside human walls, the world that exists beyond the Rights of Way and designated public spaces, if we can't see it, hear it, touch it and experience it for ourselves? Camping one night in autumn, years ago, just north of Rannoch Moor, I was kept awake till dawn by the rutting stags which were belling in the darkness around me. It was a haunting, powerful noise from the animal kingdom, a raw, timeless awakening to the world outside human ken. In Scotland, this magic is my birthright. In England, it is a crime.

The case in Scotland does demonstrate the problem of opening up the land, however. As soon as you are given the right to roam, you can see for yourself the vast swathes of coun-tryside that have been walled off for so long. This leads inevit-ably to questions about other rights to the land, about its use and its value. When Scotland introduced its first Land Reform Act in 2003, it also introduced the right of a community to buy land as a co-operative. Now, almost twenty years later, nearly 500 community bodies own more than 500,000 acres in common, and the government has set a target for a million acres by 2020. Give people an inch of freedom, and they'll want to know what happened to the mile.

In 2017, the Scottish government released the Scottish Land Rights and Responsibilities Statement, which proposes a vision of a Scotland with 'a strong and dynamic relationship between its land and people, where all land contributes to a modern and successful country, and where rights and responsibilities in relation to land are fully recognised and fulfilled'. The heart of this document is an acknowledgement of land as inherent to the rights of the people that live on it and as fundamental to the equality of society. It recognises the power of land ownership and defines the land as an asset of the country, and not just its owners. Its principles set out a guideline for all political decisions regarding land use: it states that the legal framework of land rights should exist to promote a fairer society, that land should be used to contribute to public interest and wellbeing. It calls for a more diverse pattern of land ownership, with more opportunities for individuals and groups who lease land to own it. It calls for landowners to exercise their rights in the light of their responsibility to higher stewardship. It calls for complete transparency of land data.

What is striking about this document is its decision to keep much of the framework open to change: it will be reviewed every five years. Land reform, it says, 'is constantly evolving' and its legislation must be open to hybridity, to the constant mutability of the factors that influence it. It calls for balanced judgement, encourages good communication between owners and communities, and in this listed set of ethics it starts to sound a lot like Edward Soja's Thirdspace. Or more historically, the commons.

It is the dead of night. There is a whoop from the other side of the river, an owl hunting in Home Park. But so far, no sight of Herne. My sausage grill was highly successful and I'm now watching the embers of the fire glower, mesmerised by its gentle exhalations. With my belly full of hot food, snug in my sleeping bag, I could fall asleep right now, but I'm here to keep watch for Herne. I layer up the fire with thick twigs to get the flames going, add a few arms then place on top the large wooden claw I found by the bridge, a root stock from a fallen elder tree. The flames creep up its scaffold, my cove brightens and the smoke furloughs out onto the river where it rests, colder, heavier, like a mist. I watch the full moon rise above Windsor Castle, see its reflection fall from behind the trees, cheesy yellow, into the water.

This is where the world as we know it turns upside down: what if the land itself were to be defined as a human right? The Scottish Report acknowledges that rights to land are 'central to the realisation of key human rights, particularly economic, social and cultural rights'. Three years earlier, the United Nations High Commissioner for Human Rights wrote a report that declared: 'Land is a cross-cutting issue that impacts directly on the enjoyment of a number of human rights. For many people, land is a source of livelihood, and is central to economic rights. Land is also often linked to people's identities, and so is tied to social and cultural rights.'

According to this report, poverty reduction, disaster prevention, food security, access to affordable housing, the fulfilment of women's rights are all aided by an improvement in people's rights to land. Likewise, climate change, rapid urbanisation, the battle between subsistence and private profiteering: all of these are directly related to the current definition of private property rights, the total dominion given to owners. And the same spell of enclosure that first bound England continues to spread throughout the world: the report cites estimates that, over the past twenty years, between 280 million and 300 million people worldwide have been affected by development-related displacement (hydroelectric dams, mines, oil and gas installations, gentrification). By taking the land from these people, they have taken their rights. Yet, so far, international human rights law has not taken any steps to provide for a universal 'human right to land'.

The health benefits of access to nature may be self-evident, but to be taken seriously in legal circles they must be proven. Recently, science has been providing a growing wealth of evidence to show that exposure to nature can reduce children's symptoms of attention deficit disorder and hyperactivity, and help reduce or prevent obesity, myopia and vitamin D deficiency. Other reports suggest that time spent in nature can improve social bonding, stimulate learning and creativity and reduce the symptoms of stress, anxiety and depression. In 2012, the World Conservation Congress of the International Union for Conservation of Nature produced a resolution stating: 'Growing up in a healthy environment and connecting children with nature is of such a fundamental importance for both children and the conservation of nature and the protection of the environment, that it should be recognised and codified internationally as a human right for children.'

The resolution marked a profound cultural shift in the science of ecology: rather than walling off people from nature, to create conservation sites empty of human footprint, the way forward is to encourage greater connectivity between people and their environment, to re-establish that link. As Cheryl Charles, a human rights lawyer, said, 'we were beginning to realise that people need to connect with nature personally in order to care about it'.

The park is silent and the trees are still. The moon has conquered the night: the sky blazes with a royal blue; the land is cast in silver. With the gamekeepers in their beds, with the world's principal landowner snoring into her pillow, the cult of exclusion lies temporarily dormant. The land is unmasked; its truth shines clear as day.

'So simple and so clear is this truth, that to see it fully once is always to recognise it.' Henry George wrote these words in 1879. He was an American political economist, journalist and sometime-beggar whose experiences on the breadline of America led him to write *Progress and Poverty*. The book was an investigation into the apparent paradox of how a nation could sustain economic and technological growth while simultaneously increasing poverty and inequality. His conclusions presented land as both the cause and the remedy for society's ills: 'The great cause of inequality in the distribution of wealth is inequality in the ownership of land. The ownership of land is the great fundamental fact which ultimately determines the social, the political, and consequently the intellectual and moral condition of a people.'

For George, land was the bedrock of society, and those who controlled the rights to the land controlled the rights of the people who had nowhere else to be but the land. He was the first to acknowledge the importance of land to the economic equality of its inhabitants, to suggest a single tax on the value of the land, which went on to influence Winston Churchill and Lloyd George in their 1909 budget. In the decade after its publication, his book sold millions of copies and his theories spread quickly through America and northern Europe. Political parties, think tanks, institutions and alternative communities sprouted from his seed of thought, and he won support from left and right, including figures such as Milton Friedman, Benjamin Franklin and Winston Churchill. But however clear his theory was to his followers, it somehow remained veiled under the orthodoxy of private property.

His followers, the Georgists, used a popular meme of the time to explain this illusion: *can you see the cat?* In the early twentieth century, this phrase had become synonymous with pointing out truths that were hidden in plain sight. It referred to a popular illustration of the time: a simple pen and ink sketch, it depicted a tree in the foreground, a corner of a cottage and three rats in the foreground. Beneath the image were the words: *can you see the cat?* It was an optical illusion. For some, the cat was instantly visible, for others, they needed the sentence to prompt them, but most denied the presence of any cat whatsoever. Yet there, in the negative space between the boughs of the tree, was the silhouette of a cat, crouching, ready to pounce. As George said: 'this relation, once recognised, is always afterward clear.' For the followers of George, it was a useful metaphor to explain the importance of land rights to every other freedom – almost always overlooked, but once you've seen it, you can't unsee it.

Lying here in the moonlight, awake while all others are asleep, this truth seems self-evident. And yet, by day, when society is in full swing, it remains obscured. The cult of exclusion is an optical illusion of walls and words that has drawn our eyes away from the cat. Its definition of property is so ingrained in our collective consciousness that we fail to recognise its extremism, the total dominion it grants its owners over the absolute void of rights for those who live in or around its parameters. Its spell hides the land with walls, it camouflages its importance to us, it naturalises the unnatural. And every one of its signs, fences, dogmas and doxas that direct us away from the land also point us away from its importance, because, once you've seen it, you can't unsee it.

While the issues of inequality continue to be treated as disparate, disconnected concerns, the advance of social equality will still be bound, like the land, in wire. In Sheffield, the moment that each individual street campaign collectivised into one united movement, when they saw their concerns in its wider context, was the moment the spell was broken and the campaign gained the force it needed to create change. STAG was a network of lines that reconnected people, an architecture of commoning that allowed the Sheffield campaigners to share ideas, tactics and solidarity and claim their right to the city they lived in. If only

England would follow Sheffield's lead. If only the individual groups that campaign for greater rights to housing, food production and agriculture, mental and physical health, that fight against divisions of class, race and gender, could see that their concerns are all inextricably linked to the one issue that underlies them all: our rights to land.

The sky is lighter now, a dark blue cloth with a stage light behind it; a couple of birds are chirping tentatively – dawn is on its way. The English language has myriad names for the transition of day into night, twilight, dusk, the gloaming, the witching hour, but we have nothing for when night passes to day. For the Portuguese, this is *madrugada*, essentially 'the beginning of a process'. The light is like twilight, but brightening, and with tiny flickers of perception, I sense a distant birdcall, a scurry in the undergrowth behind me. The process is beginning. The land is awakening.

In my strange, sleep-deprived state of mind, my psyche chimes with my surroundings – I am unbelievably excited, my blood is rising. But like a mushroom trip, the energy suddenly turns and I suddenly feel overwhelmed with anxiety, not butterflies but wild geese flapping in my belly. I've read about this.

The most lyrical, magical chapter of *The Wind in the Willows* is 'The Piper at the Gates of Dawn', which so inspired Syd Barrett of Pink Floyd that he named their first album after it. Ratty and Mole come across Otter, who is panicking, searching for his lost child. They offer to go out through the night to search for him and eventually, at dawn, they follow a soft piping music to find him curled up and sleeping beneath the strangest sight the pair of them have ever seen: Pan.

And then, in that utter clearness of the imminent dawn, while Nature, flushed with fullness of incredible colour, seemed to hold her breath for the event, he looked in the very eyes of the Friend and Helper ... All this he saw, for one moment breathless and intense, vivid on the morning sky; and still, as he looked, he lived; and still, as he lived, he wondered.

'Rat!' he found breath to whisper, shaking. 'Are you afraid?'

'Afraid?' murmured the Rat, his eyes shining with unutterable love. 'Afraid! Of Him? O, never, never! And yet – and yet – O, Mole, I am afraid!'

I know exactly how they feel. In the later years of the Herne legend, in the eighteenth and nineteenth centuries, Herne was occasionally sighted not as a horned, horse-backed spectre, but as a man, mustachioed, with bright devilish eyes. This seems to be where the legend of Herne meets the myth of the gypsy. He would be sighted, just fleetingly, passing like a shadow on your grave, and be gone. I am quietly resolved that if I see anyone at all on the Thames path behind me, at this ungodly hour, then it is Herne and my entire framework of existential scepticism will implode in an instant. Quickly, I modify this resolution to exclude joggers (because Herne would never wear Lycra).

In my right mind I know these stories are not real. I know they are just creative expressions of the awe and excitement their authors have felt while being vividly alive in the wild. But when they connect with actual places on the land, Home Park for Herne, Cadbury Castle for King Arthur, any forest in England for 'Rooster' Byron, the stories become the connective fluid between the minds of humans and the non-human. They are magic spells that link us with the land, and, though based not in science but in folklore, they can still have a profound effect on the world around us.

In 1999, a motorway was being built to bypass the town of Newmarket-on-Fergus in Co. Clare, Ireland. A local storyteller by the name of Eddie Lenihan came across the bulldozers and warned the construction workers of a sacred grove of hawthorn trees just a little way ahead of them. He cautioned them that if they were to cut down this grove, or *'sceach'*, which was a meeting point for the Kerry fairies, then, as the tradition went, they would never get a full night's sleep again. On top of this, the fairies would see to it that mischief would be made on that stretch of road for ever more. 'It is sacred ground,' said Lenihan, 'it doesn't revert to being a normal place.'

Lenihan, who also sports a Gandalf beard, wrote to the *Irish Times* explaining the danger, and the letter was picked up by news channels around the world, the BBC, French and Swedish news channels, CNN, the *New York Times*. The story about a story became a meme, went viral and eventually, under immense public pressure from across the globe, the £100 million motorway was re-routed, saving the *sceach* of hawthorn trees. Magic works; stories have power.

Whether or not the Kerry fairies were real is a moot point compared to the undeniable effect of their story. Lenihan's claim drew on a deeply rooted tradition of folklore, a web of story-telling that linked the identity of a people with their landscape. From Co. Clare to Boston and New York this fairy tale triggered a collective memory of vernacular storytelling that expressed the value of the land as it was defined by the people who lived on it, who came from it, and not just the people who owned it. Such stories tell an entirely different tale of ownership, that the land does not belong to us, but that we belong to it.

These stories are spells that change the way we experience the world. A spell is simply the Anglo-Saxon word for story, a derivation we find in the name Gandalf is called by Grima Wormtongue in the fourth book of *The Lord of the*

Rings: Láthspell. A variant of the Old English láðspel, Láthspell means evil story, the opposite of godspell, or gospel. Of course, whether the spell, or story, is good or bad depends on who defines it. Gandalf is a magician, a wizard and a witch because he is a storyteller, a weaver of alternative stories that threaten the established narrative of the land.

These are the stories of the commons, folk stories, the stories that come not from the castle, but from the plains, the collective voice of the people. They are the stories of insurrection and civil disobedience, the histories of the collective action that won us our rights, the stories that are rarely told or taught in schools. They defy our division, they tell us that people, as one, have power. But these stories that we have told for centuries, that consecrate an alternative relationship with the land, are silenced by the monotone blast of private property. The fences and walls that are strangling our land are constricting our connection to the stories that can heal us, the magic that can link us once again to the land and to each other. In more ways than one, they've got Gandalf in a chokehold.

It's time to get going. The birds are waking up; this little patch of thistle and dock, sticky willy and bushels of wild mustard has become a jungle of life. I am happy and surprised at my ingenuity: an hour or so ago, I fanned out my damp swimming trunks on a springy frond of willow, smoking them like a kipper over the fire, and now not only have they dried, they are warm to wear. I test the kayak for air, top it up, and still entirely unsure what I'm going to do when I get there, I slide into the water and set off towards the Herne Oak.

I'm paddling hard to counter the cold. Coming up to Queen Elizabeth's Walk, the line of lime trees that leads to the Herne Oak, my nerves are getting the better of my resolve. A year in prison is a long time to regret a walk. There are thousands of oak trees in England worthy of the story of Herne, and this youngster, which is not even the actual Herne Oak, is probably the least impressive of the lot. *But*, says the horned god on my shoulder, *the park is silent; it is completely empty; you can get away with this*. Because Harry and Meghan had just moved in here, I expected armed security, tripwires, anti-aircraft guns; but there's nothing, just those words on the sign that spell the land: 'Trespass on this site is a criminal offence.' And the silent expectation of compliance.

I still have my eyes peeled for Herne. In this half-light of *madrugada*, it feels entirely plausible that I might see him. If he's in Home Park, he will be galloping through the trees, leading his wild hunt. By the seventeenth century, the story of the wild hunt had expanded its scope. Herne no longer led just the other gamekeepers of the park, but a motley line of vagabonds and outcasts. Stories were told across Windsor about the men and women who galloped behind him, how their intestines hung from slashed bellies, how their heads were on backwards. Some were missing hands and arms, some had holes branded in their face.

These ghoulish riders were part of a larger European tradition of the Wild Hunt, something which emerged from the collective consciousness whenever a nation was in some kind of crisis. They were seen clattering down the streets of Paris on the eve of the French Revolution, led this time by Harlequin. The leaders varied from nation to nation, but their riders remained the same: they were the excommunicated, the ostracised, the witches, the gypsies, the lost souls who had been partitioned from society's grace and favour. They were the vagrants.

Today, the national crisis that grips the land is not Brexit, but the spell that binds 92 per cent of the land and 97 per cent of the waterways in England from public use. If England really wants to take back control, it should take it from the anachronistic system of ownership that has left so many of its people dispossessed of their rights. Today, Herne leads the immigrants, the Diaspora, the hippies, the fracking protesters, the small farmers who commit suicide at the rate of one a week, the ramblers, the entire rental market, the ravers, anyone in England who is ostracised by their lack of access to the value of the land. But in the Herne legend at least, they have horses, they have power and they have finally risen – change is on its way.

We don't need to look to Scotland for the alternatives. They are here already. There are any number of projects already running in England that seek to make the land more accessible to all. There has been a recent renaissance in not just rewilding spaces, but re-commoning them, opening them up not just to nature, but to community as well. From food-growing projects, to schemes that occupy empty buildings for cultural events put on for and by locals, people find the cracks in property law, the corners of waste ground in cities, and reclaim them for the community. There are already 330 community land trusts in England and Wales which have bought land for housing, food growing and workspace. Owned by the community, they work to make their spaces affordable to all, linked to local wages and not global finance markets.

And it's not just a bunch of hippies. Land has always been a cross-partisan, intersectional issue. Land reform is not anti-capitalist, or against a free market – instead, it shines a light on the fact that with land as a walled-off monopoly the property market has never been free. Land reform encourages the entre-preneurship and flow of earned capital that is so important to the Conservative mindset. Since 2018, an all-party parliamentary group has been meeting to discuss the most radical idea of them all, investigating how Henry George's theory that a tax on the value of the land could improve housing development, stabilise house prices and reduce income and wealth disparity – and pos-sibly replace all other taxes. In some circumstances, this tax has already been used, albeit in disguise. A quarter of the Crossrail development was financed by a Land Value Tax, raising the money to build it through a levy on the increase in land value around it. Though structured around the logic of a land value tax, this levy was given the euphemism 'supplementary business rate' to stop the priests of the orthodoxy falling off their chairs.

Of course, landowner lobby groups present land reform as anarchy. When Labour commissioned Land for the Many in 2019, a report which studied how changes might be made to how 'our fundamental asset is used, owned and governed', the response was hysterical. Its proposals were compared to the Soviet Union, Zimbabwe and Venezuela and the financial website This Is Money, owned by the Daily Mail Group Trust, described it as a 'frightening land ownership move ... straight from the Marxist playbook'. Once again, land reform was depicted as an extreme threat to the order of our land. But far from overturning the state, or reordering England into some goggle-eyed Stalinist state, one of the most radical uses of land in England is already here, right in front of me, at the heart of the monarchy: the Crown Estate.

The Crown Estate is a highly successful alternate vision of how land can be managed. Its accounts, the parameters of its holdings, are available for public scrutiny; it is transparent. It owns the entire coastline of England, Wales and Northern Ireland, from the shore to twelve miles out to sea and has used this property to become a world leader for renewable wind energy. Its website, like the Scottish Responsibility statement, recognises the intrinsic relationship between social equality and access to land – it talks of the mental health benefits to land, and how class affects access to the property industry. And while 25 per cent of its profit goes to fund the monarch, 75 per cent goes directly to the Treasury. In 2017, Crown Lands contributed

£329 million to the common purse, enough to pay the basic salary of almost 15,000 nurses.

Most cultures in the world have at some point held the notion that land cannot belong exclusively to individuals. In Islam, the Koran says: 'Unto Allah belongeth whatsoever is in the heavens and whatsoever is in the earth', while in Christianity and Judaism the Old Testament states: 'The land shall not be sold forever: for the land is mine, for ye are strangers and sojourners with me.' There is a Native American aphorism that expresses the same concept with a combined poetry and ecological pragmatism: you don't inherit the land from your ancestors, you borrow it from your children.

In some ways, Crown Land is the real expression of these values. It belongs in name to the monarch, but in practice to the state: it gives value to all the citizens of England. It belongs to no one and everyone. But if that is the case, then why are its lands still subject to the cult of exclusion? For these 336,000 acres, this seems particularly indefensible. For the next step in the journey towards unspelling the land, at the very least we need to extend the Countryside Rights of Way Act to include the land we already own: the Crown Land.

I have finally arrived at the avenue of limes. The park is still, but the sporadic tingle of birdsong is beginning to animate it. I think of Shakespeare's lines:

Why, yet there want not many, that do fear
In deep of night to walk by this Herne's oak.

This morning it is another story, equally preposterous, that makes me scared to walk this land. It is the story that redefines a walk as an act of aggression, that pretends that what lies inside the fence has nothing to do with those on its outside; the story that sees the land portioned into empires of private space and luxury, at the direct expense of public amenity; the story that privileges one person's rights over the land at the expense of every other. It is a story told by the powerful to the powerless, a story they enshrined in law. It must be retold – by everyone.

So, maybe now I take my chance. Maybe I tie the rope of my kayak to its paddle, place the paddle on the clipped grass of Home Park and quietly haul myself up onto the bank. Maybe, looking left and right, heart thumping, for the first time in my life a certifiable criminal, I walk barefoot up that avenue of limes. Maybe I reach the Herne Oak, climb its pointless picket fence and read the plaque beside the tree that says: 'This tree was planted 29th January 1906 by command of his majesty the King Edward VII to mark the original position of Herne's Oak.' Maybe I place my hand on its bark, my forehead on its trunk, close my eyes and, for a lingering moment, pray to Herne to lift this spell from the land.

Or maybe not. Maybe I find the inscription in an old book about Windsor. Maybe I decide that this tree, or the walk to it, is not worth the penalty they put on it, the words they use to define it. Either way, back in my kayak, I earn my year in prison. Looking to improve on my last visit's single blade of grass, I paddle along the bank and pluck a small variety of wild weeds that have escaped the mower on the plush lawn of Home Park. Wild mustard, ivy, some kind of marjoram, a small sprig of cow parsley. A bouquet of crimes.

The birds now are loud, and the trees either side of me are a chaos of song, a wild, dissonant ringing chorus which reflects off the surface of the river with the first light of the day. I feel the touch of the sun as it rises over the tips of the leaves on the tops of the Buckinghamshire trees. And I feel, in more ways than one: the land is awakening.

RESOURCES

To purchase prints, including those featured in this book go
to the author's website, foghornhayes.com, and Instagram, @
nickhayesillustration. Check out #trespassbook for photos of
the trespasses in this book

www.landjustice.uk
A network linking all those with a vested interest in a new
approach to our rights to land, from farmers, to town planners,
artists and computer programmers.

landinournames.community
A group that seeks to reinvent a land system in the UK that is
fair and open to the Black community.

righttoroam.org.uk
A campaign seeking to open up the privatised land of England
and Wales to a new right to roam

Can you see the cat?

ACKNOWLEDGEMENTS

First and foremost, thanks to my family and friends for putting up with me festering in my bedroom for so damned long; it'll be nice to see you again. To Mum, Dad, Celeste, Benny-boy, Katherine, little Wilfred and a huge and excitable welcome to Otto. To Cristine and Jack for their support, not to mention a fat dose of the Greenham blood.

And on the ground, first and foremost to the principal shamans of fireside joy, Riot and MCsquared, whose music and conversation and brimming souls are the full moon to my moth. To the fire rabble, Lisa, Helen, Tori, Bradon, Tara, Nico, Stefan, Will, Masha, Georgie and to Tom Nancollas for the provision of the finest craic in town. To the West Berks crew, Darren, Pete, Ian, James, Will F, Will T, Leo, Griffin and Ruairidh Maggs, and to the two people that bred the last three, Dave and Helen. To the land crew, Robin Grey, Guy Shrubsole, Marion Shoard, Anna Powell-Smith, Tom Kenny, Roo Bramley, Kate Huggett, Maria and Luca Sanders, Jo and Holly from Black Bark Films, for their help, advice and comradeship and in particular to Robin and Guy for reading drafts of this book. A shout out to Mike, Gill and Simon of the Land magazine and to Three Acres and a Cow, the magnificent show that weaves together 1000 years of land rights history with excellent folk song and storytelling.

To my beautiful housemates, Leo Kay, Sam Campbell and the master, Alex de Texeira de Silva, not least for bearing that foul hum that emanated from my room. To the people that helped me with my book and its rambles, to John Padwick, Louisa Adjoa Parker, Vanessa Kisuule, Richard Collins, Dave Baum, Chris Sharp, James Morgan, Gwennie von Einsiedel, Sam Lee and Robby Mac, who gets a mention in every book I've done, because he's proper lush. To Jackie Morris and Jay Griffiths, for literally everything they have ever done. To Elise and Ivor Colledge, Nilofar Shirvani, to Tribidabo and Simon Reithoffer, whose gypsy guitar is unmatched by any other, except perhaps that picker in Paris. To Eli Hynes, Lydia Gluck, Emily Dickie, and to Farmer Ambler, who gave me his time and permission to be on his land. To Jasmine, Titus, Anouk, Electra and of course Hercules and his magnificent auto-felation, which I am proud to have finally commemorated in print. To Jonathan, Iris, Sky and Anna, to James, Edwin, Ottie and Nicola. To Lawrence and Amelia, whom I met on the banks of the Thames, and (lucky for me) came armed not with an axe, but with food and Georgist insights. To Gandalf and the STAG gang, whose names are legion, and whose persistent resistance has been truly inspiring. To Rob Heron and the Tea Pad Orchestra, to Lankum, Ye Vagabonds, Eliza Carthy, the Bothy band, Paul Brady, Nic Jones, Andy Irvine, Donal Lunny and Kevin Burke, who formed the soundtrack to my solo rambles, and especially the song Martin Wynn/The Longford Tinker, which is the heart and soul of this book. To Jessica Stiles and the meadow we share.

Thank you finally to my editor Marigold Atkey, whose support and expertise throughout was especially appreciated, and to my agent, Jessica Woollard, for all her words of wisdom and humour. I literally couldn't have done it without you both.

Thank you all! xxx

NOTES

BADGER

Pages

8   'In Africa some ... walking upright...': Clive Williams, *Basildon, Berkshire, An Illustrated History* (self-published), p. 15.

12   'copses, dells, quarries ... for exploration': Kenneth Grahame, *The Wind in the Willows* (London: Methuen & Co., 1908), p. 49.

12   'It seemed ... and contentment': ibid., p. 67.

13   'The person who casts ... are supporting them': harrypotter.fandom.com/wiki/Mobilicorpus

14   'any unjustifiable intrusion ... of another': researchbriefings.parliament.uk/ResearchBriefing/Summary/SN05116

15   'create a deterrent ... had been committed': www.gov.uk/government/publications/trespass-on-protected-sites-sections-128-131-of-the-serious-organised-crime-and-police-act-2005

16   'Here's the heir apparent': Jon Ronson, 'And for your encore, Mr Bin Laden', *Guardian*, 26 July 2003.

16   'any circumstance ... injurious consequences':
      thelawdictionary.org/aggravation

17   'There is no requirement ... disrupt or deter by
      intimidating': www.cps.gov.uk/legal-guidance/
      trespass-and-nuisance-land

19   'If the defendant ... half a mile on it': swarb.co.uk/
      ellis-v-loftus-iron-co-1874

20   'the danger of mob law ... thousands of ramblers':
      Manchester Evening Chronicle, April 1932.

23   'land remained the index ... power was erected': E.
      P. Thompson, *Customs in Common: Studies in Popular
      Culture* (New York: The New Press, 1992), p. 16.

FOX

Pages

25   'wild and uninhabited ... the beach': PIERSON
      v. POST, Supreme Court of Judicature of
      New York, 3 Cai. R. 175; 1805 N.Y. LEXIS 311,
      sites.oxy.edu/whitney/xaccess/ec357/cases/
      property/pierson_v_post.htm

27   'it is either so simple ... as to defy definition':
      legal-dictionary.thefreedictionary.com/ownerships

27   'there is no word ... than possession': *National Safe
      Deposit Co. v. Stead*, 232 U.S. 58, 34 S. Ct. 209, 58
      L. Ed. 504 [1914].

28   'No fences parted fields ... But all was common':
      Virgil, *The Works of Virgil: Containing His
      Pastorals, Georgics, and Aeneis, Volume 3*, trans.
      John Dryden (London: J. Tonsen, 1721), p. 219.

29   'Remus ... "So shall it be henceforth with every one
      who leaps over my walls."': Livy, *Praefatio*, Book 1,
      Ch. 7, online at Latin Texts and Translations,

Perseus under PhiloLogic, perseus.uchicago.edu/
perseus-cgi/citequery3.pl?dbname=PerseusLatinTe
xts&query=Liv.%201.7.5&getid=1

32   today there are over ... younger riders: www.tatler.
com/gallery/british-hunting-life-uk

36   'the perfect Science of Lines ... his owne': John
Dee, *The Mathematical Preface to Elements of
Geometry of Euclid of Megara*, www.gutenberg.org/
files/22062/22062-h/main.html

36   'this fellow might be ... full of fine dirt?':
William Shakespeare, *Hamlet*, V.i.102–6,
shakespeare.mit.edu/hamlet/full.html

36   'I think the gentleman ... Men's Consciences':
Proceedings in the Commons, 1601: December 7th,
www.british-history.ac.uk/no-series/parliament-
proceedings-eliz1/pp288-310

36   'God hath not sette you ... not theye necessaries':
Andrew McRae, *God Speed the Plough: The
Representation of Agrarian England, 1500–1660*
(Cambridge: Cambridge University Press, 2002),
p. 147.

38   'Mending Wall': Robert Frost, 'Mending Wall',
North of Boston (David Nutt, 1914), p. 11.

42   'ownership anxiety' ... 'first possession': Carol
M. Rose. 'Canons of Property Talk, or,
Blackstone's Anxiety', *The Yale Law Journal*,
Vol. 108 (1998), digitalcommons.law.yale.edu/
cgi/viewcontent.cgi?article=7977&context=ylj,
p. 605.

42   'property (dominium) ... properly his own': Hugo
Grotius, *The Rights of War and Peace*, (Liberty
Fund, 2005), files.libertyfund.org/files/1425/
1032-01_LFeBk.pdf, p. 154.

42   the first person ... claim it as their own: Samuel von Pufendorf, *On the Duty of Man and Citizen According to the Natural Law* (1673; Cambridge University Press, 1991), p. 90.

43   'Though the earth ... thereby makes it his property': John Locke, *The Second Treatise on Civil Government* (1689), online at Norton publisher's archive, wwnorton.com/college/history/archive/resources/documents/ch04_03.htm

44   An infamous YouTube video ... to assert authority: Goddess of Oddness, 'Middleton's George Winn-Darley seems upset', 29 Jan 2019, www.youtube.com/watch?v=RApPTurIMBM ; see also www.dailymail.co.uk/news/article-5144495/Clash-landowner-hunt-saboteurs.html

45   'The right to destroy ... in international law': John G. Sprankling, 'The Right to Destroy', *The International Law of Property* (Oxford: Oxford University Press, 2014) p. 293.

46   'In mad fury I descended ... this fair people': Ordericus Vitalis, *The Ecclesiastical History of England and Normandy*, archive.org/details/ecclesiasticalhio3orde/page/n8/mode/2up

47   'They have become ... as owners of their own land': John Berger, *Ways of Seeing* (London: BBC, 1972) www.youtube.com/watch?v=Z7wi8jd7aC4

50   'Members of the public' ... 'It is not for me to express an opinion': Richard Alleyne, 'David Cameron's hunt convicted as judge questions RSPCA's prosecution costs', *Daily Telegraph*, 17 December 2012.

51   'These people are vigilantes ... tin of beans': ibid.

52   'Since property was a thing … the ownership of
       things': E. P. Thompson, *Whigs and Hunters: The
       Origin of the Black Act* (London: Breviary Stuff
       Publications, 1975), p. 195.
52   'open country, untenanted land': *OED*.
53   'The only question … from the use of
       it': William Blackstone, *Commentaries on the
       Laws of England* (1765–1770), files.libertyfund.
       org/files/2140/Blackstone_1387-01_EBk_
       v6.0.pdf, p. 308.
57   'Gainsborough's painting … of the English
       countryside': Olivia Rudgard, 'Famous view in
       "Mr and Mrs Andrews" under threat as council
       plans bypass through Gainsborough countryside',
       Daily Telegraph, 10 March 2018.
57   'Law is not so … the real world': Clifford Geertz,
       *Local Knowledge: Further Essays in Interpretive
       Anthropology* (New York: Basic Books, 1983),
       p. 173.

DOG

Pages
61   'We talked about … fire sites, drink cans etc':
       Roger Deakin, *Notes from Walnut Tree Farm*
       (London: Penguin Books, 2008), p. 247.
64   'the myth of a barbaric, immoral and outlaw
       class … working class life': Michel Foucault,
       Discipline and Punish: The Birth of the Prison
       (New York: Vintage Books, 1979), p. 275.
64   'MIGHTY oaks from little acorns grow … living
       tree in East Anglia': Russell Claydon, 'Oak Tree

Largest Recorded In Region', *East Anglian Daily Times*, 3 March 2010.

67 'by the mid-1500s ... in which they had no part': Gill Barron, 'Tinker, Vagabond, Journeyman, Tramp', www.thelandmagazine.org.uk/articles/tinker-vagabond-journeyman-tramp

67 'children of Belial ... without minister': John Gore, *The Poor Man's Hope* (Thomas Alchorne, London, 1635), p. 22.

67 'these coney-catchers [rabbit hunters]... state of England': Robert Greene, 'The Second Part of Cony-Catching' in *The Complete Cony-catching* (1592), online at Wattpad.com, www.wattpad.com/411154761-the-complete-cony-catching-by-robert-greene-the

68 'degrees of superiority and inferiority in our society': Thomas Dekker, *The Bellman of London* (1608).

72 'a country that hath yet her maidenhead': Sir Walter Raleigh, *The Discovery of Guiana*. (1848; Project Gutenberg, 2006), www.gutenberg.org/files/2272/2272-h/2272-h.htm

73 sentenced to ten years ... another landlord tycoon: Lynn Barber, 'Nasty Nick', *Observer*, 15 January 2006.

73 When they were alive ... 'Lowlife. Drug dealers, drug takers and queers. Scum': 'An Emissary of Beelzebub', *Evening Standard*, 22 July 2002; Robert Verkaik, 'Van Hoogstraten hired "dangerous thugs" to kill business rival, judge rules', *Independent*, 20 December 2005; David Millward, '"Emissary of Beelzebub" who revels in his own notoriety', *Daily Telegraph*, 20 December 2005.

74   'the scum of the earth': 'UK Ramblers "Scum of the Earth"', news.bbc.co.uk/1/hi/uk/233644.stm

75   'Let them waste their time and money,' ... 'in your garden?': Cole Moreton, '£200m thug tramples on footpath law', *Independent on Sunday*, 20 August 2002.

75   'Herberts wasn't actually my word ... I said perverts, the dirty mac brigade': 'Even Nastier Nick', *Guardian*, 8 September 2000.

76   In 2014, three men ... in north London: Amelia Gentleman, 'Three charged with stealing food from skip behind Iceland supermarket', *Guardian*, 2 January 2014.

76   A year later ... asked for a quid: Cahal Milmo, 'Sussex Police "criminalising rough sleepers by using plain clothes officers to catch people begging"', *Independent*, 8 February 2016.

77   'We are all incandescent with rage because of that tweet': Izzy Lyons, 'Surrey Police under fire for tweet sympathising with "uprooted" travellers', *Daily Telegraph*, 9 August 2018.

77   'The council also ... their stay': Christopher Hope and Izzy Lyons, 'Make trespassing a criminal offence to stop travellers moving onto private land, demand backbenchers', *Daily Telegraph*, 12 August 2018.

77   'They are a great nuisance to everybody': Katherine Quarmby, *No Place to Call Home: Inside the Real Lives of Gypsies and Travellers* (London: Oneworld Publications, 2013), p. 33.

77   'although nobody so far ... to a lingering death?': Raymond Wills, *Where the River Bends* (Lulu.com), p. 168.

80   'It is hard to believe ... a few decades later': ibid., p. 172.

80   'combines nationality ... dress or eating': unstats. un.org/unsd/demographic/sconcerns/popchar/ popcharmethods.htm

83   'an aboriginal droveway ... cleared for agriculture': Richard Mabey, *Nature Cure* (London: Chatto & Windus, 2005), p. 101.

86   'Nightingales no longer nest ... no birds sing': *Diss Express*, 16 February 1981.

87   'The forest came to be known ... and the ash have sprung back': Richard Mabey, *The Common Ground* (London: Hutchinson, 1980), p. 60.

SHEEP

Pages

88   'You do realise this is private property?': Roger Deakin, *Waterlog* (London: Chatto & Windus, 1999), p. 30.

88   'I got changed as languidly ... mean anything to you?': ibid., p. 31.

89   'I say "rights" to point up ... or to swim in the sea': ibid., p. 33.

89   'He does have an extremely ... a bloody chance': Cole Morton, '£200m thug tramples on footpath law', *Independent*, 20 August 2000.

92   'This makes me feel like a schoolboy and want to break bounds': Roger Deakin, *Notes from Walnut Tree Farm* (London: Hamish Hamilton, 2008), p. 223.

92   'Sleeping one time in Burgate Wood ... How
      deep do roots go?': Roger Deakin, *Wildwood*
      (London: Hamish Hamilton, 2007), p. 12.

94   'When you've seen one wall, you've seen them all':
      holmleighnyd, 'West Bromwich Albion in China
      1978', March 2011, www.youtube.com/watch?v=
      HCvLrMQHLJ8

96   'these walls look less ... lucrative trade routes': Julia
      Lovell, *The Great Wall: China Against the World, 1000
      BC–AD 2000* (London: Atlantic Books, 2007), p. 21.

96   'I will build a great wall ... Mark my words': *Here's
      Donald Trump's Presidential Announcement Speech*,
      time.com/3923128/donald-trump-announcement-
      speech

97   A study published in 2005: C. C. Carbon and
      H. Leder, 'The wall inside the brain: overestimation
      of distances crossing the former Iron Curtain',
      Psychonomic Bulletin and Review, 12:4 (August 2005).

98   'half the value of the whole land': quoted in M. Postan,
      Mediaeval Trade and Finance (Cambridge: Cambridge
      University Press, 2002), p. 342.

99   'unifying the identity of the believers and dividing
      them from the non-believers': Thomas Nail,
      Theory of the Border (Oxford: Oxford University
      Press, 2016), p. 60.

100   'heretics, sceptics ... of all kinds': Richard Rex,
      The Lollards (Macmillan International Higher
      Education, May 2002), p. xiii.

101   'They burnt his bones ... dispersed the world
      over': quoted in Brian Moynahan, *The Book of Fire*
      (London: Little, Brown, 2002), p. 494.

102   'to honour and obey ... all my betters': Alexander
      Nowell, *A Catechism*, trans. by Thomas Norton

(Cambridge University Press, 1853), archive.org/
details/catechismwrittenoonoweuoft/page/n9/
mode/2up, p. 130.

102 'all were admonished to obedience ... of god': ibid.

103 At the time ... by the rude oiks of the land: The
Venerable Bede had begun a translation of the
scripture in Old English in the seventh century
and Aldhelm had translated the Book of Psalms.
The Lindisfarne Gospels were a translation of
the Gospels into Old English, as were the Wessex
Gospels in 990.

103 'Ye ploughman should plow ... material things
from you': 1 Corinthians 9:11.

103 The line of Moses' legislation ... 'You shall not
muzzle an ox when it treads out grain':
Deuteronomy 25:4.

104 'Tyndale did euyll in translatynge ... and cheyte
in to loue': quoted in Brian Moynahan, *The
Book of Fire* (London: Little, Brown, 2002),
p. 105. In modern English: 'Tyndale did evil in
translating the scripture into our tongue ... he
regularly changed the word church into the word
congregation and the word priest into elder, and
charity into love.'

106 'I will put my laws in their hearts; I shall inscribe
them on their minds': Hebrews 8:10, 10:16.

111 'You take with you a little ... the fact of private
property': Stephen Graham, *The Gentle Art of
Tramping* (Robert & Co. Ltd, 1927), p. 51.

113 'Not to swear, nor to offer violence ... fair
works': Roger B. Manning, *Village Revolts: Social
Protest and Popular Disturbances in England, 1509–
1640* (New York: Clarendon Press, 1988), p. 235.

113 'In an enquiry in the August ... had lost their homes': Steve Hindle, 'Imagining Insurrection in Seventeenth-Century England: Representations of the Midland Rising of 1607', *History Workshop Journal*, No. 66, Autumn 2008.

114 'most odious figure': ibid.

114 'the depopulation and the daily excessive conversion of tillage to pasture': ibid.

115 'Sr Anth. Mildmaay ... a very great number hurt': Edwin F. Gay, *The Midland Revolt and the Inquisitions of Depopulation of 1607* (Cambridge: Cambridge University Press, 2009), p. 216.

117 'The long wall ... the moon shines for no one': quoted by Julia Lovell in *The Great Wall* (London: Atlantic Books, 2007), p. 155.

120 'between 1725 and 1825 ... late eighteenth century's crisis of poverty': Peter Linebaugh, *Stop, Thief!: The Commons, Enclosures, and Resistance* (Sunderland: PM Press, 2013).

120 'This proposal is ... glad to embrace it': B. Bellamy, *Geddington Chase: The History of a Wood* (Irthlingborough, 1986), p. 46.

121 'The first person ... true founder of civil society': Jean-Jacques Rousseau, *On the Origin of the Inequality of Mankind* (1754; Project Gutenberg, 2004), www.gutenberg.org/cache/epub/11136/pg11136-images.html

121 'what people cannot be ... overwhelming evidence': Moti Nissani, 'A cognitive reinterpretation of Stanley Milgram's observations on obedience to authority', *American Psychologist*, 45:12, (1990), pp. 1384–1385.

COW

Pages

124   'During my four years ... a Dorset landmark':
Richard Drax, 'The Wall', 9 July 2010,
www.richarddrax.com/news/wall

124   We are at the ... 14,000-acre estate: whoowns
england.org/2020/01/04/the-ten-landowners-
who-own-one-sixth-of-dorset

127   'Here then is the origin ... consequence of
slavery': Eric Williams, *Capitalism and Slavery* (Chapel
Hill: University of North Carolina Press, 1994),
p. 19. Copyright © 1944 by the University of North
Carolina Press, renewed 1972 by Eric Williams.
New introduction by Colin A. Palmer © 1994 by
the University of North Carolina Press. Used by
permission of the publisher. www.uncpress.org

127   'The air of England ... breathes it': Somerset v
Stewart (1772).

131   'Racial differences ... slave labour possible': Eric
Williams, *Capitalism and Slavery* (Chapel Hill:
University of North Carolina Press, 1994), p. 19.

131   'But all our phrasing ... cracks bones, breaks
teeth': Ta-Nehisi Coates, *Between the World and Me*
(London: Spiegel & Grau, 2015), p. 10.

132   The Act didn't work ... and 1692: J. Handler,
'Slave revolts and conspiracies in seventeenth-
century Barbados', jeromehandler.org/wp-content/
uploads/2009/07/Revolts-82.pdf, pp. 20-28.

137   'a desert of magnificence ... his getting rid of it':
William Hazlitt, *Sketches of the Picture Galleries of
England* (London: Templeman, 1824), p. 284.

141   'will not waste a moment ... all property whatsoever':
quoted in Nicholas Draper, *The Price of Emancipation,
Slave Ownership, Compensation and British Society at
the End of Slavery* (Cambridge: Cambridge University
Press, 2010), p. 79.

142   'If confiscation is to be ... as that of the West
Indies?': ibid., p. 80.

145   'Without connections, without any natural interest
in the soil, the importers of foreign gold have
forced their way into parliament by such a torrent
of corruption as no private hereditary fortune can
resist': William Pitt, 1st Earl of Chatham, *The State
of the Nation* (speech to the House of Lords, 1770),
en.wikisource.org/wiki/The_State_of_the_Nation

146   'An opulent city lay at my mercy ... stand astonished
at my own moderation!': Michael Edwardes, *The
Nabobs at Home* (London: Constable, 1991), p. 59.

146   'conscious and deliberate bleeding of India': Will
Durant, *The Case for India* (London: Simon &
Schuster, 1930), online at www.vifindia.org/sites/
default/files/139221701-The-Case-for-India-1930.
pdf, p. x.

147   'whether it should go into a black man's pocket or
my own': Michael Edwardes, *The Nabobs at Home*
(London: Constable, 1991), p. 37.

150   'cruelties unheard of ... haughtiness and insolence':
Edmund Burke, opening speech of impeachment
of Warren Hastings, quoted in Shashi Tharoor,
Inglorious Empire: What the British Did to India
(London: Penguin, 2018) p. 15.

151   'Posterity looking back ... to this country': *The
Parliamentary History of England from the Earliest*

Period to the Year 1803, Volume 29 (London: Hansard, 1806), p. 278.

151   'it's been much more ... history of slavery': www.ucl.ac.uk/lbs

151   'You can see their eyes ... no longer hear us': Reni Eddo-Lodge, *Why I'm No Longer Talking to White People About Race* (London: Bloomsbury Circus, 2017) p. ix.

151   'A false conceit of Interest ... than Rocks of Adament': Thomas Tryon, 'Friendly advice to the gentlemen-planters of the East and West Indies in three parts' (1684), quod.lib.umich.edu/e/eebo/A63791.0001.001?rgn=main;view=fulltext, p. 77.

151   'So I don't think ... apologise for': Nicholas Watt, 'David Cameron defends lack of apology for British massacre at Amritsar', *Guardian*, 20 February 2013.

152   'I can't be held responsible ... and I ignore it': Adrianne Maslen, 'Election 2010: Drax hits backs at slave "smear"', *Daily Echo*, 6 May 2010.

152   'A lot of people think ... you must have been asleep': Rants'n'Bants, 'Talk About Racism!!', www.youtube.com/watch?v=gLOCaSuyP5U&t=143s

153   'the Select Committee ... for other expenses': William Cobbett, *Parliamentary History of England from the earliest period to the year 1803* (London: Hansard, 1813), p. 655.

153   'modern invention ... the new idea ... believe they are white': Ta-Nehisi Coates, *Between the World and Me* (London: Spiegel & Grau, 2015), p. 7.

154   'WE the immigrants ... your conscience is not clean': Joshua Idahen and Sons of Kemet, 'Sons of Kemet – Your Queen Is A Reptile', www.youtube.com/watch?v=YEpziXD-SDk

155   'should be content ... rather than the cash': Shashi Tharoor, *Inglorious Empire: What the British Did to India* (London: C. Hurst, 2017), p. xx.

156   'we just don't have ethnic ... We're the last bastion of Englishness and I want to keep it that way': Anita Singh, '*Midsomer Murders* creator suspended after calling show "the last bastion of Englishness"', *Daily Telegraph*, 14 March 2011.

156   'were often treated with suspicion ... for some, multiculturalism': Neil Chakraborti and Jon Garland, 'It's the Outdated Notion of the Countryside Preserved in the Fictional Midsomer that should be murdered', Leicester Exchanges, leicesterexchanges.com/2011/04/06/it%e2%80%99s-the-outdated-notion-of-the-countryside-preserved-in-the-fictional-midsomer

157   'It was an African ... in nature. We are here!': *Black Men Walking* (London: Oberon Books, 2018), p. 72.

SPIDER

Pages

160   'be very justly divided among his wife and children': Law Codes of Cnut (1020), *Early English Laws*, earlyenglishlaws.ac.uk/laws/texts/cn-1018/view/#edition/translation

161   By marriage, the husband and ... she performs every thing': William Blackstone, *Commentaries of the Laws of England* (1765–1770), *Online Library*

of Liberty, oll.libertyfund.org/titles/blackstone-commentaries-on-the-laws-of-england-in-four-books-vol-1, p. 443.

162 'Our English housewife must be ... but not bitter or talkative': Gervase Markham, *The English Hus-wife*, ed. by Michael R. Best (1661; McGill-Queen's Press, 1994), p. 8.

164 'cow ... that goes to bull every moon, with what bull she cares not': Thomas Harman, *A Caveat or Warning for Common Cursitors* (1566; Project Gutenberg, 2012), www.gutenberg.org/files/38850/38850-h/38850-h.htm, p. 67.

165 'The midwife and the nurse well made away, / Then let the ladies tattle what they please': William Shakespeare, *Titus Andronicus*, IV. ii, shakespeare.mit.edu/titus/full.html

166 'the superior learning of witches ... deadliest blows at her': Matilda Joslyn Gage, *Women, Church and State*, (1893; Project Gutenberg, 2014), www.gutenberg.org/files/45580/45580-h/45580-h.htm, p. 105.

167 'The witch hunt ... and energy away from work': Silvia Federici, *Caliban and the Witch* (New York: Autonomedia, 2017), p. 194.

168 'These decrees ... power and wealth': Plutarch, *Life of Solon*, classics.mit.edu/Plutarch/solon.html

169 'on the ground ... was a trespasser': Harrison v Duke of Rutland: CA 1893.

169 'Many of the poorer parishioners ... eye to overlook them': John Graunt, *Natural and Political Observations* (1662), p. 383, en.wikisource.org/wiki/

Natural_and_Political_Observations_Made_upon_
the_Bills_of_Mortality_(Graunt_1676)/
Chapter_10

170   'Burn me the same way / into the square, and
       spoke': Claire Askew, *How To Burn A Woman*, not
       yet published.

172   'a monstrous malicious woman … a plaine atheist':
       Sarah F. Williams, *Damnable Practices: Witches,
       Dangerous Women, and Music in Seventeenth-
       Century English Broadside Ballads* (Farnham:
       Ashgate, 2015), p. 9.

173   'The closed incestuous … and central
       government': Tracey Borman, *Witches: A Tale of
       Sorcery, Scandal and Seduction* (London: Jonathan
       Cape, 2013), p. 145.

173   Across Europe … (in Iceland, it was 92 per
       cent): Rolf Schulte, *Man As Witch: Male
       Witches in Central Europe* (London: Palgrave
       Macmillan, 2009), pp. 70-73.

175   'The building itself … breath away': BBC Two
       documentary: *The Last Dukes*, October 2015.

176   'All they asked about … all that carbon
       monoxide': Barbara Harford and Sarah Hopkins,
       eds, *Greenham Common: Women at the Wire*
       (London: The Women's Press: 1984), p. 3.

177   'As far as I'm concerned' … 'as long as you
       like': ibid., p. 17.

180   'Since 2010 … events & activists': www.
       diggersanddreamers.org.uk/communities/
       existing/grow-heathrow

181   'Our living room … the communal bedroom':
       Barbara Harford and Sarah Hopkins, eds, *Greenham*

Common: Women at the Wire (London: The
Women's Press, 1984), p. 78.

182   'The media have quite … without the other':
        ibid., p. 4.

184   'It is part of the accepted lie … a sort of liberal
        pastime': ibid., p. 39.

184   'The fragile docile image of our sex must die /
        And we don't give a damn': 'Songs from the Peace
        Camp', *Guardian*, 05 September 2006.

185   'a type of secular magic': Tim Cresswell, *In Place/
        Out of Place: Geography, Ideology, and Transgression*
        (Minneapolis: University of Minnesota
        Press, 1996), p. 124.

185   'Taking down the fence … privilege and
        deprivation': Barbara Harford and Sarah Hopkins,
        eds, *Greenham Common: Women at the Wire*
        (London: The Women's Press, 1984), p. 159.

187   'An analysis of the media … environment of
        the camp': Tim Cresswell, *In Place/Out of
        Place: Geography, Ideology, and Transgression*
        (Minneapolis: University of Minnesota
        Press, 1996), p. 104.

188   'fish paste and bad oysters': Peter Stallybrass and
        Allon White, *The Politics and Poetics of Transgression*
        (Ithaca: Cornell University Press, 1986), p. 23.

188   'being ordered … calculatingly stink': *Daily Mail*,
        14 November 1983, quoted in Tim Cresswell,
        *In Place/Out of Place: Geography, Ideology,
        and Transgression* (Minneapolis: University of
        Minnesota Press, 1996), p. 107.

188   'Dirt is matter out of place': Mary Douglas, *Purity
        and Danger: An Analysis of Concepts of Pollution and
        Taboo* (London: Routledge, 1966), p. 36.

189   'their role is to create … still more illusory':
Michel Foucault, *Of Other Spaces* (1967),
foucault.info/documents/heterotopia/foucault.
heteroTopia.en

190   'There's an almost tangible feeling of doom and
desolation. People have given up and moved away':
Conal Urqhart, 'Village that defied Heathrow is
slowly dying as BAA buys up homes', *Guardian*, 16
June 2012.

191   'Previous attempts … land a trespasser':
Observer, 25 February 1983, quoted in Sarah
Hipperson, *Greenham: Non-violent Women v.
The Crown Prerogative* (Greenham Publications,
2005), p. 136.

193   'In court,' said the longest resident … 'we had to be
listened to': Barbara Harford and Sarah Hopkins,
eds, *Greenham Common: Women at the Wire*
(London: The Women's Press, 1984), p. 142.

194   'Greenham was powerful … world of unstoppable
women': Suzanne Moore, 'How the Greenham
Common protest changed lives: "We danced on top
of the nuclear silos"', *Guardian*, 20 March 2017.

195   'They are free to express … business decision':
Nadia Khomami, 'BP to end Tate sponsorship after
26 years', *Guardian*, 11 March 2016.

196   'the women never … to the inevitable': Tim
Cresswell, *In Place/Out of Place, Geography,
Ideology, and Transgression* (Minneapolis: University
of Minnesota Press, 1996), p. 118.

196   'while no doubt Grow Heathrow … trespassing
on the land': Andy Dangerfield, 'Grow Heathrow:
Green-fingered squatters' eviction fight', *BBC News*,
June 2012.

PHEASANT

Pages

202   'As Julian Fellowes has said ... hangs over one a bit': *Secrets of Highclere Castle*, Netflix, 2013.

203   'They turn up here ... real Earl and Countess': ibid.

203   'we are whisked into a world ... the done thing': David Kemp, *Vanity Fair*, December 2012.

204   'It is a likely speculation ... phonetic proximity to cunt': Geoffrey Hughes, *An Encyclopedia of Swearing: The Social History of Oaths, Profanity, Foul Language, and Ethnic Slurs in the English-Speaking World* (New York and London: M.E Sharpe, 2006), p. 111.

205   'the prettiest park ... to hold half a village': William Cobbett, *Rural Rides* (1822; Project Gutenberg, 2010), www.gutenberg.org/files/34238/34238-h/34238-h.htm, p. 9.

206   'He willingly imposes duties ... those who will come after him': Viscount de Toqueville, quoted in Peregrine Worsthorne, *Democracy Needs Aristocracy* (London: Harper Perennial, 2010), p. 47.

207   'Most certainly ... did it pass that test?': ibid., p. 24.

207   'They went on being taught ... marrow of their bones': ibid.

208   'I love that faith ... shine in that way': Raymond Zhong, 'The Anti-Snobbery of Downton Abbey', *Wall Street Journal*, February 2013.

209   'The gentry in many ... to be founded': Harry Hopkins, *The Long Affray* (London: Papermac, 1986), p. 71.

213   'To be bred in a place of estimation ... without which there is no nation': Edmund Burke,

Letter From The New To The Old Whigs (1791), socialsciences.mcmaster.ca/econ/ugcm/3ll3/burke/Works04.pdf, p. 121.

214 'Those who share the aristocratic empty ... rewards fecklessness and irresponsibility': Lord Carey, 'My fellow bishops are wrong. Fuelling the culture of welfare dependency is immoral', *Daily Mail*, January 2012.

214 'So long as they may be ... to no kind of labour': Elizabethan surveyor, quoted in H. P. R. Finberg and Joan Thirsk, eds, *The Agrarian History of England and Wales* (London: Cambridge University Press, 1967), p. xxxv.

215 'Instead of bearing the burthen ... have laid it on the people': John Wade, *The Black Book, Or, Corruption Unmasked* (1788; *The Lawbook Exchange*, 2004), p. 257.

218 'Brown's early work ... the touch of reality': John Phibbs, *Place-making: The Art of Capability Brown* (English Heritage, 2017), p. 57.

218 The twenty-four ... acres between them: Guy Shrubsole, Who Owns England blog, May 2017, whoownsengland.org/2017/05/08/the-dukes-their-tax-breaks-an-8million-annual-subsidy

219 'After being brutally evicted ... several times over': George Monbiot, 'Farming subsidies: this is the most blatant transfer of cash to the rich', *Guardian*, 2 July 2013.

219 'the English gentleman ... the soul of the people': Dr Dibelius, quoted in Peregrine Worsthorne, *Democracy Needs Aristocracy* (London: Harper Perennial, 2010), p. 82.

220   this accounted for ... in private hands: J. M. Neeson,
       *Commoners: Common Right, Enclosure and Social
       Change in England, 1700–1820* (Cambridge:
       Cambridge University Press, 1996), p. 17.

221   'use in competitions ... or activities': 'Gamebirds
       and welfare', *Veterinary Record*, 166: 376,
       veterinaryrecord.bmj.com/content/166/13/376

223   'In the UK ... out of the atmosphere': Jeremy
       Hance, 'Ultimate Bogs: how saving peatlands could
       help save the planet', *Guardian*, 28 July 2017.

224   'Suggestions of readdressing ... environmental
       benefits!!': Mark Avery, *Inglorious* (London:
       Bloomsbury Natural History, 2015) , p. 154.

225   'the only unsubsidised upland land use on offer':
       Jonathan Young, 'Marshalls of the Moor', *Daily
       Telegraph*, 11 August 2007.

226   'It's all dependent on the moors' ... 'the moorlands
       alive': ibid.

227   'fully engaged with ... North of England is
       limited': 'Briefing note: Grouse Moors and
       Flooding', Moorland Association, www.
       moorlandassociation.org/wp-content/uploads/
       2016/01/Briefing-Note-Grouse-Moors-and-
       Flooding1.pdf, p. 3.

227   A 2016 study: Nick Odoni, 'A modelling study
       and investigation into how annual burning on the
       Walshaw Moor estate may affect high river flows in
       Hebden Bridge'.

227   found a direct correlation between ... down in
       Hebden: ibid.

231   'We are not selling up to some rich man': Gordan
       Rayner, 'Highclere Castle is not for sale, Earl tells
       Lord Lloyd-Webber', *Daily Telegraph*, 13 July 2010.

231 'classes never actually ... universe to themselves':
David Cannadine, *Class in Britain* (London:
Penguin Books, 2000), p. 11.

231 'The corporation's legally ... cause to others':
Joel Bakan, *Corporation* (Robinson Publishing,
2005), p. 1.

232 'The point is, have we overlooked something, some
source of revenue, previously untapped ... if only
we had some coal, or gravel, or tin!': ITV, *Downton
Abbey*, Season 3, Episode 2.

233 Since 1995 ... 50 per cent of the wealth of the UK:
'The Invisible Land, The hidden force driving
the UK's unequal economy and broken housing
market' (August 2018), www.ippr.org/files/2018-
08/cej-land-tax-august18.pdf, p. 9.

COCKROACH

Pages

236 'throwing cans of Castlemaine in an Aussie version
of sharia stoning': Katie Hopkins, 'Rescue Boats?
I'd use Gunships to Stop Migrants', *Sun*, 17
April 2015.

237 'poor fact checking, sensationalism and flat-out
fabrication': Jasper Jackson, 'Wikipedia bans
Daily Mail as "unreliable"', *Guardian*, 8 February
2017.

237 'Dull doesn't sell newspapers. Boring doesn't pay
the mortgage': Alex Morrison, 'Profile: Paul Dacre,
Daily Mail editor', *BBC News*, 2 October 2013.

238 'the idea of the self-made man: it had worked, I'd
got there': Paul Dacre on BBC Radio 4's *Desert
Island Discs*, 30 January 2004.

238   'The "Swarm" On Our Streets': Claire
        Ellicott and Stephen Wright, *Daily Mail*, 30
        July 2015; see www.politics.co.uk/comment-
        analysis/2017/04/03/call-out-daily-mail-s-
        hypocrisy-over-asylum-seeker-attack

238   'millions of Africans with the economic motivation
        to try to get to Europe': Francis Perraudin,
        '"Marauding" migrants threaten standard of living,
        says foreign secretary', *Guardian*, 10 August 2015.

240   'However, I will waste as many gooks ... turns out
        to be a very necessary tool': Ken Burns and Lynn
        Novick, *The Vietnam War* (Florentine Films, 2017).

241   'Nouns convey greater permanence ... certainty,
        and predictability': Aleksandra Cichocka, Michał
        Bilewicz, John T. Jost, Natasza Marrouch and Marta
        Witkowska, 'On the Grammar of Politics, or Why
        Conservatives Prefer Nouns', *Political Psychology*,
        January 2016.

243   'Indifference to objective truth ... what is actually
        happening': George Orwell, *Notes on Nationalism*
        (London: Penguin, 2018), p. 16.

243   This fence cost the British taxpayer £2.3 million:
        Matt Broomfield, 'Calais Jungle wall is completed
        two months after all the refugees were driven out',
        Independent, 13 December 2016.

243   just a fraction of the £316 million: 'How much
        is the UK spending on security at Calais?', 19
        January 2018, fullfact.org/immigration/
        uk-spending-security-calais

250   'The factors that led ... as sovereign territories':
        Reece Jones, *Violent Borders: Refugees and the Right
        to Move* (London: Verso, 2016), p. 90.

251   'Qualitative data suggests … gas by local police':
       Surindar Dhesi, Arshad Isakjee and Thom Davies,
       'An Environmental Health Assessment of the
       New Migrant Camp in Calais', (University of
       Birmingham, 2015), p. 24.

255   'some nationalists are not far from schizophrenia,
       living quite happily amid dreams of power
       and conquest which have no connection with
       the physical world': George Orwell, *Notes on
       Nationalism* (London: Penguin, 2018), p. 17.

258   'because Britain has got jobs, it's got a growing
       economy it's an incredible place to live': 'David
       Cameron criticised over migrant "swarm"
       language', *BBC News,* www.bbc.co.uk/news/uk-
       politics-33716501, 30 July 2015.

258   'borders are the worst invention ever made by
       politicians': David Hughes and Kate Ferguson,
       'National borders are "the worst invention ever",
       says EC chief Jean-Claude Juncker', *Independent,*
       22 August 2016.

259   'The newspaper reader … hallmark of modern
       nations': Benedict Anderson, *Imagined
       Communities: Reflections on the Origin and Spread of
       Nationalism* (London: Verso, 2006), p. 36.

260   'It would not be impossible … clothe ideas and
       disguise': *The Goebbels Diaries, 1939–1941* trans.
       by Fred Taylor (New York: Putnam Publishing
       Group, 1983) quoted in Garth Jowett and Victoria
       O'Donnell, *Propaganda and Persuasion* (SAGE,
       2006), p. 230.

260   'these small works … women accused of
       witchcraft': Tracey Borman, *Witches: A Tale of*

Sorcery, Scandal and Seduction (London: Jonathan Cape, 2013), p. 205.

263   A report from the EU policy lab ... migration into Europe: 'The Future of Migration in the European Union', EU Policy Lab, 2018, publications.jrc. ec.europa.eu/repository/bitstream/JRC111774/ kjnd2906oenn.pdf, p. 20.

263   'I believe, as do many of my constituents, that this country is full': 'MP Richard Drax gives warning on immigration', *Daily Echo*, 11 September 2012.

264   In England there are 216,000 empty houses: Julia Kollewe, 'Number of empty homes in England rises to more than 216,000', *Guardian*, 11 March 2019.

264   Instead, 57 per cent ... poorest third of the country: Kaye Lyons and Pamela Duncan, '"It's a shambles": data shows most asylum seekers put in poorest parts of Britain', *Guardian*, 9 April 2017.

265   'ants, scurrying ...in July and August': Michael Dower, *Fourth Wave: the Challenge of Leisure: A Civic Trust Survey* (Civic Trust, 1965), quoted in Marion Shoard, *Theft of the Countryside* (Maurice temple Smith, London, 1980), p. 196.

266   Its owner, Viscount Rothermere, is himself a migrant ... non-domicile: David Leigh, 'A who's who of Britain's legal offshore tax avoidance', *Guardian*, 10 July, 2014. Note: France automatically became the domicile of Viscount Rothermere when he was born because of his father's resident status.

266   according to Private Eye, ... Bermuda: 'Selling England by the offshore pound', *Private Eye*, 2016, online at www.private-eye.co.uk/pictures/special_ reports/tax-havens.pdf, p. 9.

266   Similarly, Paul Dacre ... received a minimum of
£460,000 of CAP payments: Calculated to 2016
exchange rate. See Kevin Rawlinson and Jasper
Jackson, 'Daily Mail editor received £88,000 in EU
subsidies in 2014', *Guardian*, 30 March 2016.

267   Per year, that's the same as the maximum limit of
welfare for four households in Britain: see www.
gov.uk/benefit-cap

268   In the three months ... rose by 147 per cent: Mark
Townsend, 'Homophobic attacks in UK rose 147%
in three months after Brexit vote', *Guardian*, 8
October 2016.

269   'the genius of monarchy ... Theirs, yours, ours':
Nigel Farndale, 'A nation united as one family',
Daily Telegraph, 10 June 2012.

HARE

Pages

273   '[Social] space is a [social] product ... a means of
control, and hence of domination, of power': Henri
Lefebvre, *The Production of Space* (Oxford, UK,
and Cambridge, USA: Blackwell, 1974), p. 26.

273   'spatial politics'... 'central theme of modernity':
Michel Foucault, *Of Other Spaces: Utopias and
Heterotopias*, trans. by Jay Miskowiec (1967), web.
mit.edu/allanmc/www/foucault1.pdf

274   the hare is almost always described by reference to
what it is not: George Ewart Evans, *The Leaping
Hare* (London: Faber & Faber, 2002), p. 205.

276   'The grip of the land ... or greedy money-bag':
William Morris, *Justice* (1884), online at www.

marxists.org/archive/morris/works/1884/
justice/07geo.htm

276   'But to me it brings ... frantic striving with it':
Octavia Hill, *Space for the People, Homes of the
London Poor* (London: Macmillan, 1883), infed.
org/mobi/space-for-the-people.

277   'unenclosed and unbuilt ... of the people': Epping
Forest Act 1878.

277   release chemicals called phytoncides which boost
the immune system for up to thirty days after
immersion: Margaret M. Hansen, Reo Jones
and Kirsten Tocchini, 'Shinrin-Yoku (Forest
Bathing) and Nature Therapy: A State-of-the-Art
Review', www.ncbi.nlm.nih.gov/pmc/articles/
PMC5580555/

279   'radical openness ... all oppressively Othering
categories': Edward Soja, *Thirdspace: Journeys to
Los Angeles and Other Real-and-imagined Places*
(Oxford: Wiley-Blackwell, 1996), p. 84.

279   *Yearning: Race, Gender and Cultural Politics*: bell
hooks, *Yearning: Race, Gender and Cultural Politics*
(Boston: South End Press, 1990), p. 152.

285   'And all ... are brilliantly alive': William
Morris, 'Under an Elm-Tree, Or, Thoughts
in the Country-Side', *Commonweal*, Vol. 5,
No. 182, 6 July 1889, online at www.
marxists.org/archive/morris/works/1889/
commonweal/07-elm-tree.htm

288   and now only about 0.5 per cent of its original
extent survives: Charles Tyzack, *Wychwood and
Cornbury* (The Wychwood Press, 2003), p. 97.

290   the fair 'shall be DISCONTINUED': *Jackson's Oxford Journal*, September 1830, online at 'History of the Fair', *The Wychwood Project*, www.wychwoodproject.org/cms/content/history-fair

290   'It is understood that his Lordship ... as private property': ibid.

293   The most recent example of ... where the public are barred from 90 per cent of woodlands: 'Oxfordshire's Trees and Woodland, Today and Tomorrow', www2.oxfordshire.gov.uk/cms/sites/default/files/folders/documents/environmentandplanning/countryside/treesandwoodland/forestrystatement.pdf, p. 3.

294   'wilderness is a ferocious ... the volcanic heart of life': Jay Griffiths, *Pip Pip: A Sideways Look at Time* (London: Flamingo, 2000), p. 269.

295   'Dancing on the Green ... to their Superiors': *London Magazine* (1738), pp. 139–140, quoted in E. P. Thompson, *Customs in Common* (Merlin, 1991), p. 47.

298   Though entirely fabricated ... on new arrivals: Kevin Arscott, 'Winterval: The unpalatable making of a modern myth', *Guardian*, 8 November 2011.

298   'what the fuck do you think an English forest is for': Jez Butterworth, *Jerusalem* (London: Nick Hern Books, July 2009), p. 98.

301   'A New Generation of Vagabonds': quoted in Tim Cresswell, *In Place/Out of Place, Geography, Ideology, and Transgression* (Minneapolis: University of Minnesota Press, 1996), p. 62.

301   'social groups create deviance ... rules and
sanctions to an offender': Howard S. Becker, *The
Outsiders: Studies in the Sociology of Deviance*
(Cambridge: The Free Press, 1963), p. 9.

303   'Complaint of loud music in Tisbury ... area
checked, private party on private land. No criminal
offences:' Lexi Finnigan, 'Granddaughter of one
of the Mitford sisters causes uproar after 21st party
keeps locals awake all night', *Daily Telegraph*, 26
September 2016.

304   'The beauty of the landscape ... the most
grovelling commercialism': William Morris, 'Under
an Elm-Tree, Or, Thoughts in the Country-Side',
Commonweal, Vol. 5, No. 182, 6 July 1889, online at
www.marxists.org/archive/morris/works/1889/
commonweal/07-elm-tree.htm

TOAD

Pages

306   'It is observable that water ... the language of the
law': William Blackstone, *Commentaries on the
Laws of England* (Philadelphia: J.B. Lippincott Co.,
1893; The Online Library of Liberty, 2011), files.
libertyfund.org/files/2140/Blackstone_1387-01_
EBk_v6.0.pdf, p. 314.

307   'is most defenatly [sic] NON-NAVIGABLE':
George Monbiot, 'We have no right to our rivers
while Richard Benyon's interests are served',
Guardian, 4 April 2013.

307   In England, if you're by a river ... to be there:
www.britishcanoeing.org.uk/go-canoeing/access-
and-environment/access-to-water

309 'The Angling Trust ... canoeists have legal access': 'Benyon rejects canoeists campaign to paddle over angler's rights', *Angling Trust*, 13 December 2012, www.anglingtrust.net/news.asp?section=29&from =2012/12/01&to=2013/01/01&itemid=1444

309 there is no empirical ... the passage of canoes': Dr Keith Hendry and Angus Tree, 'Effects of canoeing on fish stocks and angling', *Environmental Agency*, January 2000, p. 24.

310 In the fifty years ... financial yield of their property: Matthew Wilson, 'Why Britain's historic hedgerows should be conserved and cherished', *Financial Times*, 13 June 2014.

310 'While we want ... the only way forward': Angling Trust, 'Benyon rejects canoeists campaign to paddle over anglers' rights', *Angling Trust*, 13 December 2012, www.anglingtrust.net/news.asp? section=29&from=2012/12/01&to=2013/01/01 &itemid=1444

312 'The law of the ... non-tidal waters': David Bailey, 'The fight for England's rivers: Canoeists call for greater access', *BBC News*, 12 July 2013.

312 Both aspects need to be proven 'before ... owners': David Hart, 'Regarding the law of navigation on non-tidal inland waters in England and Wales', 28 September 2015, www. anglingtrust.net

314 'a person who enters ... commits a trespass': W. A. Shumaker, *The Cyclopedic Dictionary of Law* (Nabu Press, 2010), p. 922.

315 'Recognise and accept ... and riparian owners': 'QC's legal advice proves there is no general public right

to navigate non-tidal rivers in England and Wales',
Angling Trust, 24 January 2017, www.anglingtrust.
net/news.asp?section=29&itemid=3624

315   'while there is no public right ... can navigate it':
www.riveraccessforall.co.uk/what_is_the_issue.php

318   'any number of arms dealers ... knew too much
about': Richard Brooks and Christian Eriksson,
'Selling England (and Wales) by the pound',
Private Eye, 2016, www.private-eye.co.uk/
tax-havens

327   'in real life I believe ... you have your guard up':
Trump: An American Dream (72 Films, 2018).

332   'the smugglers swore ... a toad': E. P. Thompson,
Whigs and Hunters: The Origin of the Black Act
(London: Breviary Stuff Publications, 1975), p. 149.

332   'I've done nothing criminal ... interfere with
my private life?': '£87,000 claim MP rails at
public jealousy of "Balmoral" home', *Metro*,
21 May 2009.

334   'It is not the individual ... and correct the
practice': Winston Churchill, 'The Mother of all
Monopolies', speech on 17 July 1909, quoted in
Andy Wightman, *The Poor Had No Lawyers: Who
Owns Scotland and How They Got it* (Birlinn, April
2013), p. 380.

337   he was suspected ... drop the case: Charlie Cooper,
'Wildlife minister Richard Benyon under fire in
another game-shooting case', *Independent*, 30
May 2012.

337   'He can disarm ... earnest and likeable': Rob
Wilson, 'Richard Benyon MP on having "the crap"
beaten out of him', *Total Politics*, 2 April 2013.

Pages

352   'The splendours of the castle ... immortal Shakespeare': Edward Jesse, *Scenes and Tales of Country Life: With Recollections of Natural History*, (John Murray, 1844), p. 40.

358   In an independent survey ... deemed perfectly healthy: savesheffieldtrees.org.uk/key-facts

360   'we don't have laxatives ... in that department': '"Teagate" poisoning probe leaves bitter taste for Sheffield tree campaigners', *Yorkshire Post*, 28 March 2018.

362   'a meeting point for building collective life': Henri Lefebvre, *Le droit à la ville* (Paris: Editions Anthropos, 1968), online at link.springer.com/article/10.1007/s11266-018-0030-y

365   'pie-in-the-sky': Jamie Blackett, 'Who Owns England? by Guy Shrubsole review: pie-in-the-sky solutions to the housing crisis', *Daily Telegraph*, 8 May 2019.

365   'conspiracy at every turn': Owen Patterson, 'Rewilding is fashionable nonsense – private owners can be trusted to look after Britain's land', *Daily Telegraph*, 5 May 2019.

365   'A more rigorous editor ... about who runs it': Edward Lucas, 'Who Owns England? by Guy Shrubsole review – a £72 million question', *The Times*, 19 April 2019.

368   'Sweden has no Eiffel Towers ... This is our monument': visitsweden.com/freedomtoroam

369   'to enable those living ... unreasonably disturbed': www.outdooraccess-scotland.scot/

act-and-access-code/scottish-outdoor-access-code-
rights-and-responsibilities

370   'normal people': John Stevens, '"Marxist" Labour
       garden tax would hit ten million families: Plans
       buried in the party's manifesto plan to replace
       council tax with a charge based on land value',
       Daily Mail, 5 June 2017.

372   In 2017 ... Responsibilities Statement: www.gov.
       scot/publications/scottish-land-rights-
       responsibilities-statement

374   'Land is a cross-cutting ... cultural rights': Land
       and Human Rights, www.ohchr.org/EN/Issues/
       LandAndHR/Pages/LandandHumanRightsIndex.
       aspx

375   'Growing up in a healthy ... right for children':
       Annelies Henstra, 'Child's right to connect
       with nature and to a healthy environment',
       WCC-2012-Res-101-EN, www.ohchr.org/
       Documents/HRBodies/CRC/Discussions/2016/
       AnneliesHenstra_en.pdf, p. 1. Copyright © 2016
       United Nations. Reprinted with the permission of
       the United Nations.

375   'So simple and so clear is this truth, that to see it
       fully once is always to recognise it': Henry George,
       Progress and Poverty (1879), p. 135.

376   'The great cause of inequality ... condition of a
       people': ibid.

379   'And then, in that utter clearness ... O, Mole,
       I am afraid!': Kenneth Grahame, *The Wind in
       the Willows* (London: Methuen & Co., 1908),
       p. 136.

380 'It is sacred ground ... a normal place': Gordon Deegan, 'Fairy bush survives the motorway planners', *Irish Times*, 29 May 1999.

383 the small farmers ... one a week: John Swire, 'More than one farmer a week in the UK dies by suicide', *Farm Business*, 15 February 2018.

384 'frightening land ownership move ... straight from the Marxist playbook': Alex Brummer, 'Should owners be forced to sell development plots cheaply? ALEX BRUMMER says Labour's frightening land ownership move is straight from the Marxist playbook', *This Is Money*, 4 June 2019.

384 In 2017, Crown Lands ... common purse: 'The Crown Estate announces £329.4m income returned for the public finances', Crown estate website, 28 June 2018.

385 'Why, yet there want not many, that do fear / In deep of night to walk by this Herne's oak': William Shakespeare, *The Merry Wives of Windsor*, IV, iv, www.opensourceshakespeare.org/views/plays/play_view.php?WorkID=merrywives&Act=4&Scene=4&Scope=scene&LineHighlight=2234#2234.

INDEX

NOTE ON THE TYPE

The text of this book is set in Fournier. Fournier is derived
from the *romain du roi*, which was created towards the end of
the seventeenth century from designs made by a committee of
the Académie of Sciences for the exclusive use of the Imprimerie
Royale. The original Fournier types were cut by the famous
Paris founder Pierre Simon Fournier in about 1742. These types
were some of the most influential designs of the eight and are
counted among the earliest examples of the 'transitional' style
of typeface. This Monotype version dates from 1924. Fournier
is a light, clear face whose distinctive features are capital letters
that are quite tall and bold in relation to the lower-case letters,
and *decorative italics, which show the influence of the calligraphy of
Fournier's time.*